Between Freedom and Progress

Conflicting Worlds

New Dimensions of the American Civil War

T. Michael Parrish, Series Editor

DAVID PRIOR

Between Freedom and Progress

THE LOST WORLD OF RECONSTRUCTION POLITICS

LOUISIANA STATE UNIVERSITY PRESS
BATON ROUGE

Published by Louisiana State University Press

Manufactured in the United States of America
First printing

Designer: Laura Roubique Gleason
Typeface: MillerText
Printer and binder: Sheridan Books

Library of Congress Cataloging-in-Publication Data

Names: Prior, David, author.
Title: Between freedom and progress : the lost world of Reconstruction politics / David Prior.
Description: Baton Rouge : Louisiana State University Press, [2019] | Series: Conflicting worlds : new dimensions of the American Civil War | Includes bibliographical references and index.
Identifiers: LCCN 2019018891 | ISBN 978-0-8071-6968-1 (cloth) | ISBN 978-0-8071-7243-8 (pdf) | ISBN 978-0-8071-7244-5 (epub)
Subjects: LCSH: Reconstruction (U.S. history, 1865–1877) | United States—Politics and government—1865–1877.
Classification: LCC E668 .P945 2019 | DDC 973.8—dc23
LC record available at https://lccn.loc.gov/2019018891

The paper in this book meets the guidelines for permanence and durability of the Committee on Production Guidelines for Book Longevity of the Council on Library Resources. ♾

For Tiffany and Isaac

Contents

Acknowledgments

I would have never finished this book without the support of my friends, family, colleagues, and several institutions. This book developed out of a seminar paper on the Cretan Insurrection from early in my time at the University of South Carolina, where several faculty members, including Tom Brown, Larry Glickman, Gerasimos Augustinos, and Kendrick Clements, volunteered their time to read it. I owe a special thanks to my mentor Mark M. Smith for encouraging me to start my research by looking for a topic off the beaten path. I'm not sure he realized that this would become the guiding principle of the dissertation he ended up chairing. Kendrick Clements, Bobby Donaldson, Don H. Doyle, Lacy Ford, Carol Harrison, Ann Johnson, and Patricia Sullivan pushed me to refine my ideas and expand my horizons through graduate courses. Drs. Clements, Donaldson, and Doyle served on my dissertation committee, deeply enriching the project. Eric Foner of Columbia University graciously served as the outside reader. Well before graduate school I was fortunate to have passionate and devoted teachers, and should give special thanks to Michael Ardantz, who went out of his way as a high school teacher to discuss American history with me. I had many excellent professors at Hamilton College and owe special debts to Douglas Ambrose and Elizabeth Jensen.

I am also grateful to several institutions that supported this project. At the University of South Carolina, I was privileged to receive a Graduate School Fellowship for the duration of my studies, as well as a two-year postdoctoral teaching fellowship. The skilled staffs at the Thomas Cooper Library, especially the offices of Government Information and Maps and Interlibrary Loan, as well as at the Irvin Department of Rare Books and Special Collections, greatly aided my research. At Indiana University, thanks are due to the staff of the Herman B. Wells Library, again with an extra word of gratitude to the department of Interlibrary

Loan. At Indiana, I also benefited from the chance to present portions of chapter 3 to the History Department's U.S. History Workshop, and thank Wendy Gamber for the invitation. At the University of New Mexico, my colleague Caleb Richardson offered the chance to present at the department's History Colloquium, again on portions of chapter 3. Our department chair, Melissa Bokovoy, facilitated a semester of research leave. The university's Zimmerman Library has been immensely helpful in tracking down often obscure sources. Oxford University Press graciously allowed me to republish portions of my article "'Crete the Opening Wedge': Nationalism and International Affairs in Postbellum America," *Journal of Social History* 42, no. 3 (June 2009): 861–87, as did Kent State University Press with my article "Civilization, Republic, Nation: Contested Keywords, Northern Republicans, and the Forgotten Reconstruction of Mormon Utah," *Civil War History* 56, no. 3 (September 2010): 281–308. Fordham University Press also permitted the republishing of some brief sections from my essay "Reconstruction, from Transatlantic Polyseme to Historiographical Quandary," 172–208, in my *Reconstruction in a Globalizing World* (New York: Fordham University Press, 2018). I thank series editor T. Michael Parrish, Catherine Kadair, and everyone at LSU Press for their wonderful support for this volume. I am also grateful to Chase McCarter for building an excellent index.

Like all historians currently researching the nineteenth-century United States, I owe a debt to a range of private and public entities that have invested resources into digitizing historical documents and making them publicly available. I started this project with microfilm and, in one remarkable case, six bound volumes of a postbellum newspaper delivered through interlibrary loan. By the time I finished my research, a truly staggering amount of sources had become available online, and were often word-searchable. Such online collections work best when fleshing out leads discovered in the archives, and this volume owes a considerable debt to research libraries and repositories. Special thanks are due to the staffs at the Manuscript Reading Room at the Library of Congress, the State Department collections at the National Archives and Record Administration, the Perkins School for the Blind, the Houghton Library at Harvard University, the Drexel University Archives, and the Special Collections and University Archives at Mercer University. A one-month Mellon fellowship at the Library Company of Philadelphia provided much-needed time and resources to advance my chapter on Paul

Du Chaillu. The library's seminar discussions and conversations with Philip Lapsansky proved invaluable.

At these institutions and elsewhere, my colleagues helped sustain me and my project. At South Carolina, I owe a special debt to my fellow graduate students, especially Josh Burgess, Ehren Foley, Kathleen Hilliard, Meeghan Kane, Jay Richardson, Chris Scott, Kathryn Silva, Michael Woods, Melissa Jane Taylor, and Aaron Marrs, the latter two of whom later invited me to present portions of chapter 2 at the Office of the Historian at the Department of State. At Indiana University, Susan Eckelmann Berghel, Claude Clegg, Nick Cullather, Konstantin Dierks, Wendy Gamber, Jacob Lee, Alex Lichtenstein, Jason McGraw, Kaya Sahin, Eric Sandweiss, Christina Snyder, and Ellen Wu welcomed me as a postdoc. The staff of the *Journal of American History*, including Steve Andrews, Nancy Croker, Ed Linenthal, Elizabeth and Kevin Marsh, Carl Suddler, Paula Tarankow, Jordan Taylor, and Cynthia Gwynne Yaudes kept me on my toes during my time there as assistant editor. At the University of New Mexico, I thank all my departmental colleagues, past and present, especially my fellow U.S.-Americanists with at least one foot in the nineteenth century, Durwood Ball, Cathleen Cahill, Paul Hutton, Andrew Sandoval-Strausz, Virginia Scharff, and Sam Truett. Sarah Davis-Secord, Fred Gibbs, Erika Monahan, Mike Ryan, and Shannon Withycombe have always made themselves available for needed distractions. Several colleagues have commented on papers at conferences, including Leslie Butler, Enrico Dal Lago, Justin Nystrom, Michael Perman, David Quigley, Heather Richardson, Mark Summers, and Elliott West. Mitchell Snay and Frank Towers have long been important interlocutors for me. Although I did not realize it at the time, a late-in-the-game discussion with Patrick Kelly proved critical to prompting me to rethink portions of this book.

My deepest debts are to the friends and family who not only got me through this project but helped make me into who I am today. Many a friend deserves more gratitude than I can give here. The older I get the more I realize how rare enduring friendships are and how lucky I am to have so many of them. I should give an extra word of thanks to Tony Coudert, Emily Scursso Hamel, Peter Holden, Amy Lawrence, Andrew Orzel, David Salmon, Kulmeet Sandhu, and Aleem Siddiqui for not only tolerating me during some of the most stressful periods of my life but also hosting me during archival visits and conference trips. My aunts

Alice and Ann did the same, for a full month. To my parents and sisters, all I can say is I love you and thank you for all the support over the years. Tiffany and Isaac, you lift my spirits during even my darkest moments and fill my life with joy. You mean the world to me. I never could have done this without you.

Between Freedom and Progress

Introduction

Reconstruction's Partisan World

On April 9, 1867, the *Memphis Daily Avalanche* announced the opening of its new five-story building on one of the city's main thoroughfares. During the Civil War, occupying Union forces had compelled the *Avalanche* to shut down. After the war the paper's editor, Matthew C. Gallaway, who had served as an officer in the Confederate Army under Nathan Bedford Forrest, returned to the city and reopened the paper. The paper initially had few resources and operated out of "a dingy one-story house built amid the surroundings of an obscure alley." Over the next few years, Gallaway used the *Avalanche* to defend the honor of the former Confederacy and fan the flames of southern white supremacist resentment, in the process helping spark the horrific Memphis race riot of May 1866. Despite facing five competing conservative newspapers in Memphis—the *Appeal, Argus, Bulletin, Commercial,* and *Public Ledger*—Gallaway rebuilt the *Avalanche* into an influential voice and a viable business. The paper's new home was "built in the most substantial and artistic manner . . . with an eye to all the requirements of a first-class daily newspaper."[1]

The building would soon include a series of statues to ornament the city and present the newspaper's understanding of the world. Above and to the right of a projecting window on the second floor would be a woman representing "America" and the "savage and nomadic condition of her people before Anglo-Saxon civilization came to her." Standing next to a crocodile, she would hold a cornucopia, be armed with a bow, and be nude to the waist except for a "barbaric headdress." To the left of the window would be "Africa," helmeted and holding a hunting horn and bow with a lion crouched at her feet, looking "as classic as the negro's features can be made." Above them, on the fourth floor, two more statues would flank a central window. "Europe" would stand on the left, "fully draped," with "Intelligence and Civilization regnant upon her coronetted brow," and holding a book and laurel wreath to crown her wisdom. A knight's helmet at her feet would show that force had been subordinated to "the behests of intelligence and peace," while her right hand held "the scepter of power." To her right would be Asia, wearing a turban "clasped with a cluster of jewels, emblematic of the richness of the East." Yet Asia would also be half-nude "to express the semi-civilization of her people" and adorned from her neck to her hips with "a costly chain," showing that her wealth was ultimately "barbaric." By her feet would be a lamp, "symbolizing the light she has shed upon the world," and a second chain indicating "the present condition of her millions of people." At the top of the building would be one final piece. At its center would be "a globe girdled with telegraph wires," above which would hang a golden "star of empire" shining its light on two wreaths representing "the reward of merit, industry, and art." Two adjacent cornucopias would signify the wealth and prosperity that had blessed the country "before Abe," meaning Lincoln, "came and let slip the dogs of war," and that would return with true peace.[2]

The *Avalanche*'s building underscored how readily Reconstruction's partisans—those who struggled over and with Reconstruction—situated themselves in the world.[3] Gallaway and his staff expressed no concern that their building's global focus might detract from their ability to speak on behalf of the fallen Confederacy or to help inspire terrorist campaigns against newly freed African Americans. And why should they? Like others of their day, they presumed that developments from across and beyond the United States would validate their arguments closer to home. The editors' prejudices, far from inhibiting this way of thinking, inspired them to make claims about the world. By no means content to simply report news, the *Avalanche* was an interpretive enterprise. The new building's "*sanctum sanctorum*," the paper explained, was its richly decorated and comfortable editorial office, equipped with its own library, all to "allow the intellectual to have full play."[4]

These self-described intellectuals, like others across the United States, made and remade daily Reconstruction's world. This book recovers and analyzes that world—a world part real and part fantasy that Reconstruction's partisans imagined themselves in as they struggled with each other over the nature of their post–Civil War, postslavery settlement. It was a world made possible by the remarkable technological and commercial transformations centered on Europe and North America during the middle of the nineteenth century. Steam engines, telegraphs, and the industrial production of print created a constant stream of news, description, and storytelling from across and beyond the nation. Intense political antagonism combined with shared but contested ideas—about freedom, progress, and the world's peoples—to motivate Reconstruction's partisans to vie with each other to make sense of this information. As writers, lecturers, editors, travelers, moral reformers, racists, abolitionists, politicians, suffragists, soldiers, and diplomats, Reconstruction's partisans made competing claims about their and their country's place in the world. Understanding how, why, and when they did so grounds our understanding of Reconstruction in its contemporary intellectual context, which is at once historically related and yet alien to our own ways of thinking.

What Was Reconstruction?

To understand Reconstruction's world, we need to first ask what Reconstruction was. This has proven to be one of the oddest issues in the study of the history of the United States. On the one hand, scholars have long treated the term in a casual manner, assuming that its meaning was self-evident. On the other, when scholars have attempted to define Reconstruction, they have rendered an increasingly complex set of divergent perspectives. As a result, we have a tremendous volume of scholarship devoted to describing and analyzing Reconstruction but a vague and eroding consensus about to what this term refers.

Most scholars would likely concur that Reconstruction concerned issues stemming from the Civil War, but beyond this there is little agreement. We have arguments about whether Reconstruction was a process, a period, or both;[5] what its geographical scope was;[6] when it began and ended, with competing answers differing by several decades;[7] and whether the term referred to the reunion of the country or the transformation of the South.[8] Along with these we have works that use the term "reconstruction" metaphorically to refer to any number of Civil War–era changes and reforms, often with little regard for contemporary usage.[9] Two recent, closely related interpretive trends have been particularly important in layering new meanings onto the term Reconstruction. The first sees Reconstruction as a name for a postbellum process of contesting the nature of U.S. citizenship, and seeks to address African Americans and other excluded, marginalized, and disfranchised groups, including women, Chinese immigrants, Native Americans, and Latinos. The second, overlapping trend attempts to reframe Reconstruction as continental in scale, with special emphasis on including the western United States.[10] Individually excellent, these studies cumulatively add further confusion about Reconstruction's basic definition. To ask what Reconstruction is, therefore, is to wade into a discussion that is reaching the point of collective incoherence.

The challenge now facing historians is to disentangle how people at the time understood Reconstruction from the increasingly divergent scholarly understandings of it. This is no easy task, since the word held multiple, if not infinite, meanings at the time. Indeed, the lack of consensus in modern scholarship about what Reconstruction was stems from, but should not be simply equated with, an ambiguity surrounding the term as it entered into the social and political lexicon of the United States. As early as the 1840s, well before it became a name for something specific to the United States, the word "reconstruction" referred to two distinct historical processes. First, it often denoted the resurrection or rebirth of individual polities—states, nations, and empires—that had been conquered, dissolved, or divided. Here the term often came up in British and French discussions of Poland, which some thought could be reconstituted from its partitioned provinces to prevent Russian expansion.[11] Second, "reconstruction" could refer to the idea of transforming the very fabric of society, especially as advocated by socialists and other radical reformers. In this sense, the term came loaded with negative associations for many in the United States.[12]

When people in the United States started using the term to refer to something specific to the country, they drew on both meanings. Often, they used the term to refer to the reunification of the North and South, the reestablishment of federal authority over the rebellious states, and the latter's reintegration into the federal electoral system.[13] In that sense, the term Reconstruction was about the triumph of the nation over its threatened dismemberment, and clearly spoke to the idea of reconstruction as national resurrection. Yet they also often used Reconstruction to refer to the destruction of slavery and the cowing of southern slaveholders, as well as the reordering of southern life that came with the expansion of civil and political rights to former slaves.[14] Here, the term reflected the idea of reconstruction as social transformation. What made this even more confusing was that these two sets of postbellum processes were inextricably interconnected. The abolition of slavery and the expansion of African American rights across the South was only possible with the defeat of the Confederacy and the reestablishment of federal authority. The reintegration of the Confederate states into the Union ultimately became contingent on Confederates' acceptance, however superficial, of abolition and the expansion of African American rights.

Acknowledging the term's original ambiguity allows us to dispense with two well-established approaches to defining Reconstruction. First, we should hold in check the impulse, particularly prominent in the last few decades, to seek new insights by continually redefining the term. This promises to bring us further away from how people at the time understood the concept and to force future scholars to work within a definitional labyrinth. Second, we need to abandon the older conceit that Reconstruction was a unitary historical thing with precise contours and a single meaning. This will only produce jockeying over which subset of issues, especially those pertaining to the South or the nation, really defined Reconstruction. Instead, we should understand Reconstruction as an evolving term with multiple but concrete meanings, two of which, national resurrection and social transformation, dovetailed with major postbellum policy crises revolving around reunion and abolition. As Reconstruction became a name for a part of the history of the United States, discussions of it were complex and often confused from the get-go, but this complexity took historically specific forms. Reconstruction was neither boundless in its meanings nor a single, cleanly delineated historical process or moment. At its heart sat two interconnected conflicts—over how to remake the Union and how to remake the South—that shared a single name. The expansive and divisive nature of these challenges laid the foundation for Reconstruction's world.

Freedom, Progress, and the World's Peoples

The two conflicts at Reconstruction's heart suggest that it was quintessentially domestic, even regional, in nature. From the challenges of remaking the Union and of remaking the South flowed a series of issues, all of which were understood to be internal to the United States. On what terms would the southern states reenter the Union and participate in federal elections? What rights would former Confederates have and what process would they go through to return to full citizenship? What was the legal status of former slaves as well as people of color more generally? What was the nature of American citizenship? Which branches of the federal and state governments had authority over these issues? Unlike with the diplomacy of the Civil War, which raised questions of international recognition, mediation, and intervention, there was no presumption on the part of any foreign power of possible legal grounds to intercede in these questions. The 1860s and 1870s, moreover, lacked the elaborate network of humanitarian and developmental organizations that now routinely attend to crises around the globe. Indeed, since these issues concerned the southern states and since the West remained lightly settled by voting citizens compared to the eastern United States, many scholars treat Reconstruction as a saga largely staged in one half of the United States. So then why did Reconstruction's partisans imbue the world with so much meaning? Why did far-flung developments matter to so many of Reconstruction's partisans?

The answer lies in the then pervasive conviction that developments in the United States held their deepest meanings as part of global struggles for freedom and progress. Echoes of this way of thinking can still be heard today, but it was at heart a product of mid-nineteenth-century understandings of history, society, and humanity. This way of thinking borrowed the Enlightenment's sweeping intellectual ambition and love of universal analytical concepts and embedded these within the vibrant popular politics of the Civil War–era United States. The result was a broadly based system of social and political thought that lived and breathed in public venues and media. The resulting intellectual style grew out of the Atlantic exchanges of the eighteenth and early nineteenth centuries, but had more routine access to and routine confidence about global information. It fed into the intellectual and cultural world of the Gilded Age and Progressive Era, but centered on a different set of political divisions and policy questions and lacked the latter's concern for academic expertise.

At the heart of this way of thinking about the world were two beliefs, each of which had its own constituent parts. The first of these was that the essential contours of world history were readily identifiable.[15] In this view, two struggles sat at the heart of human history, lending it common parameters if not the same course of development around the globe. Civilization was locked in a global struggle against barbarism, and republicanism likewise contended against despotism and aristocracy.[16]

These ideas had deep lineages that brought with them a complex array of assumptions about their relationships with race, commerce, technology, and social change.[17] As a result, these were capacious concepts, subject to interpretation and perfectly suited for contrary intellectual ends. After the Civil War, as throughout the nineteenth century, these oppositional abstractions infused everything from elaborate, sophisticated analyses to petty bigotry and political sloganeering.[18]

Civilization and republicanism provided ways to speak of both specific societies and abstract historical forces. In the specific sense, a civilization was minimally a society that had developed sedentary agriculture. In its abstract sense, civilization simultaneously referred to a higher level of societal development and a continuous process of development, and in the latter sense was often used interchangeably with "progress."[19] When civilization referred to a level of social development, its antithesis was found in barbarians, or nomadic illiterates who plundered without producing. When civilization referred to a process, it was more common to contrast it with barbarism and savagery. These terms took barbarians' worst qualities—ignorance, myopia, cruelty, and selfishness—and implicated them in societal stagnation and degeneration. Historians of the United States have most often approached these concepts in reference to views and policies toward Native Americans and Gilded Age discourses about race, immigration, and empire.[20] These were essential to these concepts' contested meanings, but the civilization-barbarism distinction had a much broader career and pervaded the whole of nineteenth-century political and cultural life in the United States and beyond. Indeed, although it takes us a little far afield from the focus of this study, the distinction between civilization and barbarism was the mantra for the self-consciously modern in much of the world from the late eighteenth century into the middle of the twentieth. During the Civil War era, the distinction was ubiquitous in popular politics.

As an individual society, a republic was minimally one that had a class of citizens who had a substantive say in how they were governed. The abstraction "republicanism" was, like that of civilization, more complicated. It at once referred to the ethos that radiated from free societies and the matrix of practices and institutions that sustained them. Contrary to how many scholars have used the term, mid-nineteenth-century Americans did not take republicanism to be a name for an ideology concerned with the common good that was supplanted by the more individualistic philosophy of liberalism.[21] Indeed, when Reconstruction's partisans mentioned liberalism, which they certainly did, it was typically synonymous with republicanism in referring to the transcendent cause of freedom, although both terms, like all, could be appropriated for more precise political ends.[22] Republicanism's opposites were despotism and aristocracy, both of which generalized the alleged personality traits of tyrants, including their selfish lust for power and impulse to dominate, into a political and social ethos antagonistic to freedom.[23] More conservative voices also warned that excessive democracy could usher in tyranny as reckless masses destroyed the foundations of republican order. In these senses, republicanism came loaded with built-in notions of class that were simultaneously political, economic, and cultural. Whereas barbarism by its nature broke apart social ties, despotism, aristocracy, and anarchy had an underlying hostility to civil and political rights.

As diverse as Reconstruction's partisans were, they largely shared these terms and agreed that civilization and republicanism were causes to fight for and forces in history. Indeed, the transatlantic origin of these terms meant they also facilitated international conversations, debates, and collaborations, although subtle differences in interpretation and tenor were sometimes lost in translation.[24] It is little wonder that individuals like Domingo F. Sarmiento, Robert Brown Elliott, Mathilde Anneke, and a great many others could forge transatlantic political and intellectual partnerships during the Civil War era.[25] A more complicated question is the place of these ideas in the oppositional culture of southern rural African Americans. As Mia Bay has demonstrated, enslaved African Americans often used the racial terminology common in the nineteenth-century United States without embracing formal theories of racial difference.[26] We simply need more research into the specific ways that the political lexicon and ideologies of southern rural African Americans were related to, differed from, and merged with those common in federal politics. As chapter 4 of this volume suggests, on this front the postbellum years constituted a period of intellectual cross-fertilization through the near-creation of a durable, regionally integrated, and self-consciously "black" or "colored" network of African American readers, authors, and editors.

If broadly circulated, the concepts of civilization and republicanism did not encourage consensus, instead serving primarily to sustain diverse and antagonistic perspectives on the world. Political rivals agreed on the terms' definitions, but not about the precise configuration of values, institutions, and practices that sustained and advanced freedom and progress. These concepts made Reconstruction's partisans remarkably at home with the idea that their own history only made sense as part of the world's, while the terms' contested natures left them perpetually ready to argue about how this was so. These debates built on those of the broader Civil War era as well as a matrix of assumptions and concerns that ran back decades and, in some cases, centuries. Was slaveholding necessary for collective material prosperity and citizens' republican independence? Or was it an antiquated form of exploitation bound to collapse before the advancing forces of modernity? Did commerce put barbarism on the retreat by bringing the backward, isolated parts of the globe into contact with the more enlightened regions? Or did it put far-flung people in harm's way before the merchant's savage greed? Did the rise of industry represent a definitive moment in civilization, ushering in a new era of perpetual progress rooted in new technological marvels and wealth? Or was it foremost a threat to republican freedom because it immiserated the masses, eroding the economic foundations of their political freedoms? Were the institutions and practices that expanded freedom the same that drove forward progress? Perhaps too much civilized progress in the form of material growth could drown a people's republican spirit in corrupting wealth. Perhaps too much freedom created the risk of a breakdown in the social and political order necessary for civilization.[27]

The second belief at the heart of Reconstruction's world stood in creative tension—not to say contradiction—with the assumption that the course of civilization and republicanism defined the contours of history around the globe. Much as Reconstruction's partisans were inclined to compress all of history down to two interconnected struggles for freedom and progress, they also believed history was about distinctive and coherent populations. History belonged to these groups and these groups made history move. Reconstruction's partisans understood that individuals could change faiths, learn languages, have diverse ancestors, and shift allegiances. Indeed, across the nineteenth century, many looked forward to the conversion of the world, or at least Europe, to what they took to be their own special republican civilization, which was itself a new creation. But a fascination with the personal experience of being culturally transgressive, common now, was rare at the time. Likewise, there was little doubt that the identities of the world's peoples reflected genuine differences in who those people were. The era lacked the ironic disposition and deconstructionist methods integral to today's analyses of group identity. In their line of thinking, the world's peoples were collective actors and not simply abstractions, social constructs, or convenient shorthand terms. To describe someone as "French" or "Oriental" or "Negro" was not simply to make a linguistic, geographical, or phenotypical distinction, but to stake a claim about that person's character and place in history. The world's peoples were the essential agents in the struggles for civilization and republicanism and were in turn shaped by those struggles. The world, in this view, had not so much a people's history as a peoples' history.

As with the concepts of civilization and republicanism, the widespread belief that humanity was composed of discrete and readily identifiable peoples laid the foundation for disagreement. A shared belief that such groups existed and a common set of terms—race, nation, tribe, culture, religion—to distinguish them from each other helped frame discussion of but did not entail consensus about the day's major issues. Faced with disagreements concerning the nature of citizenship, sectional reconciliation, and the grounds of political unity, Reconstruction's partisans levied a complex series of competing claims about themselves and each other as peoples situated in world history.[28] These arguments make for a rich but confusing written record. On the one hand, Reconstruction's partisans, like others in the nineteenth century, argued about the relationships among these categories. Could a person's race or religion, for example, preclude him or her from being a member of the American nation? Could religion transcend race, making a common community of belief out of immutably different people? How changeable was a nation's character? Here, the terms clearly referred to different kinds of groups, some the product of self-conscious conviction, others cultural immersion, and still others unchangeable biology. On the other hand, Reconstruction's partisans were remarkably inconsistent in how they used these terms. Like many others in the nineteenth century, they thought of religions as cultures, described cultures as races, and used the term race interchangeably with nation.[29] This does not mean that these terms always meant exactly the same thing: the racial terms "Negro," "black," and "African," for example, in some contexts did political work by effacing claims to American nationality. Yet, however distinctive concepts like race, religion, and culture were in some contexts, in others they could all serve equally well to identify and contrast groups of people with each other. This tells us something crucial about a core assumption shaping popular thought and political debate. Since all of these types of groups referred to putatively distinct and coherent populations, there was often little need for precision when invoking these various categories of difference.

These two beliefs—that the struggles for freedom and progress transcended human history and that humanity was composed of distinct groups with their own characters—provided the foundation for Reconstruction's world. These beliefs served as core assumptions that structured the realm of thinkable thoughts, grounding political disputes in common terms and beliefs. Either belief alone would have inspired interest in broader developments. Together, they necessitated it by creating an intellectual context in which developments everywhere were essentially comparable to each other. It was the world's distinct peoples that made this history move, but the significance of a group's distinctiveness ultimately rested with its relation to the overarching struggles for civilization and republicanism. With such an outlook, making analogies among groups across time and space was not only natural but necessary to informed argument.[30] Reconstruction's partisans did not simply project their own struggles onto other peoples, places, or events. They deliberately linked their own and others' conflicts together because they understood them to be discrete components of an overarching set of global, historical processes. Indeed, in its purest form, the belief that all groups were linked together through common struggles could undermine the premise that the distinctiveness of those groups was important in the first place. Similarly, Reconstruction's partisans often measured the foreignness of a people and their institutions not by their ethnic distinctiveness but by their alleged hostility to freedom and progress. In this way, these transcendent causes both operated under a different logic to the idea that humanity was composed of distinctive groups, and yet helped constitute understandings of who those groups were.

Partisans and Print

Such abstract ideas might seem out of place in the rough-and-tumble world of Reconstruction politics. The 1860s and 1870s were, after all, the age of Boss Tweed and the Klan. But corruption and violence in fact only accentuate how concerned Reconstruction's partisans were with the public circulation of ideas. Reigning political parties funneled resources to allies writing on their behalf while white supremacists in the South threatened and attacked Republican writers and editors. Reconstruction's issues fired intense bickering across the United States that ranged from the shallow to the sophisticated. The lifeblood of partisan debate was a decentralized publishing industry that churned out a mix of argumentation, storytelling, and description. Competing understandings of civilization, republicanism, and the world's peoples suffused and helped drive these discussions, with authors seeking to demonstrate their superior understanding of these broader themes. In sharp contrast to our own academic style, this made Reconstruction's partisans more comfortable embracing wide-ranging topics than not.

This polemical landscape was deeply prejudicial in content and structure. Claims about who was capable of being progressive and free brought with them arguments about who was not. Readers encountered an unbroken stream of characterological commentary about the world's peoples, often negative, as groups as disparate as Yankee mudsills, former slaves, French workers, Hindus, the British, Chinese immigrants, and sundry others came in for abuse. Even the most strident humanitarians believed the world's population divided into distinctive and coherent groups, they just held less stringent views about those groups and a greater sense that they could potentially change.[31] Nearly everyone who participated in Reconstruction's partisan world of print was willing to pass judgment, often severe, on the putative character of one group or another. Pointing this out does not imply a moral equivalency across the day's political spectrum. There was a vast difference between a white supremacist who condemned "Negroes" as beasts and an antipolygamy crusader who saw Mormon patriarchs as slaveholders. But it does call attention to how a shared way of thinking about the world and its peoples transcended the political divides of the Civil War era.[32]

What is more, the means to engage in Reconstruction's nationwide debates were distributed unequally. Publishing entailed the institutional means to produce and circulate text to an audience, ideally on one's own terms. Conditions favored the larger, wealthier North over the South, although by 1870 the southern states had roughly as many newspapers as they had in 1860.[33] Lower literacy rates, poverty, and dispersed settlement meant that southern Republicans, including freedpeople and scalawags, often struggled to sustain their own periodicals. In addition, African Americans and racial egalitarians who worked as authors and editors in the South faced persecution from white supremacists.[34] As a geographically scattered intellectual minority, supporters of women's suffrage sustained journals only with constant experimentation, support from benefactors, and ties to larger abolitionist networks.[35] Writing patterns, more so than reading patterns, were heavily gendered. Literature and poetry were rare fields open to female authors.[36] A tradition of female editors developed over the late eighteenth and nineteenth centuries, with publications often but not always oriented toward home life. Even so, at any one point in time the vast majority working in these fields were male, all the more so with journalists. A political newspaper like the *Clayton Herald,* which was both opposed to woman suffrage and edited by a woman, R. S. McConaughy, was a rare enterprise for the postbellum decade.[37] Especially in the North, where public education was common, the working class was largely literate and by most accounts read avidly. As such, working-class concerns filtered into pamphlets, newspapers, and dime novels. But, in contrast to a few decades later, there were few publishing organizations that were working class from the ground up and that had far-reaching circulation.[38] Northern Republicans, ranging from racial egalitarians to conservative Unionists, dominated printed debates from 1865 to 1873, with Democrats, including former Confederates and many northern white supremacists, providing the main counterpoint.

If unequal, this commercialized and politicized publishing industry was also lively, and that liveliness is integral to understanding why Reconstruction's issues gave rise to such widespread and intricate global imaginings. The polemical landscape was above all one made by extensive and complex networks of thousands of authors, editors, and publishers and millions of readers. It operated most dynamically in federal politics, engaging Reconstruction's partisans in discussions across state lines in ways that stood in awkward juxtaposition to the localized politics of the postslavery South, where white supremacist violence aimed to squelch civic debate and political engagement on the part of racial egalitarians. Its foundation lay in a combination of widespread practices of reading as consumption and a diversity of forms of production. Civil War–era Americans read in public and private and as a central act of citizenship, for their jobs, out of religious concern, for self-improvement and refinement, and for leisure.[39] Reconstruction's issues, moreover, consumed federal politics during publishing's transition from an artisanal craft to an industrialized business, and hence occupied a historical moment marked by a diversity of publications.[40]

This was especially evident in newspapers, which in the 1860s and 1870s were in a polemical golden age. Metropolitan dailies with extensive regional and national readerships existed alongside thousands of smaller local and trade papers. Already changes were afoot that would transform the newspaper industry by the 1890s. By then, smaller papers would specialize in local news and telegraphic monopolies, syndication, professionalization, sensationalism, and corporatization would diminish the range of editorial perspective even as the number of newspapers increased.[41] In the 1860s and 1870s, however, the newspaper industry was a welter, with even small-town editors interpreting national and international issues and running letters from friends traveling abroad whenever they could line them up.[42] Most papers were explicitly partisan in their outlook, with the political parties and individual politicians providing funding.[43] By the sheer multiplicity of newspapers, volume of print, thirst for news, love of opinion-mongering, and number of readers, the newspaper industry in the Civil War–era United States was unlike anything else in the world at the time.[44]

Newspapers were just one particularly important medium. Weekly, monthly, and quarterly magazines offered a mixture of literary, political, historical, and scientific content that ran from the elitist to the popular.[45] This was also an era of industrial book publishing, with national and international best sellers emerging alongside thousands of less popular works, some still published by small-time printers. History, travel literature, and novels were all popular genres whose works often had overt political messages.[46] As they long had, printers produced pamphlet literature for profit and to advance their own and their clients' causes. It was by no means hard for authors who had a ninety-page rant or wanted a sermon or speech published to find a local printer. The 1860s also saw the consolidation of a professional lecture circuit in the North and West, with authors performing their reading to large audiences, including newspaper reporters who in essence transcribed the same lectures with notes about audience reactions.[47] Finally, the government, especially the federal government, produced and distributed a tremendous volume of material, including printings of congressional speeches.[48] It is difficult to understate the centrality of publishing to the political culture of the mid-nineteenth-century United States. Most citizens listened to political speeches or participated in parades at most a few times a year. They read their politics weekly, often daily.

Undergirding Reconstruction's elaborate realm of partisan bickering was an infrastructure for circulating text that militated against the isolation of diverse communities. Commercial publishers developed regional and national distribution systems. Texts circulated more quickly and in greater abundance near cities, which were plastered with the printed word. But canals, steamships, railroads, and express companies made it affordable to ship bulky goods over long distances, allowing, for example, for the rise of magazines with national readerships.[49] Newspaper editors read each other's works through a government-supported exchange system and borrowed material from any source they found interesting, with no concern for copyright. The post office also shipped newspapers and, after 1851, magazines at reduced rates. A newspaper or magazine article could "go viral" as editors borrowed and reprinted it.[50] Readers themselves helped make this infrastructure by handing off cheaper texts as public property while sharing and gifting valuable ones with friends, relatives, and neighbors.[51] Libraries, sometimes just a communal bookshelf, were common in the West and North and in southern cities.[52] For commercial, political, and personal reasons, differences in genre did little to fragment discussion, and a mixture of argumentation, storytelling, and description sloshed from source to source, place to place, and reader to reader.[53] In short, the commercialized and politicized publishing industry kept Reconstruction's partisans in conversation with each other, if often indirectly as readers and listeners.[54]

This volume explores the interplay of these three factors during the pivotal years of federal Reconstruction policy-making. First, from 1865 to the early 1870s, the interconnected issues of how to remake the Union and how to remake the South exercised a powerful hold on federal politics, defining the partisan landscape and inspiring rival arguments about what was possible and what was good. The daunting nature of these issues created a sense of crisis across the political spectrum, with political discourse ranging in tone from combative to apocalyptic to euphoric. Second, though domestic in nature, these issues were refracted through two broadly held beliefs that the causes of freedom and progress defined history and that distinctive peoples with their own characters composed the world's population. These beliefs produced a disposition to think of developments from across and beyond the United States as essentially relatable to each other, encouraging an intellectual style that favored wide-ranging comparisons. Third, far from being confined to the elite, this mode of thinking and arguing about the world lived and breathed in public texts that were produced and consumed on a weekly and daily basis. This commercialized and politicized world of mass publishing was unequal in structure and content, but it was also impressively vibrant and popular. Together, these three factors made Reconstruction's world: a global landscape of information, argumentation, and imagination that derived much of its vigor from domestic political battles.

The following chapters seek to demonstrate Reconstruction's world in action, offering a corrective to much recent literature. For much of the twentieth century, historical scholarship tended to develop in regionally and nationally delimited fields of study. Important thematic conversations connected these fields, but historians, perhaps drawing on the mid-nineteenth-century tendency to see the world as divided among coherent and distinctive peoples, tended to frame their studies in terms of discrete, geographically bounded areas of specialization. Since the 1990s, historians have pushed against this tendency, building on and expanding existing research topics, pioneering new ones, and asking basic methodological questions about what we study, how we conduct research, and who we write for. This tendency has not so much obliterated older national and regional fields of study as much as made them explicitly concerned with broader patterns and connections and lodged them within even larger continental, hemispheric, oceanic, and global fields of study.[55] As a result, there is now a substantial literature that situates the Civil War–era United States in broader geographical contexts, including national approaches that address the conquest of the Far West, borderlands approaches concerned with the contact zones between the United States, Mexico, and Canada, and even farther-reaching transnational studies. We now have a much richer literature addressing what different groups in the Civil War–era United States thought about foreign events and peoples and how they engaged with them whether at home or abroad.[56]

Yet, with the Civil War era, much of this scholarship accentuates how particularly important events or groups pulled American attention in their direction and thereby altered the course of American history. Such is the case, for example, with the substantial literature about Caribbean revolutions and emancipations, the European Revolutions of 1848, and the Paris Commune.[57] Of course, these events did garner attention in their own right and they did shape attitudes within the United States, but the impression of this research is one of the outside world impinging on the interests of a people otherwise preoccupied with themselves.[58] The approach in *Between Freedom and Progress,* however, is to call attention to the constancy with which people concerned with Reconstruction, and the politics of the Civil War era more generally, linked developments from far and wide to those in the key theaters of their own conflicts. Rather than argue for a single dramatic event as upending American thinking, the emphasis is on the deeply entrenched and politicized assumption that all historical moments and developments were essentially relatable to each other and the resulting interest, constant and wide-ranging, in both nearby and far-flung developments. Like other works, this book focuses on specific people, places, and events, but its emphasis is on how these were emblematic of a broader disposition to think and argue globally in a particular fashion.

Focusing on the pivotal years of Reconstruction policy-making, *Between Freedom and Progress* zeroes in on exactly that period (1865–1874) during which time and energy for such engagement should have been most scarce. Instead, what it finds is constant and eager interest in a multitude of events, places, and individuals, several of which have been largely and even completely ignored by Reconstruction scholarship. This period was one of Republican dominance in federal politics and culture, and much of what was said reflected the power of the party's northern core. Having saved the Union and purged the United States of slavery, northern Republicans entered the postbellum period with an ebullient if sometimes anxious faith that they exemplified America and that America exemplified republicanism and civilization. In their view, Union victory and abolition laid the groundwork for a new epoch of world history in which freedom and progress would march forward together. There were underlying tensions in this worldview that would come more to the fore over time, but in the immediate postbellum years the tone of northern Republicans was routinely optimistic. At the same time, an emerging nationwide network of African American readers, authors, and editors, tied to but also distinctive within the Republican Party, promised to bridge the border-crossing analogies of federal political culture and the violent, localized politics of the postbellum South. Leading figures in this network-in-the-making shared much in common with this northern Republican outlook, but also maintained a sharper sense of how entrenched the forces of barbarism and despotism were within the United States in the form of white supremacy. Democrats, including a large minority of northern whites and most former Confederates, formed the partisan antithesis to northern Republican and African American interpretations of the world. Into the 1870s, they held that the Republican Party was filled with aspiring despots who were plunging the South into racial anarchy and barbarism. As the defenders of "black" subordination and a weak federal government, they held themselves to be the true representatives of America's republican civilization.[59]

The first chapter focuses on an insurrection by Greek Orthodox Christians on the island of Crete against Ottoman imperial rule from 1866 to 1869. Largely forgotten today, the insurrection was a geopolitical and humanitarian crisis that had the potential to trigger a broader collapse of Ottoman authority in southeastern Europe. It was also a richly symbolic conflict that spoke to ideas about race, religion, Greek and Turkish character, and national liberation from imperial tyranny. Chapter 2 uncovers the multifaceted career of Paul Du Chaillu, the most popular and controversial authority on Africa living in the United States after the war. Du Chaillu made two expeditions to the region of Gabon in equatorial West Africa during the 1850s and 1860s. After both expeditions, he traveled to Britain and the United States and published best-selling accounts of his adventures. His return to the United States after his second expedition would see him reach the zenith of his success as a popular authority on Africa. The third chapter addresses three northern Republican leisure expeditions around the length of the globe from 1867 to 1871 and the narratives that resulted from these travels. Charles Carleton Coffin, William Fogg, and William and Olive Seward all made use of an emerging global patchwork of steam-driven transportation systems. Indeed, these journeys were self-conscious celebrations of technology as a driving force behind freedom and progress as well as explorations of a world set in motion. Chapter 4 turns its attention to the African American struggle to secure an autonomous presence in Reconstruction's swirling, nationwide debates about the South, the nation, and the world. It argues that the collapse of southern slavery and the defeat of the Confederacy created an unprecedented opportunity for African Americans to coordinate a nationwide campaign against white supremacy. Integral to these efforts was the near creation of a network of African American readers, authors, and editors that bridged the North, the South, and the West, with newspapers playing a particularly important role in linking African Americans across space. The final chapter turns to Mormon Utah, a society that northern Republicans considered to be in but not of the United States. Viewing the western half of their country as a national component of a global frontier of civilization and republicanism, northern Republicans expected the region to embrace a free and prosperous future. Yet in Utah they discovered a peculiar problem of the present in the form of a Mormon society that seemed to practice barbarism in the form of polygamy and despotism in the form of the authority of the Church's hierarchy. Democrats again responded to northern Republican rhetoric, at times defending the right of the Mormons to govern their own institutions and at other times arguing that southern freedpeople were the Mormons of the South. The volume concludes by arguing that these studies highlight an important tension in postbellum northern Republican thinking that in turn helps us understand Reconstruction's place in the broader history of the postbellum United States.

1

Contested Sympathy for the Cretans

From August of 1866 to February of 1869, an insurrection against Ottoman imperial rule organized by groups of Greek Orthodox Christians on the island of Crete drew the attention of Reconstruction's partisans from California to Chania and Massachusetts to Memphis.[1] Now obscure, the Cretan Insurrection was an international humanitarian crisis that troubled British statesmen with the prospect of Russian and French intervention in the Ottoman Empire, and perhaps even the dissolution of the Ottoman Empire in Europe.[2] Along with its geopolitical significance, the insurrection garnered attention because of its rich symbolic meanings. Throughout the nineteenth century it was fashionable to celebrate the Greeks as the founders of western civilization and to loathe the Ottoman Empire as the West's Asiatic, Oriental antithesis.[3] In important ways, American sympathy for the Greek rebels on Crete was a sequel to earlier support for the Greek War of Independence in the 1820s.[4] That Christians fought against a Muslim power added yet another dimension to the insurrection's meaning.[5] Finally, the insurrection was just the kind of nationalist rebellion against an external, imperial power that nineteenth-century Americans consistently celebrated as honoring their own revolution.[6] There were few concrete connections between Crete and the United States in the form of trade, tourism, or strategic relationships, and it was ideological commitments that drove discussions of the multivalent insurrection within the United States.[7]

The Cretan Insurrection took place during the critical years of Reconstruction policy-making. In the middle of 1865, Abraham Lincoln's successor, Andrew Johnson, sketched what looked to be a stern yet moderate course for returning the Confederate South to the Union. In his plan, the political, economic, and military leadership of the Confederacy would have to secure presidential pardons before they could have their rights as citizens restored, but lesser Confederates merely had to take an oath of allegiance to the United States and accept slavery's end.

Johnson recognized the pro-Union governments of Arkansas, Louisiana, Tennessee, Virginia—established during wartime occupations—as legitimate, making them eligible to participate in federal elections. For the other seven Confederate states, Johnson moved to establish provisional governments and required them to repeal their acts of secession, repudiate their war debts, and outlaw slavery before they could participate in federal elections. In both cases, the state governments, with electorates composed mostly of former Confederates and exclusively of white men, would determine the rights of freedpeople. In its basic features, this plan might have found enough support in the North from Democrats and conservative and moderate Republicans to come to fruition.[8]

In practice, however, his plan quickly fell apart. Johnson struggled to get former Confederates to meet all of his criteria, did little when the southern states passed racist Black Codes, and issued pardons to Confederates at a blistering pace. Before the end of 1865, Republicans in Congress were preparing to investigate conditions in the South and refusing to seat newly elected senators and representatives from states reconstructed under Johnson's plan. Johnson and congressional Republicans quickly entered into a three-year-long confrontation. Johnson vetoed what Republicans considered moderate legislation necessary to secure an antislavery peace. Republicans then passed new legislation over Johnson's veto, especially after strengthening their majority in the 1866 midterm election. Johnson turned to the administrative powers of the presidency to obstruct congressional Republican plans, prompting Republicans nearly to remove him from office through a hastily prepared impeachment trial.

These next three years would see Republicans hammer out compromises within their party to pass a series of sweeping measures, including two constitutional amendments. Over this period, congressional Republicans placed the former Confederates states (excluding Tennessee) under temporary military rule, required them to rewrite their state constitutions with freedmen participating in the process, defined national citizenship as a birthright with legal protections that stood above state law, and prohibited states from limiting suffrage by race.[9] By 1871, all of the former Confederates states had civil governments and were participating in federal elections, with freedmen voting and running for office.

Coming right as arguments about congressional policies were at a fever pitch, the Cretan Insurrection became an integral part of Reconstruction's world. Its meanings within the United States became inseparable from the partisan struggles among northern Republicans, Democrats, and Andrew Johnson. Their interpretations of the insurrection shared much in common, including sympathy for the Greek Orthodox rebels and a tendency to flatten out the ethnic and religious complexity of the eastern Mediterranean into cleanly delineated groups, ignoring the existence of non-Turkish Ottomans and of Muslim Greek Cretans. But interpretations also clearly split along the same party lines informing federal policy-making toward the South. Northern Republican arguments reflected their intense confidence that abolition and Union victory had validated their views of freedom and progress and bolstered America's place in the world, but also their anxieties stemming from their confrontation with Johnson. Democrats, in contrast, saw in Crete a suffering analogous to their own experiences under radical despotism and "Negro" barbarism. Condemning northern Republican sympathy as cant, Democrats understood Crete as a tragic tale of the age, one of unmitigated suffering brought on by tyrants indifferent to the true foundations of freedom and progress. For a variety of reasons, including southern white supremacist violence, competing interest in other events such as the Morant Bay rebellion in Jamaica, and the temporary paucity of well-funded, politically oriented newspapers, African Americans left behind little printed commentary about Crete—although at least two papers did keep track of the conflict.[10] But both Democrats and the northern Republicans viewed the insurrection and the international politics surrounding it as a global struggle in which distinctive groups with their own characters contended for, with, and against the twin menaces of barbarism and despotism.

The Insurrection

Four factors contributed to the coming of the Cretan Insurrection. The first was Greek nationalist sentiment among the island's Christian population, much of which longed to join mainland Greece, which had secured its independence from the Ottoman Empire in the 1820s. Especially among much of its Greek Orthodox clerisy and in the island's interior, independence and union, or *Enosis*, was a burning cause. The mountainous region of Sphakia in western Crete had a longstanding reputation for resisting Ottoman rule, and would prove critical to the

1866 insurrection.[11] Second, the Ottoman Empire governed the island haphazardly. Crete's Ottoman governors neglected to implement a series of reforms mandated in 1856 by the Ottoman sultan, yet also made concessions to the island's Christians, including the right to own arms. The rural districts suffered under a system of tax farming, albeit one administered locally by leading Greek Orthodox Cretans in much of the island.[12] Third, social and economic developments strengthened the Greek Orthodox Cretan position. The island had a tiny Turkish population, and substantial portions of its Greek-speaking Muslim population, previously in the majority, had converted to Greek Orthodoxy in the last four decades. Greek Orthodox Cretans bought up land in the countryside while Turkish and Greek Muslims clustered near the island's coastal cities.[13] Finally Greek and European influences helped sustain revolutionary sentiment. Greek merchants, professionals, and students with experience beyond Crete likely encouraged the start of rebellion. Greek and Russian diplomats at times misled Greek Orthodox Cretans into believing that a rebellion would prompt foreign intervention.[14]

According to the most detailed account we have, which was written by the American consul on the island, William J. Stillman, the spark for the insurrection came at a fair in the mountain town of Omalos, near Sphakia, in April of 1866.[15] There, a group of local chieftains formed a council and remonstrated to the Ottoman authorities for better governance while a faction of these appealed to Britain, France, and Russia—the official co-arbiters of the region's politics—to allow unification with Greece. Diplomatic officials in Crete pressured the Ottoman governor, Ismael Pasha, not to suppress the council by force, so he instead called the island's Muslim minority into its walled cities, sparking panic. The Ottoman imperial government rebuked the council's requests as a revolutionary act and ordered the governor to arrest the leaders of the rebellion unless they promised submission. In response, leading Greek Orthodox Cretans, with encouragement from the Greek minister of war, formed a general assembly near Sphakia and declared independence and union with Greece in August. Throughout this period, tensions mounted between Orthodox and Muslim Cretans, especially in and near the cities that were now crowded with refugees. An independent revolutionary committee in Athens raised money, provided weapons, smuggled in Greek volunteers, and attempted to foment revolt in other Ottoman provinces.[16]

The conflict in Crete proceeded as a mixture of formal campaigning by Ottoman and revolutionary forces, guerrilla warfare, and localized religious violence among Christian and Muslim Cretans. The Ottoman Empire sent over fifty thousand troops to Crete, including semi-autonomous forces from its quasi-independent ally Egypt, and attempted a blockade.[17] Ottoman campaigns outraged many in Europe and America, although it remains difficult to ascertain just how ruthless these were. Our most thorough account of the fighting, again from Stillman, reflects his anti-Ottoman sentiment and his limited mobility during the insurrection. Stillman claimed that Ottoman forces routinely destroyed villages even after their surrender, with Omer Pasha—the Croatian Serb convert who had helped lead Ottoman forces during the Crimean War—personally participating in campaigns of mass rape.[18] Nineteenth-century Ottoman armies, especially their irregular contingents, had a well-documented history of civilian atrocity, including mass rape, but with Crete the Ottoman government was attentive to British diplomatic concerns that atrocities would inflame western opinion.[19] Massacres of Greek Orthodox Christians took place, but perhaps with less frequency and method than western sources, shaped by Orientalist assumptions about the cruel Turk, suggest. In the fall of 1867, the Ottoman grand vizier, Ali Pasha, traveled to Crete and offered an amnesty and administrative reforms only to have the rebels, encouraged by Greek politicians, reject them.[20] Scholarship on Greek Orthodox attacks on Muslim Cretans is virtually nonexistent in English, but these no doubt were also common. By one account, the Greek Orthodox rebels destroyed and in some cases poisoned their own drinking wells to help kill disease-stricken Ottoman forces.[21]

What is clear about the combat is that the poorly prepared and lightly armed rebels proceeded to fight an off-and-on guerrilla war for two and half years before the insurrection unraveled. Larger battles did occur, but so too did interludes as the Ottoman and Egyptian forces remained near cities in the coastal perimeter with the rebels in the mountainous interior.[22] Far-flung Greek merchants and European philhellenes supported the insurrection, including with money and arms, but never at levels that matched the scale of the Ottoman deployment. Perhaps fifty thousand women and children, nearly one-fifth of the island's total population, fled to mainland Greece and the surrounding islands; it is not clear how many Muslims Cretans fled persecution from Christians. Hunger and disease were likely the biggest killers on all sides.[23] Some covert support came from Russia and Greece, but neither state could venture open intervention with the British state backing Ottoman territorial integrity. The divided and faction-ridden Greek government seesawed between clandestinely supporting the insurrection and avoiding war with the Ottoman Empire, declining, for example, to seat Cretan delegates sent to its parliament. As the war dragged on, some Greek politicians quietly looked for a way out.[24] By late 1868, Ottoman forces on the island gained a decisive upper hand while the Greek and Ottoman states nearly came to blows. The latter crisis prompted Russia, France, and Great Britain to finally interceded and bring the crisis to an end. In a conference held in Paris in early 1869, the powers established that the Greek state would prevent insurgents from organizing in its territory while the Ottoman side would permit the rapid return of Cretan refugees.[25]

Cretan Slaves and Northern Republicans

Crete elicited northern Republican sympathy and interest in the face of some strong interpretive headwinds. In addition to the intermittent nature of the combat, the island was largely isolated from Europe, with no telegraph lines and little commerce outside of the Ottoman Empire. The Ottoman government, moreover, pressured local papers to report that the insurrection had ended, with American newspapers often reporting the same.[26] When Constantinople's English-language paper, the *Levant Herald,* printed two letters from Stillman indicating otherwise, the Ottoman government fined and then imprisoned the editor for three months.[27] The Ottoman blockade of the island further limited communication with the outside world, and the official correspondence of European and American consular officials to their home offices were sometimes the only conduit for information about the insurrection.[28] American observers frequently lamented the lack of reliable news.[29] Yet this did not stop northern Republicans from overwhelmingly presuming a connection between their American commitment to civilization and republicanism and the Cretan insurrectionists' struggle.

A handful of northern Republicans became directly involved in the uprising. Particularly active was the bold but hapless Stillman. Stillman had long supported the causes of European nationalist and republican movements, and had once run a botched secret mission for Lajos (or

Louis) Kossuth, the unsuccessful Hungarian rebel against Austrian rule. He also nearly joined Giuseppe Garibaldi's expedition to Marsala. Stillman's route to Crete began when he returned from Europe, where he had been living as a painter, to volunteer for the Union Army at the start of the Civil War. Failing the medical examination, Stillman proceeded to secure a diplomatic post in Italy, but after a brief stint in Rome he found himself transferred to Crete. There, he quickly fell into antagonisms with Ismael Pasha.[30] From the start of the insurrection, the defiant but increasingly beleaguered Stillman wrote numerous dispatches to the State Department and penned articles for *The Nation* and *Atlantic Monthly*. He finally took a leave of absence from Crete in September of 1868 to recover his nerves and take his family to safety, only to see politicking in Washington cost him his post. By the time he left the eastern Mediterranean in the summer of 1869, he was not only impoverished but had lost his wife to suicide, which he attributed to childbirth, stress, and grief for the Greek Orthodox Cretans. Perhaps reflecting these experiences, in the 1890s Stillman developed negative racial attitudes toward Greeks and other southern Europeans. He wrote *The Cretan Insurrection* in 1870 and later devoted two chapters to Crete in his *Autobiography of a Journalist*.[31]

Equally prominent was the Boston couple Samuel Gridley Howe and Julia Ward Howe. Samuel, a renowned northern reformer and long-standing philhellene who had served as a doctor and soldier in the Greek War of Independence (1821–1828), assumed the formal leadership of American relief efforts.[32] He was both an abolitionist and a believer in scientific theories of racial difference.[33] Despite tensions with her husband, Julia played an active and influential role, especially in organizing relief support. Julia also had an established interest in European nationalist and republican movements, and, as the author of "The Battle Hymn of the Republic," was a leading opponent of slavery and southern secession.[34] The Howes' efforts on behalf of the Cretans began with speeches, a pamphlet, and the organization of fundraising committees in Boston and New York that mustered $37,000 in donations, over twenty cases of supplies, and nearly four hundred breech-loading rifles.[35] Taking advantage of Greek mercantile networks that operated in New York, Britain, and throughout the Mediterranean, the Howes then traveled to Greece to distribute their aid.[36] Returning to Boston, Julia tried her hand at some poems for Crete and organized another relief fair, funds from which eventually became supplies smuggled into Crete.[37] Over the same period, the couple published a nearly monthly magazine, the *Cretan,* excerpts from which appeared in more prominent papers, including the *National Anti-Slavery Standard.*[38]

The Howes' fundraising efforts tapped into a broad base of humanitarian sympathy most evident in the prosperous and developing Republican strongholds of New England, New York, western Pennsylvania, Philadelphia, and the upper Northwest.[39] In contrast to a business- and Greek-dominated relief fund in London, donations to the Howes' Boston committee came overwhelmingly from individuals with no apparent family ties to Crete or Greece.[40] Such noteworthy abolitionists as Gerrit Smith and the committee's treasurer, Amos A. Lawrence, made contributions of $500 and $200. Less radical Unionists also pitched in. Henry Bellows, a leading Unitarian clergyman, warmly offered to give Samuel Gridley Howe what support he could and ended up serving as the president of the New York relief committee.[41] George Bancroft, who voted for Lincoln in 1864 but remained a Democrat at heart, helped organize fundraising efforts in New York City.[42] Henry Wadsworth Longfellow presented the insurrection as an abolitionist struggle, asking of Crete: "Thou sobbing captive in a sea of smiles, / Whose fairy sails on sunny errands flee, / Shall the blue waves that bless thy sister isles / Bind on thy brow the curse of slavery?"[43]

Support reached beyond these notables. The overwhelming majority of donations (roughly 460 out of 571) and over half of the $24,900.41 raised by the Boston committee came from individuals or small groups of individuals, with sums as small as 35 cents and with a median donation of $10. Many donors provided their initials or names, but others merely wrote humble or sympathetic messages like "A mite for the Cretans" ($10) and "From one who is well and comfortable" ($20) alongside their donations. Many organized their own charitable events, including a "Concert of the Ladies of Newport" ($526.90) and a sold-out "Concert in aid of the Cretans, Harvard Music Asso'n" ($2,249.22), where many of the 2,500 audience members remained on their feet throughout.[44] Other donations came from churches, schools, towns, an orphanage, and from as far away as McKendree College in Illinois ($26) and Milwaukee ($25). Though lacking a formal committee, Philadelphia contributed $1,739.54 to the Boston fund. Boston's sister committee in America's commercial capital of New York City not surprisingly drew more heavily on businesses. Again, however, small donations made their way in from individuals, a church, a school, and from as far away as Rochester, New York, Fairfield, Ohio, and Dodgeville, Wisconsin.[45] As late as January of 1869, the New York committee was imploring Americans in the voice of the Cretans to donate superfluous clothing and money.[46] With an established role in reform movements, it is no surprise that women featured prominently in these fundraising events as well as on Boston's donor rolls.[47] Upon returning from distributing aid in Greece, Samuel Gridley Howe gladly noted the thankfulness of Cretan refugees as they received clothing made and donated by "thousands of New England women and girls."[48] A second "ladies faire," which the Howes organized after distributing the aid from their first fundraising efforts, netted another $30,000, which was sent to Greece to buy food and clothes for Cretan refugees.[49]

Northern Republican sympathy for the insurrectionists reached further with the help of newspapers, magazines, and lectures. Newspapers like the *New York Times,* the *Chicago Tribune,* and the *Cleveland Leader,* as well as Republican-leaning independents like the *Sacramento Daily Union,* all offered front-page coverage when news was available.[50] These opinionated dailies quickly integrated discussions of Crete into their constant editorializing. Prominent magazines, including *The Nation, Harper's Weekly,* and *Atlantic Monthly,* likewise covered the insurrection and sought to explain its meaning. Finally, there were public speeches. Wendell Phillips and Samuel Gridley Howe were among the more notable to give speeches in Boston in January 1867 and March 1868, while Henry Ward Beecher spoke in New York City in January 1867.[51] When English author and visitor to Crete J.E.H. Skinner lectured in Chicago, the *Chicago Tribune* reported that "Everyone" in his full audience had "read and heard of" the most dramatic event of the insurrection, an attack on the monastery of Arkadi.[52] Similarly, the *New York Times* reported that when Stewart L. Woodford, a former officer in the Union Army and the Republican lieutenant governor of New York, lectured on Crete at Steinway Hall, his large audience listened "with deep attention."[53]

Stillman sounded the earliest note of what would be a mounting chorus of Republican sympathy. At the beginning of the insurrection, the Cretan rebels delivered to Stillman an appeal addressed to President Andrew Johnson, which he then sent on to Secretary of State William

Seward. Despite Stillman's expectation that the insurrection would prove futile, he stressed to Seward that "every word" of the appeal was "wrung from patriotic hearts by bitter and most unmerited oppression." Stressing his "American instincts," Stillman added that if Americans could only see how "a barbarous and licentious soldiery" drove Cretans from their homes, destroyed churches, and "paralyzed" industry, they could not help but be moved.[54] In December of 1866, Stillman again described to Seward how the insurrection had been "conducted with so much heroism and constancy on one side and savage barbarity on the other." Stillman explained, "The sympathy I ought to feel for a people aspiring to freedom was, thus, much increased by the injustice of the Government and still more by its subsequent barbarity and excessive cruelty."[55] Stillman was not alone among his peers in the U.S. diplomatic corps. Edward Joy Morris, the American minister to Constantinople, A. S. York, the American consul on the Greek island of Zante, and Mr. Rousseau, an American diplomat in Vienna, expressed similar sentiments.[56] John Hay, Lincoln's former private secretary, lectured on the insurrection while traveling in the region, and U.S. naval officers demonstrated "American" sympathy by donating money and clothing to refugees who cheered them at Athens's port.[57]

Stillman, the Howes, and the broader press articulated a free-labor Orientalism that condemned Turkish misrule for undermining economic progress and familial tranquility. Writing for *Atlantic Monthly*, Stillman repeatedly measured Ottoman misrule through the island's poverty. Towns such as Chania suffered from "dilapidation and decay," while wretched roads and "benighted restrictions" on shipping stifled farmers.[58] Likewise, the rural plain of Cydonia would return to its ancient prosperity if freed from the "Mohammedan blight."[59] The *New York Times* characterized the Ottoman Muslims as "vapid and indolent," and Stillman claimed that the Christian Cretan was the island's "only industrious citizen."[60] Ottoman despotism, in these depictions, destroyed the emotional and economic bonds that drove progress. This economic critique merged seamlessly with a sentimental notion of the household as a nurturing space that was the pervasive complement of the free-labor vision of the hardworking male citizen. The height of the Howes' revulsion was reserved for the alleged Turkish disregard for the sheltering ties of the affectionate family. Samuel claimed that Turkish treatment of "boys, girls, and women" violated civilized norms and was "often so cruel and so abominable that one can hardly find comprehensible language in which to speak of it."[61]

The November 1866 attack on the Arkadi Monastery, which was hosting approximately three hundred soldiers and six hundred civilians, mostly women and children, became the most infamous incident of Turkish barbarity.[62] In its February 2, 1867, edition, *Harper's Weekly* provided an overview of the insurrection that dwelt on Arkadi. The insurrectionists, argued *Harper's,* were motivated not only by "a common patriotic desire that Crete should be governed by Cretans," but also by a "system of continued cruelties" that had "few parallels on record." *Harper's* claimed that while both sides fought with intense hatred in the current struggle, it was the Turkish Muslims who were guilty of "slaughtering without mercy to wreak their vengeance." As *Harper's* explained, the Cretans were "enduring great suffering, and even ending their own lives" to avoid being "borne away as captives of the infidel Moslem." *Harper's* then added that "The most tragic event" in this war was the attack on Arkadi and included an account thereof from the *Levant Herald.* The *Herald* reported that a much larger Turkish force bombarded the monastery and its resilient rebels and refugee women and children for four days. When the attackers finally breached Arkadi's outer walls, the rebel soldiers fought desperately in the courtyard before taking refuge in the cellars while women and children barricaded themselves in the refectory. With these last defenses collapsing, reported the *Levant Herald,* the remaining insurgents resolved to destroy the monastery, their attackers, and themselves by igniting their powder.[63]

Harper's Weekly included a "vivid sketch" from a Cretan resident of Istanbul familiar with the monastery (see figure 1). In it, soldiers fight in the background while men and women strain to hold shut the last door between themselves and the Ottoman forces, represented by only an axe blade and a spear point. At the center of the illustration a woman clutches a naked baby to her body and defiantly stares at the door while priests standing near her ignite the powder. The sketch's message to *Harper's* readers was clear. Faced with the Turkish onslaught, the Cretan rebels fought unceasingly. Overpowered, they preferred death to having their women and children fall into the hands of the Turks, long maligned as lustful and cruel.

The *Harper's* article as well as its excerpt from the *Levant Herald* are loosely accurate and may have drawn from accounts of the attack by its

FIGURE 1. "The War in Crete—the Attack on the Monastery of Arcadi—[From an Original Sketch]," *Harper's Weekly,* February 2, 1867, 68.

few Greek Orthodox survivors.[64] But they are also one-sided. They neglect the perspectives of the diverse attacking forces, which included conscripts, officers, and irregulars from Turkey, Crete, Ottoman Europe, and Egypt. The excerpt left unmentioned that it was likely Egyptians soldiers with Ottoman bayonets at their backs, including perhaps some Coptic Christians, who breached the monastery's walls.[65] So too did *Harper's* fail to report that the monastery had been a center of revolutionary activity and that its abbot, Gabriel Marinakis, was a leading insurrectionist (whom the attackers killed and then decapitated).[66] But the woman and baby in the illustration were not pure fiction; the monastery was full of both. Months later, when British writer J.E.H. Skinner visited the monastery, he found among the corpses that of a woman clutching a baby, albeit not in the same room as where the powder was stored.[67] Certainly this was a massacre. An ossuary containing skulls of the Greek Orthodox victims, many of them visibly cracked, has become part of a sanctuary at the rebuilt monastery.[68]

The story powerfully affected northern Republicans. Within two weeks of *Harper's* Arkadi illustration, the New York state legislature passed a concurrent resolution expressing "sympathy for the Greeks, who are now struggling for freedom," and urging "our national government to protest against the barbarous and inhuman system of warfare adopted by the Turks."[69] For many Republican sympathizers, Arkadi was a definitive statement, or as Stewart Woodford described it, "the cry of all Crete for liberty or death."[70] Indeed, Arkadi demanded attention even from skeptics. *Frank Leslie's Illustrated Newspaper*, a politically independent weekly that lacked a consistent partisan ideology, initially dismissed the thought of Protestant sympathy flowing to Greek Orthodox Christians and warned against foreign entanglements.[71] Yet *Leslie's* repeatedly covered Arkadi, conceding that the insurrection was "exciting great attention all over the civilized world."[72] Nearly a year after Arkadi, the magazine admitted that Crete had so "engrossed the attention and enlisted the sympathies of the public" that it had been "induced" to better cover the insurrection.[73]

There were of course many, including northern Republicans, who like the editors of *Frank Leslie's* hesitated to embrace the cause of the Greek Orthodox Cretan rebels. A mixture of ignorance about the region, busy schedules, and competing causes all limited the interest of some northern Republicans.[74] Not everyone was temperamentally inclined to sympathy; the conservative and acerbic Anglo-American editor of *The Nation*, E. L. Godkin, looked upon the insurrection with derision.[75] Overwhelmingly, however, northern Republicans felt confident assuming that by their very nature as the true Americans they understood and sympathized with the Greek Orthodox insurrectionists and their struggle. This belief proved remarkably resilient to the scarceness and unreliability of information coming from the island. The ease with which northern Republicans related to the Cretan Insurrection reflected their underlying conviction that the world's people were all involved in global struggles for freedom and progress, and could be known by the roles they presumably played in these.

Sentimental Diplomacy

The ideological fervor of northern Republican reactions is particularly evident in how they understood the diplomacy surrounding the insurrection. In retrospect, one can see that the possibility of any kind of substantial engagement on the part of the United States with the insurrection was remote; indeed, some saw as much at the time. As a matter of hallowed tradition, American statesmen did not entangle the United States in European power politics, which were clearly at play in the conflict. What is more, the United States had no military capacity to project power in the Mediterranean, especially with the Ottoman and British navies in the area. The United States could have unilaterally recognized the insurrectionists as belligerents or even as an independent country, but such a move would hardly have changed the policies of the major players in the region or developments on the ground. Yet still, as with the insurrection itself, northern Republicans confidently imbued the insurrection's surrounding diplomacy with meaning, taking it to be a pitched battle in the global struggles for freedom and progress.

Northern Republicans, well-aware of the Ottoman Empire's weakened state and precarious hold on its European provinces, at times expected the insurrection to trigger a broader Ottoman collapse. In an article titled "The Eastern Question—Crete the Opening Wedge," the *New York Times* informed its readers that the insurrection would spread revolution throughout the empire.[76] A later article, "The Clouds Accumulating—Turkey About to Fall to Pieces," stated that the backward, theocratic empire would soon collapse before the age's "irresistible spirit of progress."[77] The *New York Tribune* described Constantinople as a place where "an effete Mohammedanism struggles in vain against the aggressive spirit of Christian civilization."[78]

Such giddiness often dissolved into resentment toward Great Britain and at times France for supporting Ottoman territorial integrity in order to check Russian expansion.[79] The underlying cause of Crete's suffering in the first place, according to Samuel Gridley Howe, was that the powers had acted like "Asiatic despots" and sacrificed Crete to please Turkey back at the end of the Greek War of Independence.[80] Traditional American Anglophobia, ongoing diplomatic quarrels, and England's aristocratic tradition all fueled ire toward Britain.[81] The *Sacramento Daily Union* asserted that the English elite had a "habitual indifference to moral and human considerations" and would help sustain "A loathsome, heathen despotism" to hinder Russia.[82] When the sultan toured Europe during the insurrection—the first and last nonmilitary trip of an Ottoman sultan outside his territories—a correspondent for the *New York Tribune* referred to it as a "magnificent farce" and condemned the English for gleefully kneeling in the mud before him.[83] Once again,

Harper's Weekly gave graphic expression to northern Republican sentiment (see figure 2). Responding to the sultan's visit to England, *Harper's* portrayed John Bull stooping to kiss the hand of the sultan and singing "God preserve thee, Sultan, long; / Ever keep thee from all woes: / May thy State and thee be strong, / To dismay and resist thy foes!" The sultan, meanwhile, whispers to his grand vizier, "These infidel *John Bulls* don't see those little Massacres of their Christian brethren in Crete," while Turkish flags float over a hillside attack on Cretan Christians in the background.[84] There was some truth in northern Republican accusations. British statesmen worked assiduously to prevent intervention or any other maneuver that might result in Cretan autonomy and the collapse of the Ottoman Empire in Europe. Yet, the northern Republicans' moralistic tone led them to overlook the ways in which self-interest incentivized the British and French to urge the Ottoman Empire to avoid atrocities and to find a mediated solution to the conflict.[85] Indeed, four European powers—Russia, Austria, Italy, and France—asserted the right to transport Christian refugees from Crete on humanitarian grounds, while U.S. officials dithered about the issue, much to Samuel Howe's rage.[86]

Some northern Republicans particularly smiled on the idea that Russian, which had been a nominal ally of the Union during the Civil War, would reopen "the Eastern Question" concerning the uncertain future of the Ottoman Empire. The *Cleveland Leader* claimed that American sentiment would all be with Russia if that power sparked a broader European war. The paper, referring to the island by its older Venetian name, commented that Americans, already sympathetic toward the "oppressed and independence-loving Christians of Candia, struggling against heathen, barbarian and foreign tyrants," would feel a natural affinity for Russia. Like the United States, Russia had grievances against Britain and France, lacked allies in Europe, was a young, expanding nation, and had recently moved to end a form of bound labor.[87] Such comments were ultimately far-fetched. Russian statesmen did have concern for the insurrection on religious and geopolitical grounds, but not to the point of risking a broader war.[88]

Northern Republicans looked to those who dissented from the continent's prevailing order—Europe's liberals, radicals, and humanitarians—to stand with them in favor of civilization and republicanism. Stillman, who had worked as an artist and critic in Europe since the

FIGURE 2. "Which Is the Infidel?" asks this cartoon from *Harper's Weekly*, August 17, 1868, 528.

1850s, corresponded directly with European literati, including members of Britain's Pre-Raphaelite school of painters.[89] In particular, Dante and William Michael Rossetti—the sons of an exiled Italian radical—helped Stillman find venues for his writings and put him in contact with their wealthy Greek merchant-patrons.[90] At its zenith, Stillman's efforts included attempting to raise funds for a Greek expedition—a clear violation of consular neutrality—through Stauros Dilberoglue, a radical London merchant close to the Rossetti brothers.[91] While these efforts amounted to little, Stillman remained close to the Rossettis, lodging with them after the insurrection.[92] Through them he met his second wife, the Pre-Raphaelite artist Marie Spartali, the daughter an émigré merchant who served as consul-general for Greece in London during the insurrection and who was also connected to radicals and nationalists.[93]

The northern Republican press was also quick to point to Europeans who supported the insurrection. One close colleague of the Rossettis, Algernon Swinburne, hastily wrote a poem, "Ode on the Insurrection in Candia," and donated the profits from it to Cretan refugees.[94] The poem was a later quoted in an editorial by the *Cleveland Leader* and prompted the Italian republican Giuseppe Mazzini to write the author encouraging his efforts.[95] Similarly, when Victor Hugo wrote a letter in support of the insurrection, the *National Anti-Slavery Standard* paraphrased his declaration that "the cause of Crete is that of Greece, and the cause of Greece is that of Europe."[96] It was in this context that northern Republicans eagerly awaited word of Garibaldini who had traveled east a few years after the unification of Italy to fight on behalf of Crete. As with much else in the insurrection, northern Republicans' hopes were informed—approximately two thousand Redshirts arrived in Greece—yet unfulfilled. The Greek government compelled most to return home to avoid a diplomatic quagmire, with only handfuls making it to the island.[97] At least one French sympathizer and future Communard, Gustave Flourens, fought with the Cretans and was awarded Cretan citizenship and then elected a member of the Cretan Provisional Assembly.[98]

These pro-Cretan voices in Europe were, northern Republicans thought, rare kindred spirits in a continent otherwise committed to cynical Great Power diplomacy. Among the powers of the world, this line of thinking went, the United States had a special obligation to stand up. Stillman, for one, stepped beyond his limited consular duties to ask Secretary of State Seward, "May the friends of humanity not hope that America will lead off in a question where no political interest can stain the purity of her motives?"[99] Going further, the *Cretan* averred that prompt recognition of Cretan independence would "diffuse the lesson throughout Christendom" that America remained an uncompromising and unmatched defender of "freedom, civilization, virtue, and Christianity."[100] Although the *New York Times*, like *Frank Leslie's*, warned against formal American entanglement in the Eastern Question, it also argued, offering Crete as an example, that America had a unique obligation to master diplomacy. "Untrammeled by the traditional and selfish policy of the old dynasties," claimed the *Times*, "the friends of freedom and progress throughout the world justly expect from the United States an attitude of intelligent sympathy toward them."[101] In Constantinople, Edward Morris had hoped, to little effect, that the purity of American motives toward Crete would have an ameliorating influence on European diplomacy.[102] The *Sacramento Daily Union* was more ambitious. It suggested that Europe recognized the Union's newfound strength and reminded readers that European monarchs had long interfered in American affairs. "What if," asked the *Union*, "the republic should venture to retaliate, and begin to exercise an intervening influence in European affairs in favor of free institutions?" Surely, thought the *Union*, this could bring American diplomacy in line with "the strength and mission of the republic" without necessarily leading to war.[103]

None of the politicians, cabinet members, or bureaucrats in the U.S. government ever found the diplomatic middle road envisioned by the *Union*. Congress, the president, and the Department of State declined to take bold action. Confronting this situation, northern Republicans continued to profess national sympathies for the Cretans. The *Cretan* took President Andrew Johnson, an increasingly bitter opponent of Republican domestic policy, to be the villain behind diplomatic inaction. An address to Congress published in the *Cretan* argued that supporters of the insurrection had "the right to expect and demand, that, as soon as the existing administration is overthrown, there shall be a radical change of our foreign policy."[104] The *Cretan* similarly lambasted Johnson's secretary of state, William Seward, a Republican who had stayed on in Johnson's cabinet and who was actually sympathetic toward the Cretans, for failing to recognize the provisional government of Crete.[105] Even if the administration did not act, the Howes found consolation in their belief that the Cretan rebels were "virtually" recognized "by the American people."[106] "America can save Crete," the *Cretan* quipped with reference to Seward's purchase of Alaska, "even if Mr. Seward does not buy it."[107] Public interest became sufficiently strong to move a bedraggled Congress into issuing a Republican-sponsored joint statement of sympathy for the Cretans, introduced in the Senate by abolitionist Charles Sumner. It did not, however, go as far as Representative John Shanks (R-Ind.) urged when he requested full official recognition of the Cretan provisional government as an independent state.[108]

The idea that the United States, as an actor in the global struggles for freedom and progress, could somehow save Crete, as a victim in the same, was wishful thinking. Andrew Johnson, moreover, was not to blame. Johnson, in fact, had put up no apparent opposition to congressional statements of sympathy for the Cretans, although according to Secretary of the Navy Gideon Welles he signed them only through inattention.[109] Late in the war, during a brief discussion with his cabinet about Crete, Johnson reminded Seward that the Ottoman Empire had been a Union ally during the war and that the United States had its own matters to attend to.[110] But the brevity and tardiness of the conversation, more so than Johnson's stance, indicate the unlikelihood of any serious American action. Indeed, the Howes faced more fundamental difficulties. As with French imperial rule of Mexico (1861–1865) and the Ten Years' War in Cuba (1868–1878), northern Republicans disagreed over how exactly their unique national commitment to freedom and progress should translate into policy. In both of the latter cases, northern Republicans shared in their dislike of old-world imperial powers exercising influence in the western hemisphere, but divided in their judgments over the aptitude of the Catholic and racially mixed peoples of Mexico and Cuba to govern themselves.[111] With Crete, there was little concern about race—if anything, preconceived notions of the Greeks as "white" and the Turks as "Asiatic" helped their cause.[112] Northern Republicans like Samuel Gridley Howe were willing to abandon the national tradition of nonintervention in European diplomacy and throw America's weight, whatever it was, behind Cretan independence. At one point he even briefly pursued a scheme of embroiling the United States in the conflict by attempting to run the Turkish blockade under an American flag or, that failing, doing the same with an American crew under the Cretan revolutionary flag. Neither suicide mission, and the latter was intended as such, got off the ground.[113] One former Union cavalryman with ties to the eastern Mediterranean, Sidney DeKay, joined the insurrection, where he led a failed attempt to blow a hole in the hull of an anchored Turkish frigate.[114] A moderate Republican newspapers like the *New York Times* might laud DeKay's valor when he later became wounded (unbeknownst to the *Times,* by an accidental discharge of his own weapon), but they spurned formal American involvement.[115]

The United States was not going to save Crete, but the conceit that it could inspired multiple instances of diplomatic showmanship. Early in the conflict *La Turquie,* the sultan's official newspaper, denounced expressions of sympathy from the United States, but as the war ground on it opted for more diplomatic approaches.[116] Concerned with Stillman's negative reporting, the Ottoman Empire sent its first ever envoy to the United States during the insurrection, the French-born Ottoman consular official Edouard Blacque, whose deceased first wife had been an American.[117] He arrived at nearly the same time as the Greek government's first ever minister to the States, Alexander Rangabe, who played up the genocidal nature of Turkish campaigns and the natural expectation that Americans would be concerned with the suffering of the oppressed.[118] Rumors from the Washington press had it that Rangabe was aligned with Republicans in Congress while Blacque supported Johnson. Not to be outdone, the Cretan Provisional Assembly somehow induced Julius Bing, a former Union soldier and briefly the U.S. consul in the nearby city of Smyrna, to serve as their own diplomatic agent to the United States.[119] In November of 1868, the Greek Chamber of Deputies formally thanked the U.S. Congress and people for their sympathy.[120]

The U.S. government's response to these diplomatic moves was a predictable mix of official neutrality and seeming partiality for the rebels. It sent its first minister to Greece, with the post going to Charles Keating Tuckerman, who had served with his brother Henry on the New York City Cretan Relief Committee. As part of the same, Henry, among others, collaborated with D. W. Botassi, the Greek consul in New York, to circulate a Cretan appeal to the United States.[121] Tuckerman arrived in Greece too late to do much for the insurrection and, unlike Stillman, felt constrained by diplomatic procedure.[122] He did, however, forward to the United States a statement of thanks, later reprinted in the press, from the Cretan refugees in Athens in response to John Shanks's speech in Congress and explained to Washington that the Greek Orthodox Cretans looked to America for salvation.[123] The Greek King, George I, lauded Tuckerman's philhellenism by decorating him in 1871, although Tuckeman's willingness to side with the king against Greek liberals in the country's intrigue-wracked politics likely contributed to the honor.[124]

Such maneuvering continued through the end of the insurrection, much of it centered on Stillman. Once he stepped down as consul, the Ottoman grand vizier, Ali Pasha, recognizing his stature with the local population, sought to enlist him as an intermediary on the island. Stillman was wise to decline the position; the Ottoman leadership clearly resented his past actions. In 1870, the sultan awarded his predecessor, George Mountfort, the rank of the Imperial Order of Medidich in honor of his dutifulness and neutrality, a full eleven years after Mountfort's term as consul had ended. It was a clear jab at Stillman's partisanship.[125] In contrast, when Stillman's wife passed away, the city of Athens, still filled with Cretan refugees, held a public funeral to honor the family.[126]

Even with the deck stacked so heavily against any type of formal involvement by the U.S. government, northern Republicans thought of themselves as global actors in league with the insurrectionists in their quest for freedom and progress. To their minds, the transcendent nature of civilization and republicanism made them kindred spirits with the rebels, as with the small number of European statesmen, writers, and artists who spoke out in the name of the Cretan cause. This sense of connection affirmed the northern Republicans' belief that they exemplified America and that America exemplified the causes of freedom and progress. But, in its purest form, that same sense of connection also undermined the idea that national distinctiveness was really important in the first place. If the Cretans, Americans, and European liberals all shared the same commitment to civilization and republicanism, and if these two causes were the ones that really defined who a people were, then were they not all really part of the same group? And did not their opponents similarly compose another, rival group of barbarians and despots? The tensions between these two patterns of thought were particularly apparent in the border-crossing analogies that northern Republicans made as they discussed the insurrection.[127]

Ambiguous Analogies

Northern Republicans were quick to advance a wide range of analogies that linked the Cretans to themselves and other peoples struggling for freedom and progress and likewise lumping the Turks together with an assortment of nefarious villains. References to the Civil War, for one, came into play. Stillman, for example, stressed the connection in correspondence to Seward by explaining that he had followed developments in Crete "with no less anxiety than that I felt during our own struggle with the criminal organization of the enemies of Freedom."[128] The *Springfield Republican* compared the rebels with John Brown and other defiant antebellum abolitionists.[129] Likewise, Stewart Woodford, in his speech in New York City, argued that the Cretans were motivated by the same spirit as Garibaldi's Italians and the Union's "citizen soldiery."[130] Similarly, the Howes explained, tersely, that reports of the insurrection's demise had the "internal marks of having being [*sic*] written in Constantinople, by a copper-head employee of a republican government," who had espoused "anti-American and despotic ideas."[131] The alleged disregard of the "Turks" for the affective bonds of the sentimental family found expression through comparisons to the Confederate prison of Andersonville. As the *New York Times* declared, "We are accustomed to shrink from contemplating the miseries of Andersonville; but they were perpetrated upon men—soldiers who had braved the horrors of war." The *Times* demanded to know, "Shall such horrors go on, and the Christian world stand mute and unprotesting?"[132]

Analogies ranged as far as Mormon Utah and conquered Poland and as near as the South. Samuel Gridley Howe wrote that, while Cretan Christians could appeal to local officials, "so might once the unhappy negro in the center of Alabama (may perhaps again) apply to a white justice of the peace against his master!" Likewise, the Turkish rulers suffered under "the curse which slavery brought upon our Southern slavocrats; to wit, the power to make other men do their sweating."[133] Stillman came to see the entire Ottoman state as akin to an elaborate slaveholding enterprise that shared the same underlying spirit of despotism with the Confederacy.[134] To those who thought Crete too distant to be of interest, *Harper's Weekly* countered that many had once felt similarly about southern slavery.[135] Differences mattered too. Stillman, focusing on prosperity, lamented a Cretan waterfront that physically resembled New York harbor but supported only a "tumble-down town."[136]

The *Cretan* routinely equated the "Turks," with their allegedly insatiable lusts and disdain for sentimental family life, with Mormons, who were in turn linked to slaveholders. It printed one letter that claimed, for example, that "The English Government, the quondam champion of the slave Confederacy, sees fit to be also the champion of a Mormon Empire."[137] And the *Cretan* could only hope that America would cease indirect support for the "Mohammedan and Mormon slavocrats in the east" as it had its support for the "Southern slavocrats."[138] The *Boston Advertiser* echoed these statements, describing the Ottoman Empire as an "Asiatic dynasty, with Mormon customs."[139]

Then there were comparisons to Native Americans. When explaining how the "barbarous nature of Turkish warfare" had produced so many Cretan refugees, Samuel Gridley Howe noted, "Even the Polish peasant did not thus fly before Russian armies; and the only parallel is to be found among barbarians, or savages on our own frontier."[140] In Congress, Representative Shanks went further and argued that the Ottoman forces, desperate to subdue the Cretans, massacred them with a "cruelty of which is without parallel even among the annals of the Apache."[141] In linking Turks to Apaches, it is tempting to read these analogies as arguments tying dark-skinned people together as barbarians. Yet often the racial import seemed the exact opposite: by lumping Turks, Apaches, Mormons, and southern slaveholders together, the analogies suggested that race was not the governing category of analysis. White people could and did serve just as well as symbols of barbarism in discussions of Turkish misrule. In at least one case, however, a comparison was explicitly racial. An unidentified booster of Cretan independence in New York City, perhaps a Republican, explained to *The Round Table* that having the "inferior race" of the Turks rule the "superior race" of the Greeks would be akin to the Apaches governing New York or Vermont.[142]

These analogies were emblematic of the creative tension that sat at the heart of Reconstruction's world. The globe was populated by distinct peoples, yet who these peoples were could only be understood relative to the transcendent causes of civilization and republicanism. The analogies at once blurred the distinction between things foreign and domestic and yet affirmed northern Republicans' sense of being a people, Americans, defined by their commitment to freedom and progress.

This tension was evident in their beliefs concerning the foreignness of the Greeks. Certainly, there was little doubt about the Turks, who, as the supposed embodiment of despotism and barbarism, were despicably foreign to northern Republicans' allegedly national instincts. Describing the Greeks as independent, diligent, intelligent, and cultivated, northern Republicans rarely took Greek particularities as manifestations of barbarism.[143] *Harper's Weekly* once described the Greek Orthodox Cretans as "semi-barbarous," but blamed Ottoman oppression for this, as did Lewis Packard, a Yale professor of Greek resident in Athens.[144] British statesmen, in contrast, were much more willing to play up the Christian Cretans' barbarity and implicate them in the island's poor governance.[145] More often, as leading abolitionist Wendell Phillips argued, Cretan distinctiveness underscored claims to independence and union with Greece proper. As he asserted before a sympathetic Boston audience, "Crete stretches her arm across the Atlantic, and asks us to protest against Europe, and to advocate the American idea that every nation has the right to govern itself."[146] Nations should govern themselves because they were all distinctive, and those nations that believed this all made themselves akin to America in their love of freedom. It was one variation of the tendency of Reconstruction's partisans to see the world as divided into groups but then to undermine the importance of those groups' distinctiveness by defining the latter in terms of overarching struggles.

Occasionally northern Republicans undercut their own presumed affinities with the insurrection by criticizing the Greeks, especially for having a monarch and an established, non-Protestant church.[147] It was none other than Julia Howe who upon returning home jokingly described her work in Greece as follows, highlighting her negative views of the Greek Orthodox clergy:

> Oh! what were the projects you made, Mrs. Howe,
> When you went where the Cretans were making a row?
> Emancipation—civilization—redintegration of a great nation,
> Paying no taxes, grinding no axes—
> Flinging the Ministers over the banisters.
> These were the projects of good Mrs. Howe
> When she went where the Cretans were making a row.[148]

One cannot help but wonder whether some Greeks similarly doubted the depth of ideological accord when Samuel Gridley Howe used relief funds to establish industrial schools that, he believed, would save refugees from idleness.[149] Yet even in the face of cultural differences, northern Republicans tended to maintain a faith in the Greek potential for freedom and progress. As the *Cretan* wrote of refugee children at those American-run industrial schools: "they will be imbued to some extent with American ideas. Every scholar will grow up with a knowledge of, and partiality for, our people and for our institutions. They will be half Americans. They will be native missionaries from this generation to succeeding ones."[150] The point was not that the refugees were going to become ethnically indistinguishable from Americans, but that when it came to things that really mattered—representative government, free labor, the affective household, education—they would become like Americans, as northern Republicans understood them to be.

Given such beliefs, it is not surprising that at least a few northern sympathizers figured that American control of Crete would serve just as well, if not better, than its union with Greece. A flyer addressed to "the people of the United States" by one New York National Reconstruction Club proposed exactly this, urging the United States to acquire the island. Doing so would provide a naval and commercial outpost in the Levant, which, the flyer argued, would soon be largely free from Ottoman control. Acquisition of the island would also mean a territory "in which we may establish American Institutions." Believing erroneously that the Ottoman government could not defeat the insurrection, the club asserted that it would be glad to sell the island. "Let us acquire Candia," the flyer confidently suggested, "our commerce requires it, our mission among the Nations demands it."[151] If Americans and Cretans both loved freedom and progress, and if this defined who they were, then what did it matter whether the rebels became part of the United States or Greece?

White Cretans and Yankee Turks

Democrats, North and South, also interpreted the Cretan Insurrection and particularly northern Republican interest in it. The *Constitution* of Atlanta, the *New York World*, the *Richmond Enquirer and Sentinel*, and the *Memphis Daily Avalanche* were among those who challenged northern Republican understandings of the insurrection. For Democrats, Crete became a means of expressing both their partisan grievances—particularly against so-called "Radical" Republicans—and a rival strain of nationalism that wedded ideals to a rigid and pronounced understanding of race. While northern Republicans harbored racial prejudices, the concept of race generally remained loosely defined and latent in their discussion of the insurrection. Democrats, in contrast, stressed the irrevocable superiority of some peoples over others and the obligations of northerners to their fellow "whites" in the South.

The *Constitution* was a spirited critic, focusing its derision on "Yankee" humanitarianism. When Charles Sumner introduced a congressional resolution expressing sympathy for the Cretans, the *Constitution* described his Senate foreign relations committee as having "resolved itself into a universal sympathetic society." The "Radical party," it further complained, "sheds tears over the down-trodden everywhere, and its wailings for the distressed go forth into the uttermost parts of the earth." The newspaper lamented that underlying this sympathy was a belief that "all are bound by a common brotherhood." "No stretch of distance," it argued, "can annihilate [the Radical party's] tender feelings for suffering humanity."[152] The *Constitution* further accused the Radical Republicans of moralistic arrogance. At the heart of the Radicals' "transcendental faith" was its claim "to be the missionary through which the world shall be converted from heathenism to its progressive ideas."[153] Boston, home of the Howes and capital of abolitionism in the United States, attracted a heavy dose of criticism. She was "the center of this great moral solar system," and "arrogates to herself the lead in all schemes" to uplift the oppressed people of the world.[154] As the *Constitution* described it, Boston's perspective was that, "she being the center of the universe, all must obey."[155]

The *New York World* similarly criticized what it saw as the self-righteous grandstanding of the "Cretan Committee" in New York City. It proposed that the committee forgo the cause of Crete and instead raise funds to save a group of now-destitute missionary settlers who had left Maine for Palestine in 1866. While mocking these "Main-iacs" as religiously fanatical "Yankees of the Yankees," the paper still believed that as fellow white Americans they deserved aid. The *World,* however, doubted that Republicans would take up an issue that was "not a tempting one for orators."[156] Over a year later, it argued that Bostonians were too in love with themselves to grasp the complexities and dangers of the Cretan Insurrection.[157]

Democrats further alleged that northern Republicans were hypocritical, most obviously because they now supported an act of rebellion. After explaining to its readers that Boston was now home to "a paper devoted to the cause of the *rebel* Cretans," the *Constitution* cautioned its readers not to be alarmed. Even "cold and stoic Boston," it explained with derision, "has a heart; and even *rebels* are touching it to tenderness and tears."[158] Like northern Republicans, Democrats interpreted Crete through analogies to their domestic experiences. The *New York World,* for one, suggested that, "Being copperheads in respect to Crete," Republicans sympathizers should "show consistent courage in their opinions, and become copperheads also in respect to the South."[159]

Yet the perceived hypocrisy ran deeper still, for northern Republicans sympathized with rebels despite their domination of the South, which purportedly matched and exceeded Turkish cruelty. The *Memphis Daily*

Avalanche was sure that even the Radical Republicans could not honestly expect the rest of the world to ignore "the fact that the North is doing to the South of this country just what Turkey is trying to do to Greece." Like Turkey, claimed the *Avalanche,* the North sought to "strip a gallant race of the rights of self-government" and impose its own ideas at bayonet point.[160] The *New York World* mocked the northern Republicans' attempts to get Americans "to discriminate in a question of legitimate rule between New Englanders in black satin waistcoats holding sway in Washington, and Turks in green silk Turbans exercising dominion at Constantinople."[161] The *Richmond Enquirer and Sentinel* went further, alleging that, despite all the "usual gabble about the inhumanity of Russia to the Poles, the Turks towards the Greeks and the Cretans, &c., &c.," only the Radicals had been so cruel as to surrender a conquered people to mercies of their former slaves.[162]

Democrats claimed that they, not northern Republicans, shared a bond with the Cretan rebels. Responding to the call for aid from the *Cretan,* Atlanta's *Constitution* noted that southerners could not help but sympathize with the Cretans, for "Their condition is too much like our own." Both had fought long, brutal wars for their independence, and both remained under the control of another power. Referring to a Turkish military commander in Crete, the *Constitution* asserted that "A dozen or so Oma Pachas came upon us from their Turkish strong-holds, a few years since, with fire and sword, reducing us to skin and bones, until we languish in our native nudity."[163] And surely, the *Constitution* surmised, the Senate's statement of sympathy would meet with disregard from the Ottoman Empire. Focusing on the prominent Radical Charles Sumner much as the Howes vilified Andrew Johnson, the *Constitution* argued that Turkey would no doubt "delicately direct the attention as well as the sympathies of Mr. Sumner" to the South. For it was in Sumner's own country, asserted the *Constitution,* where "insults and outrages, tyrannies and oppressions of which the [*sic*] Crete never dreamed" continued.[164] The *New York World,* referring to the congressional Republicans' assertion of control over Reconstruction, went even further in the middle of 1868 in response to the Ottoman Empire's offer of clemency. "In what striking contrast is this action of the Grand Turk," exclaimed the *World,* "to that of the Rump Congress with *their* insurrection."[165]

Of particular concern to Democrats was the seeming disregard of northern Republicans, especially Radicals, for racial hierarchy.[166]

According to the *Constitution,* Boston's "generous nature was such" that she anticipated "that period when some of the lower orders of being, through her benign influences, shall assume a place in the family of man."[167] The *Constitution* was convinced that this "meddlesome disposition of the Radical" underlay interest in both the Cretan Insurrection and the Reconstruction of the South. The *Constitution* described how Radicals in one breath expressed "canting, sycophantic sympathy" for the Cretans while in the next they promised racial terror in the South "by the arming of negroes against the whites." Echoing longstanding Democratic complaints about the moralistic tendencies of abolitionists and Republicans, the paper saw in sympathy for Crete a kind of cultural imperialism that was in turn entangled with a confused belief in racial equality. The Radicals, the *Constitution* claimed, ultimately wanted to make "the chain of brotherhood universal" and gather "into its welded links all the different races of men, giving them the same cast, language, law, government."[168]

For Democrats, northern Republican sympathy for Crete was most aggravating because it underscored this lack of racial fidelity. In contrast to Ottoman rule of Crete, the *Constitution* stressed that southern whites suffered from wrongs that were "offered to, visited upon, and erected over a people of the same race" as and "kindred in tongue" with their oppressors.[169] The *Memphis Daily Avalanche* decried how the same people "who would enslave eight millions of their own race and color in order to control the votes of three millions of blacks who know nothing of liberty . . . are shedding tears over the struggle of Greece!"[170] Similarly, the *New York World,* in reference to the "Main-iac" missionary settlers in Palestine, stated its suspicion that Radicals in Congress would not come to their aid precisely because they were white.[171]

Distant though it was, Crete became a part of Democratic interpretations of the United States and their place in it. It allowed Democrats to lament the destruction of the Old South and deride what they understood to be contradictory and self-righteous values of northern Republicans, especially Radicals. Democrats believed, moreover, that the northern Republican desire to remake the South in accordance with its own ideals reflected an ideology whose boundless ambitions were clearly evident in sympathy for Crete. Most worrisome to Democrats was the apparent northern Republican disregard for the racial hierarchy that was the foundation—according to Democrats—of America's republican civilization. The sense of betrayal was intense enough that the *Consti-*

tution felt it could justly "warn" Bostonians that "as their eyes wander sorrowfully and their hearts heave pathetically towards the distant Cretes," they should "remember, occasionally, their own self-created Crete in our midst."[172]

Conclusion

The period of the Cretan Insurrection corresponded with the triumph of congressional Republicans over Reconstruction policy-making. Already buoyed by Union victory and the destruction of slavery, northern Republicans in 1866 through early 1869 were becoming more confident that they had overcome recalcitrant southern planters and an obstinate, conservative president to secure an antislavery reunification of the country. Through their efforts, they believed, they had purified America's republican civilization and inaugurated a new era in which the forces of freedom and progress would march together across the globe. The result was a genuine but often self-righteous concern over barbarism and despotism, which northern Republicans could perceive whether looking to the South, the West, or abroad. Democrats countered northern Republicans by asserting their own sympathy for the Cretan Insurrection. In the process, they claimed that the United States was a country dedicated to liberty but delimited by race. In their interpretation, the Cretans and the former Confederates were racially superior rebels who sought freedom from the imperious sway of outsiders. For Democrats, however, the former Confederates faced a more galling situation, for their oppressors had supposedly betrayed and subordinated a portion of their own race and nation for the sake of destroying a distinction foundational to the survival of republicanism and civilization. Democrats, like northern Republicans, found in Crete the means to articulate and affirm their understanding of their place in their nation and their nation's place in the world.

By early 1869 the Ottoman Empire had decisively suppressed the Cretan Insurrection. The Ottoman state elected to half-heartedly institute the reforms suggested by Ali Pasha during his 1867 visit. In what became known as the Organic Statute of Crete, the sultan promised better governance and granted the island a General Assembly. The Assembly was more nominal than real, eligible to meet for only forty days a year to legislate on local matters under the authoritarian control of the

Ottoman governor, and with a contrived razor-thin Christian majority chosen by local elders. Still, these changes shaped the subsequent history of the island, with the Assembly and the sultan's promised reforms becoming rallying points for increasingly organized and public resistance to Ottoman rule. In 1897, yet another wave of religious violence and revolutionary activity prompted the Greek state to attempt an occupation of the island. This proved a military disaster, but one that triggered a European intervention, which in turn saw Crete transformed into an autonomous principality in the Ottoman Empire. The last Ottoman soldier departed in 1898, and ten years later the island's legislature declared union with Greece.[173] Crete's Muslim population, already reduced, began a massive exodus from the island, with perhaps fifty thousand denizens, estimated to be over half of its remaining Muslim population, leaving in 1898–1899 alone. After 1923, Crete would have almost no Muslim residents.[174]

As a failed revolution in a tumultuous world, the Cretan Insurrection quickly fell from public attention in the United States. Many northern Republicans, even the Howes, maintained much of their optimism about the future of freedom and progress and turned their attention elsewhere—republicanism in Spain, the proposed annexation of the Dominican Republic, the spread of American civilization to the continental West. But for some, Cretan defeat demanded explanation. One answer, to which many northern Republicans turned with increasing frequency in the coming decades, was that the problem lay with the world's various peoples. Some papers, like the *New York Times,* went from cheering the rebels to arguing that they needed to win their own freedom before they could elicit any more American support.[175] Pity could quickly morph into contempt. Yet, for others, continued Ottoman rule prompted a renewed emphasis on the unity of and common threats to those fighting for civilization and republicanism. As one woman suffragist put it shortly after the insurrection ended, while pondering factionalism at home, and with wide ranging references to republicanism in Italy, reform in Britain and the United States, and the Ten Years' War in Cuba: "Was it all a mistake that we deemed that Mazzini and the Cretan, Stuart Mill and the Cuban, Wendell Phillips and Anna Dickinson were leading separate divisions of *one* army, fighting the world over for the same end, a larger liberty?"[176]

2

Paul Du Chaillu, a White Supremacist in Passing

During the 1860s, an explorer and writer named Paul Du Chaillu became one of the most popular and controversial authorities on Africa living in the United States. His success began in 1861 when he published his first book, *Explorations and Adventures in Equatorial Africa,* based on his expedition to the region around the Gabon River. It became a remarkable best seller in Britain and the United States. In 1867, after a second voyage to the region, he published *A Journey to Ashango-Land,* also a transatlantic best seller, and launched a series of lecture tours in the United States. By all accounts, he was among the most entertaining speakers of his day.

A quintessential nineteenth-century self-made man, Du Chaillu was ambitious and lucky, quick on his feet and yet seemingly incapable of escaping controversy. Largely unknown today, Du Chaillu was an integral figure to Reconstruction's partisan world, speaking to the day's debates over race based on his travels. Du Chaillu blended science, adventure, and storytelling in ways that dovetailed with current politics and played into the hands of white supremacists. In particular, he created the most pervasive and enduring symbol of barbarism to come out of the second half of the nineteenth century, one that white supremacists quickly appropriated to suit their polemical ends. He also, out of a sense of expediency, embraced white supremacy and made it, for a few short years, integral to his public career, lending his intellectual authority, dubious though it was, to Democratic critics of Republican Reconstruction measures.

The period of Du Chaillu's greatest fame in the United States, from 1861 to 1872, coincided with the dismantling of one white supremacist order and the emergence of a new one. This period saw the wartime unraveling of southern slavery, its abolition shortly thereafter, and the expansion of African American rights up through the ratification of the

Fifteenth Amendment in 1870. It also witnessed the rise of white supremacist riots in southern cities and paramilitary campaigns in the countryside on the part of clandestine groups like the Ku Klux Klan. These terrorist enterprises sought to humiliate former slaves, subordinate them to the landholding class, and isolate them from their political allies.[1] In federal politics, discussions about race reflected a mixture of continuities and changes. On the one hand, the collapse of slavery did little to erase the centuries of accumulated theories, stereotypes, and assumptions concerning supposedly distinct races. On the other, arguments about race in the United States had been inextricably linked to arguments about slavery, and slavery's destruction necessarily altered how Americans defended, critiqued, and equivocated about white supremacy. Since there had been no single pro- or anti-slavery viewpoint before the war, the collapse of the old order necessarily produced manifold shifts in perspective.

There were, however, also overarching trends in the evolving contest over the uncertain place of race in the postbellum United States. Proslavery racial arguments had tended to focus on justifying the institution as an orderly system of economic production that provided childlike "Negroes" with benevolent, Christian tutelage. With slavery abolished, southern white supremacists shifted the tenor of their arguments, emphasizing the menacing nature of unchained "Negroes" who were naturally inclined to violent barbarism. Similar rhetoric had circulated since at least the Haitian Revolution (1791–1804), but now such claims proliferated as white supremacists turned increasingly to apocalyptic rhetoric warning that freedpeople would either die off or "Africanize" the South, destroying its republican civilization. In both cases, the stress was on the inability of "Negroes" and "whites" to coexist on equal footing—a viewpoint that northern white supremacists were eager to endorse.[2]

At the same time, the Civil War associated the most virulent forms of white supremacist rhetoric and actions with the cause of the Confederacy. Widespread African American service in the Union armed forces, firsthand observations of slavery, and anti-Confederate press coverage all gave frequent if not universal pause to white supremacy. If many northern Unionists continued to think in racial terms, they also became far less receptive to particularly vulgar and brazen expressions of anti–African American sentiment.[3] These two trends put the doctrinaire and avowed white supremacists in the Democratic Party in an awkward polemical position. On the one hand, embittered by the destruction of slavery and unable to dislodge Republican majorities in Washington, D.C., they found solace in slandering African Americans and their political allies. On the other hand, they searched for intellectually and politically respectable ways to bolster white supremacy. Du Chaillu would prove to be of service on both accounts. In doing so, his career constituted a critical episode in and sheds light on the intricate struggles over race and citizenship during and after emancipation and abolition.

Comings and Goings

So who was Paul Du Chaillu? An enigmatic individual who encouraged misconceptions that he was born in New Orleans, New York, or Charleston, Du Chaillu in fact did not set foot in America until the age of twenty-one.[4] The son of a French merchant, Du Chaillu had spent the last years of his adolescence on the coast of modern-day Gabon, in equatorial West Africa, where his father managed a small trading post before accepting responsibility for provisioning the tiny official French presence in the region.[5] Du Chaillu arrived in Gabon around 1848, perhaps to escape the unrest sweeping Paris. In Gabon, Du Chaillu by chance befriended and then spent much of his time with Jane and John Leighton Wilson, a missionary couple from South Carolina who had moved to the region from Liberia in 1842. He became close with the Wilsons, learned English at their school on the Gabon estuary, and likely imbibed John's fascination with chronicling the local environment.[6] The Wilsons encouraged Du Chaillu to move to the United States, where he might secure a better future than that available in the small colony in Gabon, and helped him secure a position teaching French at a seminary in Carmel, New York.[7]

By 1852, Du Chaillu was in New York, where he quickly embraced the United States as his adoptive country. Within a few years, he became aware of how captivated Americans were by his stories of equatorial West Africa. After he wrote a series of articles about the region for the *New York Tribune,* an American ornithologist, John Cassin, contacted Du Chaillu. When Du Chaillu proposed returning to Gabon to provide Cassin with bird specimens, Cassin raised credit for an expedition through Philadelphia's Academy of Natural Sciences. By October of

1855, Du Chaillu was on his way back to Gabon.[8] Arriving in December of 1855, Du Chaillu began the first of two lengthy stays that would make him one of the best known and most controversial explorers of Africa. During his first expedition (1855–1859), the exploration of Africa became, as it would remain for the next several decades, a subject of intense popular interest.[9] It was at this time that David Livingstone returned from his first expedition and emerged, thanks to Roderick Murchison, as a British celebrity. Many parts of Africa had in fact been well-known to Europeans and Americans for centuries, especially due to the Atlantic slave trade. But large portions of Africa's vast interior had never seen a European. Over the next twenty years, a spate of expeditions kept the exploration of Africa at the center of British, European, and North American attention.[10]

In addition to traveling at a moment when the exploration of Africa was becoming a popular obsession, Du Chaillu benefited from three key factors. First, he had an excellent setting that aligned with the seemingly mysterious nature of Africa. Located on Africa's western coast, Gabon experienced wind and ocean currents that had limited European slaving and trading in the area until recently. Contact dated to the fifteenth century, but Europeans knew little of the region.[11] It also contained some of the world's most verdant rain forests, which western readers viewed as dark and mysterious jungles. Gabon made an excellent setting for a series of best-selling works.[12] Second, Du Chaillu was a considerably better storyteller than most of his peers. Fellow explorers like David Livingstone, John Speke, Henry Morton Stanley, and Samuel White Baker provided novel information and harrowing experiences, but none of them excelled at captivating popular audiences as Du Chaillu did. His knack at telling good stories would lead him to make a far greater impact on popular culture than any other African explorer, especially in the United States.[13] Third, he had the gorilla.

The outside world knew next to nothing about gorillas when Du Chaillu began his expedition. The first modern accounts of gorillas began to circulate beyond Africa in 1846, when John Wilson, Du Chaillu's mentor, got hold of a gorilla's skull from local traders. Unsure of what it was, he became fascinated with the animal but had little success learning more about it. In 1847, Thomas Savage, an American missionary in Liberia who visited the Wilsons, described Wilson's gorilla skull and a few more bones to the British naturalist Richard Owen and to

Jeffries Wyman, a former student of Owen's and the leading comparative anatomist in the United States. It would be Wyman who would have the privilege of naming the species (*Troglodytes gorilla*).[14] The adolescent Du Chaillu, who was perhaps estranged from his father, lived with the Wilsons as John worked to get more bones, eventually securing two complete skeletons, which he sent to Owen and Wyman. When Du Chaillu returned to the Gabon estuary in 1855, he shot and stuffed birds for Cassin but increasingly focused on gorillas, which in his accounts were ferocious and terrifying.[15]

Upon the conclusion of his first expedition, Du Chaillu traveled to New York, Boston, and London. In the States, Du Chaillu found himself a celebrity but struggled to secure his economic footing. He donated some of his gorilla remains to Wyman, and by early 1860 had converted the rest of his haul of hunting trophies, including stuffed gorillas, into a collection on Broadway with a 25-cent admission.[16] It was probably Wyman, esteemed in the tightly knit scientific community around Boston, who introduced Du Chaillu to Samuel Kneeland, a naturalist who agreed to help convert his journals into an English-language narrative.[17] Harper and Brothers agreed to publish the volume, *Explorations and Adventures in Equatorial Africa,* in late 1860. When it hit the shelves in 1861, it became a best seller despite the ongoing Civil War, selling nearly 300,000 copies in 1861 by one estimate.[18] Sensationalistic in nature, *Explorations and Adventures* described gorillas as beating their chests, bending guns, and mangling one of the local guides with him on his expedition.[19] It started Du Chaillu on a writing career that would in turn inspire Edgar Rice Burroughs and Merian C. Cooper to create Tarzan and King Kong.[20]

Before *Explorations and Adventures* made it into publication in the United States, Du Chaillu found himself invited to London by Richard Owen upon the urging of Wyman. Owen was then locked in a debate over Darwin's recently published theory of evolution through natural selection, which had already prompted references to some of Du Chaillu's specimens.[21] In part because of religious concerns, Owen hoped that Du Chaillu's expertise could help prove that mankind could not possibly be evolutionarily related to apes, a point implied but not argued in Darwin's *On the Origin of Species.* With little formal scientific training, Du Chaillu probably cared little about the debate, but he got on well with Owen, which opened doors in British high society.[22] When Owen's colleague Roderick Murchison extended the opportunity to speak at the Royal Geographical Society, Du Chaillu took it and won over Britain's educated elites with some animated and self-effacing performances. Du Chaillu soon gifted Owen one of his gorilla skins. These same contacts led to the chance to publish *Explorations and Adventures* with John Murray, Britain's leading publisher, who rushed it into production ahead of Harper and Brothers. It rapidly became the most popular book in Britain.[23] Ironically, Owen's influence was most marked in the American edition, which, as Du Chaillu's most recent biographer has demonstrated, contained a hastily added section stressing the gulf between men and apes.[24]

In Victorian scientific circles, Du Chaillu earned applause for providing new and fascinating information but also sparked controversy. One writer in the United States questioned Du Chaillu's expertise during his brief post-expedition stint in the United States. In London, criticism proved withering. Particularly damning was a critique by one of Owen's and Murchison's rivals, John Edward Gray, who uncovered some plagiarized illustrations in Du Chaillu's rapidly published book and questioned whether he had traveled to Gabon's interior.[25] A London scientist, Frederick Smith, demonstrated that Du Chaillu's description of ants borrowed heavily from an earlier work by Thomas Savage. Many of Du Chaillu's claims were worthy of skepticism, such as his argument that in addition to the gorilla he had discovered a new nest-building primate, the *nshiego-mbouvé,* and another with a human-like head, the *kooloo kamba.* At one scientific meeting, Thomas Malone, a chemist and leading photographer, repeatedly interrupted Du Chaillu as he made comments on a paper to argue about Du Chaillu's description of a harp. Du Chaillu confronted Malone and spat on him.[26] Controversy worsened as the press got hold of it.

This was only the start of his problems. Many suspected that Du Chaillu had embellished his accounts of the gorilla, as well as the frequency of cannibalism in Gabon's interior.[27] Du Chaillu had neglected to measure his location while traveling and exaggerated his distances, sparking ridicule in a community obsessed with precise scientific mapping. An old acquaintance from Gabon, R.B.N. Walker, who now wanted to capitalize on the "gorilla craze" himself, wrote a public letter accusing Du Chaillu of being a charlatan and alleged that he had changed his last name to obscure some disreputable origins. People began to question everything about Du Chaillu.[28] Winwood Reade, an unsuccessful novelist from a wealthy family, traveled to Gabon to investigate Du Chaillu's claims and argued, erroneously, that his descriptions of the gorilla were based only on local stories. One of Du Chaillu's few allies, the globe-trotting polymath and iconoclast Richard Burton, also traveled to Gabon from his consular post at Fernando Po and found Du Chaillu's work largely accurate.[29]

Du Chaillu sold what remained of his specimens, pooled his resources, and lined up some funds from Harper and Brothers to support a second trip to Gabon, where he planned to redeem his reputation. After putting himself through a rigorous training program with the most advanced exploratory techniques, Du Chaillu returned to Gabon in 1863 with an elaborate collection of instruments. His journey would be marked with mixed results, including losing several of the instruments and nearly getting killed, but also traveling farther into Gabon's interior. There, he was the first known European to encounter "dwarf negroes," sometimes still referred to as pygmies, in this case the Bongo. He also collected pages' worth of precise geographical data. When he returned to England, he restored his allies' faith in him and won over some detractors. With the help of Henry Walter Bates, a respected British explorer of the Amazon, Du Chaillu converted his journals into a second travel narrative, *A Journey to Ashango-Land* (1867). Like the first, it would prove to be tremendously popular in Britain and the United States. Then, right as Du Chaillu had the chance rejoin British elite society, he left for New York.[30]

The Gorilla as a Racist Symbol

The image of the gorilla as a dangerous beast helped reshape white supremacy during Reconstruction by weaving together two strands of racist thought. The first was the idea that "Negroes" were not fully human and were more akin to primates. This line of thinking predated Darwin's theory of evolution through natural selection and took a variety of forms, all of which held "Negroes" to be mentally inferior to white people. The second was that "Negroes" had a natural disposition toward violence and anarchy and that, if left without white supervision, would lapse into barbarism. This latter belief, though long present in the United States, became far more salient in racial thinking following emancipation and abolition.[31] Since gorillas, especially as Du Chaillu described them, were far more intimidating than other primates, the animal became a distinctively apt metaphor for both of these discourses. Initial popular interest in the gorilla led to its rapid emergence as a polyvalent symbol, sometimes with obvious racist import.[32] Yet the gorilla's evolving meanings also reflected changing political circumstances, and it was not until after the Civil War that it became a pervasive symbol of racial menace.

The gorilla's potential as a racist symbol was apparent almost immediately after the publication of Du Chaillu's *Explorations and Adventures*. When Du Chaillu established his Broadway museum, it prompted a better-established nearby rival, P. T. Barnum, to immediately open his own gorilla-inspired exhibit. A clear sign of the racist imagery to come, Barnum purchased an African American man who suffered from microcephaly and had difficulty walking and dressed him in black fur, repeatedly asking viewers, "*What is it?*"[33] As much was also evident in a cartoon in *Vanity Fair* that appeared shortly after Du Chaillu's return from his first voyage (see figure 3). The cartoon made a big-enough impression that almost a year later newspapers in Ohio and Vermont excerpted its text without reference or explanation, suggesting that the editors believed their readers knew the cartoon well.[34] The gorilla as a racial epithet also quickly made its way south. In the middle of the war, the *Memphis Daily Appeal* reprinted an article that described slaves fleeing to Chicago as "about as ignorant as the African gorilla."[35] And yet part of what is striking about this rhetoric is that while it tapped into longstanding ideas about the close relations between "Negroes" and primates, it did not draw on Du Chaillu's descriptions of the gorilla as a violent beast. Even the "gorilla" in the *Vanity Fair* cartoon was more farcical than intimidating in its threat.

Indeed, much of the gorilla craze that followed on the heels of Du Chaillu's first expedition had little to do with race. References to the gorilla proliferated, with *Explorations and Adventures* advertised as "'The Gorilla Book'" and excerpted widely in the press.[36] One student at Williams College sparked local anxiety by dressing up as a gorilla and haunting local residents, with the good people of Stamford, Vermont, chasing him from town. The ruse eventually came to an end but provoked laughs as far away as Tennessee and Ohio.[37] Newspapers in the United States followed Du Chaillu's discussions of the gorilla in England

PROFESSOR.—THIS, LADIES AND GENTLEMEN, IS THE GORILLA, OR MAN-MONKEY, THE GREATEST LIVING CURIOSITY IN THE KNOWN WORLD. HE WAS CAPTURED BY A PARTY OF TRAVELLERS ON THE BANKS OF THE SENEGAMBIA WHILE—*(stick accompaniment.)*

GORILLA *(indignantly.)*—JEM BRIGGS, IF YOU PUNCH ME AGAIN WITH THAT STICK, I'LL COME OUT THERE AND LAM YER OUT OF YER BOOTS!

FIGURE 3. No title, *Vanity Fair,* May 26, 1860, 350.

and reported on his second voyage. Several papers noted when London evangelist Charles Spurgeon lectured about the gorilla to his congregation with Du Chaillu and one of his stuffed gorillas on stage in October of 1861.[38]

The gorilla did quickly become a symbol for barbarism, but often without explicit racial meaning. Indeed, it was far more common to see Democrats and Confederates accuse Abraham Lincoln and Republicans in Washington, D.C., of being gorillas than it was to see them hurl the epithet at African Americans.[39] Already by 1861 it was de rigueur for Confederates and northern Democrats to make reference to the "Gorilla Government," a practice that continued throughout the war.[40] One could argue that this rhetoric was implicitly racial, especially since Democrats and Confederates routinely spoke of "black Republicans" and associated the party with abolitionism, "miscegenation," and African American rights. Yet even when Confederates and Democrats made arguments about racial inferiority within their discussions of Republicans as gorillas, they rarely applied the term to African Americans.[41] Instead of focusing on race, it was far more common for articles using the term "gorilla" to highlight the Lincoln administration's alleged greed, incompetence, brutality toward southern civilians, and infringement on civil rights.[42] Accompanying these comments was often related hyperbole about Lincoln as a tyrant or despot.[43]

This focus on Lincoln and Republicans remained in place, moreover, even after the preliminary Emancipation Proclamation turned the war toward a crusade against slavery.[44] At the Democratic Convention of 1864, C. Chauncey Burr, the conservative editor of *Old Guard,* remarked on how incredible it was that the Union had found men willing to enact "the infamous orders of the gorilla tyrant that usurped the Presidential chair."[45] Those claiming Lincoln was a gorilla did not invariably describe him as antislavery, and in fact in at least one case an author sought to discredit Lincoln as a principled opponent of slavery.[46] When Republicans responded to such rhetoric, they typically focused on mocking Confederate pretenses to eloquence, not the politics of race.[47] When Republicans turned this rhetoric around and accused Confederates of being gorillas, they accentuated Confederate cruelty to civilians or made puns about guerrillas.[48] The latter strategy was apparent in a series of humorous album cards by Henry Louis Stephens that featured a conscripted Zouave rabbit who ended up decapitating the leader of a band of Confederate guerrillas (see figure 4).[49] Altogether, it is striking how rarely white supremacists used the gorilla as a metaphor for the violent threat of racial barbarism during the Civil War.

Public discussions of the gorilla abated as the years passed. By the end of the war, references to the animal were rare.[50] Had Du Chaillu decided not to return to the United States after his second expedition, the gorilla might have waned as a popular symbol. Instead, Du Chaillu not only returned but also quickly emerged as arguably the most

FIGURE 4. Scenes 9 and 10 of Henry Louis Stephens's album cards, *The Adventures of a Conscript as Told by Himself.* Library of Congress, Prints and Photographs Division.

popular public speaker of his day. His popularity soared just as white supremacists were shifting away from proslavery rhetoric about "Negro" docility and "white" benevolence toward an emphasis on "Negroes" as inhuman beasts. Even more so than after his first expedition, Du Chaillu now emerged as a celebrity, with the gorilla central to his career.

His success was closely tied to *A Journey to Ashango-Land,* which many reviewers thought redeemed his reputation while again providing engaging stories. The *Albany Journal* said of it that no other recent travel narrative, not even those of Livingstone, appeared "so well calculated to please and instruct."[51] The *San Francisco Bulletin* said that it was "intensely interesting, abounding in curious and sprightly sketches of African character."[52] Mobile's *Nationalist* reprinted a *Cincinnati Gazette* review arguing that the book constituted "one of the most remarkable cases of the contest of an author with his critics, and of his complete victory."[53] When in 1869 one writer contrasted Du Chaillu's "notoriety" with Livingstone's "fame," James Redpath, who did business with Du Chaillu, came to his defense, arguing that "No one can read his second volume . . . without being convinced of the injustice done to him by the old slanders."[54] This success buoyed Du Chaillu's status on the lecture circuit.

In contrast to Britain, where Du Chaillu spoke before small gatherings of gentleman scientists, in the United States he encountered a popular lecture industry active across the North and West. In fact, his second expedition and the well-advertised talks and publications that followed, much like Stanley's search for Livingstone on behalf of the *New York Herald*, constituted a commercialization of African exploration for consumption in the United States.[55] After arriving in New York in April of 1867, Du Chaillu soon began making appearances, beginning with select venues and audiences in the city but moving quickly to wide-ranging tours.[56] Du Chaillu's lectures had an element of the exotic. The *Daily Press* of St. Paul, Minnesota, described his narrations as "so unique" and "dissimilar from the usual routine" that they were no doubt the most engrossing available.[57] As a lecturer, it may have helped that Du Chaillu cut a distinctive figure. In its account of his speech on cannibalism, for example, the *New York World* depicted Du Chaillu, "the celebrated African traveller," as "a small sized, dark complexioned, gentlemanly man" who "spoke with a French accent, and not very fluently, but in a simple, direct and pleasing manner"[58] (see figure 5).

Yet Du Chaillu was more than just peculiar. He was an intense, charismatic, and sociable figure who thrived in public and seemed willing to speak just about anywhere.[59] One former journalist commented that Du Chaillu was "so genial, so vivacious, and so witty" that he felt bad calling attention to the speaker's foibles, including his tendency to exaggerate.[60] One paper noted his "very easy and entertaining" manner of speaking and his superb dry humor, and another noted that his fresh, lively style "keeps one's attention constantly chained."[61] A dose of cynicism allowed the *Troy Weekly Times* to nail Du Chaillu's style best of all. "Here at Congress Hall is Du Chaillu," quipped the paper, "making every body's acquaintance, magnifying his adventures, a pleasant, gossipy, flattering talker, with a hand to science and both eyes to cash, who has gone farther with his tongue than his legs will ever carry him."[62] Du Chaillu was especially skilled at captivating children without losing the attention of

FIGURE 5. Du Chaillu speaking in Boston on the gorilla, which is depicted bending a gun. *Harper's Weekly,* March 6, 1869, 148.

adults.[63] Edward Clodd, an English friend, explained how his own children received from Du Chaillu an unforgettable account of his adventures complete with a frightful imitation of the gorilla.[64] The *Boston Advertiser* described the "hundreds of boys and girls who sat before him leaning forward, with half-open mouths and sparkling eyes" at one lecture.[65] Not one to miss an opportunity, Du Chaillu wrote several books for young adults.[66] It was no surprise that Du Chaillu was constantly in demand, with listeners braving the elements and waiting for hours to hear him.[67] According to Clodd, when Du Chaillu refrained from speaking about the gorilla at a backwoods Baptist church because it was Sunday, his audience implored him and the deacon urged him, "'Brother Paul, did not the Lord make the gorilla, and can it be wrong to talk about His works in His House and on His own Day?'"[68] Du Chaillu's prominence was further aided by newspapers, which regularly reprinted or summarized his lectures.[69]

Tailoring his writings and speeches to appeal to his audiences, Du Chaillu reignited the gorilla craze and blurred the boundary of scientific knowledge and popular entertainment. By 1868 a museum in San

Francisco, California, was boasting that it had one of Du Chaillu's gorillas on display.[70] In the same year, Democratic politician and polymath John R. McConnell attempted to prove that the animal that had tempted Eve in the Garden of Eden was a gorilla.[71] In 1869, an obscure author, Emanuel Herzberg, published his *Gorilla Catechism,* a meandering, misanthropic satire featuring human-like gorillas who fancied themselves devoted to reason but were in fact captives of custom and religion.[72] As the *San Francisco Bulletin* noted in 1871, when Du Chaillu first offered his descriptions of the gorilla he was mocked as a fraud. Now, however, New York taxidermists were using cowhide to make stuffed gorillas, of "the most gigantic size and hideous features," in such numbers that "every family can have one."[73]

This renewed fascination combined with the charged racial politics surrounding congressional Reconstruction measures to bring to the fore the gorilla's potential meaning as a racial epithet. Civil War rhetoric about white Republican politicians as gorillas largely disappeared, and references to southern freedpeople and northern African Americans as gorillas multiplied. Du Chaillu was not directly involved in this transformation, in part because he was not much concerned with electoral politics in the United States, although he sometimes claimed to be a Republican. He also was unlikely to invoke the gorilla as a racial symbol because of his intellectual ties to Richard Owen.[74] Indeed, during his second voyage, Du Chaillu collected over one hundred human skulls for Owen, who was still arguing against evolution and theories of stark racial difference.[75] Instead, it was Democratic partisans who appropriated the gorilla and turned it into a symbolic rallying point that encapsulated their beliefs that African Americans were inferior, that they were menacing, and that empowering them had plunged the South into barbarism.

As congressional Reconstruction measures went into effect, Democrats gladly turned to the gorilla as a leading symbol of the absurdity of expanding African American rights. Democratic invocations of the gorilla as a racial epithet ran from the comedic to the contemplative to the apocalyptic. The *Tarboro' Southerner* in the North Carolina lowcountry described one carpetbagger, David Heaton, as coming to the city to "cavort and play Gorilla for the negroes" to secure their votes as he ran for Congress.[76] The *Patriot* of Harrisburg, Pennsylvania, claimed in October of 1867 that "The Radical gorillas carried Louisiana by 75,000 and

Alabama by 80,000," but that radical journals in the North were not celebrating the fact because Ohio had just rejected its own measure on "gorilla voting."[77]

When P. T. Barnum made a second attempt to capitalize on the gorilla, popular references demonstrated well the braiding of racial politics and popular entertainment. By the fall of 1867, Barnum had convinced many onlookers and part of the press that he had purchased a gorilla from Africa for $18,000. In fact, he had purchased a baboon already resident in New York City and originally from southern Africa (see figure 6). Barnum nonetheless created quite a stir, in part by fabricating stories about the animal's impressive strength.[78] Democratic papers were quick to add references to Barnum's gorilla in their attacks on "the Negro." In 1868, *Round Table* magazine noted Du Chaillu's relevance to the national debates over race and equated the noblest gorilla with "the most debased black troglodytes." Noting correctly that Barnum's specimen was a baboon, the magazine suggested that the distinction hardly mattered. Either way, if freed, the animal would likely rise to the pinnacle of society because the principle of equal rights had required society to abandon all sense of ethnological distinction.[79] Similarly, when Barnum's "gorilla" died, the *Richmond Enquirer* lamented the passing of "the most distinguished native of Africa" to visit the United States and then suggested that the animal should have run for president since the "Radical" Republicans, lacking constitutional scruples, would have voted for a foreigner. The paper then added that the gorilla had violently resisted "the manners and customs of our people," but that it would have felt at home among southern freedpeople.[80] General Rufus Rowe, speaking in California against congressional Reconstruction measures, claimed that Du Chaillu and others had demonstrated that some Africans had tails, insinuating that African Americans were closely related to primates. If P. T. Barnum had not recently retired, Rowe added, he could have provided "the gentleman who presides over the deliberations of the sovereign State of Louisiana," likely referring to Oscar Dunn, "with a stuffed specimen of his ancestors."[81]

The centrality of the gorilla to Democratic campaigns against the expansion of African American rights was especially apparent to French newspaper correspondent and future prime minister Georges Clemenceau. Reporting on a Democratic campaign rally in Manhattan in November of 1867, he explained: "The best point of attack for the

FIGURE 6. An illustration of Barnum's "gorilla" attacking its keeper, who survived. *Frank Leslie's Illustrated Newspaper,* October 19, 1867, 77.

Democrats is the negroes. Any Democrat who did not manage to hint in his speech that the negro is a degenerate gorilla, would be considered lacking in enthusiasm. The idea of giving political power to a lot of wild men, incapable of civilization, whose intelligence is no higher than that of animals! That is the theme of all the Democratic speeches."[82]

Such rhetoric was popular among Democratic loyalists, but could also offend moderate voters. Indeed, when in 1868 the Democratic vice presidential nominee Francis P. Blair Jr. devoted a tour to disparaging the idea of African American equality—in this case his preferred form of racist slander was to describe African Americans as Mormons—it proved a disaster for the campaign.[83] Indeed, northern Republicans condemned Democratic uses of the gorilla as a racial epithet, and at moments turned them against Democrats themselves. When African

Americans voted in city elections in Washington, D.C., for the first time, the *New York Tribune,* in an editorial reprinted by Philadelphia's *Telegraph,* criticized the Democrats for starting off their campaigns "calling negroes gorillas" and ending with equally absurd "fraternal demonstration of attachment."[84] The *New Orleans Republican* mocked Democrats for belatedly deciding that African American voters were welcome as long as they voted for their party while still holding that those who voted for Republicans were "negroes, baboons, gorillas, apes, etc."[85] The neighboring *New Orleans Tribune,* an intra-party rival to the *Republican,* received one letter from its Washington correspondent arguing that it was people who could not let go of an antiquated belief in white supremacy who were "conceited barbarian[s]" and "gorilla[s]."[86] In Congress, Republicans still chortled at puns involving Confederate guerrillas.[87] In what must have often been a self-conscious inversion of white supremacist usage, Republicans, including the leading cartoonist Thomas Nast, frequently presented the Irish, who were largely reliable Democratic voters, as gorillas.[88]

African Americans similarly responded to Democratic rhetoric about the gorilla. After the 1867 city election in Washington, D.C., a local man referred to a crowd of African Americans at a grocery store as "African gorillas," prompting criticism by George Dyson, an African American member of the Seventh Ward Republican Club.[89] In 1872, the *Weekly Louisianian* ran an editorial on the colored man's capacity for self-government that pointed to the democratic overthrow of Edmund Roye in Liberia, who the paper took to be an aspiring tyrant. "If the advocates of the Monkey-and-Gorilla origin of the negro" could orchestrate such a peaceful political change, the paper commented, "we should like to hear the evidence."[90]

Perhaps the tartest Republican retort came from the *San Antonio Express,* which began an article by reprinting a description of Barnum's gorilla from the *Houston Telegraph.*[91] Male gorillas, the *Houston Telegraph* explained, with overt racism, "'are exceedingly fond of negro women'" and occasionally abducted them from African towns to perhaps eat them but, more likely, to live with them "'in a state of enforced concubinage.'" The *Express* responded that, if it had not been for the word "gorilla," a reader would have thought that the article referred to the "customs of the chivalry prior to the rebellion." "The treatment that the Telegraph says the gorilla uses towards the negro women," continued the paper, "is an exact picture of the state of society as it existed in the South during the palmy days of slavery."[92]

The White Supremacist International and the Fate of "the Negro"

If it was Democrats who transformed the gorilla into a racist symbol, Du Chaillu found other ways to throw himself into postbellum debates about white supremacy. Arriving at the height of controversy over African American rights, Du Chaillu encountered a polemical landscape in which Democrats were searching for information about Africa and the African diaspora that they could take as proving their negative appraisals of "the Negro." Especially for white supremacists, who believed that "the Negro" had the same underlying character anywhere he was, evidence from Africa could demonstrate what lay in store for the South now that the slaves were free. In his second volume and in some of his more prominent lectures in the United States, Du Chaillu would speak to these concerns, offering, for a brief moment in his long career, white supremacist arguments based on his observations of African life.

Searching for a place in both British scientific circles and with popular audiences in the postbellum United States, Du Chaillu fashioned himself into a white supremacist when it seemed opportune to do so. He had spent his formative years in a tiny European community on the coast of Gabon where he interacted with equatorial West Africans on a regular basis.[93] By his own account, he conversed with equatorial West Africans frequently enough to develop an imperfect hold of multiple local languages.[94] His closest companions, the Wilsons, were missionaries who, although by no means free from racism, devoted their lives to saving Africans' souls.[95] Du Chaillu may very well have learned English alongside equatorial West Africans.[96] In his first volume and in his public lectures in Britain, he rarely if ever addressed the subject of race. Du Chaillu often had condescending views of equatorial West African beliefs and rituals, but so too did missionaries and philanthropists who disavowed racism. His closest ally in Britain after his first expedition, Richard Owen, tended to argue on the behalf of human equality and was critical of Darwinian attempts to view "the Negro" as an intermediate step between the gorilla and "Caucasians."[97]

So when and why did Du Chaillu come to espouse white supremacy?

His publicly stated views about race changed when he returned from his second voyage. Starting with a final chapter of his *A Journey to Ashango-Land,* which stands out from the rest of the book, Du Chaillu took a much more categorical stance on race and much more negative views of "the Negro." Indeed, *A Journey to Ashango-Land* as a whole offered copious and sometimes nuanced descriptions of equatorial West African cultures. Du Chaillu was by no means uniformly positive in his views of equatorial West Africans, and was troubled by superstitions, especially fetish worship and belief in witchcraft.[98] These, he believed, impaired economic development among "primitive negroes" and led to frequent deaths, particularly of those accused of witchcraft.[99] Yet even here he once attributed these "superstitions" to "busy brains" and an active imagination.[100] Du Chaillu also had praise for many of the equatorial West African ethnic groups he encountered.[101] He expressed sympathy for the equatorial West Africans who contracted smallpox upon contact with his expedition, including one of his traveling companions, Macondai, whom he had known for years.[102] Finally, Du Chaillu, perhaps in part to underscore the truthfulness of his first travel narrative, noted the old friends he came across during his second voyage.[103] In short, a reader who skipped the final chapter might have found plenty of positive if patronizing accounts of equatorial West Africans as well as bluntly negative ones in *A Journey to Ashango-Land.*[104] The main body of the book was sufficiently ambiguous on race that one African American newspaper, San Francisco's *Elevator,* could excerpt a passage from it in good conscience.[105] His descriptions outside of the final chapter to *A Journey* can be classed with those by fellow explorers, such as Benjamin Anderson, Richard F. Burton, and David Livingstone: biased but rich with detail. Modern scholars of Gabon continue to cite them.[106]

Du Chaillu's ethnological chapter stemmed from his deepening contact with scientific racists in Britain after his first expedition, when controversy surrounding his *Explorations and Adventures* alienated him from much of the scientific community.[107] Spurned after the savaging of his first book, Du Chaillu began socializing with a group of irreverent British writers who dubbed themselves the "Cannibal Club."[108] A member of this group, Richard Burton, in turn connected Du Chaillu to James Hunt, who with Burton founded the Anthropological Society of London (ASL) in 1863. Like Richard Owen, Burton and Hunt were, at the time, critics of Darwin's theory of evolution. Unlike Owen, however, they were leading proponents of polygenism in particular and scientific theories of racial inferiority more generally. They founded the ASL to free themselves of what they took to be Victorian strictures and piety, including the belief that all humans shared a common ancestor created by God.

Hunt and Burton were energetic advocates of these ideas. Burton offered a series of negative accounts of East and West African societies based on his travels. In addition to publishing his *On the Negro's Place in Nature* (1863), dedicated to Burton, Hunt had the ASL translate the works of several continental scientific racists. Hunt also connected with Henry Hotze, a Swiss-born Confederate propagandist who, upon the invitation of Mobile polygenist Josiah Nott, had translated Arthur de Gobineau's *Essai sur l'inégalité des races humaines* (1853) for American readers in 1856.[109] With the American Civil War raging, Burton argued that slavery was necessary to civilize Africans and in 1864 defended Hunt's racial views in his *A Mission to Gelele,* which was based on further travels in West Africa. Du Chaillu himself became wrapped up in these efforts, speaking at the ASL and finding himself defended by Hunt and Burton in meetings and in print. By association, Du Chaillu was now part of a white supremacist international centered on Hunt and Burton that included authors in the United States. Hunt, for example, cited the work of New York white supremacist John H. Van Evrie, and Van Evrie printed an American edition of Hunt's *On the Negro's Place in Nature* (1864) as part of his campaign against abolition and African American rights.[110]

Burton and Hunt's emphasis on the incapacity of "the Negro" for civilization and progress was particularly apparent in Du Chaillu's final chapter, "Ethnology." He opened by stating that in the interior of equatorial West Africa one found the African "shut up from the world around him."[111] There, Du Chaillu claimed, one could see the inherent tendencies of the race. From his observations, he concluded that all the evidence pointed to a population that had never been civilized and that was now dying off. Du Chaillu averred that, contrary to the arguments of other explorers, this could hardly be the fault of European slave raiders and alcohol-peddling merchants.[112] In fact, writing "in defense of the white man," Du Chaillu stated that he had noticed a population decline even among those tribes "who had seen no white man and his fiery water." Instead, Du Chaillu stressed that it was disease, the "barrenness of women," and especially the Africans themselves that were to blame. Du Chaillu conceded that the coastal trade certainly did see traffic in alcohol and slaves, but added that the latter were traded only by Africans operating out of nearby Portuguese-controlled islands. Where these forces took their toll, "the negro"—Du Chaillu left the term uncapitalized—was himself to blame. More important to understanding the inevitable demise of the race was the popular belief in witchcraft. This, he believed, took away "more lives than any Slave Trade ever did." Arguing, without citation, that accounts from other parts of Africa proved the same, Du Chaillu asserted that the population was declining across the continent, assumed that "the negro race has run its course," and added that the "Southern States of America" were "the only country in which the negro is known to have increased."[113] Such claims were patently absurd since, if true, it would be impossible to explain why there was a population of "Negroes" anywhere on the planet.

The root cause of these problems, according to Du Chaillu, was "the Negro's" inability to change. Here, Du Chaillu noted that equatorial West Africans worked iron and used looms, but added that their methods were so simple that they did not indicate a capacity for progress. Everything, Du Chaillu wrote, "tends to show that the negro is of great antiquity, and has always remained stationary." When it came to "his future capabilities," Du Chaillu struck an odd compromise between those who judged that "the negro will never rise higher than he is" and those who believed "he is capable of reaching the highest level of civilization." Du Chaillu believed that "the Negro" could in fact be made "a more useful member of mankind," but that it would take constant effort on the part of whites. "The negro," he argued, had positive characteristics, including being "the most tractable and the most docile" of the "uncivilized races of men." One had to conclude, however, that if left alone "he will soon fall back into barbarism, for we have no example to the contrary." What little optimism Du Chaillu had about "the Negro's" capacity for progress was mitigated by an underlying pessimism about his long-term survival. If "the Negro" could be uplifted, thought Du Chaillu, he could not, ultimately, be saved from extinction. Given the inevitability of this outcome, Du Chaillu suggested that whites should nonetheless "be kind to him and try to elevate him."[114]

When lecturing in the United States, Du Chaillu reiterated his ethnological claims in multiple venues with newspapers present to record and circulate his statements.[115] He lectured on diverse topics, including the gorilla, but when he addressed race he was unequivocal. The most detailed account we have of his lecture on "Races and Types of Mankind" comes from the *New York Times*'s summary of the last of his 1868 lectures at Steinway Hall. The talk began with a discussion of the "habits of the various tribes that dwell in Equatorial Africa." It then turned to Du Chaillu's arguments about race, beginning with his claim that "travelers have searched in vain for anything to remind us that the negroes ever enjoyed a higher state of civilization than that which they now present." Du Chaillu pondered the polygenist thesis that Caucasians and Africans were of separate creations, and decided in favor of a common origin with differences resulting from evolution, although he did not reference Darwin or natural selection. This process must have taken a very long time, Du Chaillu suggested, to explain the marked inequality in intelligence between Caucasians and "the lower types of races of men, such as Hottentots, Bushmen, Oboungous, Australians, and various tribes of negroes."

Du Chaillu then returned to his argument for extinction from *A Journey to Ashango-Land,* adding that not only "the negro" but "all races of men, except the progressive Caucasian, are destined to extinction." "Civilization" could not save these races, he stated, "for it is impossible to raise up these inferior races to the standard of their superiors." Whenever two distinct races came into contact, moreover, he believed they would necessarily come into conflict, with the more intelligent one triumphing. Du Chaillu then turned to miscegenation, arguing that while different groups of whites benefited from intermixture with each other, procreating with other races hurt Caucasians and produced a "mongrel or hybrid" offspring that "will soon die out." Du Chaillu then reiterated his argument that Caucasians should care for the inferior races even as they faced inevitable extinction. Finally, he concluded by claiming that Caucasians would one day "overspread the whole earth" and "reign with a glory of which we can have no perception."[116] Since Du Chaillu's main point of contact with white supremacy came in Britain, the ease with which his ethnological analysis translated to an American audience was a testament to the transatlantic nature of scientific racism.

That he struck a nerve with debates within the United States over race and citizenship was evident in the reactions to his chapter and lectures. Since many northern Republicans were ambivalent about race and others were outright scientific racists, it is not surprising that some entertained his arguments. Indeed, Du Chaillu's claims about miscegenation, if not total extinction, could have just as easily come from Samuel Gridley Howe, who believed "mulatto" offspring were sterile and that most "colored people" in North America would eventually disappear from the continent.[117] *Harper's Weekly* noted that learned Americans had "highly appreciated" Du Chaillu's lecture on "Races and Types of Mankind."[118] The more conservative *New York Times* concluded its review of *A Journey to Ashango-Land* by quoting Du Chaillu's dismal appraisal of "the Negro's" future and noting that his ethnographic claims, grounded in firsthand observation, warranted attention.[119] But there was also much criticism of Du Chaillu's arguments on religious and secular grounds that pushed against his stringent white supremacy. These criticisms often mixed an underlying faith in universal humanity with a tendency to still think of humanity as divided into distinctive groups, including racial ones, with their own comparable characters.

One review of *A Journey to Ashango-Land* for the American Colonization Society's monthly, the *African Repository,* considered the work stale and used Du Chaillu's own evidence to pick apart his argument that Gabon's demography pointed to an inevitable extinction. Dense local forests and an outbreak of small pox explained the scattered and seemingly declining population. If anything, recent immigrations to the region suggested a "redundancy of population in Central Africa." If African beliefs and customs were responsible for the declining population, why had not Africans perished as a race long ago? The reviewer did commend Du Chaillu for his "sympathy with the native tribes," and agreed with his judgment that "the negro is tractable, docile, and has many excellent qualities."[120] A subsequent comment in the same publication simply ran roughshod over Du Chaillu's ethnographic argument to claim that his book demonstrated that "All of this country . . . is populous and healthy," that "the cessation of the slave trade is having a favorable effect on the natives," and that the region had a "capacity for civilization and intercourse, for agriculture and trade, much in advance of what has been dreamed."[121]

The racial politics of Reconstruction informed these and other reactions to Du Chaillu's arguments, often explicitly. Boston's Methodist newspaper, *Zion's Herald,* made as much clear in its response to a lecture by Du Chaillu. Whereas Du Chaillu had argued that miscegenation "poisoned" entire populations, such as those of Santo Domingo and Mexico, *Zion's Herald* countered that admixture strengthened them, pointing out that Frederick Douglass was Maryland's most gifted son. The paper also mocked the idea of a superior white race that included "the Irish semi-savage from the bogs of Allan" and poor southern whites who still lived like medieval serfs. "Negroes" had proven themselves an intelligent, "emotional race" inclined toward Christianity and, far from going extinct, would join in a common human destiny of "the unification of all races."[122] Similarly, the editor of the recently founded evangelical literary magazine *Hours at Home* found Du Chaillu's ethnological views "very superficial" and averred that not only was the race going to survive, but missionary experience in Africa as well as evidence from the United States and West Indies showed that it had "'the power of progression.'" Whereas the Indian "seems to have but little capacity for the higher state of civilization," the editor noted, "the Negro" was being elevated by the joint projects of enfranchisement in the United States and proselytization in Africa.[123]

More secular critiques of Du Chaillu were also prevalent. Like the evangelical ones, they were both at peace with racial categories in general and critical of the most severe prognostications of white supremacists. The most prominent critique came from Horace Greeley's *New York Tribune* in response to Du Chaillu's 1867 lecture at the Cooper Institute in Manhattan. The *Tribune* acknowledged Du Chaillu's talents as an explorer but placed his views on extinction on the scientific fringe. The *Tribune* was willing to concede, perhaps for the sake of argument, that "the negro race" was incapable of progress, but found this to be a far cry from demonstrating his inevitable disappearance. What is more, the *Tribune* stressed that while inferior races were "disappearing in certain parts of the world," this reflected expropriation of aboriginal lands and the introduction of civilized vices without the controlling influence of Christianity. Not only would the African race survive, thought the paper, but it would flourish in the "burning tropics," as evidenced by the recent population growth of the British West Indies following emancipation. If entertaining enough when addressing gorillas and cannibalism, Du Chaillu was "simply intolerable when he begins to philosophize about the appointed fate of the negro race."[124]

The *Tribune*'s editorial itself became a point of contestation, no doubt due to the paper's renown. The *Enquirer* of Columbus, Georgia, reprinted an article by South Carolina's *Charleston News* that derisively summarized it. Claiming that the *Tribune* "lectures M. Du Chaillu on his lecture," the *News* offered a brief excerpt of Du Chaillu's talk at the Cooper Institute that underscored his racial paternalism. Immediately following the excerpt, the editorial again stressed what it took to be the *Tribune*'s arrogance, stating that the paper "tells M. du Chaillu that he may be a very good hand at telling travellers' tales, but should confine himself to that, and not deal in generalization."[125] The *Brooklyn Daily Eagle* provided a fuller critique that lambasted the *Tribune* as a radical Republican organ. The *Tribune*'s problem, the *Eagle* argued, was with Du Chaillu's facts, not his philosophizing. By seeing "the negro in his native land as he is, and not as the friends of the black man think he ought to be," Du Chaillu had demonstrated that slavery had saved "the negro . . . from the most odious barbarism." Granting that slavery degraded most races, the *Eagle* stated that "the negro alone had been elevated through it," to the point where slaves in the United States "had been civilized and Christianized and stood higher in the scale of civilization than any four millions of their race the world ever saw." The *Eagle* believed the *Tribune* could not countenance the coming extinction because it would mean "No great reformers, no upholders of the eternal verities, no abolition societies, no opportunity for vindicating the inherent sovereignty of manhood! . . . A world without sun and life without purpose!" Seeing radicals as both self-righteous and calculating, the *Eagle* alleged that, for all their rhetoric over African Americans, they cared little for vote-less Native Americans.[126]

Democrats took pleasure in integrating Du Chaillu's ethnographic statements into their rhetorical assault on Reconstruction. The *Richmond Enquirer and Sentinel*, for example, reprinted an editorial by the *Journal of Commerce* in New York that took Du Chaillu's claims to be but the latest affirming a remarkable consensus among explorers that "there is no evidence of present or past civilization among the negro race in Africa." Du Chaillu, the editorial reported, "found a total absence of civilization" and abundant evidence that "there has been no progress in the race for thousands of years." Echoing Du Chaillu, the editorial noted that travelers to Africa found the population to be declining and added that the same was now true in the United States. With a clear turn toward America's Reconstruction, the *Journal* concluded by suggesting that "By the time that philanthropists have established the doctrine of the equality of the races, it will not be strange if there are no negroes left to enjoy the new status."[127] The *Enquirer and Sentinel* subsequently printed Du Chaillu's ethnographic arguments once they became widely available through his speech at the Cooper Institute.[128] Likewise, it endorsed the claims of another paper that the president of Haiti was "an unadulterated negro of the Congo breed," that the people of Haiti were "unwashed Africans," and that referred to "savages" of the island's interior as "about as near the status of the gorilla as anything of the *genus homo* discovered by Du Chaillu in Equatorial Africa."[129]

The *New York Herald,* perhaps the most popular paper of its day, offered a prominent endorsement of Du Chaillu's views.[130] The *Herald* began by reflecting that Du Chaillu arrived in America with new information about Africa right as "the public mind is profoundly moved about the status of the negro in our political and social life." After reviewing Du Chaillu's recent successes touring the West and listing his publications, the *Herald* explained that Du Chaillu had gone to equatorial Africa not for sport but "as a *savant* to study . . . the races of men and animals, and especially the negro in his primitive condition and home." Du Chaillu, it argued, should go to Congress to lecture its pro- and anti-negro elements, where the former would have the most to learn. "It may be profitable," the paper continued, connecting Du Chaillu's ethnographic claims with rhetoric about the gorilla, "for our negro-worshipping Congressmen to learn how far the gorilla and negro of Africa are removed from the white Caucasian race of this country." The race, the paper claimed, had never been civilized in "his long history," and "returns to barbarism from even a partially civilized state when left to himself." Amalgamation produced hybrids who could not survive, and whenever social and political equality among races had been attempted, it had led to anarchy. Such experiments, the paper continued, hurt the white race while doing nothing for "the black man," who would eventually be "pushed out of existence." The *Herald* could only hope that Du Chaillu would express these points not only in Congress but across the entire nation in his upcoming lecture tour.[131] Much as Democratic papers countered the *Tribune*'s critique of Du Chaillu, they seconded the *Herald*'s editorial.[132]

Du Chaillu's ethnographic arguments became so widely known that references to them required little explanation. John Codman, a merchant from the United States who traveled to the Caribbean island of St. Thomas in 1864 and then Brazil in 1866, demonstrated as much in his resulting travel narrative. The overarching theme of his volume was that "Negroes" were foolish, ugly, irrational, and that, if slavery itself was injurious to labor, "Negroes" could not govern themselves and should only be free if held as wards of the state.[133] He concluded his volume by commending plans under discussion in the Brazilian government for a gradual, compensated emancipation that would, he hoped, avoid the pitfall of enfranchising non-whites to the benefit of one political party. He even contemplated Brazil's becoming a "black empire" as its white denizens languished in the tropical heat and the coolie trade supplied more dark-skinned laborers. Yet Codman seemed not to have much hope for the distant future of Brazil. He closed his volume by pointing out that the Brazilians already knew from experience what Du Chaillu had had to teach some Americans based on his time in Africa. Codman concluded with a long quotation from one of Du Chaillu's talks averring that "whites" might uplift "the Negro" in the short term but could not save him from his fate.[134]

Conclusion

Du Chaillu gave white supremacists two things they wanted—a means to slander African Americans, and intellectual legitimacy—and at points even managed to fuse the two together. The full import of Du Chaillu's postbellum career may have only become apparent as Reconstruction's partisans listened to his more casual lectures about his travels in Africa. Often focusing on titillating, frightening, and humorous descriptions of fetish worship, cannibalism, polygamy, and slavery in equatorial West Africa, his stories about equatorial West Africans played upon his reputation as both a scientist and an entertainer. In one lecture, Du Chaillu stated that equatorial West African mothers sold their own children without guilt, that the men beat their women into making love to them, that "the great ambition of the African negro was to eat," that they had few domesticated animals, and that polygamous African men continued marrying younger women even if one hundred years old.[135] Such arguments blended expertise with humor. Editors often called attention to Du Chaillu's witticisms or offered their own. The *Marysville Daily Appeal* of California ran one typical short note entitled "Barbaric Economy" contending that "the cannibal tribes of Africa" never wasted a corpse. "Women are among them, as with us, considered tenderest."[136]

Comedy often works by resolving anxiety, and in the late 1860s a great many white supremacists were anxious about the future of racial distinctions in the United States. Herein lay the key to much if not all of Du Chaillu's popularity. The *Crisis*, a rabidly racist newspaper from Columbus, Ohio, reprinted a summary of a lecture by Du Chaillu in New York in which the correspondent indicated the audience erupting into laughter over twenty times:

> I succeeded in collecting fifteen chimpanzees, . . . more than two thousand birds, thousands of insects and shells. I succeeded also in collecting one hundred and twenty skulls of negroes. [laughter] . . .
>
> The natives are very lazy and make their wives do everything for them. [laughter] . . .
>
> They all believe in witchcraft. Whenever a man dies they kill several of his relatives, because of jealousy. The estate there consists altogether of women and wives, but principally wives. [laughter] . . .
>
> The largest number of wives I ever knew one to have was two hundred, and when I inquired of his majesty how many children he had, he condescended to say he had six hundred. [laughter] . . .[137]

Not every audience member in New York or every reader in Columbus was a white supremacist. Nor did all of Du Chaillu's jokes poke fun at equatorial West Africans. But many listeners and readers certainly took extra satisfaction from Du Chaillu's comments, believing that to laugh at a dark-skinned person from equatorial West Africa was to laugh at a freedperson in the South. In that sense, Du Chaillu's career helped firm up white supremacist confidence that the racial group of "the Negro" was readily identifiable and its character fixed. At a time when events put the legal and cultural status of racial distinctions in flux, Du Chaillu offered white supremacists reason to feel confident in their views and laugh off the ideas of their political opponents.

We know little about what Du Chaillu thought of all this, but he must have laughed too, at points. It was not until 1916 that Edward Clodd, Du Chaillu's English friend, revealed that "Like more than one eminent man, [Du Chaillu] invented more than one birthplace for himself. One day it was New York; another day it was Paris, while according to the obituary notice of him in *The Times* (May 1, 1903), it was New Orleans. The truth is that he was born in the island of Bourbon or Reunion. His father was a Frenchman, clerk to a Gaboon trader, and his mother was a mulatto."[138] Far-fetched though this story may seem, the detailed research of Henry Bucher Jr. has confirmed that Du Chaillu's father, Charles-Alexis Duchaillu, worked on the island, located off the coast of Madagascar, in the early 1830s. After a hiatus of uncertain length, he returned by 1840, at which point he owned seven slaves. From there he eventually moved to equatorial West Africa. Du Chaillu's middle name, Belloni, was common among Réunion families of mixed descent. While Du Chaillu's father appears to have never listed Paul as his legal child in French records, the two met up in Gabon, where what evidence we have suggests emotional distance between them.[139] From there, Du Chaillu met the Wilsons, missionaries from the proslavery state of South Carolina who incidentally helped launch the career of a man of mixed descent who would become Reconstruction's most popular white supremacist.

3

From North and South to East and West

From 1867 through 1871, three expeditions, each composed of northern Republicans, traveled around the length of the globe. The detailed narratives that resulted from these journeys shed light on tensions lurking just beneath the surface of northern Republicans' optimism about freedom, progress, and the world's peoples. Eager to witness firsthand how technology and commerce were reshaping the world, these travelers expected to see civilization and republicanism marching forward together in the form of American and more broadly western influence on the benighted "East." Freedom and progress, they believed, would advance as the far-flung regions of the world became more tightly connected with "the West."[1] Much of what these travelers witnessed seemed to affirm this expectation, yet at points they also recognized the existence of a more inchoate set of changes that were shaping societies with their own complex patterns of intermingling, subordination, and segregation. At moments, they even felt their certainty about the future course of human history give way to a more open-ended sense of possibility.

These journeys came at the zenith of northern Republican power. From 1867 to 1871, northern Republicans asserted control over Reconstruction policy-making, implementing a series of measures that secured the reentry of the former Confederate states on antislavery terms. To many northern Republicans—especially those who were at best ambivalent about racial equality, and who therefore wanted to push the transformation of the South only so far—their party appeared to have resolved the two major crises at the heart of Reconstruction. Slavery was out of the South and the South was in the Union.[2] What is more, this period witnessed the consummation of the sweeping program of economic development that the party had inaugurated during the war. The completion of the transcontinental railroad in 1869 capped off a series of initiatives that included homestead legislation to speed the settlement of the West, a transcontinental telegraph, a new system of land-grant colleges to support agriculture and mining, and a high tariff to encourage industry. All this, thought northern Republicans, promised to unite the country in a shared prosperity centered on individual choice. This confident vision was never purely economic in nature, and rested in good measure on a belief that contact would bring cultural conversion. Southern whites, freedpeople, immigrants, and Native Americans would all, the most optimistic believed, ultimately embrace the purified version of America being promulgated by northern Republicans. But what if they did not? The northern Republicans, in destroying the legal foundations of a formal system of human subordination, slavery, and seeking to unite and integrate the country around an open, mobile economy, raised the prospect that they would be left with few means to regulate the interactions among the world's peoples. In this way, they laid the foundation for anxieties rooted in their own prejudices over the coming decades, deeply shaping the politics of the Gilded Age.

The Global Steam Frontier

The middle decades of the nineteenth century witnessed steam-driven technological changes that accelerated economic integration and deepened contact across space.[3] These trips came at the zenith of this process, as four engineering projects brought the "golden age of steam power" (1830s–1870s) to new heights.[4] The most important of these to northern Republicans was the Pacific Railroad, completed in May of 1869, which created the world's first transcontinental rail system.[5] Every bit as transformative was the Suez Canal, which was operational by November of 1869 thanks to steam-powered dredging equipment and which made steam shipping from Europe to East Africa and South Asia cost-effective.[6] Starting in 1867, the Pacific Mail Steamship Company, kept afloat until 1875 by U.S. mail subsidies, connected the western United States to East Asia, where European-owned steamship lines were well established.[7] More remote to Americans but nonetheless integral to these three expeditions was the Great Indian Peninsula Railway, which in 1870 connected Bombay on the west coast of India with the Ganges Valley and Calcutta on the east coast.[8] As many then realized, and as several scholars have noted, these four projects made it practical to travel the length of the world almost entirely by steam.[9] The eccentric northern Democrat George Francis Train capitalized on these developments by traveling around the world in eighty days (or so he claimed) in 1870, but he wrote little about it.[10] Jules Verne, inspired in part by Train's trip and in part by one of these Republican travelers, quickly wrote his novel *Around the World in 80 Days*.[11] By 1872, Thomas Cook, an English entrepreneur, was selling his first round-the-world tourist packages.[12]

Of these three sets of travelers, the first to leave was Charles Carleton Coffin, a Civil War journalist and New England abolitionist. He departed for England in July of 1866, spent a year in Europe, and then set off around the rest of the globe in November of 1867.[13] Carleton, to go by his pen name, scheduled his trip to arrive in Egypt with the Suez Canal under construction, in central India ahead of the completion of the Peninsula Railway, and then in Utah in time to see the completion of the Pacific Railroad.[14] He dedicated his volume, *Our New Way Round the World*, to his wife, Sally, who traveled with him, but rarely mentioned her in his five hundred-page text.[15] The other two expeditions began shortly after the completion of the engineering projects, traveling in the opposite direction but along mostly the same route. William Fogg, a Republican journalist of New England extraction, departed from Cleveland, Ohio, in the fall of 1870, reached San Francisco in November, and then made his way across Asia, arriving in Cairo by September 4, 1871.[16] Fogg not only traveled with a copy of Carleton's rapidly published volume, but lifted without attribution a few brief passages from it—an act that might not have outraged fellow journalists of the day.[17] His narrative, the shortest of the three, appeared first as a series of dispatches for the *Cleveland Leader*, one of the city's Republican newspapers, and then as a 237-page souvenir volume for close friends that included photographs and illustrations.[18] Both Carleton's and Fogg's volumes avoided discussing Europe, a well-worn topic, and focused instead on their travels to and through the East.[19]

The third expedition, the most prominent of the three and the most complex in its route and composition, centered on former Secretary of State William H. Seward. Seward left his home at Auburn, New York, on August 9, 1870, not to return until October 9, 1871.[20] He traveled with a varying assortment of relatives and associates and was often welcomed by foreign dignitaries and American consular agents.[21] Seward's party dwindled as it went, but included a handful of individuals throughout.[22] One was William Freeman, a recently hired African American servant who suffered from some loss of hearing and who appeared frequently but always briefly in Seward's narrative.[23] Also with Seward were Olive and Harriet Risley, the daughters of Hanson Risley, a low-ranking political ally from New York who joined the group as far as San Francisco.[24] The relationship between William Seward, who was sixty-nine years old at the start of the voyage and who had recently lost his wife and daughter, and Olive, who was twenty-six, involved a degree of mutual adoration, although it is unclear if they ever wanted or found any kind of romantic fulfillment.[25] To avoid the controversy that came with traveling with two younger unmarried women, William "adopted" Olive (but not Harriet) while in Asia, even though her father was alive.[26] Their relationship was partly intellectual: William had mentored Olive in her studies and Olive wrote for William, who had been injured in a carriage accident and then the three-part assassination plot that killed Lincoln.[27] Olive's private correspondence stressed as much, as when she explained to Seward's sister-in-law that "I never imagined that I could learn as much as I have on this journey."[28] The volume that resulted from their trip, *William H. Seward's Travels around the World*—which sold over sixty thousand copies—was based largely on Olive's journal, which included her extensive transcriptions of William's comments and, at points, experiences that she had apart from William. Olive worked alongside William and his son Frederick to prepare the volume for publication and continued to move it forward after William's death on October 10, 1872. Arguably, she was his coauthor, but the volume lists her as its editor.[29]

Steam, Commerce, Progress

When Carleton described his narrative as a "book of observation," he captured the intellectual scope of all three travel accounts.[30] Their works focused on recording their reactions to what Fogg described as "the strange and curious nations of the Orient" as they were becoming integrated into capitalism's global steam frontier.[31] As Carleton, Fogg, and the Sewards set off to see "what is to be seen along the new highway of the world," they expected to find deepening contact bringing freedom and progress to the benighted East.[32] Western technological marvels would, they believed, revolutionize hierarchical eastern societies while commerce, consensual and mutually beneficial in their minds, would pull easterners out of the stagnant past and into the dynamic present.[33]

Indeed, Carleton, Fogg, and the Sewards were often downright giddy about the precision and scale of western technology.[34] The Sewards, making their Pacific crossing in September of 1870, recorded as the voyage's "Great Event" the spectacle of a mid-ocean meeting of their steamer with the *America* at precisely the hour predicted by their ship's captain (see figure 7).[35] Similarly, Fogg gushed at how his ship's engine steadily "pushed our leviathan forward" against a typhoon, lauding the vessel as "a triumph of skill and brains over the elements, of science over nature."[36] Carleton compared the Pacific Railroad's route over the mountains to "the work of the Titans."[37] Such enthusiasm extended as well to non-American projects. The Sewards praised the Suez Canal as well as the railroad and telegraph lines connecting it to the Nile.[38] Carleton, the pithiest of the lot, painted with the broadest brush strokes. At the end of his narrative, he celebrated "Coal, the stored-up sunlight of a million years" as the "grand agent" in uniting the world in the march of progress. "Liberty," he continued, "lights the fire, and Christian civilization is the engine which is taking the whole world in its train."[39]

These travelers' reverence for technology, especially in facilitating

FIGURE 7. "Meeting of the Steamers in Mid-Ocean," from Seward, *William H. Seward's Travels*, 33.

commerce, was also apparent when they moved beyond the steam frontier. Both Fogg and the Sewards, for example, were impressed and amused by the bustling scenes along Japan's well-maintained eastern thoroughfare.[40] More often, however, frustration marked such experiences. Carleton devoted an entire chapter to his 160-mile ride in a horse-drawn dak between Nagpore and Jubbulpore, where the Great Indian Peninsula Railway was still under construction. Moving at night to avoid the worst heat, Carleton took three days to complete the trip, which involved repeated delays due to bolting and balking horses, a persistently faulty wheel, and a driver who refused to work until threatened (see figures 8 and 9).[41] The Sewards, reaching the port of Tien-Tsin while en route to Peking, noted that "Here steam-navigation ends. We must stop and see what next." What followed was five chilly days of traveling by single-cabin, flat-bottom riverboats that crawled their way up the Pei-ho River at about a mile-and-a-half per hour, mostly without heat.[42] Along with the steam engine, lighted streets and the telegraph also marked the boundaries of modernity. When Fogg arrived in Singapore, he stated that "For more than three months I had been beyond the range of telegraphs, out here once more we seem to touch civilization."[43] Earlier, after traveling in Canton, China, after dark, Fogg explained how the coolies carrying his and his guide's sedan chairs groped their ways through the city's deserted and unlit streets and compelled porters to let them pass through the wooden gates that sealed off the various wards. Finally arriving back at the city's foreign quarter, Fogg commented, "I felt that I had left behind the dark, hideous barbarism of the East, and, almost by enchantment, had reached the bright and cheerful civilization of the nineteenth century."[44]

Such negative judgments noted, the major theme of their narrative was their gushing optimism about the possibilities for the future. Integral to this vision was a belief that technology, in promoting commerce, would break down the isolation and tear up the traditions that kept the East mired in the past. The Sewards, reflecting on the use of courier pigeons in China while in Peking, pondered, "What a change must come over the empire, when this postman gives place to the railroad, the express, and the electric telegraph!"[45] A month later, while preparing to travel up the Yangtze River onboard the American-built and American-staffed steamer *Plymouth Rock,* the Sewards exclaimed: "Plymouth Rock, a name identified with the civilization of America, now employed

FIGURE 8. "Getting Under Way," from Coffin, *Our New Way Round the World*, 125. The dak's awning reads, "Deccan Horse Dak."

FIGURE 9. "Dead Set," from Coffin, *Our New Way Round the World*, 129.

to signalize an American regeneration of China!"[46] Arriving at Suez, the southern entry point for the canal, the Sewards stated that the city, "like Omaha, is a great place in the future."[47] Upon his departure from Calcutta, Fogg noted the rapid growth of rail mileage in British India, explaining that previously a voyage into the interior would have been prolonged and perilous. But, more than simply convenient, he continued, railways mattered because they were having a "great moral effect" on India by "weakening the ties of caste," a development which he considered potentially more important than even the railroad's economic benefits.[48] Traveling in Egypt, Carleton claimed that while the country had not yet experienced "moral or mental elevation," it was advancing in ways that promised these in the future. "Commerce, railroads, steamships, telegraphs, the influx of travellers, contact with European nations, and Christianity," he argued, "will yet work a wonderful change in this old land."[49]

Each of these travelers assumed that this technology-driven transformation of the East would entail the spread of Protestantism and the retreat of non-Christian religions and cultures. Like Fogg, Carleton and Seward celebrated what they saw as the railroad's assault on the caste system in India, with Carleton linking this explicitly to the decline of Hinduism as a religion. As he put it, "The locomotive . . . is cutting up a faith whose roots run down deep into bygone ages."[50] Later, when Carleton saw the flood-damaged banks of the Ganges River in the Hindu holy city of Benares, India, he described it as a "fit emblem of the change which has already commenced in the Hindoo religion, which is being swept away by the mighty current of Christian civilization."[51] Fogg struck a similar note about Islam when traveling in northern India, reflecting on the transformations wrought by "the all-civilizing locomotive" over a land once "swept by the devastating hordes of Timour the Tartar" and subsequently controlled by the "Mussulman dynasty" of Akbar the Magnificent.[52] Preparing to depart from Bombay a month later, Fogg commented that he had only become more fascinated with India, home to one-sixth of humanity, as "a land where western ideas and a Christian civilization are now struggling for a foothold, but must eventually replace the effete idolatry and paganism of the past."[53] These travelers were not missionaries, and they recorded no instance of personally exerting themselves to convert the people they met. Indeed, even as they invoked religious distinctions, much of what they said about these groups was secular in nature, and they tended to see proselytizing as part of a broader conversion process that would be a natural aftereffect to global integration. Seward, in fact, went so far as to emphasize that commerce and not Christianity would inaugurate China's rebirth. "I look," he stated at a reception in his honor in Hong Kong, "chiefly to commerce for the regeneration of China—that commerce to come across the American Continent and the Pacific Ocean," no doubt by steam.[54]

Yet at other points these travelers betrayed an undercurrent of uncertainty, focusing instead on what they took to be the pervasiveness and persistence of so-called heathen superstition. The Sewards, describing some of the practices and beliefs affiliated with various temples in Japan, opined that "Superstition, though abating in Japan, is nevertheless far from extinct."[55] Fogg, like Carleton, visited Benares's riverfront, but instead of seeing Hinduism swept away, he was struck by its tenacious hold. There, he commented on how male and female Hindu pilgrims came to bathe, some nude, in the river's "filthy stuff" while deceased Hindus floated down river and burned in nearby funeral pyres. "No where in the world unless in Central Africa," claimed Fogg, "can be seen such besotted superstition and idolatry coupled with such intolerant fanaticism."[56] In Allahabad, also along the Ganges, Carleton described how one could encounter Muslims prohibited from eating pork within three minutes of Hindus who "bow down to the image of the sacred hog Baraha." All of this, he thought, was evidence of how "man wallows in degradation" without Christianity.[57]

Their assumption that technology, commerce, and Protestant Christianity would march forward in close company explains why both the Sewards and Carleton took time to discuss Egypt's Viceroy Ismael Pasha.[58] On the one hand, the viceroy served as evidence of western influence because he had been educated in Paris and was an enterprising booster of steam-driven progress. Remarking on the network of railways the viceroy was developing, Carleton stated, "Thus far he has shown quite as much enterprise as any ruler in Europe."[59] The Sewards went further, declaring, "No nation has a bolder projector, or more liberal patron, of internal improvements."[60] On the other hand, the viceroy was a Muslim, and his commitment to progress might undermine these travelers' assumptions about the relationships among technology, commerce, enlightenment, and the spread of Protestant Christianity. Instead, they presented the other side of the free-labor Orientalism espoused by Stillman and other northern Republicans in response to Ottoman rule in Crete. If the island's economic underdevelopment was associated with alleged Asiatic backwardness, then Egypt's dynamism suggested its ruler was only so Eastern. Carleton took faith in his belief that, while the viceroy was not a Christian, his infrastructure projects would benefit missionaries. Commenting on the viceroy's plans to extend his Nile railway past the river's first cataracts, Carleton claimed: "The Valley of the Nile is the natural highway to the heart of Africa, by which commerce and Christian civilization are yet to reach Ethiopia. The work which Ismael Pasha is doing will be as far reaching in its results as time itself."[61]

At times these travelers lent a clear nationalist edge to their celebrations of technology and commerce, lauding both how advanced and active Americans were and the especially beneficial nature of their resulting influence. But there was also a more abstract sense in which these two forces were intrinsically progressive and irresistible. Indeed, envisioning commerce as a product of mutual consent and seeing technological advances as willful and benign, these travelers took these forces of civilization to be naturally supportive of freedom as well.

In Two Hemispheres and of Two Minds

Such optimism, however, existed alongside tensions inherent in these travelers' view of freedom, progress, and the world's peoples. Like most northern Republicans, Carleton, Fogg, and the Sewards disliked arbitrary hierarchies, especially among men, and the coercive acts that sustained them. Freedom from such systems of subordination, they believed, allowed societies to be ordered by consent, was at the heart of modern progress, and was one of the virtues of their own newly purified nation. Yet presumptions about human difference—racial, religious, national, and cultural—also shaped their thinking. As they traveled, Carleton, Fogg, and the Sewards oscillated between condemning hierarchy—often with an emphasis on universal humanity—and endorsing notions of ingrained and often innate difference.[62] The result was a deep ambivalence about European imperialism in the East.

These travelers' contempt for hierarchy found ready expression in their comments on social relations in eastern societies. Fogg, the most flippant egalitarian of the bunch, relished mocking the pretenses of Japan's sword-wearing nobility. The countenance of a passing nobleman in Yokohama, he commented, "shows that he is proud and overbearing," adding that the nobleman no doubt viewed Japanese commoners as "*scum*" despite their being "honest, industrious, and polite." While it was customary to bow to such a figure, he and some unspecified fellow travelers merely stared back at his glance without flinching, "as an 'American sovereign' should."[63] Fogg's comments were not an ethnic or racial critique of the Japanese but a political and economic one of the "servile abuses of the feudal system" that denied the people prosperity much as it did, he noted, in Spain. He hoped that Japan's recent civil war had seen the people "cast off the manners of slaves" and that they would soon claim a voice in their government.[64] Carleton took a different view of the Japanese civil war, but also thought it shed light on Japan's feudal baggage. He averred that the Japanese people had little interest in the conflict because it was "like the dispute between York and Lancaster, or the old struggle of France as to which party shall have the Dauphin." "Civil war in this country," he reiterated, "is as chronic as it was in Europe under the feudal system."[65]

They also condemned the actions of domineering Europeans and Americans, at points critiquing racial privilege as aristocratic. Carleton recoiled at British haughtiness in India, lamenting that local merchants—individuals who could draw upon "the Bank of England for millions of dollars" and who could read "the Rig Veda, or Shakespeare, Racine, Humboldt, Cicero, and Homer in the original"—had to step aside and bow to "the merest stripling of an ensign with epaulets on his shoulders!"[66] Fogg commented similarly when in Hong Kong, which was then policed in a particularly rigid and biased fashion.[67] Fogg described how late every night he could hear drunken sailors singing in full chorus down the middle of the street. The police, Fogg reflected, "never seem to interfere with such demonstrations on the part of *white men*."[68] Fogg again mentioned race in northern India by stating, "Here your skin is your patent of nobility and passport, all in one." With a love for performative flair, Fogg drove his point home by relaying how, when encountering bowing natives and servile coolies, he flouted local conventions by bowing in return "with a civil and polite 'salaam.'"[69]

The imperious behavior of an American carriage driver in Yeddo, Japan, troubled the Sewards. The man cracked his whip over "the bare heads of the native crowd" and traumatized Japanese onlookers by mangling a litter of sleeping puppies. "'It will never do to stop for such things,'" the driver pontificated, to William's disgust, "'let them learn to keep their streets clear.'" Pondering this and other events on their way from Japan to China, the Sewards expressed their concern about both the personal arrogance and the military posturing of western powers in Japan, whose people the Sewards praised at length.[70] No mere personal experience, the Sewards saw the incident with the carriage driver as emblematic of western arrogance. "Intimidation and menace naturally provoke anger and resentment," they commented, adding, "Though the eye of the Japanese is long and curved, it sees as clearly as the foreign eye, which is round and straight. Human nature is the same in all races." Believing that the long-isolated Japanese nation could only survive the shock of modern civilization with western mentorship, the Sewards hoped that the United States would embrace a broader philanthropy and begin sending teachers instead of military forces to Japan.[71]

When Carleton and Fogg both became exasperated to the point of violence in British India, both admitted so with apparent unease. Carleton, during his travels by dak in central India, became stranded for over an hour and a half in the town of Seonee, in part because his driver disappeared into the crowd of a religious festival. Carleton and his wife wandered the crowd helplessly until they came across an Englishman, who advised them to act menacingly. Deciding to take his advice, Carleton and his wife found their driver's boss and waved their fists "within an inch of his nose" (see figure 10). Directed by the boss to their driver, they grabbed him by the shoulder, spun him in circles, shook their fists, and screamed at the top of their lungs. The technique worked but left Carleton and his wife laughing, not at the driver or "Hindoos" more generally, but at "the ludicrousness of the whole affair."[72] Fogg also recorded verging on violence when, after having been drenched by freezing rain, he attempted to procure hotel rooms in a nearly deserted Himalayan town. As he noted apologetically, "I am afraid I flourished my rattan threateningly over the heads of the native servants in charge of the establishment to expedite their movements."[73] In the same letter, and at the same hotel, however, he took pride in the restraint that a fellow American demonstrated when a hotel employee accidentally incinerated his boots. The employee, familiar with English behavior, anticipated "a volley of curses, emphasized by some missile," but received instead only a "mild reprimand." His friend, Fogg added, "is a gentleman, an American, and a New Yorker."[74] It would be naive to assume that these accounts constituted the full story, but in presenting the authors as unaccustomed to menacing subordinates, they conform with the authors' critiques of hierarchy.

FIGURE 10. "Stirring up a Hindoo," from Coffin, *Our New Way Round the World,* 135.

When race served as a justification for subordination and exploitation, these travelers could be sharply critical. Indeed, Fogg even included, without offering any defense for his country, a blunt comment from an Afro-Jamaican police officer in Hong Kong. Addressing some quick inquiries from Fogg, the officer explained that he had never been to the United States and "thought there was too much prejudice against color there to suit him."[75] Yet these travelers also frequently invoked mid-nineteenth-century racial terminology, blithely describing unfamiliar, diverse, and complex populations as "Caucasians," "Malays," "Mongolians," "Asiatics," "Aryans," and "Negroes." These categories, as well as broader distinctions between white and nonwhite peoples and those from temperate and tropical climes, had a way of appearing almost at random in their comments. Their critiques of racial hierarchy notwithstanding, they frequently proved themselves sufficiently comfortable with the idea of racial difference to reference it without explanation or justification. Carleton was a prime example of this. Discussing medieval Egypt, he explained how twelve thousand Circassian slave-soldiers purchased by the sultan from Genghis Khan "had Northern blood in their veins" and eventually overthrew the sultan, founding the Mamluk dynasty.[76] Surveying the Japanese civil war, he similarly claimed that the conflict was "a question of the supremacy of climate, race, and blood," with the southerners having "tropical blood" from the Pacific islands while the northerners "are from a vigorous clime; they face the cold wintry winds which sweep down the sea of Ochotsk from Kamtchatka."[77]

The Sewards issued forth a particularly perplexing series of comments and actions concerning race. What little they said in their narrative and private correspondence about William Freeman, the African American servant who traveled with them, suggests that they were comfortable with viewing him as a subordinate and marginal member of the group, esteeming him to be dutiful without expecting him to be servile.[78] Beginning their voyage in August of 1870, only six months after the ratification of the Fifteenth Amendment, the Sewards twice noted that Freeman was now a voting citizen of the United States. Crossing the Missouri River early in their voyage, the Sewards asked their readers whether Freeman did not "feel his importance" when garrulous passengers asked him to participate in a political discussion.[79] Yet the Sewards did not bother to follow through on the subject by asking Freeman about the experience or recording his thoughts. The Sewards later awkwardly attempted to equate the time Freeman spent stranded atop an elephant in India, after everyone but William Seward forgot about him, with the wait he had "for the fifteenth amendment to bring him to the citizenship of the United States."[80] The fact that they named the wrong amendment—it was the Fourteenth Amendment that granted citizenship—and that they trivialized the struggle for African American equality to laugh off their forgetting of Freeman suggests both that they thought they should be sensitive on the matter of African American rights and that they were clearly failing to be so. Likewise, when the Sewards attended a ball in Shanghai, China, they were pleased to see "'John Brown's soul marching on'" in the form of a "modest and intelligent" former slave, Mr. Butler, who attended on equal footing with the other guests and who was making a healthy salary in the freighting business. Again, however, they paid no apparent attention to what Mr. Butler himself thought about his situation. The Sewards were proud of their commitment to equality and yet struggled to think of African Americans as worthy of their own voice.[81]

The Sewards' ruminations about the role of race in world history demonstrated similar inconsistencies. En route from Singapore to Batavia, for example, the Sewards contrasted the various members of the boat's crew, speculating that Europeans had a "closer ethnological affinity" with "the Hindoo and Malays nations" than with "Mongolians."[82] But the Sewards also later described "the Malays" as "intellectually as well as physically feeble," and judged that their incredible skills with irrigation, as evidenced in hillside rice cultivation, must stem from an instinct instead of technological mastery.[83] It could have been Du Chaillu discounting the skills of central African ironworkers and weavers. At the Nile's first cataract at Assouan, the Sewards commented on the "diversity and strangeness" of the area's population, finding Assouan to be heavily "African" and yet under the commercial control of "superior races," in this case "Berbers, Abyssinians, and Libyans."[84] The Sewards' most sweeping theorizing came as they steamed up the Red Sea, viewing along the way a rare part of the globe untouched by the force of progress. The Sewards postulated that the area was the historic contact point between "the two great divisions of the human family, the white race and the dark races." Instead of comingling across history, the Sewards argued, these two groups had parted ways, "perhaps by consent, more probably by instinct," with "the dark races" remaining in Africa and moving across South Asia while Caucasians left these to their "dark competitors" and moved to Europe, the Atlantic, and then the Americas.[85] Somehow this was to have happened with the "Malays" being ethnologically closer to whites than the more northerly "Mongolians."

At other times, Carleton and the Sewards—here Fogg had little to say—placed greater emphasis on how differences reflected an underlying human nature. Attempting to trace the rise of the Hindu caste system in northern India during antiquity, Carleton argued that while the system's hold over its followers was unparalleled in history, its origins lay with the instinctive human need for religion.[86] Observing dervishes in Cairo prompted the Sewards to think of the practices of Shakers in the United States and wonder at the origins of both "in a common principle of human nature."[87] Later, after visiting the ancient ruins of Abydos, Egypt, they speculated that ancient Egyptian religion informed Jewish practices and beliefs, the mythologies of classical Greece and Rome as well as modern India and China, and the asceticism and monasticism common in Christianity and in the East. Such musings suggested that the Sewards also believed that, far from going their separate ways, "the white and dark races" shared a common religious heritage. They closed their reflections by asking whether the human capacity for religious knowledge was limited and whether the world's religions were not all based "on some intuitive idea or abused revelation?"[88] So often explicit in judging other races, nations, religions, and cultures inferior, the Sewards also persistently called attention to shared human nature. Such inconsistency should not be read as evidence of an underlying lack of interest in the nature of humanity. As Seward wrote privately to his son Frederick after traveling up the Nile, encountering the "relics of the earliest civilization of our race" left him tormented by philosophical questions.[89] Such inconsistency was in line with the broader tension in these narratives between upholding human equality and condemning hierarchy, on the one hand, and assuming the existence of profound differences among the world's peoples on the other. Both end points of the ethnological imagination—universal equality and immutable difference—had to be squared with the notion of expanding, unifying forces of civilization, including commerce, technology, and most controversially empire.

Imperial Musings

These travelers' conflicted beliefs shaped their views of European imperialism. British rule in India—which had long prompted a complex range of opinion within the United States—elicited a convoluted set of comments from each of these travelers, as did Dutch rule in Indonesia from the Sewards.[90] In each narrative there was a tension between impressions based on encounters with imperialism on the ground and their reflections about imperialism as a historical process. For all three, as well, the Great Mutiny of 1857 and the end of the corrupt and cruel administration of the British East India Company constituted key developments. The complexities of their narratives affirm historian David Wrobel's cautioning against flattening out the vast body of European and North American travel writing by treating it as intrinsically imperial in nature.[91]

Fogg said less than Carleton and the Sewards, but what he did say underscores that he shared their ambivalences about race, equality, and therefore empire. Although he repeatedly skewered the British as arrogant, Fogg also defended their presence in the East. His lengthiest comment came from a conversation with an English civil servant who meekly asked Fogg if the United States was going to ally with Russia, a rival power in central Asia. Dumbfounded by the question, Fogg proceeded to offer his readers a rare geopolitical discourse. British concerns were justified, he explained, as the two powers were already "almost face to face" in the region. Unwilling to predict the outcome of a conflict, Fogg was certain that British rule in India was preferable to a Russian conquest or to Indian autonomy. The "intelligent natives" would delight at seeing the English "thrashed" by the Russians, but would be no better off for it. Russia itself was "An organized barbarism, of Asiatic origin," staffed by corrupt officials and incapable of effective or enlightened rule. Independence would return India to its centuries of bribery, during which corruption had eaten "into the national character so deeply that many people believe it can never be washed out." The majority of Indians, he continued, cared little about who ruled them as long as taxes remained low, with criticism of the British reflecting "merely the hatred that easterners always bear their masters," adding that "masters the Hindoos will always have." British rule, much reformed since the mutiny, brought with it "incorruptible" judges and civil servants and a growing number of schools and colleges that ensured that "young men are growing up with western ideas."[92] It was a head-spinning series of statements in which the national term Indian was equated with the religious one of "Hindoo" and in which the racial category "Asiatic" applied to them as well as Russians. The Indians, moreover, were both incapable of change and yet were imbibing western ideas. British rule should be welcomed, but only because it had become less exploitative.

Carleton's most extensive comments on the British Empire came in response to a discussion with an English engineer in central India. The engineer had resided in India for twenty years and knew at least one native language. He had also lived through the massacre of British subjects at Cawnpore during the Great Mutiny of 1857, where he witnessed his wife and two children get "'cut to pieces,—literally chopped up.'" Yet the engineer, haunted by the past, focused on the arrogance of his countrymen, not the cruelty of the Indian rebels. While the local population was kind and loyal, Englishmen refused to learn local languages, flew into fits of rage and violence, and indulged themselves at the houses of wealthy natives only to later snub them. Most so-called Christians, moreover, made a mockery of their religion while offending "Hindoo notions of morality and religion." Carleton provided an accompanying illustration of a hypothetical scene of a British officer attacking a native

Indian with the derisive caption "The Master Race" (see figure 11).[93] In a later passage Carleton continued to reflect on British rule, echoing the criticisms of his interlocutor but also offering a qualified apology. Certainly, Carleton noted, the British East India Company had treated India terribly, with its rule probably constituting one of the darkest pages in history. But, Carleton added, India had never been well-ruled, lacked an indigenous tradition of patriotism, and was currently seeing marvelous improvements under the new regime.[94] Like Fogg, Carleton reconciled himself to the British presence in the East by accentuating its reformed nature. Unlike Fogg, however, Carleton held out hope for a degree of eventual self-rule, arguing that "Christian civilization" would energize a people who were not "Asiatics" but "ancient Aryans."[95]

The Sewards also expressed a mixture of concern and ultimate support for European empires, even as they stayed as the guests of Governor-General Myer in Java, were hosted by William's friends Lord and Lady Napier in southeastern India, and were welcomed by Viceroy Lord Mayo in Calcutta.[96] Such connections made for frequent privileged access to places, audiences, and modes of transportation, as when the British government in Bombay fitted out a special steamer to take the

FIGURE 11. "The Master Race," from Coffin, *Our New Way Round the World*, 131.

Sewards down the coast to see Goa.[97] But it did not cause the Sewards to refrain from criticism. As Jay Sexton has demonstrated, the Sewards tended to welcome a reformed imperialism built around the expansion of infrastructure and commerce and the expansion of Anglo-American values, including nationalism, to putatively less advanced regions.[98]

The Sewards became acquainted with Dutch imperialism on the heavily populated island of Java, home to the colonial administration in Batavia. The Sewards' impressions were mostly positive, in part because they visited the centerpiece of the Dutch trading empire during what was a tranquil and prosperous period compared to the preceding two centuries of greed, corruption, and turmoil. They were impressed with what they took to be the contentment and docility of the native Malay population and the success of the Dutch in orchestrating the island's agricultural production. While in the interior of the island they encapsulated their views by stating that "Dutch colonization has a story as simple as its results are wonderful," followed by an account of how the Dutch government masterfully came to control the island by force and cooption once it took the reins from the Dutch East India Company.[99] Although the Sewards conceded that the Dutch ruled despotically, even witnessing troops embark to suppress a rebellion, they considered Dutch rule "a great and beneficent success." Indeed, the Dutch government had, they claimed, "practiced far less severity and cruelty toward the natives" of Java than Spain, Great Britain, and the United States had practiced in America.[100]

Yet there were limits to their support of Dutch rule, as became apparent when the Sewards stayed as the guests of Wiranarta Kalsoema Radhe Adepathe, a noble on the colonial government's payroll in the island's interior. The Sewards initially held a negative opinion of Radhe Adepathe, believing him to be a petulant and overbearing local despot.[101] But over time they found themselves liking their host "vastly" between his episodes of gout. When a young, unnamed Dutchman who was traveling with the Sewards questioned an account that Radhe Adepathe was providing of his "great ancestry," the Sewards found themselves critical of the Dutchman. Explaining that they had observed that the Dutch were constantly worried about treachery from the regent, the Sewards reflected that "suspicion is the punishment for usurpation."[102] If never fully comfortable with some of Radhe Adepathe's behavior, they found themselves asking whether it would be treasonous for "this humiliated and pensioned wearer of twelve diamond-hilted ancestral swords, to strike with them a blow for the lost sceptre of his tribe?"[103] Even with all the benefits of Dutch rule, the Sewards pondered whether the Javanese did not have a right to rebel.

The justifications the Sewards offered for Dutch imperialism also underscore just how conditional their support for imperialism was. In their view, the Dutch were to be lauded not for having their empire per se, but because it was one that, they believed, kept Java free from pauperism, raised the Malays to "the partial exercise of political function," tolerated all religions while encouraging missionizing, and supported widespread literacy. Indeed, for all their negative commentary about the Malay race, the Sewards would have preferred that Dutch colonial subjects had a greater exposure to sentiments of "personal liberty and national independence." They closed their reflections on Dutch rule by affirming their belief in "the ultimate civilization of the whole human race" while accepting that progress toward that end was "slow, and seemingly uncertain."[104] Much as with Fogg and Carleton, their statements on the "Malays" and the Dutch were consistently conflicted, both pointing to the advantages of European rule over an allegedly backward people and yet preferring greater independence and progress for all.

As in Dutch Indonesia, the Sewards' endorsement of imperialism in British India and elsewhere was qualified. Speaking before a racially exclusive and mostly British audience at Bombay's socially prestigious Byculla Club, William Seward urged Britons and Americans to embrace each other in what was for these travelers a conventionally ambivalent statement. On the one hand, he identified the two as Anglo-Saxon empires, suggesting an underlying racial perspective. On the other, he lauded both for being above the "blandishments of despotism" and concerned with "universal progress." As cordial allies, the two would encircle the earth with the British love of rule of law and the "American love of educated liberty."[105] His speech was, like many of the comments by Fogg and Carleton, critical of unbridled imperial power. He reminded his listeners that whatever governments they established "amid the *débris* of Asiatic empires or in the chaos of America," those governments should exist "for the welfare and happiness of the native races among whom they are founded." It was the allegedly reformed, benevolent empires of the modern era that Seward had in mind when he urged his audience that "The inventions of steam, railroads, telegraphs, and missionary colleges and schools" now allowed empires to carry on their work "peacefully and humanely" instead of through haphazard violence.[106]

From Many, What?
A World between Coercion and Conversion

As Seward's comments suggest, at their most optimistic these travelers believed that the technology-driven progress of the present was so spectacular that imperial violence could, largely, become a thing of the past. Easterners might need to be prodded and mentored, this line of thinking went, but they would eventually convert in both a religious and cultural sense to western ways. A clear current of doubt about the racial capacities of groups like "Hindoos" and "Malays" existed, but it was not so powerful as to reverse these travelers' giddy expectations for the future. Yet, this same optimism could evolve into a second concern that focused on the peoples of the East as autonomous actors. Without coercion, what was there to ensure that the large, diverse, and complex societies of the East would move down the path that these travelers believed the West was pointing to? What if neither their optimistic expectations for nor their civilizational pessimism about the East's conversion captured what was happening as the world became more tightly integrated? Only as they made their way did Carleton, Fogg, and the Sewards appear to consider that the East's past might weigh as heavily on its future as the West's present. So too was it slow to dawn on them that as commerce mixed together the world's peoples it might produce something entirely new.

Expecting to find peaceful commerce, buoyed by advancing technologies, wearing down old antagonisms and uniting the world's peoples behind western-led progress, these travelers remarked frequently on the recalcitrance of ethnic, religious, and national divisions in the East. The prevalence of urban segregation, for example, routinely captured their attention, with the Sewards noting it in Jerusalem, Fogg in Singapore, and Carleton in Bombay.[107] Indeed, they found these patterns of segregation nearly universal in the East. In Patna in northern India the Sewards stated that the city, "like all towns and villages on our road," was divided between Hindus and Muslims.[108] Carleton noted that Cairo, "like other Eastern cities," was divided into walled ethnic quarters, including ones for Copts, Jews, and Franks, while in China he noted Peking's division into walled Tartar and Chinese sections.[109] Such segregation was doubly troubling when it applied to westerners, as the Sewards made clear while in the small foreign settlement of Yokohama, Japan, where social interactions with neighboring Japanese were limited by treaty stipulations and western condescension.[110] Perhaps reacting as well to the divisions internal to the foreign settlement, which included a separate Chinese quarter, the Sewards found themselves surprised by the settlement's contrast with "the intermingling of all classes, conditions, and races" under common mores that they knew from home.[111] After a ball in the foreign quarter of Yokohama, the Sewards repeated this theme, accentuating those treaty stipulations, stating that "Of course, not one Japanese of either sex was there. . . . Caste and race are unrelenting antagonists to universal civilization."[112] When the Sewards visited Saigon, perhaps unaware of recent French campaigns to pacify the surrounding regions, they were struck by finding a city with amicable relations across ethnic lines.[113]

Equally worrying was that commerce might exacerbate ethnic tensions. The Sewards in particular, but also Fogg, took interest in the attitudes of and toward the Chinese. Fogg, in Yokohama, noted that the city's hundreds of well-dressed and successful Chinese immigrants considered themselves "very much above the natives."[114] Fogg similarly commented on animosity toward Chinese merchants and sailors in the Malacca Strait, where Malay pirates targeted Chinese junks and where his ship's Malay sailors antagonized its Chinese servants and firemen. Only "the control of English officers, backed by their revolvers," maintained order among "these semi-savages."[115] The Sewards held more favorable views of the Chinese and lamented anti-Chinese sentiment as hindering progress. In Java, the Sewards were glad to see the cessation of Dutch complicity in local anti-Chinese policies, favored by the island's Muslims.[116] In Singapore, the Sewards noted that half of the city's population was Chinese, and that "It would be an effectual antidote to the California croaking against the pagan Chinese" to see how British officials encouraged and protected their immigration.[117] Indeed, as Jay Sexton has pointed out, the Sewards' comments here were not fleeting thoughts but instead reflected William's belief that Chinese immigration to the United States was integral to the growth of America's trans-Pacific commerce.[118] In his private correspondence, William was similarly praiseful of the Chinese he encountered.[119]

Yet these travelers were also struck by just how mixed together the complex and diverse populations of the East were and were becoming. Port cities, along with a few other urban centers, showcased how the tides of history were pressing people together in surprising and befuddling combinations. In Cairo, the Sewards reflected on how, without any apparent strife, "The Italian, the French, the English, the American, and the German jostle alike the children of Ishmael and the children of Israel, the Greek, the Copt, the Berber, the Abyssinian, the Nubian, the Soumalan."[120] Similarly, in the city of Suez, Carleton described "a swarthy crowd of Arabs, negroes, Nubians, Hindoos, Italians, Spaniards, Germans, Frenchmen, Englishmen, Russians, and Turks."[121] Fogg noted that Hong Kong's "motly" [*sic*] population included not only British and Chinese, but also Sikhs from the Punjab serving as Sepoys, Parsee merchants originally from India, and approximately three hundred Afro-Caribbean police officers in the Crown's service.[122] In Singapore, Fogg explained that "In the streets and shops we see every shade of color and every caste of race . . . Java and Ceylon, Hindostan and Burmah, and every island of the East Indian Archipelago has here its representatives" while the Sewards noted seamen "of many Oriental races, natives of Goa, Javanese, Hindoos, Malays, Burmese, Siamese, Cingalese, Abyssinians, and negroes."[123] Such ethnic commotion obviously intrigued these travelers, but it also defied an easy narrative of western influence on a uniform East. This was particularly apparent in their split reactions to Alexandria, Egypt. The Sewards, arriving after traveling the Nile, noted the city's well-dressed Europeans, English and French carriages, and Italian opera, stating, "It seems as if we had already entered Europe, and left Egypt behind us."[124] Carleton, coming from Europe, was more struck by the blurring of lines. "The Occident has invaded the Orient," he remarked, "and the two civilizations are so intermingled that it is impossible to say where the one begins and the other ends."[125]

Would all this yield western influence, greater divisions and antagonisms, or something new? It was hard to find a clear answer. Steaming from Aden to Bombay, Carleton found more evidence of a world mixed together when his ship's crew formed a band featuring "a red-faced Englishman" on trumpet, "a full-grown Malay scraping a violin, and a little Hindoo boy tooting a flageolet." As the volume of the music increased, "An Irishman and a negro" waltzed together, "amid enthusiastic cheers of the admiring crowd" (see figure 12).[126] Less open than this scene but every bit as mystifying was the Calcutta derby. There, Fogg found "Europeans and Bangalese, Turks and Arabs, Hindoos and Mohometans," arriving in all manner of contrivance and dressed in all manner of fashions. Yet, Fogg noticed, "no person . . . unless of pure European blood, is admitted to the inner circle, or near the grand stand." Among the excluded were India's often wealthy and educated "*Eurasians,* or English-speaking half castes," who were shut out from high society and in turn snubbed even "wealthy natives of full Indian blood."[127] Segregation and intermixing were themselves mixed up together.

As Carleton, Fogg, and the Sewards traveled, moreover, each encountered evidence that western technology and commerce could work against one-way influence. In Egypt, Carleton found the very technologies that were supposed to convert easterners doing the opposite, with Russian, Austrian, and Egyptian steamers taking Muslim pilgrims to Mecca.[128] When in Singapore, Fogg reflected on what he saw as the commercial triumph not of westerners but the Chinese. "Every steamer and junk," he claimed, "brings a crowd of the emigrants from Chinese ports" who through hard work and frugality were able to return home

FIGURE 12. "The Jolly Mariners," from Coffin, *Our New Way Round the World,* 79.

wealthy.[129] Also of interest to Fogg was the career of Mr. Whampoah (originally Hoo Ah Kay), "a millionaire Chinese merchant."[130] As Fogg explained, the middle-aged Whampoah received him in his European-style counting house in polite, perfect English. There, Fogg could observe a table covered in correspondence in multiple European languages and a staff that included "a Bengalese and a Parsee, and several others whose dress and complexion indicate either Portuguese or mixed European and Asiatic blood."[131] Mr. Whampoah reflected not the unilateral influence of the West upon the East but the ability of people in the East to master the West to make something new. Carleton, passing through a teahouse in the gardens of a Chinese merchant in Singapore, likely the same Mr. Whampoah, was similarly struck by how contact yielded, to him, unappealing intermixture.[132] As he described it, "the proprietor has Italian vases, French clocks, Japanese carved work, windows of German stained glass, floors of English encaustic tiles, flower-pots from the potteries of his native land, arranged with little taste or order."[133]

Indeed, the selective appropriation of western ideas, contacts, and institutions often appeared to be the norm. In Allahabad, in northern India, Carleton was perplexed when he visited an American Presbyterian mission. There, he discovered that a western education, though coveted, did little to facilitate conversion. Speaking of one of the mission's local benefactors, Carleton explained that "this man is not a Christian. Although he does not worship idols, he has not embraced the Christian religion. He has arrived only at a state of *betweenity*."[134] Fogg had a similar experience while being toured around the holy city of Benares by a well-educated "high-caste Brahmin." Fogg explained that his guide "laughed at the superstition of his countrymen and professed to disbelieve in *Brahma* and his namesake *Shiva*," but Fogg "could not make out that in objuring [*sic*] Paganism he had embraced Christianity."[135] The Sewards also confronted the selective appropriation of western ways when observing a lesson at a mission school in South India with Lady Napier. There, they reflected that while the children, speaking in "the Tamil dialect, others in Telugu, others in the Hindostanee," answered Bible questions as well as American children, very few of the thousands in the region so educated became Christians.[136]

What would be the ultimate outcome of the present, overflowing as it was with possibility? Amid all their confidence about the triumph of freedom and progress, at least one of these travelers found a little room for open doubt. Contemplating his travels to and in Egypt, Carleton described how wealthy Muslims living around the Mediterranean went to Paris and enjoyed that "paradise of the West." Rigid in their religious observance at home, in Paris, he claimed, "they forget all about Mecca," and after returning to Cairo or Constantinople proceeded to "observe the sacred fasts with roast-turkey and champagne." Here was a conversion of a different sort that, if only briefly, led Carleton to wonder: "The world is moving in more sense than one; but where is it going to?"[137]

Carleton, Fogg, and the Sewards, usually confident that the East would conform to the ways of the West, found reason to be fascinated, perplexed, and perhaps even intimidated. The East's diverse peoples were distinctive from and often antagonistic to each other, suggesting that the East, vast and complex, was ordered more by its own history than by western influence. And yet the East could appear hopelessly jumbled together, with sundry eastern and western peoples crowded together in combinations that dazzled the onlookers. Finally, western contact might lead to the selective adoption of technologies, practices, and institutions, only to see them put to unexpected ends.

Conclusion

Confident but inconsistent, these travelers put on display tensions lurking just beneath the surface of northern Republican thinking. Like their peers at home, they expected that deepening contact among the world's peoples would promote freedom and progress and were opposed to formal systems of personal subordination among men. Their vision of the postbellum United States, and ultimately of the world, was of a prosperous whole united by consensual, benign commerce, which was in turn buoyed by the marvels of well-intentioned technological innovation. Yet these travelers were also ambivalent about human equality, condemning arbitrary hierarchy while casually invoking racial categories and at times advancing arguments about various groups' innate inferiority. The result was two conflicting sources of doubt. At times, as with the Sewards on "the Malays," Fogg on "the Hindoos," and Carleton on the southern Japanese, there was little or no faith in the capacity of some peoples to keep up with the wondrous changes sweeping the globe. But at others there was a clear sense of the complex societies of the East as moving in their own directions. Whether in terms of the persistence of old-world ethnic antagonisms, freewheeling cultural intermixing, or the selective appropriation of western practices and technologies, these travelers at points realized that global integration did not guarantee unilateral western influence.

These tensions marked the northern Republicans' postbellum political hegemony in subtle but profound ways. Committed to destroying arbitrary hierarchies and to deepening the commercial integration of the country and the world, northern Republicans begged the question of what forces, if any, would moderate contact among the world's peoples going forward. At their most confident, northern Republicans expected the irresistible forces of freedom and progress to ride roughshod over the national, cultural, racial, and religious boundaries dividing the world's peoples to render a unified, uniform world. They also, however, had persistent doubts, including about African Americans, Irish Catholics, and Native Americans, and their giddy optimism was always at risk of sliding into contempt for and fear of those who seemed opposed to the right kind of change. As a result, the northern Republican hegemony produced a country that was, for over a decade, remarkably if not completely free from legal restraints on human movement, and yet whose citizens were increasingly concerned with controlling the direction of influence. Over the coming decades, northern Republicans repeatedly proved themselves willing to contemplate tighter control of immigration, the forced confinement of Native Americans on reservations, and local and state regulations on ethnic groups and African Americans. These views represented not so much the spurning of postbellum ideals as northern Republicans' shift from a state of confidence to one of anxiety.[138] Their vacillations set northern Republicans off from the uncompromising white supremacists of the Democratic Party.

Perhaps no moment captures this difference between northern Republicans and Democrats better than William Seward's visit to the Great Wall of China, where he paused to offer some historical reflections. Seward observed that the wall had failed to prevent the eventual Mongol and Tartar conquest of China and argued that, after much terror and bloodshed, it had "ceased to be needful." Conquerors and the conquered became "reconciled, assimilated, and contented" under Manchurian rule on the one hand and the influence of Chinese "morals and manners" on the other. Seward reflected: "How little can human foresight ever penetrate the remote future! . . . Is it not well that human power cannot bind or control for an indefinite future the destinies of any nation?"[139] A former statesman and politician who had lived through the Civil War, nearly been killed by a Confederate assassin, and witnessed emancipation and the triumph of the Union, Seward was perhaps thinking of sectional reconciliation between the conquering Union and the purportedly genteel planters of the southern states. The two sides, he was suggesting, like the Manchurians and Chinese, would become one people. As such, his comments may have reflected an underlying preoccupation with the fate of white America and therefore an at best secondary concern for freedpeople and racial minorities more generally. But it is equally striking that Seward did not bother to qualify or limit the scope of his comments, which stressed that the prejudices of the present would not dictate the future course of human history. Doctrinaire postbellum white supremacists would have blanched at the very idea.

4

"Our Papers"

If one imagined a book perfectly designed for Reconstruction's partisan world, it would look like Benjamin Anderson's *Narrative of a Journey to Musardu* (1870). This well-crafted account of exploring Liberia's interior by an African American émigré was rich with detail and had a distinctive backstory. Anderson's expedition was the Liberian state's second attempt in a decade to reach the city state of Musardu, located in modern-day southeastern Guinea.[1] We know little about nineteenth-century Musardu, but Liberia's leaders had multiple reasons to want to visit. Liberia's borders were then more extensive and ill-defined, so the expedition served to explore and assert control of Liberia's interior. The city was also known to belong to the Western Mandingoes, a reportedly educated and civilized people who might become allies. Finally, contact could open up direct trade with the interior, including its gold fields.[2]

The expedition would not have been successful without Anderson, an ambitious, free-born African American who left Baltimore, Maryland, for Liberia in late 1851 at the age of sixteen to escape racial prejudice. In Liberia, Anderson quickly rose to prominence, first working as a clerk for a local business and serving in militia campaigns. He continued his education, standing out for his skills with mathematics and surveying. Anderson soon entered politics, briefly holding the post of secretary of the treasury in 1863, before the age of thirty. He would hold the post again in the 1870s and serve as secretary of the interior in the 1880s, with his political alliances transcending Liberia's acrimonious Republican-True Whig divide.[3] In need of more funds than the cash-strapped Liberian state could spare, Anderson returned to the United States shortly after the Civil War.[4] There, he secured $200 from Henry Schieffelin of New York, who was an active benefactor of Liberia and Liberia's chargé d'affaires to the United States.[5] Schieffelin's donation, along with $100 from another benefactor, allowed Anderson to return to Liberia and depart for Musardu by early 1868.[6]

Anderson's resulting narrative was rich in detail, much of which pointed to a vibrant commercial civilization in Liberia's interior. He described a country featuring productive farms, iron-working, markets, well-defended towns and cities, and wicker suspension bridges.[7] Musardu itself lacked its former grandeur, but was still the capital of the Western Mandingoes and "an exceedingly healthy place" with over seven thousand inhabitants.[8] Anderson encountered native Africans who he deemed sagacious, solemn, learned, pious, polite, handsome, generous, and intelligent.[9] He understood the seemingly "tyrannical and bloodthirsty" nature of local rulers to be a performance necessitated by political circumstances and saw through some of the most horrifying stories that one local leader, eager to control trade, invented to intimidate Anderson's porters from moving inland.[10] Yet Anderson's narrative was not uniformly positive. He regularly described his porters and native groups as uncivilized.[11] Likewise, his volume was full of descriptions of native Africans as greedy, dithering, violent, duplicitous, drunk, and superstitious, especially when local leaders and traders attempted to slow his progress.[12] Finally, Anderson chronicled the local practice of slavery, including the sadistic repression of a slave revolt.[13]

It is easy to imagine how Reconstruction's partisans might have incorporated Anderson and his narrative into their running arguments. Proponents of racial equality could see in Anderson's expedition proof of the blessings of interracial cooperation and of African Americans' dynamic role in bringing progress to Africa. White supremacists might have mocked Liberia for depending on white philanthropy and have claimed that Anderson demonstrated that "Negroes," if free, were best off in Africa, away from white competition. Anderson wrote his narrative with a careful eye to the day's scientific standards, earning it a place on Roderick Murchison's bookshelf, so its quality alone might have challenged white supremacists.[14] But the details of Anderson's narrative had ambiguous polemical value, and proponents of racial equality and white supremacy might have both drawn selectively on them to bolster their claims about race, freedom, and progress. Some white supremacists, familiar with minstrelsy stereotypes, would have laughed when Anderson noted that he performed the song "Dixie" to West Africans.[15]

But Anderson's narrative garnered only brief mention in a handful of publications, largely because of how it was published.[16] Schieffelin secured support for the volume through the Smithsonian Institution, as well as later incorporating portions of it into his collection, *The People of Africa* (1871), which aimed to promote the spread of civilization and Christianity in Africa.[17] Joseph Henry, the head of the Smithsonian Institution, supported the expedition but, in contrast to Schieffelin, because of his negative views of "the Negro." Believing that people of African descent could not compete against Anglo-Saxons in the world's temperate zones, he had long seen little hope for their survival in most of the United States. Having once commented that his only hope for the "black man" to become civilized rested on a process of selection that would take eons, he saw Liberia as offering the opportunity for a grand "experiment" featuring the mass migration of former slaves.[18] Henry must have seen little reason to promote the volume in the United States, and Schieffelin, seeing Anderson's volume as useful to Liberia, sent most copies of it there.[19]

A distinctive figure on the postbellum polemical landscape, Anderson nonetheless encountered challenges familiar to African American readers, authors, and editors. He was able to publish a substantive work that served his desired ends, yet only under conditions controlled by people with their own racial agendas. In that sense, his work was both emblematic of how Reconstruction's federal political culture embraced wide-ranging global imaginings and indicative of how it offered at best deeply unequal access to the means to circulate claims about civilization, republicanism, and the world's peoples. Postbellum African Americans confronted a society that expected citizens to be informed and concerned about the global course of freedom and progress, but that offered few means for them to engage with these topics on their own terms. These issues came into sharpest relief with the near-creation of a nationwide African American publishing network built around newspapers and, for four key years, centered on the editorial persona of Frederick Douglass. This network faced immense logistical and political challenges as well as existential and strategic questions about whether and when to identify using racial terms like "black" and "colored." Given the long, often difficult history of interracial collaboration in the abolitionist movement in the North, the postbellum currents that were tenuously buoying racial egalitarianism, and the perilous nature of African American political mobilization, this network-in-the-making faced intense pressures from within and without.[20]

The New National Era *and Postbellum African American Publishing*

Nobody in the postbellum United States was better acquainted with these challenges than Frederick Douglass. Douglass had been a leading figure in the making of an independent African American press before the war. Building on an earlier tradition of abolitionist publishing pioneered by figures like Samuel Cornish, Douglass believed that African Americans had to secure an unmediated presence in the open, combative realm of print even as they continued to collaborate with white abolitionists.[21] After the war, he and two of his sons, Lewis and Frederick Jr., renewed this struggle through the *New National Era* of Washington, D.C. (originally entitled the *New Era* and later briefly renamed the *New National Era and Citizen*).[22] Founded by a local group of leading African Americans and initially edited by abolitionist and Douglass ally J. Sella Martin, the *New National Era* quickly entered a budgetary crisis. Douglass, his finances strengthened by the lecture circuit, bought out the proprietors and took control of the paper. He proceeded to run it with Lewis and Frederick Jr., who both had experience in the printing trade, managing much of the day-to-day operations.[23] The opportunity was especially poignant for Lewis, who had recently lost a fight to join, and thereby integrate, the Washington branch of the typographer's union.[24]

Frederick Douglass assumed control of the paper begrudgingly. He had turned down an invitation to edit it upon its launch because he thought circumstances called for a better-funded journal that could rival the country's leading metropolitan dailies.[25] Moreover, this was an exceptionally busy and in ways frustrating time in Douglass's life. Over the life of the paper he would continue to lecture, be appointed by President Ulysses Grant as a low-ranking member on a fact-finding commission to the Dominican Republic, serve on Washington, D.C.'s Legislative Council, learn that his house in Rochester burned to the ground, become president of the insolvent Freedmen's Savings and Trust Company, and manage a large and sometimes struggling family. Throughout this period, he witnessed white supremacists conduct brutal campaigns to curtail African American civil rights while northern support for and federal guarantees of the same weakened.[26] For all these demands on his time and energy, Douglass and his sons built on Martin's work to develop the *New National Era* into an ambitious enterprise. The paper would become a key venue for the Douglasses to elaborate notions of a racially inclusive version of American identity, condemn white supremacy, and urge African American progress, about which Douglass was often anxious.[27] Running under the family's control from late 1870 to 1874, the paper became, as one fellow African American editor in California put it, "the National organ for colored Americans."[28]

As that comment suggests, the full significance of the *New National Era* lies with its ambition to speak to and for a larger community of African Americans who were in turn a constituency in federal politics. Confederate defeat and abolition opened the possibility for the first time of a coordinated, nationwide movement against white supremacy. Even before the war ended, northern educational, denominational, and political organizations with varying racial politics began moving South. If often condescending toward the culture of the formerly enslaved, these organizations quickly became vehicles for political mobilization and alliance-making. Forms of public organizing well established in the North, including cultural and political associations, public rallies and parades, and political conventions, braided with patterns of clandestine resistance developed by enslaved communities in the South.[29] A nationwide network of African American readers, authors, and editors promised to consummate this process, ensuring the steady exchange of information across regions and providing a weekly or even daily presence in national debates about the South and the world of which it was a part. What made a publication "black" or "colored" and who got to say was itself an intrinsically difficult, political topic, but one that did not so much negate as complicate the value of a greater African American presence in the fractious realm of debate.

The *New National Era*, along with other postbellum African American newspapers, helped just such an extensive network to begin to cohere, bridging the violent, localized racial politics of the post-emancipation South and the world-wandering arguments commonplace in federal politics. Newspapers served as natural nodes in this emerging network. They required less capital to establish than a publishing house or a magazine and could grow or shrink in terms of print runs, page length, and frequency of publication to match demand. Printers could use their equipment for odd jobs to make extra money. In terms of labor, newspapers could function with a tiny staff or grow into substantial enterprises. Newspapers had multiple potential sources of revenue, including subscriptions, advertising, local sales, government printing contracts, community investment, and political boosters. Newspapers were also particularly well-suited to incorporate multiple perspectives and circulate them to multiple audiences. Even a small newspaper could feature guest editorials, correspondence from travelers, poems, and, although it was less common than today, letters from concerned readers. This combined with the readiness with which editors reprinted material from other papers, magazines, books, and other sources. Indeed, such borrowing could help keep costs down. At one point, one leading African American paper derived two-thirds of its content from other publications.[30] African American editors, like others, swapped newspapers with each other through voluntary exchanges, forging connections across space and providing a circuit for intellectual exchange.[31] In the 1860s and 1870s, if African Americans wanted to write for a magazine, go on a lecture tour, or publish a bound, book-length work, they, with very few exceptions, had to work with white Americans, a challenge that African American women had compounded by gender discrimination.[32] Such collaborations did not always mean strife, and publishing with African Americans did not guarantee accord. But the rise of a regionally integrated African American press nonetheless promised to create greater intellectual autonomy, shape patterns of public debate, and undermine arguments that African Americans were incapable of progress.[33]

Even with the versatility and flexibility of the format, the hurdles facing African American newspapers were immense. In the South, the vast majority of African Americans lived in rural settings that stretched over an area larger than western Europe and were at constant risk of white supremacist violence.[34] Compounding this problem were the low literacy rates and lack of financial resources consequent of slavery. As is well known, freedpeople demonstrated an intense commitment to mastering literacy and could draw on longstanding clandestine and communal reading practices that allowed texts and information to circulate broadly. This no doubt magnified the influence of African American newspapers, but by itself did little to alleviate their immediate financial troubles.[35] Republican newspapers in general struggled to find subscribers and advertisers in the South, becoming largely dependent on government printing contracts for survival, which often went to rival factions. Republicans in Congress briefly attempted to bolster southern Republican newspapers by extending government printing contracts to two newspapers in each state, but they declined to sustain such efforts.[36] In the North and West, the problems were different but nearly as daunting. African Americans in the North had played a pioneering role in the abolitionist movement, and their experiences there had honed skills as speakers, authors, and editors.[37] But the North and the West had only a tiny African American population, much of it impoverished and geographically dispersed. Previous experiences under slavery and exclusion from public schools in the North meant that perhaps around half of northern African Americans were illiterate.[38] As a result, African American newspapers in the North and West struggled with finances nearly as much as their southern peers.

Counterbalancing these factors was a clear sense of urgency to establish newspapers that could interject an autonomous perspective on racial issues, organize political efforts, and advocate for civil rights in the fractious realm of public debate. This impulse led to the rapid establishment of African American newspapers across the country, although also the equally rapid folding of many of them.[39] In the North and West, there were a handful of vibrant weekly newspapers that were immersed in economically struggling communities. Such was true, for example, of the *Weekly Anglo-African* of New York City, founded by the brothers Thomas and Robert Hamilton in 1859 alongside their short-lived *Anglo-African Magazine*. Despite some support from the American Methodist Episcopal Zion (AMEZ) Church, the paper closed shop near the end of the Civil War.[40] In Cincinnati, local African American leaders worked together to found the *Colored Citizen* in 1863, with ministers and activists contributing to the paper. When it closed remains uncertain, but it lasted at least into the late 1860s, printing local notices, supporting African American contributions to the Union war effort, condemning local discrimination, and debating white supremacists.[41] Less typical was the *Elevator* in San Francisco, which ran from 1865 into the 1880s thanks to the commitment of its editor, Philip A. Bell, and support from the region's small but well-organized African American community.[42]

Most northern and western African American newspapers foregrounded an explicit racial consciousness. The *Colored Citizen* of Cincinnati, for example, described itself as "conducted by colored men for the special benefit of colored men."[43] Such racial consciousness often found expression in a dual commitment to fighting white supremacy and advocating racial uplift, as was the case, for example, with Bell's *Elevator.*[44] Most northern African American newspapers were also avowedly political, orienting significant portions of their news and editorials toward engagement in the day's expansive and acrimonious discussions of freedom, progress, and the world's peoples. An important exception to this trend was the *Christian Recorder* of Philadelphia. A publication of the African Methodist Episcopal (AME) Church, the *Christian Recorder* had an enviable financial stability and an impressive number of subscribers for an African American newspaper of its day. But its editor during most of Reconstruction, Benjamin T. Tanner (1868–1884), focused on spiritual and denominational matters, offering only intermittent discussion of politics. In the 1860s the paper was a dynamic force in African American culture, publishing, for example, Julia C. Collins's *The Curse of Caste; or The Slave Bride* (1865), likely the earliest novel by an African American woman. But its most consistent and ambitious periods of political engagement came before and after the pivotal years of Reconstruction policy-making.[45]

In the South, African American newspapers often focused on community issues, with many, such as the *Colored Tennessean* and the *Southwestern Christian Advocate,* providing a crucial service by running advertisements for African Americans looking for lost family members.[46] The most financially stable southern African American papers, and the most expansive in their coverage, were located near coastal cities that had large rural African American populations nearby and local free populations of mixed descent that benefited from greater prewar access to education and property. The *Louisianian* of New Orleans, for example, ran under the guidance of its founder, southern-born and northern-raised P.B.S. Pinchback, from 1870 until he sold the journal in 1874.[47] Financially, it sustained itself through local sales, advertising revenue, state printing contracts, and its political backers.[48] The *South Carolina Leader* (initially the *Missionary Record*), founded by Richard Harvey Cain, a northern AME missionary and future South Carolina politician, similarly benefited from its proximity to Charleston and the predominantly African American lowcountry.[49] Many African American political leaders, including Cain and Pinchback as well as Bruce K. Blanche, Robert Brown Elliott, Alonzo J. Ransier, James T. Rapier, and Hiram Revels, ran newspapers to support their careers.[50] Some newspapers were deliberately short-lived, such as those run by northeasterner George T. Ruby in Texas and Louisiana during elections and legislative sessions.[51]

The racial politics of the postbellum South, marked by both alliance-making across the color line and rampant white supremacist violence, made for a complex series of negotiations. African American editors in the South sometimes disavowed the idea that their enterprises were "black" or "colored" in nature. Ruby, for example, did so and even alienated some African Americans by favoring white leadership of the local Republican Party.[52] Pinchback's *Louisianian* likewise initially denounced claims that it was a racially delimited paper, positioning itself as an interracial Republican organ, although months later it changed course and played up its African American ownership and editorial staff.[53] Such disavowals reflected both desires to create a color-blind society and the factionalism in the southern branches of the Republican Party, which often required such rhetorical maneuvering.[54] Whatever stance these editors took, they no doubt understood themselves to be fighting for racial equality with firsthand experience of discrimination. Indeed, at points the southern African American press gestured toward the possibility of an Afro-diasporic publishing community that reached beyond the nation. William G. Brown, one of Pinchback's editors, had spent much of his early life and received his education in Jamaica.[55] Robert B. Elliott, the influential South Carolina politician who ran Cain's *South Carolina Leader* as a political paper for two years, was likely born and educated in Liverpool, England.[56] Both papers took interest in developments abroad, with the *Louisianian* addressing labor in the Caribbean and the *Leader* editorializing about the Morant Bay Rebellion in Jamaica.[57]

In other cases, editors presented newspapers as having a unitary racial identity when they were in fact fraught interracial and cross-class collaborations. The *New Orleans Tribune,* for example, at points proclaimed its independence from white influence, but such declarations were neither accurate nor served to make public the paper's complex alliances. The paper's founder and associate editor, Dr. Louis Charles Roudanez and Paul Trévigne, were highly educated members of New

Orleans's free colored population and active members in an interracial, pro–civil rights faction of the state's Republican Party. Its lead editor, Jean-Charles Houzeau, had a slightly dark complexion and allowed people to believe he was also of mixed descent, admitting later that he never denied the rumor and once testifying as colored under a false name. But he was born in what would soon be Belgium to an aristocratic family. In Belgium and then Paris, he imbibed and advocated socialism and universalism, ideas that would deeply shape the *Tribune*'s arguments.[58] A series of interracial and cross-class alliances among backers, editors, contributors, and readers—the last of which likely included at least some of the city's numerous European immigrants—were integral to the paper's operation. Indeed, those alliances soon frayed due to tactical disagreements between Houzeau and Roudanez concerning the 1868 election, with Roudanez, in contrast to most freedpeople, allying with Democrats against the Republican ticket, ultimately costing the paper its two government printing contracts.[59] The *Mobile Nationalist* in Alabama had an outright acrimonious history due to antagonisms across and within racial and class lines.[60]

The *New National Era*, before and after Douglass took it over, reflected and shared the ambitions and challenges facing other African American newspapers. Like its peers, the *New National Era* was of necessity small, offering only a four-page weekly edition on Thursdays. It had a steady if modest flow of advertising customers, including patent medicine companies and local businesses, such as boarding houses and dry goods stores.[61] Annual subscriptions cost $2.50, and the paper had twenty-eight subscription agents in 1871 and forty-two in 1874, with several in the former Confederacy.[62] It is unclear what the geographic distribution of subscribers was, but if the paper was typical for its day, most would have been local. The paper also benefited from a city printing contract.[63] Ideologically, the paper was explicit in its commitment to offering an African American political perspective. Douglass tended to see other African American newspapers as local in nature, which contained an element of truth in some cases but also understated the scope of some editors' interests and ambitions.[64] It was therefore with a touch of proprietary aggrandizing that Douglass explained that the *New National Era* would allow 5 million African Americans to speak for themselves—as though they could not otherwise do this.[65] Later, the paper justified its role more pointedly, claiming that the interests of

African Americans "cannot be safely intrusted [*sic*] to any journal which holds divided allegiances."[66]

This emphasis, however, hardly meant abandoning alliances with white racial egalitarians. Indeed, the paper was a consistent Republican Party organ that stood by Ulysses S. Grant throughout his corruption-wracked administrations.[67] Before and after Douglass assumed formal control, the *New National Era* promised its readers a distinctive antislavery, pro-equality perspective that foregrounded the concerns of African Americans but also promised to remain of interest to all who loved justice, to address the nation at large, and to defend the cause of universal humanity.[68] Nor did it mean refraining from disagreement with other African American and pro–civil rights publications. The paper, for example, had a brief debate with two other African American newspapers, Bell's *Elevator* and the *Progressive American* in New York, over the Republican Party's initial failure to secure passage of Charles Sumner's Civil Rights Act in 1874.[69] It also had a far more contentious series of exchanges with the AME Church's *Christian Recorder* concerning Douglass's views on race and religion.[70]

The paper grounded its arguments in the day's ideas, and as a result had a clear global consciousness. Particularly salient here were its arguments stressing the inclusiveness of American nationality, the barbaric and despotic inclinations of southern white supremacists, and the capacity of African Americans for progress.[71] As elsewhere, these themes bridged easily into discussions of developments in the West and abroad. Haiti, which the United States had only recently granted diplomatic recognition and where it sent its first African American diplomatic official, Ebenezer Bassett, garnered frequent comment.[72] No country earned more attention than "Santo Domingo," or the Dominican Republic, which Ulysses S. Grant proposed to annex.[73] Douglass served as the assistant secretary to the president's fact-finding mission to the country, where Samuel Gridley Howe again made an appearance. Douglass, as several historians have noted, was an enthusiastic supporter of the annexation scheme, in part as a means to push forward the cause of racial equality and inclusion.[74] The *New National Era* addressed annexation or reprinted related content at least thirty-two times in its thirty-five issues from December 1870 through July 1871.[75] But the paper's coverage also ranged far beyond the Dominican Republic. European wars, political struggles, and diplomacy garnered such frequent attention as to defy easy summation.[76] The paper also evinced a conventional interest in foreign curiosities, such as when it reported a story about Chinese tea makers cutting their product with doctored willow leaves.[77]

The *New National Era* exemplified the power of newspapers to incorporate multiple sources and voices and connect readers, authors, and editors across space. Even before Douglass took over, the paper was emerging as a dynamic forum for African American authors, and here too its global consciousness was apparent. Within its first few months alone it included several contributions with an international focus. Frank J. Webb called for an international industrial exhibition in the United States in which "colored men" could demonstrate that they "have not been left in the rear in the march of progress."[78] Martin Delany editorialized on the evolution of civil rights in France, England, and the United States.[79] George B. Vashon offered a lengthy historical reflection on the Nile from its first empires to the recent discovery of its headwaters.[80] Such contributors underscore the predominance of men in the world of newspapers. Douglass was, however, a long-standing proponent of women's rights, and turned to Ottilie Assing—with whom he had a long and complex relationship—for regular contributions to the paper's columns and worked at least occasionally with Mary Ann Shadd Cary.[81]

Contributions also included letters from African American and white racial egalitarians as they traveled. One anonymous traveler provided a description of the hurricane-wracked island of St. Thomas.[82] David T. S. Fuller wrote a series of letters from Paris, including one on the charming gatherings held at the house of Sainte Suzanne Melvil-Bloncourt, an Afro-Gaudelupean deputy to France's National Assembly familiar to Douglass, and another on the city's Haitian quarter.[83] One of the Fisk Jubilee Singers wrote from England about their series of performances, including at the Annual Fete for the National Temperance League and a smaller one at a royal lunch.[84] Like others, the paper reprinted diverse content, including news items from the similarly titled *New Era* of Monrovia, Liberia, an article from London's *Cornhill Magazine* on the cultural and physiological diversity of Africans, and a St. Louis paper's analysis of Russian attempts to conquer the central Asian city of Khiva.[85] The *New National Era,* perhaps more so than any African American newspaper of its day, exemplified the ability of newspapers to address diverse subjects, showcase multiple contributors, and engage with other publications.

The *New National Era*, along with other postbellum African American newspapers, helped a nationwide network of African American readers, authors, and editors begin to cohere, thereby bridging the violent struggles for civil rights in the South with the globe-straddling arguments of federal politics. In doing so, the *New National Era* was both emblematic of its times and yet occupied a distinct position in the postbellum polemical landscape. The paper was a conventional partisan organ staking claims about freedom, progress, and the world's peoples, but it also played a leading role in carving out a public venue for African Americans to address these topics before a national audience. Closely aligned with the Republican Party, the organ expressed a shared faith in the onward march of civilization and republicanism, yet also proved itself to be more concerned than many of its intra-party peers where slavery and racism were involved. Two topics prominent in the paper capture well this interplay of partisan affiliation and minority perspective. Sharing the anti-Catholic sentiment spreading across the North in the late 1860s and 1870s, the *New National Era* took a typical Republican approach to condemning the Church and its followers. Yet the paper also aspired to help pioneer an openly African American movement in support of Cuban abolition during the Ten Years' War on the island.

Infallible Progress

The *New National Era* ran a sustained editorial campaign against the Catholic Church.[86] In part, the *New National Era*'s animus reflected the racism and Democratic allegiance of many Catholics in the United States, especially immigrants from Ireland.[87] In this, the *New National Era*'s comments on the Catholic Church reflect the paper's close ties with the Republican Party, which increasingly sought to shore up its base by drumming up fears about Catholic immigrants and their Democratic Party allegiances. At the center of northern Republican anxiety were Catholic campaigns at the local and state level to secure greater voice in the religious, presumptively Protestant, practices common in schools and other public institutions. But this issue was never purely domestic. Ward M. McAfee has argued that these issues prompted interest in educational reforms by Otto von Bismarck, and Timothy Verhoeven has recently stressed that anti-Catholicism within the United States drew on deep, transatlantic currents of thought as well as the mid-century Vatican's opposition to liberal ideas about freedom and progress. Far from focusing on only developments and conflicts in the United States, northern Republicans consistently stressed Catholicism's reach and watched developments in Europe, the Caribbean, and Latin America.[88] For many, including the *New National Era,* the Church was, paradoxically, both a threat at home and, globally, a backward institution bound to retreat before the spirit of the age.

The *New National Era*'s campaign began with an editorial in its first issue by Reverend J. E. Rankin that defined the Church as a threat to America's "Bible Civilization." Rankin argued that ongoing struggles on the part of American Catholics to create a separate system of schools put the foundation of America's free and progressive civilization at risk. This foundation lay in the existing system of common schools, which, Rankin continued, raised American children to have ethics that derived from a proper understanding of the Bible. Such ethics were in harmony with and essential to the existence of "American institutions" that were different from those of the "civilization of Catholic Europe," which tended to sink "the individual man, the free man," under the distinctions of "class, grade, and caste," and leave him "overridden by king, noble, priest." "This is no question of *religions,*" Rankin stated, but instead one "of *civilizations.*" Tying his arguments more directly to Reconstruction, Rankin claimed that "European civilization, whether represented by the nobility of England, the Empire of France, or the Pope in Rome," had welcomed the prospect of Confederate independence. "Bible civilization," in contrast, "is progressive," had been on the side of the slaves and had seen the Union to victory, and looked forward to a coming millennium "when man, individual man, shall have all his rights accorded him."[89] In a subsequent editorial in response to an article in the *Catholic World* that accused early Protestants of being heretics, the Douglasses hit on a similar civilizational analysis. They argued that Protestantism, in retranslating the Bible from original sources, had the more authentic faith, and hence brought "progress, morality, intelligence, liberty, and general prosperity" as it spread.[90]

Without taking its eye off of Europe, the *New National Era* paid close attention when Catholics in the United States criticized African Americans. In one instance, a priest in St. Louis piqued the *New National Era*'s ire by alleging that "Only the Catholic Church," and specifically not the Baptist or the Methodist Churches, "can control the fiery passions of the negro." The *New National Era* countered that Catholics were hardly suited to serve as moral guides. Describing Catholics as "bigots" with a long history of slaughtering Protestants, the paper suggested that it would behoove them to remember that "there is quite as much morality, religion, civilization, and prosperity in the United States, England, and *Prussia,*" which had recently defeated the forces of Napoleon III, "as in Mexico, Spain, and *France,* to say nothing of Italy and Austria." Statistics from New York City, the paper added, demonstrated that "very much the largest portion" of crime there was "committed by Roman Catholics."[91] Likewise, the paper later analogized between foreign and domestic foes. As the editors explained it: "The difference between the Republican party and the Democratic party very considerably resembles the difference between the Catholic Church and the Protestant denominations—one has the best ideas, and the other the best organization." While this might seem to pass as a half-hearted compliment, the editors added that the Democratic Party, and by implication the Catholic Church, "would be nothing without its rigid discipline and party domination over the individuals composing it."[92]

The *New National Era* was ever eager to document the retrogressive nature of Catholicism in Europe, taking particular interest in the First Vatican Council, called by Pope Pius IX, and its decision to define and declare papal infallibility Church doctrine. The idea that the Catholic Church was considering such a decree was enough to irk the editors, as it did other northern Republican and independent newspapers. When reports arrived suggesting that the advocates of the decree within the council were preventing their opponents from voicing criticisms, it only added icing to the anti-papal cake.[93] The paper followed and editorialized about dissenters within the council and their alleged marginalization.[94] When the council finally declared the Pope infallible, the paper reprinted the council's statement, noting, "We are left to the alternative of swallowing its enormities with unquestioning credence, or being cursed after the usual popish fashion."[95] Over a year later, when a press in Wurzburg, Germany, published a collection of passages by Frederick the Great on the topic of infallibility, the *New National Era* demonstrated its continuing interest through some short excerpts.[96] Within three days the paper again condemned the Church for excommunicating Dr. Ignaz Döllinger of the University of Munich, whose book criticizing the council's decision, *The Pope and the Council,* became popular in England and the United States after its publication in English. Again the paper compared the Church with the Democratic Party, arguing that both were unable to come to terms with "the necessary results of the enlightenment and civilization of the nineteenth century" and move beyond their delusions concerning papal authority on the one hand and slavery and white supremacy on the other.[97]

The Vatican's inability to fend off Italians troops from Rome made a mockery of papal authority. In August of 1870 the paper was happy to report rumors that the Pope was anxious over the possible departure of the French forces that had been defending the city.[98] When Rome fell less than two months later, completing the unification of Italy under King Victor Emmanuel II, the paper hailed it as a triumph, provided a description of the papal territories, and offered a lengthy editorial.[99] Most striking to the paper was not the final collapse of the Pope's last bastion of temporal power or the geopolitical significance of the conquest, but the failure of Europe's Catholic powers to come to the Pope's aid. The paper took their inactivity to be a "cheering symptom of the times" and argued that it demonstrated that the Church, as "the hereditary and ancient enemy of liberty, enlightenment, and science," was doomed, with Pius IX having hastened the downfall. All of this, it added, paralleled the foolish attempts of America's retrograde slave owners to make slavery "the absolute power" in the United States before the Civil War. While progress might be slow, it would nonetheless be steady, and the editorial concluded that "in the natural and inevitable course of events, in some centuries, sooner or later, the Vicar of Christ will be a tradition of by gone days."[100]

The paper saw events in the United States as similarly demonstrating the Church's retrograde nature, but often with a greater sense of menace. When a riot against Irish Protestants took place in "that extremely Catholic and Democratic city" of New York in 1871, the second in two years, the *New National Era* suggested that, while the local clergy had condemned the violence, they did so only to advance their own power. Instead of "denouncing the foul spirit of intolerance" that had led to the riots, the paper argued, the local clergy had "turned the occasion to the service of their ghostly superstitions" by warning their parishioners against following false teachers, in essence discouraging them from following the commands of civil officials. In doing so, the paper averred, the local clergy were "forcing their divinity and infallibility into things political as well as spiritual." Ultimately, the paper concluded, the "Celtic

Catholics" of New York were merely following the principles of their religion by enacting the retrograded philosophy of religious bigotry "in accordance with ancient divine example."[101] When, several months later, the *Irish People* of New York City encouraged Catholics to consider using violence against Irish Protestants if they ever dared to parade through the city, the editors of the *New National Era* were again happy to underscore the prejudiced extremism of Irish Catholics.[102]

The *New National Era* also cheered Otto von Bismarck, normally associated with European conservatism, when he pressed the Prussian Chambers to end the Catholic clergy's control over education in parts of the newly unified Germany. The paper accepted Bismarck's assertion that the Catholic clergy and their allies had begun a conspiracy to destroy Germany, which the paper judged "the greatest Protestant power in the world." Yet, energetic though these Catholic conspirators might be in their attempts "to arrest the march of progress and enlightenment," they had little hope in the nineteenth century, which was defined by advancing civilization. As the editorial claimed in conclusion, "If this priestcraft, superstition, fanaticism, and reactionism should come in conflict with the enlightenment, the knowledge and the progressive tendencies of the century, the triumph of the latter is certain," especially when backed by an ascendant Germany.[103] In a subsequent editorial, the paper argued that the Church had succeeded in manipulating France and Austria into an anti-German alliance, while ensuring the neutrality of Russia, a country that, as a representative of "political and religious absolutism," was a natural ally with the Pope. Ultimately, however, the paper found such maneuvering pointless. Even if without a talented leader like Bismarck, who was acutely aware of the conspiracy against his country, "the progress," and "the growing enlightenment of the nations of Europe," made a restoration of Catholic supremacy impossible. The only question for the paper was why Bismarck and the German people could not see the necessity of going beyond the mere expulsion of the Jesuits to declare a formal separation of church and state. Believing that "the beneficent working of our system, which has stood the trial of nearly a century, must have become manifest to the whole world," the paper could only express amazement that the Germans, "as progressive a people as any other," rejected by large majorities proposals for separation.[104]

It is tempting to see such consistent and unapologetic anti-

Catholicism as out of step with the paper's pro–civil rights politics. Far from it, the *New National Era* linked its condemnation of the Church to its abhorrence of slavery and white supremacy, and did so with the kind of historical logic conventional for the time. If the Church opposed freedom and progress as slaveholders and white supremacists did, the two groups must have the same underlying character. It mattered not that the two manifested their barbaric and despotic spirits through different practices and institutions. To modern historians looking for precise points of comparison, such reasoning can seem odd. But in a world defined by overarching struggles for civilization and republicanism, it was perfectly natural to see Frederick Douglass and Otto Von Bismarck as fighting the same battles.

Cuban Freedoms

Nowhere were the inequalities at the heart of Reconstruction's polemical landscape more apparent than in the paucity of African American newspaper coverage of bound labor abroad. The 1860s and 1870s witnessed several abolition measures, including in Russia, the Dutch Caribbean, Brazil, and Puerto Rico. The same period saw as well a massacre of freedpeople in post-emancipation Jamaica and overlapping revolutions in Spain and its slave colony of Cuba.[105] Given these and other developments, African American newspapers addressed race, servitude, and emancipation abroad when they could. The San Francisco *Elevator*, for example, argued with the moderate Republican *Philadelphia Press* over the meaning of the abolition of serfdom in Russia and of slavery in the United States.[106] In 1865, a reader of the *Black Republican* of Louisiana was predicting that African Americans, natural civilizers abroad, would soon be fighting for freedom in Cuba, Haiti, Liberia, and the rest of Africa.[107] When a traveling Englishman lauded the abilities of Haitians to a London paper, the *Colored Citizen* of Cincinnati took the praise as condescending and expanded on the accomplishments of African Americans.[108] But African American newspapers also struggled to muster the resources to offer more regular, detailed engagement with these and similar events. The *New National Era*'s coverage of the Ten Years' War in Cuba (1868–1878) exemplified both the difficulties facing African American newspapers and their drive to establish their own presence in debates on these issues.

A complex conflict, the Ten Years' War involved a rebellion against Spanish authority led by some of the island's slaveholders but opposed by others, a conflicted rebel program of recruiting slaves that at moments embraced abolition, and a mixture of force and conciliation from the Spanish government that ultimately suppressed the rebellion.[109] Attitudes toward the conflict within the United States were similarly complex. Cuba, desired by proslavery expansionists before the Civil War and a refuge for former Confederates after it, had long been wrapped up with political controversy.[110] African Americans and abolitionists more generally had long been concerned for the island's enslaved population, and many hoped that the post-emancipation United States would pursue an antislavery foreign policy. Other northerners suggested purchasing the island or otherwise annexing it. But under the guidance of its cautious secretary of state, Hamilton Fish, the Grant administration dismissed such schemes, avoiding intervention even when Spanish forces executed U.S. citizens aboard the *Virginius* in 1873.[111] The *New National Era* took a clear interest in the conflict and began to emerge as a forum for African Americans and some white racial egalitarians to discuss it.

The paper began its coverage under Martin's editorship, including arguments from contributors, accounts of Cuba and the progression of the conflict, and its own opinions. In March of 1870, its third month of operation, it ran a pro-independence letter from New York explaining that Spaniards "act in the name of despotism and barbarity" and that their rule had hindered the advance of the colony "in civilization and progress."[112] In April the paper ran two letters from an American traveling in Cuba that mixed descriptions of the island's culture and economy with a closing wish for Cuban independence.[113] In June, the paper published two pieces, one noting the failure of an anti-Spanish expedition that departed from New York and the other supporting President Ulysses S. Grant's decision not to recognize Cuban belligerency.[114] The Spanish government's promise to implement a gradual, post-natal emancipation measure piqued the paper's interest. In October of 1870, the paper ran a short article that described the emancipation law going into effect in Cuba and Puerto Rico, but did not reflect on it.[115] Two years later, the paper would return to the topic, criticizing the Spanish government for failing to faithfully implement the measure in Cuba.[116]

The paper continued its mixture of updates, accounts, and editorials under Douglass's leadership. Often the paper reprinted content from other sources without appending its own opinions, suggesting that its small editorial staff was stretched thin. In early 1871 it provided a short editorial on the prospect of the United States buying the island from Spain, advising against entertaining the idea with any urgency.[117] In May the paper printed without comment an exchange of letters between Carlos Vie, the Spanish consul in New Orleans, and Harrison Reed, the northern-born Republican governor of Florida, discussing the benefits of emancipation.[118] In the summer and fall the paper reprinted articles from an English periodical, *Harper's Monthly,* and the *Baltimore American,* but without adding its own opinion.[119] In February of 1872 the paper again ran original content, publishing a poem by Ulysses B. Vidal, an African American supporter of Cuban independence in Philadelphia, that addressed the Cuban quest for freedom from Spanish political despotism.[120] In October of the same year the paper lent its support to the Spanish Abolition Society when it condemned the Spanish government for its failure to abolish slavery. The Spanish, the paper believed, seemed to have a "domineering and tyrannical spirit" built into their national character, and hence stood opposed to the facts that "Cuba must someday belong to the Cubans" and "slavery is doomed everywhere."[121]

The *New National Era*'s coverage expanded in 1873 due to its continued role as a forum for discussing the rebellion. In January, the paper began running a series of unsolicited letters by white northern Republican and former Union soldier William A. C. Ryan, who had been fighting for the rebels and who the Spanish would execute as part of the *Virginius* expedition by year's end.[122] Calling attention to the rebellion as an antislavery struggle, his letters urged African Americans to hold a national convention to rally aid for Afro-Cuban rebels, described the horrors of Spanish rule, and demanded that the federal government recognize the rebels as belligerents.[123] Along with the first letter, the paper ran two other pieces. The first was a short editorial that equated the revolution with a struggle for abolition by arguing that "the independence of Cuba is the independence and freedom of the black men of that isle." The second was a reprinted piece from the *New York Times* expressing frustration with the Spanish government.[124] This prompted a letter by D. A. Straker, an Afro-Caribbean lawyer originally from Barbados, arguing that international law stood against U.S. involvement in the conflict, which Straker then followed up with a second letter clarifying that his argument was not pro-slavery but pro-peace.[125]

The *New National Era*'s coverage crested as it offered an editorial of its own that struck a moderate tone while echoing Ryan's call for African American action on the behalf of the rebels. The paper laid out an ambitious agenda. First, African Americans, who understood the plight of enslaved Cubans from their own experiences, "should meet throughout the nation and arouse public sentiment" so that "the Cuban negroes may take heart, the insurgents gain new courage, and the American politicians secure sanction therefrom." "A National Convention of colored men" in Washington, D.C., the paper added, would be beneficial. To shore up support for the Cuban rebels in the southern states, the paper suggested that every Republican newspaper in the South reprint the Cuban constitution, which abolished slavery. "If there be apathy among our people," the paper commented, "it is simply because of a lack of information." This step could support the growth of "Cuban Associations" among African Americans, which could generate "thousands of dollars" and hundreds of African Americans who "might voluntarily surrender the great boon of American citizenship to join their fortunes with those of their suffering brethren."[126] Not unlike the 1865 contributor to the *Black Republican,* the *New National Era* envisioned African American men, many of them former Union soldiers, carrying forward struggles for freedom and progress abroad.

This agenda points to both the potential to engage southern freedpeople with the wide-ranging causes swirling together in Reconstruction's cultural politics and also the forces working against the fulfilment of that potential. An extensive and interconnected community mobilized around sympathy for people abroad would hardly have been out of place at the time. But in 1873 southern freedpeople were already locked in a desperate struggle of their own against white supremacy. Northern African Americans had neither the political clout nor the resources to induce southern Republican papers, which were already scarce in 1873, to publish the Cuban Republic's constitution. A convention of African Americans concerned with Cuba did occur, although it was small, assembled on an impromptu basis, and quickly unraveled.[127] Similarly, a delegation of leading African Americans, including Frederick Douglass, had earlier met with President Grant to urge recognition of Cuban belligerency, but to little effect.[128] The mobilization across the South never took place, although there were proposals for a convention of African American men in New Orleans "to consider the best means for setting at liberty all persons of color now held in slavery upon the

American continent."[129] When a convention took place there in 1872, Cuba appears to have garnered only brief mention, with domestic politics taking primacy of place.[130] Broader grassroots African American mobilization took place in the North, including a public meeting at the Cooper Institute in New York, but these efforts never amounted to a sustained, regionally integrated campaign.[131] Indeed, editors of the *New National Era* were spread so thin that they struggled to follow up on their initial proposal for concerted action with additional editorials. Their subsequent coverage of the rebellion consisted of a noteworthy but diminishing volume of reprinted content as well as a few letters to the editor from African Americans sympathetic to the rebels.[132] The paper's readers and editors were concerned for the plight of Cuban slaves, but lacked the resources to cultivate that concern into a far-reaching African American movement.

In seeking to carve out an autonomous African American space on the postbellum publishing landscape and to help forge an interconnected African American press capable of coordinated political action, the paper was not rebuking the Republican Party, divided as it was over how to handle the Ten Years' War. Indeed, if anything, the Douglasses likely saw their views as in conformity with, if on the leading edge of, Republican opinion. The paper's racial egalitarianism was also, strange as it may seem to us, at peace with its anti-Catholicism, with slavery, the Church, and the Spanish Empire all standing in opposition to both freedom and progress. Such was clear as well in the paper's views of Dominican annexation, which it promised would both push the bounds of American citizenship and save the Dominicans from their own religion.[133]

Conclusion

As the *New National Era* explained in one 1871 column, of the many African American newspapers to fail in the last thirty years, almost all were crippled by a combination of limited resources and insufficient popular support.[134] In 1874, in the midst of a searing economic depression, its ally, Bell's *Elevator* in San Francisco, published an article entitled "Our Papers" that surveyed the state of African American periodicals. Prompting this effort was the *Elevator*'s inability to find any recent issues of the *New National Era*. "What," it asked, "has become of the *New*

National Era?" Looking across the nation, the *Elevator* found fourteen newspapers edited by African Americans and committed to presenting African American political viewpoints, with names ranging from the upbeat titles *Grand Era* (Baton Rouge, Louisiana) and *Our National Progress* (Harrisburg, Pennsylvania) to the more anxious *Freedmen's Monitor* (Athens, Tennessee) and *Watchman* (Mobile, Alabama). An undercurrent of anxiety marked the *Elevator*'s survey as the paper addressed advertising, subscribers, and suspensions. Such concerns were not misplaced. The *New National Era*, after four years of operation, had closed shop in October with mounting debts and declining subscriptions. In a society with thousands of newspapers, a rare African American organ fell silent.[135]

The nationwide network of African American readers, writers, and editors that began to emerge in the postbellum decades was in a state of perpetual flux, with a constant risk of failure on the part of any one organ existing alongside a shared dynamism. Indeed, the *New National Era*'s closure came right as this network seemed to be moving toward stabilizing and solidifying. In 1875, a first ever "Convention of Colored Newspaper Men" took place in Cincinnati with the backing of Frederick Douglass, P.B.S. Pinchback, and John Mercer Langston. The convention's first object, according to opening comments by Pinchback, was "to make colored people's newspapers self-sustaining." There were many familiar names among the seventeen men in attendance, including George T. Ruby, J. Sella Martin, now running the *True Republican* in northern Louisiana, Lewis Douglass, now employed at the *Elevator*, and William G. Brown, Pinchback's former editor at the *Louisianian*.[136]

The convention had high ambitions. Its attendees laid out proposals to create a Colored Press Association, to endorse a newspaper as "the organ of colored people," and to organize a collective for purchasing newspaper machinery. The attendees also aimed to produce greater political coordination among African Americans across the nation by calling for an 1876 convention with over 330 representatives in Nashville, Tennessee.[137] Finally, they set their eyes on the 1876 Centennial Exhibition in Philadelphia, sketching plans for an eighteen-volume history of the race, a campaign to persuade the organizers to include the work of African Americans, and a statue "in the name of the colored women of America" from Edmonia Lewis, an African American sculptor living in Rome.[138] Amid all this other work, the convention took time to unanimously endorse a statement honoring the birth of the Irish nationalist and abolitionist Daniel O'Connell. One supporter of the measure stated his hope that it would "soften the prejudices and hostilities of the Irishmen to the negro race."[139] Yet these plans met with only mixed success over the coming year. The AME Church helped fund Lewis's statue, but otherwise the convention lacked the means to follow through on its sweeping agenda. A National Convention of Colored Men did take place in Nashville in 1876, with another following in 1879, although with the latter, where we have extant sources, attendance was lower than the newspaper men likely would have hoped for and skewed toward the surrounding region.[140] Indicative of the bittersweet promise of the long postbellum campaign for civil right was the national Centennial Exhibition itself. There, Frederick Douglass appeared on the grandstand alongside President Ulysses S. Grant and other dignitaries, but only after the city's police nearly denied him entry.[141]

The middle and late 1870s witnessed the combined forces of economic depression and white supremacist violence undermine the cross-regional ties at the heart of this emerging network of African American readers, authors, and editors. Yet these forces never managed to fully close the institutional and associational possibilities opened in the 1860s and early 1870s. By the 1880s, a new cadre of African Americans was forging connections across regions. Many were former slaves or their children who found early support from postbellum schools, universities, church organizations, and civic and political associations. These same organizations played critical roles in supporting southern African American newspapers and magazines.[142] Douglass, in the twilight of his career, was still forging connections with new editors and authors, including the anti-lynching crusader Ida B. Wells.[143] White control of publishing ventures still presented a considerable problem, and the new linkages that began to form among African Americans in the North, South, and West remained tenuous. As late as World War I, African American railroad porters had to smuggle the *Chicago Defender*, edited by a child of former slaves, Robert Sengstacke Abbott, into the Deep South.[144] But these connections allowed for news to flow among African Americans across regions, shaping patterns of emigration from the South, campaigns against Jim Crow, and an expanding range of opinions about freedom, progress, and the world's peoples.

5

Mormon Utah, the Blossoming Plague-Spot

The entire western United States was, to northern Republicans, from conservative Unionists to racial egalitarians, a national component of a global frontier of civilization and republicanism.[1] With energy and resources freed up after Union victory, northern Republicans redoubled their efforts to bring this vast territory under the control of the federal government and into conformity with their vision of America.[2] But in the middle of this landscape of the future was a peculiar problem of the present. Mormon Utah, unlike the allegedly "savage" Native Americans in the region, constituted its own strange, semi-civilized society. During the Civil War there had been only modest federal presence around Salt Lake City, and the Mormon leadership governed the region without much interference. Now that the war was over, northern Republicans were convinced that this needed to change. In the three decades following Appomattox, the Republican Party would, when it had firm control of the federal government, attempt to break the power of the Mormon Church in Utah and compel it to abandon the practice of polygamy. The period from 1865 to 1874 represented the first wave of these efforts, which northern Republicans tied explicitly to Reconstruction by linking the allegedly barbaric and despotic practices of the Church to those of southern slave owners.[3] Northern Republican concerns were never about just polygamy or the authority of the Church in a narrow sense, but linked these practices to an understanding of the Mormons as a people with their own character, which northern Republicans often deemed to be foreign to that of Americans.

To their Democratic critics, northern Republican rhetoric and policies smacked of intolerance, of self-righteous Yankees demanding that the whole world conform to their values and customs. Such arguments, which appeared as well in Democratic reactions to northern Republican sympathy for the Cretans, had a complex political backdrop. As was more fully evident here, in the immediate wake of abolition, they constituted a lingering proslavery defense of the Old South that held it to have been a distinctive society crushed by northern Republican closed-mindedness. Such claims also pointed to the complicated ways in which Democratic white supremacy was wrapped up with a one-dimensional tradition of toleration. Long opposed to the moralizing tendencies of abolitionists, northern Whigs, and Republicans, Democrats were often more welcoming to the diverse cultures—and votes—of white immigrants. In a political context where anti-Catholicism and nativism were powerful forces, Democrats embraced Irish and German immigrants on the same racial grounds that they persecuted African Americans, expropriated Mexican and Native American lands, and discriminated against Chinese immigrants. Writing against what they saw as a foolishly race-blind northern Republican cultural imperialism, Democrats at times extended their defense of white immigrants to Mormons. At a few moments they even became careful observers of them. Yet Democrats also struggled to stomach a public defense of polygamy, which was a form of marriage and social organization broadly associated with nonwhite peoples. Indeed, in the coming decades, southern whites would repeatedly lynch Mormon men, often missionaries, as a perceived threat to their women.[4]

Twin Relics of Barbarism

Northern Republicans turned their attention to Utah because they believed that, with polygamy, the Mormons had resuscitated a barbaric form of marriage that gave reign to male lust and made victims of innocent women and children.[5] Rooted in a set of gender conventions that exalted manly restraint in place of the masculine virility and prerogative often championed by their political opponents, northern Republicans labeled polygamy "patriarchal" and presumed it to therefore be inherently and irresistibly exploitative.[6] The result, they were certain, was that the Mormon household could never be a nurturing home that contributed to progress by raising girls into caring mothers and boys into diligent workers.[7] In its essence, northern Republicans thought, polygamy was akin to another exploitative and retrogressive domestic institution: slavery. Such conclusions built upon popular anti-Mormon novels from the mid-1850s, which came off the presses shortly after and drew heavily on the depictions of female servitude in antislavery novels. These novels also featured depictions of Mormon fathers as lustful, violent slave owners and Mormon proselytizers as slave procurers.[8] As early as their first national platform in 1856, Republicans had declared polygamy and slavery to be "twin relics of barbarism" and vowed to prevent their expansion into the territories of the American West.[9] In fact, the accusation that polygamy was, like slavery, an un-American barbarism constituted, as J. Spencer Fluhman has recently shown, an important transformation in anti-Mormon sentiment.[10] Northern Republicans did considerable injustice to Mormon beliefs and practices. Fatherly authority was central to nineteenth-century Mormon family life, and the wives of Mormon men were sometimes shocked and aggrieved to learn that their husbands had entered plural marriages. But northern Republican depictions tended to ignore the religious nature of the institution, the easy availability of divorce for discontented Mormon wives, and the strong sense of community and voice in the Church that Mormon wives cultivated, whether they were in polygamous marriages or not.[11]

Northern Republicans expected to oversee the abolition of this other peculiar institution. In 1862, early in their congressional ascendancy, Republicans passed the Morrill Act proscribing polygamy. Abraham Lincoln prudently decided not to further antagonize the Mormons in the midst of a civil war, but his private secretary and future biographer, John G. Nicolay, spent his limited free time in the White House working on an anti-Mormon novel, portions of which he outlined on Executive Mansion stationery.[12] Union victory brought renewed attention to the territory. Fueled by hopes of "civilizing" the western "wilderness," growing immigration to the territory, the completion of the transcontinental railroad, and the actions of the Mormons themselves, congressional Republicans debated numerous bills to weaken the Mormon Church, pressure polygamists, and strengthen the hand of federal officials and "Gentiles" living in the territory.[13] Years of corrupt leadership, rising class conflict, and the debilitating financial crisis of 1873 would all dampen but not fully extinguish northern Republican optimism and confidence in their ability to institute reform. Ultimately, it would take the landslide Democratic victories in the election of 1874 and their ensuing control of the House of Representatives to halt the northern Republican campaign against Mormon Utah. Not until the 1880s would their political assault on polygamy resume, finally forcing the Church to abandon the practice in 1890.[14]

Both the phrase "twin relics of barbarism" and the linking of slavery and polygamy featured prominently in postbellum Republican criticisms of Utah. John Beadle, a Republican and one of the most prolific and popular postbellum critics of Mormon Utah, attempted to describe the similarity between "Slavery and polygamy" as "'twin relics'" in his introductory essay to a jailhouse confession by Bill Hickman, one of Brigham Young's alleged "Danite" assassins.[15] Both institutions, according to Beadle, prompted an all-consuming selfishness among men. In the case of polygamy, claimed Beadle, a patriarch's willingness to bring open shame upon his first wife and unnatural misery upon the women of his household moved him "a long way on the road towards doing any other mean thing which will give him an advantage over his fellow-men."[16] Leading abolitionist Harriet Beecher Stowe, in a triumphal preface to an autobiographical exposé of Mormon life by Fanny Stenhouse, took it for granted that polygamy was a form of slavery. Lauding the "glorious breaking of fetters" that came with emancipation and Union victory in the Civil War, Stowe asked her readers: "Shall we not then hope that the hour is come to loose the bonds of a cruel slavery whose chains have cut into the very hearts of thousands of our sisters—a slavery which debases and degrades womanhood, motherhood, and the family?"[17]

By the end of the Civil War, in fact, the belief that polygamy was a form of patriarchal slavery was widely familiar, and could be referenced briefly. In his weekly travel article "Across the Continent. Overland Scenes" in the popular New York weekly *Frank Leslie's Illustrated Newspaper,* Thomas W. Knox, a Republican newspaper correspondent, invoked northern stereotypes when describing the trip of a Mormon farm family to Salt Lake City.[18] Portraying the family's husband as evincing "an air of determination" that "convinces the beholder that his will is law," Knox explained that, instead of lingering in the market to allow his wives to "inspect the fineries," the husband merely did his business and then loaded up his ox-wagon with his "animate and inanimate goods and chattels" to return home.[19] *Frank Leslie's* itself seemed to take the equation of the two for granted when, in a subsequent editorial, it casually referred to polygamy as the Mormon's own peculiar and patriarchal institution and claimed that the Mormons had hoped to see Confederate victory ensure states' rights.[20]

Even when they wrote about polygamy in greater length, northern Republicans often took their conclusions for granted. Consider, for example, the writings of Samuel Bowles, the influential editor of the *Springfield Republican* who, along with Schuyler Colfax, the Republican Speaker of the House of Representatives, and Albert D. Richardson, a radical Republican correspondent for the *New York Tribune*, made their way across the West by overland stage in 1865.[21] Bowles, although he wrote pages about the Mormons, could condemn polygamy without much need to justify his arguments, as when he asserted that, under it, a wife "becomes simply a servant and serf, not the companion and equal of man; and the inevitable influence of this upon all society need not be depicted."[22] Another Republican, General James F. Rusling, was similarly confident in his 1867 army quartermaster's report to the House of Representatives.[23] Based on his three weeks inspecting the U.S. Army fort overlooking Salt Lake City, Rusling concluded that, "'Peculiar Institutions,' whether slavery or polygamy, breed the same results, whether in South Carolina or Utah," presenting outsiders with a choice between "acquiescence or emigration." When Rusling turned to the impact of polygamy on domestic relations, he argued that it led Mormon patriarchs to refer to women as though they were domestic animals, "or as our southern slave lords used to speak of their 'likely young niggers.'" Here, Rusling, like Bowles, felt no need to elaborate, concluding that "nothing more need be said than that the whole thing is simply an organized insult to Christianity and an outrage against the civilization of the age—in very truth," polygamy was "slavery's hideous and exquisite 'twin relic of barbarism.'"[24]

Republican descriptions of Mormon wives and children highlight their belief that polygamy corroded the affective, gendered relationships that supposedly made northern households nurturing homes. When Carleton, while on his trip around the globe, visited Salt Lake City in the months before the completion of the transcontinental railroad, he asserted that the Mormon Church taught women that "concubinage is ordained by God" and that to reject the advances of even an "old, hateful," and "repulsive" polygamous husband would be heresy. The result was that, when in Salt Lake City, "You see nature's protest in the sad and care-worn countenance of every woman you meet."[25] Schuyler Colfax echoed these sentiments, believing, as did others, that lustful Mormon patriarchs were totally unrestrained. Unable to escape their "remote" and "mountain-walled" society, Colfax claimed, Mormon women faced "marriages of 3 sisters to one husband—of a mother & all her daughters—of nieces—even of one's own half sister." Nor could wives stop their husbands from abandoning them for girls "in the first bloom of maidenhood."[26]

Not surprisingly, it was two Republican territorial officials appointed by Ulysses S. Grant, a reliable opponent of the Mormons, who supported Ann Eliza Young, one of Brigham Young's wives, in her efforts to secure a divorce and publicly denounce polygamy. Likewise, James B. Pond, a militant abolitionist who had fought alongside John Brown in Kansas and who was in Utah working with the increasingly anti-Mormon *Salt Lake Tribune,* managed Ann Eliza's early public speaking career and accompanied her to Washington, D.C., in 1874. There, her speech before Congress helped inspire the Poland Act, strengthening the hand of federal officials in the territory.[27]

An illustration of communion in the Mormon Tabernacle in Salt Lake City in *Harper's Weekly* gave graphic expression to these concerns (see figure 13).[28] In it, wives and their children occupy the foreground, surrounded by shaded rows of older men and stern-looking Mormon patriarchs distributing communion water. In the lower left-hand corner, the viewer confronts the faces of a young girl in peaceful repose, a Mormon mother, and, over their shoulder, two leering, gruff Mormon men, one of whom stares back at the reader. In the center, the shadowed face of a long-haired Mormon man looms over a young child too small to lift a communion cup. If not a depiction of overt exploitation, the illustration's juxtaposition of youthful innocence and patriarchal control would have nonetheless resonated with northern Republican understandings of Mormon society.

Underlying Republican equations of polygamy and slavery was a presumption, shared across the political spectrum, that barbarisms manifested the same spirit and had the same effects whether in the South, the West, or abroad. This was evident in the northern Republicans' willingness to make the kind of world- and history-straddling analogies so common to the day. The Sewards, when they visited Salt Lake City in August of 1870 on their way around the world, argued that

FIGURE 13. "Sacrament in the Mormon Tabernacle, Salt Lake City, Utah," *Harper's Weekly,* September 30, 1871, 912–14

"Polygamy is antagonistic to, and incompatible with, the existence of the family." These two institutions, he added, were on the brink of an "irrepressible conflict" that had already played out "in all the nations of the East," where the harem had triumphed, leading "not merely to the degradation but the enslaving of women, and the demoralization and corruption of the entire social body."[29] Herman Snow, writing for the travel magazine *Overland Monthly,* explained that just as polygamy gave "to the Turk his stolid self-conceit, as he indolently surveys his extensive harem of human toys," and filled "the American Indian with haughty vanity, as he stalks along in paint and feathers" with his laboring squaws behind him, so to did it cause the Mormon patriarch "to vaunt himself with outrageous self-conceit."[30]

References to slaveholders, Native Americans, and Turks were only the start for some. Catherine Waite offers one clear example. She moved to the territory when her husband, Charles, a Chicago Republican, was appointed associate justice of the territory in 1862. Her *The Mormon Prophet and His Harem,* which went through at least five editions from its first publication in 1866 to 1868, argued that misogyny and polygamy were endemic to heathen and otherwise degraded nations, pointing to Muslims, Jews, Native Americans, Hungarians, and some earlier Christians for evidence. Shortly thereafter, she claimed that whether one looked at the ancient or modern world, one found that "the most enlightened and prosperous nations" revered women and practiced monogamy, that the "practice of polygamy is adverse to free institutions," and that "The love of the home" strengthened "the love of country and of liberty."[31] Such rhetoric was sufficiently common that Mormons sometimes turned it on its head, with one Apostle, George Q. Cannon, arguing in 1869 that polygamy was the foundation for the longest standing civilizations on the globe, those in Asia.[32]

John Beadle offered a similarly wide-ranging analysis. Marriage, according to Beadle, existed for three reasons: reproduction, companionship, and, most nobly of all, so people could love divinely through "a complete intercommunion of soul and interchange of pure affection." The polygamous, however, only exercised animalistic lusts tied to reproduction.[33] Beadle attempted to prove his assertions "by a comparative view of polygamous and monogamous nations." The "Indian and native African," wrote Beadle, "know nothing of the softer sentiments," and understood women to be merely "a superior beast of burden." The "Hindoo," among the "partially civilized races," considered women's lot in life so poor that "it is thought no particular harm to drown a female infant." Meanwhile, the "Mohammedan races, generally" had no institution of "Home, as known by us," and instead kept harems. Only the practice of monogamy, argued Beadle, could allow for all three forms of attachment, and only with them would men begin to value women as anything other than objects of lust. Beadle's analysis then probed history to demonstrate that "In the march of progress" polygamous nations had been and remained unable to compete with "the hardy vigor of Western Christians." The pre-Christian Greeks, with their "fixed principle" that "the dignity of woman is the strength of the state," had "overran" the "effeminate Persians and Hindoos." Likewise, the Romans had reigned supreme until conquered peoples within their realm eroded a six hundred-year-old tradition of matronly honor and dignity. Then Rome, "in turn, fell before the hardy monogamists of Northern Europe." Later still, when the conquering "Mohammedans" turned to Europe, the Germans "left the plains of Poictiers [Poitiers] covered with the corpses of three hundred thousand polygamists." Yet Mormon polygamy was worse than all of these, for in addition to the common baseness of "that of the Jews, Turks, and Hindoos," it "consists in the grosser forms of incest, the intermarriage of near relations." If the Mormons drew any inspiration from their contemporaries, believed Beadle, they must have done so from "the Utes and Shoshonees who surround them."[34] In his table of contents, Beadle described the subject of this section as "Turk, Persian and African *vs.* the Christian White," demonstrating how easily religious distinctions blurred into racial ones.[35]

Mormon Despotism

Connected to polygamy, in northern Republican condemnations, was the alleged theocratic despotism that the Mormon Church had created in the territory.[36] This despotism, Republicans asserted, was a monstrosity not only for its particular religious doctrines, but also because it eroded the distinction between church and state and concentrated power into the hands of a power-hungry, aristocratic priesthood. Because Reconstruction's partisans of all kinds believed that the world was composed of distinct and coherent groups of people, they could ultimately relate polygamy and despotism back to the underlying character of the Mormons. Here, however, there was also room for disagreement, especially concerning the relationship between the Mormon people and the small priesthood who ruled over them.

Republican journalists, jurists, and politicians heaped scorn upon the allegedly despotic Mormon leadership and its deluded following. Although Catherine Waite framed *The Mormon Prophet and His Harem* as a balanced but critical investigation into polygamy, she nonetheless dedicated over a third of it to the political history of Mormonism in hopes of alerting America to "the dangerous character of this monarchy growing up in the midst of the Republic."[37] Longstanding New York Republican James McKean, who President Grant appointed chief justice of Utah in 1870 to challenge Church authority, captured the intensity of the revulsion. Near the start of his confrontational, four-and-a-half-year tenure at the post that would see him attempt to try Brigham Young, he exclaimed, "Utah is a Theocracy, a spurious Theocracy in the heart of the Republic!"[38] Similarly, Robert Baskin, an Ohio lawyer long active in anti-Mormon political efforts within Utah and Washington,

D.C., wrote in his reminiscences that the "sole motive" behind the 1870 founding of Utah's Republican-aligned Liberal Party had been "to correct the abuses prevalent in Utah, and to establish republican American rule in place of the usurped rule of the priesthood of the Mormon church."[39] John Beadle, not surprisingly, also condemned Mormon despotism. As he explained in his first popular book on the Mormons, *Life in Utah,* the fundamental preconditions necessary for the Mormon Church to stand "forth complete as a theocratic absolutism" had been met in Utah by the creation of an all-powerful Mormon priesthood and an ignorant laity.[40] Two years later, Beadle accused Mormon leaders of holding multiple political posts and quipped that "A plurality of offices as well as of wives obtains in Utah."[41] Charles Nordhoff, traveling through Salt Lake City on the way to California, folded arguments about polygamy into a critique of Mormon hierarchy by asserting that the former was, like slavery, a naturally "aristocratic institution" reserved for the elite. Set on preserving the privilege to "gratify their bestial propensities," the Mormon leadership, Nordhoff argued, had led their coreligionists to a wasteland.[42]

Many Republicans criticized the followers of the Mormon Church. The *New York Times,* for example, blamed the Mormons' troubled past on their hive mentality when describing "The Mormonism of Salt Lake" as "a despotism growing up in the midst of a free state," and "an autocracy confronting a society where the will of the people is supreme."[43] William Elkanah Waters, a Union army officer who visited Salt Lake City while inspecting conditions at nearby Camp Douglas, took a relatively cautious position. Perhaps because of his political conservatism, he was inclined to view the more sensationalist renderings of Mormon society critically.[44] Yet he still shared the basic beliefs of most Republican anti-Mormon writers, and repeatedly described the Mormons as deluded, fanatical, and ignorant.[45] George L. Woods, one of the founders of the Republican Party in Oregon and the territorial governor of Utah for five years during the Grant administration, argued that while he supported woman suffrage in theory, he could not endorse it in Mormon Utah. There, where the Mormon-dominated territorial legislature extended suffrage to women in 1870 as a symbolic response to proposed congressional legislation, Woods found it to be largely irrelevant, since, "by the order of the priesthood all Mormons vote as directed by the Church." "[I]t is a common thing," he added, "to see a Mormon priest with 6, 8, 10 & sometimes more wives & concubines go to the polls to vote together."[46]

As the alleged despot of this theocracy, Brigham Young often elicited ridicule from Republicans. Some, such as *Harper's Weekly,* drew attention to how Young won a fanatical loyalty from his followers. Describing services at the Mormon Tabernacle in Salt Lake City, *Harper's* explained how Young, in his sermons, "as in private," wielded a "strange magnetic influence" on "his disciples."[47] The rise of Brigham Young was a pivotal moment in the history of the Mormons according to John Hay, one of Abraham Lincoln's other private secretaries during the Civil War (along with John G. Nicolay) and a Reconstruction-era diplomat and editorialist. Writing on Joseph Smith's 1844 execution for the *Atlantic Monthly,* Hay concluded by briefly surveying the succession of Brigham Young. As he put it, Young "exerted himself to gather all the reins of government into his own hands; and there was not in all the slavish East a despot more absolute than he" when the Mormons fled mob violence "into the vast and tolerant wilderness."[48] Jacob Boreman, another Grant-appointed federal judge in Utah, found Young to be "the general 'boss' of" Salt Lake City in religious and especially temporal matters. "The people," he believed, "appeared to look to him with fear and as if he were an iron ruler."[49] Some who met Young, like Schuyler Colfax, thought despotism permeated his being. According to Colfax, Young had "a short & powerful neck, & a chin & lips that betoken commanding will, inflexible determination, & an exaction of submission to his authority & demands."[50] A verse from an undated campaign song styled on the Union tune *Marching through Georgia* illustrates how Utah Liberals viewed themselves as locked in a struggle against a Mormon aristocracy:

> "Orland's boys with carpet bags will never take Salt Lake!"
> So the royal families said, but that was their mistake,
> We'll show them at the ballot boxes who will "take the cake,"
> While we go marching through Zion.[51]

Republicans often questioned whether the Mormon Church could survive without Brigham Young's controlling leadership. Upon rumors that he had fled Salt Lake City in 1871 to escape federal prosecution, *Harper's Weekly* anticipated troubles for the Church. *Harper's* suggested that the Mormons would either follow Young in another "hegira" or disperse, for there seemed "to be no successor of *Young* who can command the people by his personal power."[52] Republicans who moved to the southern states during Reconstruction could take their anti-Mormonism with them, and the editor of the *Morning Republican* of Little Rock, Arkansas, concurred with *Harper's*. Believing that Young was well on his way to Mexico, the *Morning Republican* asserted that "His retreating from his stronghold . . . has solved the problem of polygomy [*sic*] on the American continent."[53] Others, however, were not so optimistic. Fred W. Loring, a New Englander traveling through Salt Lake City on the Union Pacific, asked in *Appleton's Journal,* "But, after Brigham Young, what?" Would polygamy and Mormonism survive the passing of a man Loring described as a corpulent tyrant? Uncertain, he concluded that "time only can decide."[54] In February of 1867, Union general William B. Hazen, who had close ties to Ohio Republican James Garfield, reported on federal military power in Utah to the House Committee on Territories. In doing so, Hazen discussed the Mormons, alleging that Young drew power from his "perfect organization, religious fanaticism, and despotic power." Unlike others, however, he suggested that the Mormons were not about to disappear. "The same thing was believed when Joe Smith died," pointed out Hazen, "but look at the results."[55]

As with the barbaric patriarchy of polygamy, Republicans felt at ease ranging across the globe and history when discussing Mormon despotism and fanaticism. John Beadle, for one, compared the fate of the Mormon Church to that of the papacy in recently unified Italy, asserting that they were both prone to fall before the onward march of progressive nations. As he explained it, "as the Pope's temporality could not continue in the middle of Victor Emanuel's kingdom, so an ecclesiastical organization like that of the Mormon Church cannot peaceably continue in America."[56] Charles H. Brigham, in a fourteen-page article for Boston's *Old and New,* evaluated the prospects of the "Mormon State" and found that on balance its future looked dim. For while the "Mormon power" could count on a number of strengths, Brigham argued, it was, ultimately, "an absurdity and an anomaly in this age and country." In the course of his overview, Brigham found space to equate the Mormon Church, in its disdain for outside civilization, to the Roman Catholic Church, its "tribunals" to the "Inquisition of the Middle Ages," Brigham Young to a domineering Napoleon, the educational philosophy of the "Mormon priesthood" to that of the "Roman priesthood," and its members to fanatical "Huguenots of France," "Covenanters of Scotland," and "Moslems of Damascus," as well as eccentric "Shakers, and Mennonites, and Second Adventists."[57]

Debating Mormon Policy

Given the diversity of the Republican coalition and the strains it underwent in the decade following the Civil War, it is hardly surprising that there was occasional discord among northern Republicans concerning Mormon Utah. Such differences developed around questions about gender relations in the rest of the United States, the role of the Mormons in settling the West, their future in the United States, and what measures could and should be applied against polygamy and the Church's temporal authority. Yet, genuine though they were, these disagreements developed within and ultimately highlight the common framework through which northern Republicans interpreted Mormon Utah. They judged Mormon Utah relative to a northern understanding of American character that was in turn indexed to global struggles for freedom and progress.

Some woman suffragists, for example, agreed with standard northern Republican condemnations of polygamy but turned them toward a critique of America for not bringing its gender conventions into conformity with the country's commitment to freedom and progress. Anna Dickinson, an abolitionist, suffragist, and one of the most popular pro-Union public speakers during the Civil War, demonstrated as much in her postbellum anti-Mormon speaking tour.[58] Dickinson drew on her mastery of lyceum conventions and echoed other northern Republicans in condemning Brigham Young as a despot and polygamy for replacing the nurturing power of the home with the lusts of patriarchs. Indeed, her descriptions of the Mormons were as categorical as any, arguing that polygamy caused infant mortality and relating a story of a woman who married the same man as her aunt.[59] But Dickinson stressed that Mormon polygamy was rooted in ideas about women common across the country and the world, especially that they were suited to be only mothers and wives.[60] At least a few publications, including the *Revolution* and the *National Anti-Slavery Standard,* summarized her speech and supported its argument, with the latter also publishing a glowing letter from a subscriber in Pennsylvania who heard the speech a few months later.[61] Another suffragist, Abigail Scott Duniway, made a more roundabout connection. She argued that the introduction of female voting rights in the Wyoming Territory had driven out prostitution, suggested that exclusive male voting rights coincided with the exploitation of women, and asked readers of her Portland newspaper, the *New Northwest,* "Isn't Brigham Young a fit example of the dire consequences of man suffrage?"[62]

Northern Republicans also divided over how to explain Mormon success in settling what they considered to be a remote and difficult portion of the American "frontier." Here, they found a genuine interpretive snare, for while they considered Mormon practices and beliefs to be retrogressive, such "civilizing" of the western "wilderness" was integral to their understanding of America's national mission. Confronting this quandary, some gave credit to the Mormons while others sought to downplay their accomplishments.

Praise for Mormon achievements, in fact, was hardly rare among northern Republicans. Writing in August of 1866, *Harper's Weekly,* despite its revulsion at polygamy, provided its readers with a description and accompanying illustration of the successes of the Mormons in Salt Lake City. These included an affordable school system, some substantial buildings, a number of well-established stores, a theater, gardens, and a life-giving irrigation system. Their esteem for this orderly and prosperous society is apparent in their illustration, which depicts a cityscape centered on a broad, active, and straight street surrounded by the neat angular rooftops of Mormon buildings and leafy tree canopies (see figure 14). Above the cityscape, portraits of well-attired Mormon leaders look forward without any apparent malice, while to their sides are sketches of prominent Mormon buildings. As *Harper's* noted in conclusion, whatever one thought about the Mormon religion, "the great virtue of labor can not be denied to the Mormon population." *Harper's* also praised Brigham Young, arguing that it was his "executive ability" that had "redeemed the wilderness, made it a fruitful field, and 'made the desert to blossom as a rose.'"[63]

Similarly, Samuel Bowles, in 1865, optimistic that the Mormon Church would abandon polygamy, at one point positively gushed over the Mormons' leadership and achievements. Surely the Mormons had had "great worldly wisdom" presiding over them, with their leaders showing "tact and statesmanship." Among the Mormons at large, he

FIGURE 14. "Brigham Young and the Twelve Apostles of the Mormon Church," "The City and Valley of the Great Salt Lake, Utah," and other drawings, *Harper's Weekly,* August 18, 1866, 520–21.

continued, "there have been industry, frugality and integrity" that produced "such progress, such wealth, such varied triumphs of industry and ingenuity and endurance."[64] The *New York Times,* while condemning Brigham Young, claimed the Mormons as a people were "mainly thrifty, industrious, full of enterprise and vigor," had contributed to the wealth of the country, and had "taught us what could be done with the far deserts."[65] Charles Nordhoff found Salt Lake City shabby but saw some merit in Mormon claims that the Church had transformed destitute European converts into virtuous laborers, and advised railroad capitalists interested in settling the West to take note.[66] William Seward was to the point: "In the aspect of political economy, Utah is a wonderful success."[67]

Some, however, read Mormon achievements as a product of despotism and fanaticism. General William Hazen, for one, seemed to waver, describing Mormon laborers as "probably the most universally industrious" people in America, while warning that the Church hierarchy "extends to every hamlet, and controls the actions and influences the thoughts of every individual," regarding agriculture, religion, and politics. As he said in reference to the Church's leadership, "Implicit obedience is their first rule."[68] Four years after initially singing the praises of Mormon energies, an embittered Samuel Bowles noted how visitors to Utah would be impressed not by the merits of Mormon efforts and ingenuity, but by the "power of a religious fanaticism, directed by a lordly will and organizing a faithful, simple industry." If these fanatics "set in motion many of the elements of progress and civilization," they could not be said to embody them.[69] When Mormons built thirty-four miles of railroad to connect Salt Lake City to the transcontinental line, Thomas W. Knox argued that they did so under the command of Brigham Young. As he stated it, "The Mormons are not without energy, driven as they are by the spiritual whip of their prophet and chief, Brigham Young."[70]

Some downplayed Mormon accomplishments. Considering public education to be a key source of progress, it is not surprising that, contrary to *Harper's* passing compliment, northern Republicans more often expressed concern for and criticism of Mormon-run schools in Utah.[71] Some, like John Beadle, claimed that Mormon industry was largely a myth, and alleged that Mormon farmers had "built houses, barns and fences, but such as they were absolutely forced to have in order to live at all."[72] Fred W. Loring, on his transcontinental railroad trip, began his article on Salt Lake City by expressing relief at finally having reached an oasis of civilized comfort. But in the evening, away from the main hotel, Salt Lake City's dimly lit buildings appeared shabby, its theater "cheerless and dingy in the extreme," and its actors of "unrivaled badness." The following morning his impressions only worsened. Echoing others, Loring also added that Brigham Young kept the Mormon people "ignorant" and that if they practiced "habits of industry and thrift," this spoke to Young's tyranny and not their own virtues.[73] Catherine Waite took a slightly different tack, accusing Brigham Young of disrupting the concord between labor and capital that sat at the heart of free-labor ideology when he "misjudged human nature" and sparked class antagonisms in his "already inharmonious kingdom" by attempting to fix prices over the protests of mechanics and laborers.[74]

When Republicans did find merit in the Mormons' industriousness, the result was ambivalence, which sometimes manifested itself in descriptions that presented Mormon Utah as in but not of the civilized world. Such a distinction rested on the dual meanings of civilization as both a level of development and a process of continual progress. In one editorial, for example, the *New York Times* conceded that the Mormons were a "civilized community," but then condemned them as the only one of "the present day" that practiced polygamy, which it claimed outraged "the decencies of modern civilization."[75] Similarly, Schuyler Colfax described how Utah had become the Mormons' home because it was the only place in the "civilized world" where they could practice polygamy. Yet, a few pages later, Colfax recounted that he had told Brigham Young in a frank but open meeting that polygamy had "arrayed the civilized World against" the Mormons.[76]

Northern Republicans differed further over how to explain and address the rise of a polygamous and theocratic society within the United States. How could they explain the flourishing of barbarism and despotism, of all places, on the American frontier? Some northern Republicans skirted this question by focusing on the high number of foreign émigrés among the Mormons. John Beadle argued that "at least seven-eighths" of the Mormons were foreigners, and that they came from the "lowest and most ignorant classes" of Europe straight to Utah. Such people, claimed Beadle, were not Americans, and could not become Americans, because they were people who merely had "Mormonism grafted onto Europeanism."[77] Anna Dickinson likewise noted while on tour that "the great rank and file of the people . . . are Swedes, Finns, Danes, Germans, French, the great majority of them English and Welsh, the most vicious and degraded of the peasant class of Europe."[78] In a similar vein, Samuel Bowles, in 1865, claimed that, while there were a few attractive women and "strong-headed" men apparent in a Mormon service he attended, the "great mass" were destitute foreigners who ranked below even the most impoverished of the East Coast working classes in appearance and condition.[79]

At other times, however, it mattered less where the Mormons were from and more that their institutions were offensive to the nation's honor and spirit. Because the Mormons practiced barbarism and despotism, they could not be Americans and furthermore embarrassed the United States before the civilized world. Schuyler Colfax had hoped, in 1865, that strong enforcement of federal laws and non-Mormon immigration to Utah would bring an end to the "illegal, barbaric & woman degrading Institution, which now stains our National escutcheon."[80] Likewise, when *Harper's Weekly* heard rumors that Young had fled Utah in 1871, it hoped that his exit promised the death of that "'peculiar institution' which made Utah a plague-spot on the map of our country."[81] Similarly, Fred W. Loring described Young's rumored wealth as "a disgrace to our government, and a blot on our fair fame as a nation."[82] Though Samuel Bowles had earlier mentioned the poor condition of European Mormon immigrants, when he traveled across America again in 1869 he offered the readers of *Atlantic Monthly* a more concise and moralistic indictment of Mormon Utah. While travelers might be charmed by Salt Lake City, Bowles assured his readers that no organization of any stripe in Europe or America was as "foreign to all our principles of life and growth" as Brigham Young's Church. Even a little knowledge of "our national instincts and faith in progress," claimed Bowles, would allow an observer to see the inevitable collapse of the Church before "the advancing tide of American emigration and American civilization." Both the "theories and practices" of the "autocracy" in Utah, he argued, outraged "our American fundamentals."[83] For some, the foreignness of Mormon culture could underscore that African Americans formed a part of the national mainstream. One letter to the *Elevator,* the African American newspaper in San Francisco, argued with reference to polygamy that "It seems plainly impossible to isolate our race, like the Indians, the Mormons, or the Chinese."[84]

Confronted with a national problem, Republicans varied in what they thought was the optimal response. Many Republicans were willing to flex the power of the federal government, as evidenced by several Republican-sponsored bills, opposition to the seating of the polygamous George Q. Cannon as Utah's territorial representative to Congress, and repeated rejections of Utah's application for statehood. The first round of proposed bills subsequent to the Morrill Anti-Bigamy Act of 1862 began in 1866 and lasted until 1870. In June of 1866, Benjamin Wade introduced to the Senate a bill that would have asserted federal control over the Utah militia and jury selection, prohibited Church officers from officiating marriages, and removed territorial tax exemptions for the Church. It failed to pass and was followed by the proposed Cragin Bill of 1867, reintroduced in 1869, which went further and called for the abolition of jury trials for bigamy cases. Representative Shelby Cullom's slightly less drastic 1869 bill passed through the House of Representatives but floundered in the Senate. Representative James Ashley proposed dividing much of Utah's land among the surrounding territories, only to prompt concerns that the Mormons would thereafter manage to increase their influence. A second round of proposed legislation then started in 1872, with a multitude of bills coming mostly from Republicans, such as John Logan and Frederick Frelinghuysen in the Senate and William Wheeler in the House of Representatives. Daniel Voorhees was an aberrant Democrat in the mix, and James Blair a stray Liberal Republican. With the exception of the Poland Act of 1874, these bills failed to pass, in part because of expectations that the completion of the Pacific Railroad made them superfluous and in part because of uneasiness from conservative Republicans and Democrats over the expansion of federal power. Proposals for anti-Mormon legislation largely came to a stop between 1874 and 1880, a period of diminished Republican power in Washington, D.C.[85]

Some, like General James Rusling, found the Mormons to be not only un-American but downright seditious, and called for more than legislation. He confessed to having "great faith in the moral power of bayonets, when exhibited on the right side." Rusling explained his rationale, linking slavery and polygamy in the process: "The nation found it necessary to invoke [bayonets] against slavery when nothing else would suffice, and I am not clear that we shall not yet have to invoke them against polygamy, the other 'twin relic,' before we are well quit of that diabolism."[86] Others, however, cautioned against such brash measures. General Hazen, in a report from the previous year, warned against the use of military force. He found the Mormons to be "in spirit a separate and distinct nationality" from Americans, and claimed that "No one can be in Utah long without feeling that they are among a foreign people."[87] Yet he found that they were too shrewd to do anything overtly hostile, that they were "too valuable a portion of the nation to be destroyed if they can be utilized," and that "extermination" could not be a viable option at "our age of civilization." Hazen hoped that the federal government would strengthen its authority in Utah gently, while reaching out to the Mormons, educating them, and hopefully making them "feel that they are a part of us."[88]

Some believed that Mormon polygamy could be ended through theological debate, but most focused on secular issues even as they condemned a society defined by religious belief. Much as J. E. Rankin had described the difference between Catholics and Protestants as one of civilizations, with Mormon Utah the emphasis was often on how a religiously delimited population presented secular problems. In 1870, John Philip Newman, the chaplain of the Senate during Ulysses S. Grant's presidency, traveled to Utah to challenge the biblical justification of Mormon polygamy.[89] In three hours spaced out over three days, Newman publicly debated Orson Pratt, one of the Mormon Church's twelve apostles.[90] Northern Republican reactions, however, were mixed at best. In the *New National Era,* the Douglasses asserted that such efforts were pointless. "Polygamy like slavery," it claimed, "is not to be disposed of by quotations from the Bible," which, the paper pointed out, could easily be interpreted as supporting the practice. The paper reiterated, "As with slavery so with polygamy," and argued that the institution needed to be "brought to the bar of reason and science," and that "The whole advancing force of civilization, culture, refinement, and moral purity must be marshalled against it."[91] The *New York Times* similarly suggested that biblical exegesis would prove ineffective and largely missed the point that it was the progressive nature and "decencies of modern civilization," not the ancient world of the Old Testament, that polygamy outraged.[92] Even William Waters, who was a friend of Newman's, wrote about his time in Utah upon Newman's request, and dedicated his resulting book to Newman, addressed Mormon theology briefly while stressing Brigham Young's despotism and the "practical" problems with polygamy.[93]

Many northern Republicans, not unlike Carleton, Fogg, and the Sewards, believed that freedom and progress were operating under their own steam, and therefore expected the defeat of Mormon polygamy and theocracy to be inevitable. Harriet Beecher Stowe, in her brief introduction to Fanny Stenhouse's autobiographical exposé, encouraged the women of America to express humanitarian concern to help "free her sisters from this degrading bondage." Before "enlightened sentiment and sympathy," promised Stowe, "every form of injustice and cruelty *must* finally go down."[94] Moderate Republicans uncomfortable with the expansion of federal power no doubt welcomed the idea that republicanism and civilization would advance on their own. The *New York Times,* for one, condemned calls for military force or stern legislation because it believed that they were unnecessary. Commerce and technology, embodied in the Pacific Railroad, would soon liberate previously isolated

Mormons by bringing them "a stream of penetrating and disenchanting light."[95]

Yet such optimism, if expedient for some, was pervasive in the immediate postbellum period. John Beadle found the future of the Mormon Church, as an autocratic institution, to be inherently doomed in a democratic society. Mormon religion could only persist because of the "previous mental slavery" of its followers and could not thrive amid "free institutions and free thought."[96] Like Beadle, *Frank Leslie's* believed that the Mormon merging of church and state could not survive contact with outsiders, and like the *Times* it believed that the Pacific Railroad would soon inundate Utah with non-Mormons. But instead of merely dissolving, *Frank Leslie's* thought that Brigham Young would direct his persevering followers to escape with their substantial financial resources and establish an "independent Polynesian polygamic kingdom or empire" in the Pacific, where Mormon missionaries already had a presence.[97] Noting that "Mormonism must soon give way before the advancing tide of American civilization," Catherine Waite also contemplated a Mormon exodus to the Pacific.[98] Samuel Bowles, however, had disavowed such an idea as early as 1865. "Ultimately," claimed Bowles, "before the influences of emigration, civilization and our democratic habits, an organization so aristocratic and autocratic as the Mormon church now is must modify its rule." First to go would be its "most aristocratic and uncivilized incident or feature of plurality of wives," broken down by the arrival of "mails, daily papers, railroads and telegraphs." Although "A kingdom in the sea" might perpetuate polygamy temporarily, "commerce and democracy would ultimately follow it" there too. Already, Bowles heard the "click of the telegraph and the roll of the overland stages" sounding polygamy's "death-rattle." Within a matter of years, he claimed, "the first whistle of the locomotive will sound its requiem; and the pick-ax of the miner will dig its grave."[99]

Ultimately, Republicans might compromise on the means as long as they achieved their ends. One English traveler, William Hepworth Dixon, recorded his attempts to convince a handful of militantly anti-Mormon Republicans that, when it came to matters of conscience, persuasion was preferable to coercion. Pressed, one of his Republican interlocutors, with manifest confidence, brought the conversation to an end: "Well, while we are divided in opinion, perhaps, as to the use of physical force, we are all in favor of moral force. . . . Union is our motto, equality our creed. Boston and Salt Lake must be got to shake hands, as

Boston and Charleston have already done. If you can persuade Brigham to lie down with Bowles, I am willing to see it. . . . And now pass the wine."[100]

Black Mormons and Democratic Apologists

Northern Republican commentary about Mormon Utah prompted a variety of responses that, if more limited in scope, were still telling in their range. Some found room to poke fun at northern Republicans' crusading zeal while others wrote with venom. Northern Democrats and ex-Confederates in particular offered varied responses, sometimes critiquing northern Republicans for imposing their values on others and sometimes treating the Mormon religion as a symptom of northern fanaticism. Often, Democrats turned northern Republican rhetoric on its head, alleging that it was now-unregulated "Negroes," not slaveholders, who were the South's polygamists.

Mark Twain, always more a public wit than a politico, treated northern Republicans' reforming zeal as a cause for humor. During Reconstruction, Twain published *Roughing It,* an account of his time out West during the Civil War, which included a two-day visit to Salt Lake City. Twain drolly described how, like others, he arrived in Salt Lake City ready to crusade against polygamy by getting "up the usual statistics and deductions preparatory to calling the attention of the nation at large once more to the matter." "With the gushing self-sufficiency of youth," he readied himself to plunge into the work of reform. Then, however, he saw the Mormon women, who he considered to be such "poor, ungainly and pathetically 'homely' creatures" that he could not help but that think that Mormon husbands deserved applause for their charity. Parodying the dramatic language of some reformers, Twain added that, if the Mormon husband deserved acclaim, then the "man that marries sixty of [these women] has done a deed of open-handed generosity so sublime that the nations should stand uncovered in his presence and worship in silence."[101] With his rare comedic dexterity, Twain used a simple joke about one group's physical appearance to invite readers to have a self-effacing laugh at their own moral conceits.

Others were more partisan in their efforts to debunk northern Republican rhetoric. John Codman, the same merchant who referenced Du Chaillu at the end of his travel narrative of coastal Brazil, wrote what was perhaps the most detailed and provocative postbellum defense of Mormon society in the Great Basin. Codman, like many others who wrote about the Mormons in the 1870s, visited Utah by rail as part of a trip to the West. But Codman eschewed the standard itinerary, which he described as consisting of priming oneself on anti-Mormon writings and spending a half-day in Salt Lake City viewing a handful of landmarks.[102] Instead, Codman devoted three months to traveling the Great Basin by horse, mule, and wagon, in the process lodging, dining, and socializing with Mormons, apostates, and Gentiles. Though he made light fun of polygamy and some Mormon beliefs—suggesting at one point that Mormon revelations were brought on by indigestion—he found most Republican anti-Mormon rhetoric fanciful.[103] Some things remained a mystery to Codman, including how a shrewd man like Brigham Young could come to Mormonism in his thirties.[104] On the whole, however, he found the Mormons to be cheerful and kindhearted hosts, upstanding citizens, and sincere believers who served God in their own way despite persecution.[105]

Codman also challenged popular critiques of Mormon polygamy and theocracy. Polygamy was, he gladly conceded, backward and unnatural, but it was not as horrible as commonly represented and was best if left to die off on its own.[106] Despite what some apostates claimed, Codman argued, many Mormon women and children, including those he visited and dined with, were happy in polygamous households, which were not as common as many thought anyway.[107] Brigham Young and the Church leadership did direct the energies of a reverential following, but with pragmatism and a commendable willingness to take part in the daily labors.[108] The Mormon Church, Codman added, had ceased persecuting apostates, schismatic groups, and nonbelievers, welcomed non-Mormon denominations into the territory, and treated Native Americans humanely.[109] As he concluded his volume, he went so far as to claim that "in all my voyages and travels about the world, I never before passed three months in a country more industrious, upright, honest in dealing among themselves and with others, quiet, inoffensive, loyal to government, temperate, virtuous, and religious than the Mormons."[110]

Codman was perfectly aware that his mixed but generally positive evaluations of Mormon Utah would, if noticed, garner criticism. Indeed, Codman opened his volume by noting that one "prominent literary magazine" had refused to publish his work because "it was too impartial."

Likewise, the closing lines of his volume welcomed what he anticipated would be criticism from Gentiles and Mormons. "Both verdicts," he believed would serve "as proofs of the impartiality claimed for the book."[111] Codman's book slipped under the radar of most northern Republicans, in part perhaps due to low sales.[112] Codman did, however, elicit criticism from the anti-Mormon *Salt Lake Tribune* for his continuing efforts to uphold the public reputation of the Mormons.[113]

The eagerness of northern Republicans to oversee the abolition of this other peculiar institution also prompted a qualified defense from at least one southern paper. In one wide-ranging editorial that touched on race, states' rights, and the degenerate character of the North, the *Memphis Daily Avalanche* both distanced itself from the Mormons and yet defended their right to manage their own domestic institutions. In the *Avalanche*'s embittered words, the North "is restless without *progress,* even though this may not be *improvement.* Her passion is, not to do what she ought, but to *teach others* to do what *they* ought to do. She is intolerant: hence her meddling with all the domestic relations and laws of other States. She would have the world look through her glasses, though mouldy with prejudice and conceit."[114] Lest we think that the *Avalanche* completely missed the mark, four years later Frederick Douglass's *New National Era* in essence conceded the point and then dismissed its significance. Tolerance, the *New National Era* argued, was a virtue when it came to "other people's opinions, creeds, actions, and habits." "If," the paper explained, "the Mormon believes that Salt Lake City will rise some fine day with all that is in it . . . and go right up to heaven, we are quite willing to let him rejoice in the prospect." But, the paper continued, toleration was no virtue when claimed for white supremacist perpetrators like those in the Democratic Party, which was guilty of "murder, robbery, treason, dishonesty, and fraud."[115] Douglass understood well the subtext of Democratic defenses of the Mormons' right to autonomy, seeking as they were to defend slavery's former existence and recreate something close to it.

In other cases, Democrats shared a disdain for Mormon polygamy and the power of the Church hierarchy. Such was the case when the *Memphis Daily Appeal,* one of the *Avalanche*'s local Democratic rivals, considered the 1874 Poland Bill. On the one hand, the *Appeal* thought that the bill, which would prevent polygamists from serving on juries and in civil offices in the territory, was reminiscent of Military

Reconstruction and would lead to the same results. With the majority of "intelligent" citizens removed from power, loyal but corrupt outsiders would take over the government and exploit and ruin the rest of society. Yet, the *Appeal* also found polygamy and Brigham Young to be odious, and pointed out that if religious freedom extended to otherwise unlawful acts, society would be thrown into anarchy. What if, the editorial asked, "The Africans," meaning African Americans, were allowed to establish in the South "that kind of fetishism which murders children."[116] Much like the *New National Era*, the *Appeal* concluded that toleration had to have limits, but here for the sake of condemning pro–civil rights legislation. The *Charleston Daily News* also used debates about antipolygamy legislation to both rebuke Mormons and take a shot at radical Reconstruction. The paper argued that Mormonism was contrary to Christianity and the law, but added that it would collapse if left on its own and advised that persecution had always strengthened it in the past. But if Congress were to pass a new antipolygamy law, it suggested, it should make Utah a military district send there "a few thousand Southern negroes . . . as controlling citizens." "If these things will not cause Mormonism to collapse," the paper concluded, "nothing will."[117]

Some Democrats attempted to harness the Mormons' popular negative associations to their own polemical ends. *The Star of the North* of Columbia County, Pennsylvania, ran a short satire of Union League Clubs in which one resolved to abolish education, make women men, make black people white, and grant "Free Lovers, Mormons, Shakers, and soldiers" their rights.[118] Often, Democratic publications went a step further and linked freedpeople, who were allegedly lapsing into barbarism, to Mormons as fellow polygamists.[119] The *Memphis Daily Appeal* offered one cryptic notice explaining that grand juries in Texas were "after the Mormon negroes in that state."[120] The *Public Ledger*, yet another Democratic paper in Memphis, argued that northern Republicans had set themselves up for a bureaucratic nightmare by granting pensions to Union soldiers' widows. "It never occurred to the sapient philosophers of the Radical school," commented that paper, "that when the negro was turned into a warrior he took a new wife almost every week, and became a splendid sort of Mormon."[121] The *Columbia Herald* of Tennessee offered a brief notice of a "negro fight" caused by Mormonism, meaning adultery.[122] The *Fairfield Herald* of South Carolina reported that a local black vigilante group was targeting polygamous African

Americans "who were emulating Brigham Young and the Sultan of Turkey." Such policing efforts appeared futile, argued the paper, because there were too many African American polygamists.[123] When, in 1870, the *Stark County Democrat* of Ohio caught word that Mormon polygamists had been denied the right to naturalized citizenship, it mocked the recent Fifteenth Amendment by asking if the same should not hold for "a Negro and Chinese Poligamist" [*sic*].[124] Such claims made it to the zenith of political rhetoric, warranting frequent mention, for example, in the controversial speeches of Francis P. Blair Jr. in his 1868 campaign as the Democratic vice presidential candidate.[125]

Democratic arguments appealed to some racially conservative Unionists, including no doubt some Republicans. One scalawag paper, the *Nashville Union and Dispatch,* for example, described an African American whose wife caught him with another woman as "A Negro Mormon."[126] Likewise, the conservative former Union general Jonathan Tarbell, resident in Mississippi, argued that "Mormonism is fitly compared to the depravity of the blacks," who he also described as thieving, ignorant, and incompetent.[127] But arguments that African Americans were practicing polygamists also met with Republican rebukes. Already by 1865, some Republican papers were mocking such Democratic claims. The *Chicago Tribune,* for example, asserted that the Democratic *New York World* had it all wrong when it claimed freedpeople, if allowed to vote, would convert to Mormonism. If anyone was to convert, countered the *Tribune,* it would be the former slaveholders, who had just lost their own system of concubinage.[128]

Conclusion

It took until the Poland Act of 1874 for northern Republicans to follow up on their previous legislative act concerning Mormon Utah, the Morrill Anti-Bigamy Act of 1862. That long delay reflected many factors, including a belief among many northern Republicans that such legislation was unnecessary. The forces of America's republican civilization were already marching forward under their own power, many thought, and would inevitably compel the Mormon Church to abandon its despotic leanings and barbaric form of family life. Much as Carleton, Fogg, and the Sewards tended to believe that commerce and technology were uniting the world together and thereby advancing the forces of freedom and progress, many northern Republicans believed that in modern times Mormon Utah could not long remain isolated. Once better integrated into the rest of the nation, America's republican civilization would triumph there. Yet, much as these travelers also had their moments of doubt, there were many who believed that Mormon barbarism and despotism would ultimately require some form of coercion, whether legal or martial, to be defeated.

That same long delay also witnessed and took shape from the fraying of the northern Republican hegemony in federal politics and culture. The developing industrial economy of the North, driven by precisely those technologies that were supposed to unify the nation and the world in a common prosperity, had created deep class divisions, staggering concentrations of wealth, and new levels of political corruption. These emerging Gilded Age issues both divided many northern Republicans against each other and increasingly crowded out public discussion about Reconstruction's dual challenges of how to remake the nation and how to remake the South. Many of the party's more moderate members, moreover, believed Reconstruction's twin policy crises had met with adequate resolution.[129] In 1873, the industrializing economy of the United States would enter into a severe depression and in November of 1874, just months after the Poland Act became law, Republicans would suffer crushing defeats in congressional elections. The Republican Party held a thin majority in the Senate but lost control of the House, denying Republicans the ability to pass the kind of sweeping legislation that had marked the apogee of their power in the late 1860s. As white supremacists mounted increasingly brazen attacks on the South's fledgling interracial democracy, the postbellum northern Republican hegemony in federal politics and culture came to an end. Their reforming impulse itself did not disappear, and northern Republicans, with some Democratic support, would eventually coerce the Mormon leadership into suspending polygamy. But the giddy optimism of the postbellum years would give way to a less confident view of the world that had greater doubts about whether freedom and progress would span the globe together.

Conclusion

When Peter K. Cole arrived at Yokohama, Japan, no later than May of 1867, he was one of only a handful of African Americans in the small, relatively isolated foreign enclave that the Sewards would lament three years later. Perhaps encountering prejudice and discrimination in the United States had inured Cole to social isolation in ways that made him comfortable with the challenges of living abroad, for he was a seasoned traveler. In an earlier voyage, he had traveled to the Old World for seven years, spending much of his time in China and Japan and learning to speak and write Japanese. Cole, about whom we unfortunately know little, likely decided to return, or at least to return when he did, because of the inauguration of regular steamship traffic across the Pacific in 1867.[1] While in Japan, he wrote a series of letters to Philip Bell's *Elevator* in San Francisco. If mostly concerned with local business and industry, Cole also took time to reflect on the forces reshaping Japanese society.[2]

Cole was strikingly optimistic. He saw tremendous promise for a world united by commerce and technology, especially with America in the lead. "American commerce, ideas, and inventions," he believed, would have already formed the leading edge of progress in Japan had it not been for the Civil War. With Japan now connected to the United States through regular steamship traffic, the Japanese had become smitten with the "industry, perseverance and prolific inventive genius of the American people."[3] Once they recovered from their wonder, Cole believed, the Japanese would, thanks to American influence, emerge as "the leading country of the East."[4] Reacting to the arrival of the Pacific Mail Steamship *China* in Yokohama, Cole gushed of Americans, "Oh! what a people; what a progress," and looked to a future when a still more magnificent, humanitarian, and free America had united the world together.[5]

To sustain such optimism, Cole had to come to terms with the antiforeign violence that Europeans and Americans encountered in Japan. When eleven French sailors were massacred after making landfall, Cole did exactly this. Believing the attack to be "horrible" and "atrocious" and of a kind all too common in Japan, Cole admitted that it seemed to call for "speedy and summary vengeance" from the western powers. Yet Cole also urged caution, pointing out that westerners had only recently arrived in Japan, whose people had an insular culture built around strict obedience to the land's ruler. Indeed, there was already evidence of change, with commoners opening up to trade and gradually embracing western views despite the dangers of doing so. It was this change, he believed, that so frightened Japanese elites and prompted them to confront westerners with violence. It was, he thought, "The impossibility of stopping the onward march of civilization," which would in time bring equality between "prince and peasant," that so animated Japan's ruling caste. Such violence therefore suggested not Japanese hostility to change but the impending collapse of the country's feudal order and the complete opening of Japan to the influences of western civilization.[6]

Yet that same inevitability also had a darker side. Cole took it for granted that some peoples, and not just hidebound aristocrats, would lose out before the onward march of progress. When the Japanese government, upon the request of resident Europeans and Americans, opened already settled and cultivated lands for public auction only to see them grabbed up by speculators, Cole seemed reconciled to the inescapable nature of the outcome. As he noted: "the native here, like the poor Indian of America, must leave the spot of his childhood and the land his forefathers tilled from time immemorial, to make room for the European civilization which while it enriches at the same time impoverishes."[7] If increasing equality would form a part of the onward march of civilization, so too would dispossession for those who stood in its way.

These two sides of Cole's view of the triumph of progress encapsulate a central tension in northern Republican thought. One side of his thinking had progress as an enlightening force that was inextricably linked to the advance of freedom at home and abroad. Technology and commerce would bring the distant corners of the world into deepening contact with the advancing spirit of the nineteenth century, exemplified by a purified America. This, by itself, would break apart the hierarchical relationships that mired Japan in a feudal past. It could have been Carleton writing about India, Bowles about Utah, Douglass on the Vatican, or Stillman about Crete. Freedom and progress were in harmony with each other. Where one went, so went the other. The only way to stop the advance of progress among a people was to oppress them. The only way to keep a people unfree was to isolate them from the forces of progress.

The other side of Cole's view of the inevitable march of progress hinted at a different course for history. If the onward march of civilization was inevitable, what would happen to those who failed to embrace it or, in the case of the Japanese near Yokohama, were simply in the wrong place at the wrong historical moment? Here, Cole maintained a critical perspective. He expressed sympathy for the dispossessed and argued for the imperfect nature of European, meaning here "western," civilization. Even so, he did not dwell on the injustices done so much as state them as a matter of fact. Many northern Republicans would lack Cole's discerning eye, and among them the same faith in the inevitability of progress could not only dampen sympathy but produce contempt for and outrage at those who seemed to stand in the way.

Northern Republicans' postbellum faith in the onward march of civilization could both bolster and undermine hopes for the universal enjoyment of republican freedom. In its optimistic version, the natural harmony between civilization and republicanism promised to unite the world's people in the forward march of history. Adhering to this view did not necessarily require a belief in the complete equality of all races, cultures, religions, or nations. Indeed, it typically presumed that the most backward peoples of the world would change the most, losing much of what made them distinctive. In the pessimistic version, the inability of some of the world's peoples, perhaps most, to embrace the changes required by progress meant that they had little hope of ever being free, if they even managed to survive well into the future. This pessimistic version of northern Republican thought offered a different dystopian vision from the one Democrats had espoused after emancipation, in which liberated "Africans" threatened to drown the region in barbarism. Both saw little grounds for hope for the backward peoples of the world, but one centered on a vision of progress as an unstoppable force and the other on impending cataclysm.

Historians have long pondered the conundrums of postbellum politics. How could the same northern Republicans who destroyed slavery and expanded civil and political rights in the South turn their backs on African Americans just a few years later, and right as southern white supremacists were waging their most brazen campaigns of terror? How could the same party that destroyed slavery orchestrate a series of lengthy wars against Native Americans in the western states and territories? Examining Reconstruction's world underscores a crucial point about postbellum northern Republicans. Along with their Democratic foes, they believed in historically transcendent struggles for civilization and republicanism and in the organization of humanity into distinctive peoples with their own characters. While they believed in according rights to individuals, they still judged those individuals as members of putatively coherent groups, whose fates they could not evaluate without reference to the idea of progress. To speak of a people enjoying freedom made little sense to northern Republicans outside of that people's ability to embrace and promote civilization. In this way, northern Republican's faith in any of the world's peoples, including Mormons, African Americans, Irish Catholics, Chinese immigrants, southern whites, and Native Americans, was intrinsically fickle. The same giddy optimism about the triumph of freedom and progress could slide into doubt about the ability of any one people to make progress and to therefore benefit from freedom.

Already by the early 1870s, Reconstruction's two issues—how to remake the Union and how to remake the South—were beginning to exercise less control over federal politics. Other issues, including wars with Native Americans in the arid West, political corruption, the money issue, and class conflict were increasingly demanding attention. Many northern Republicans who had an at best tepid commitment to racial equality had good reason to believe that Reconstruction's two issues had found adequate resolution and that the country was ready to move forward to other concerns. When the economy entered a prolonged and severe recession in 1873, it further marginalized Reconstruction's issues in federal politics. To say that this development "ended" Reconstruction presumes that it was a unitary historical thing with a clear beginning and end instead of a polysemous name for two interconnected, evolving conflicts that different partisans breathed life into as they argued over who they and others were. As late as the 1960s, southern white supremacists were still describing themselves as "unreconstructed" as they defied federal attempts to support African American civil rights.[8] In that sense, Reconstruction's issues of national reunification and the transformation of the South never completely disappeared, and in fact periodically moved back to the fore of federal politics, most obviously during the contested election of 1876. In the South, these issues remained at the front and center of politics, although the grounds of contestation shifted dramatically through the triumph of white supremacist violence and chicanery over the electoral process.

What did end, however, was the postbellum northern Republican hegemony in federal politics and the exuberance that had come with it. This break in their power, along with a new sense of national crisis over issues of class, corruption, and the economy, reoriented and changed the tenor of federal politics. Northern Republicans who had earlier anticipated the universal triumph of republicanism and civilization drifted toward concern over the unchanging nature of Chinese immigrants, Native Americans, and Mormons in the West, African Americans in the South, and Catholic immigrants in the North and Midwest. Southern white supremacists and northern Democrats gradually, if never completely, turned away from their rhetoric of an impending racial apocalypse and toward one that presented whites as the natural protectors of a restricted freedom and the promoters of commercial and industrial progress. Reconstruction's world faded from view as new worlds—part imagined, part real—developed around the political fault lines of the Gilded Age and Jim Crow. Democrats and northern Republicans, although still deeply divided against each other, could now often understand each other's concerns about whether all the world's peoples were really capable of both civilization and republicanism and whether freedom and progress were not often at odds with each other. Against and through that intermittent consensus, members of allegedly coherent and distinctive groups at home and, increasingly, abroad would make claims about themselves as peoples.

Notes

Introduction

1. No title, *Memphis Daily Avalanche,* April 9, 1867, 2; Marius Carriere, "An Irresponsible Press: Memphis Newspapers and the 1866 Riot," *Tennessee Historical Quarterly* 60, no. 1 (spring 2001): 2–15; Stephen V. Ash, *A Massacre in Memphis: The Race Riot That Shook the Nation One Year After the Civil War* (New York: Hill and Wang, 2013), 37.

2. No title, *Memphis Daily Avalanche,* April 9, 1867, 2.

3. When referring collectively to the various groups contending over Reconstruction, this volume prefers the term "Reconstruction's partisans" to the more common "Americans" for two reasons. First, while certainly most politically engaged people living within the United States were concerned about Reconstruction, many were not; see David Herbert Donald, Jean Harvey Baker, and Michael F. Holt, *The Civil War and Reconstruction,* 3rd ed. (New York: Norton, 2001), 480–81. Likewise, some who resided in the United States and who were concerned with Reconstruction were very recent immigrants who may or may not have identified as "American." A familiar catch-all term, "American" can also be imprecise. Second, there is a broader conceptual debate about the ontological status of nations and ethnicities. Do national designations like "American" refer to actual, specific, stable groups of people that exist and act in the world as groups? Or are such populations products of perception, constituting only passing, contested figments of our collective imaginations? For an introduction to this debate, see Rogers Brubaker, *Nationalism Reframed: Nationhood and the National Question in the New Europe* (New York: Cambridge Univ. Press, 1996), 13–22; Rogers Brubaker, "Ethnicity without Groups," *European Journal of Sociology* 43, no. 2 (2002): 163–89; and Zsuzsa Csergo, "Review Essay: Do We Need a Language Shift in the Study of Nationalism and Ethnicity? Reflections on Rogers Brubaker's Critical Scholarly Agenda," *Nations and Nationalism* 14, no. 2 (April 2008): 393–98. In the context of this methodological dispute, the term "Reconstruction's partisans" provides an analytical vantage point that is outside of debates, prominent in the nineteenth century and now, over who is American and why. In that sense, "Reconstruction's partisans" is not only more precise than "Americans," but it also serves to extricate our own terms of analysis from debates over national identity, which are here a subject of analysis. My intent is, as I hope is clear, not to downplay the importance of citizenship and suffrage, which were in ways national, but to avoid the ambiguities that come with invoking national labels like "American" too cavalierly. I do at times refer to putatively coherent groups of people, including national groups, but typically when discussing matters of perception and self-perception. There are a few cases in this volume where referencing an actor's own categories of difference has seemed the only quick way to situate that person in social and political context. Political affiliation represents a special case of group identity

since parties had internal networks undergirding their communities. I take them, at least in the context of this study, to be more reliable means of identifying historical actors than nationality, especially since the Republican and Democratic parties were so deeply divided against each other during the pivotal years of Reconstruction policy-making. Party labels do warrant qualification, in part because political parties in the United States were and are coalitional by nature. This is especially true of the Republican Party when it comes to the politics of Reconstruction, where a persistently complicated relationship existed between its northern and southern wings. For this reason, I usually refer to "northern Republicans," "freedpeople," and other more specific terms instead of simply "Republicans." With Democrats, a shared commitment to white supremacy and political necessity rapidly smoothed over differences concerning the sectional conflict, rendering a fairly unified front in Reconstruction politics. In the context of this study, lumping northern and southern Democrats together under a single label often makes sense. Such categories of course do not fully encompass or fully describe Reconstruction's partisans.

4. No title, *Memphis Daily Avalanche,* April 9, 1867, 2.

5. Eric Foner et al., "Eric Foner's 'Reconstruction' at Twenty-Five," *Journal of the Gilded Age and Progressive Era* 14, no. 1 (January 2015): 13–27, 25; and Gregory P. Downs and Kate Masur, "Introduction: Echoes of War: Rethinking Post–Civil War Governance and Politics," in *The World the Civil War Made,* ed. Gregory P. Downs and Kate Masur (Chapel Hill: Univ. of North Carolina Press, 2015), 1–21, 3.

6. See Elliott West, "Reconstructing Race," *Western Historical Quarterly* 34, no. 1 (February 2003): 6–26; Heather Cox Richardson, "Reconstruction and the Nation," in *A Companion to the Civil War and Reconstruction,* ed. Lacy Ford (Malden, Mass.: Blackwell, 2005), 447–67; and Heather Cox Richardson, "North and West of Reconstruction: Studies in Political Economy," in *Reconstructions: New Perspectives on the Postbellum United States,* ed. Thomas J. Brown (New York: Oxford Univ. Press, 2006): 66–90.

7. See especially O. Vernon Burton, David Herr, and Matthew Cheney, "Defining Reconstruction," in *A Companion to the Civil War and Reconstruction,* ed. Lacy Ford (Malden, Mass.: Blackwell, 2005), 299–322.

8. See especially Mark Wahlgren Summers, *The Ordeal of the Reunion: A New History of Reconstruction* (Chapel Hill: Univ. of North Carolina Press, 2014), 1–5, 11, 13–14, 17, 395–96.

9. Downs and Masur, "Introduction," 4–5.

10. On these trends, in addition to the essays by West and Richardson above, see for example Heather Cox Richardson, *West from Appomattox: The Reconstruction of America after the Civil War* (New Haven, Conn.: Yale Univ. Press, 2007); Elliott West, *The Last Indian War: The Nez Perce Story* (New York: Oxford Univ. Press, 2009); Joshua Paddison, *American Heathens: Religion, Race, and Reconstruction in California* (Berkeley: Univ. of California Press, 2012); and Edlie L. Wong, *Racial Reconstruction: Black Inclusion, Chinese Exclusion, and the Fictions of Citizenship* (New York: New York Univ. Press, 2015).

11. For a fuller exploration of this topic, see David Prior, "Reconstruction, from Transatlantic Polyseme to Historiographical Quandary," in *Reconstruction in a Globalizing World,* ed. David Prior (New York: Fordham Univ. Press, 2018), 172–208. See, for example, "The Reconstruction of Poland," *Living Age,* April 28, 1855, 195–201; "Monthly Record of Current Events," *Harper's New Monthly Magazine,* June 1855, 112–16, 115; "The Reconstruction of Poland," *Western Democrat,* November 24, 1854; "Reestablishment of the Kingdom of Poland," *Ashland Union,* November 8, 1854.

12. See, for example, "Military Crisis in Europe," *Living Age,* March 15, 1851, 518–28,

527; "Mr. Cottle and His Friends," *Harper's New Monthly Magazine*, December 1853, 68–76, 76; Henry Smales, "French Revolution: M. Louis Blanc," *American Whig Review*, July 1848, 90–100, 97; "Social Reforms," *New Englander*, August 1850, 452–70.

13. See, for example, "Fatuity of Mr. Seward," *Liberator*, March 15, 1861, 42; Abraham Lincoln, "Proclamation of Amnesty and Reconstruction," in *The Collected Works of Abraham Lincoln*, ed. Roy P. Blaser (New Brunswick, N.J.: Rutgers Univ. Press, 1953), 7:53–56; Lincoln's message on his pocket veto of the Wade-Davis bill, in Blaser, ed., *The Collected Works of Abraham Lincoln*, 7:433; "The Last Public Address," in Blaser, ed., *The Collected Works of Abraham Lincoln*, 7:400–401; Andrew Johnson, "Amnesty Proclamation," in *The Papers of Andrew Johnson*, ed. Paul Bergeron (Knoxville: Univ. of Tennessee Press, 1989), 8:128–31, especially 8:128–29; Andrew Johnson, "Proclamation Establishing Government for North Carolina," in Bergeron, ed., *The Papers of Andrew Johnson*, 8:136–38, especially 8:137; and see *Report of the Joint Committee on Reconstruction at the First Session Thirty-Ninth Congress* (Washington, D.C.: Government Printing Office, 1866), viii–xiv, xvi, xviii, xx, xxi.

14. See, for example, "The New York Herald Gives Up for Seymour and Blair," *Lincoln County Herald*, September 3, 1868, 2; "Heraldiana," *Nashville Union and Dispatch*, August 18, 1868, 2; "The Presidential Campaign," *Democratic Enquirer*, September 3, 1868, 3; *Charleston Daily News*, August 23, 1867, 2; "The Situation at the South," *Charleston Daily News*, October 8, 1869, 2.

15. The existing literature on the nineteenth-century United States sheds little light on this belief as a popular phenomenon; helpful is Dorothy Ross, "Historical Consciousness in Nineteenth-Century America," *American Historical Review* 89, no. 4 (1984): 909–28.

16. Existing scholarship demonstrates well the importance of the idea of a historical struggle between republicanism on the one hand and despotism/aristocracy and anarchy on the other to Reconstruction's politics. See especially Mitchell Snay, "The Imagined Republic: The Fenians, Irish American Nationalism, and the Political Culture of Reconstruction," *Proceedings of the American Antiquarian Society* 112 (2002): 291–313; Andrew Slap, *The Doom of Reconstruction: The Liberal Republicans in the Civil War Era* (New York: Fordham Univ. Press, 2006); Charles W. Calhoun, *Conceiving a New Republic: The Republican Party and the Southern Question, 1869–1900* (Lawrence: Univ. Press of Kansas, 2006); Patrick J. Kelly, "The North American Crisis of the 1860s," *Journal of the Civil War Era* 2, no. 3 (September 2012): 337–68. There is relatively little Reconstruction-focused scholarship on the putative struggle between civilization and barbarism/savagery, but helpful works covering the postbellum decade include Frank Ninkovich, *Global Dawn: The Cultural Foundation of American Internationalism, 1865–1890* (Cambridge, Mass.: Harvard Univ. Press, 2009); Gordon H. Chang, "Whose 'Barbarism'? Whose 'Treachery'? Race and Civilization in the Unknown United States-Korean War of 1871," *Journal of American History* 89, no. 4 (March 2003): 1331–65; Jay Sexton, "William Seward in the World," *Journal of the Civil War Era* 4, no. 3 (September 2014): 398–430; Timothy Verhoeven, "Transatlantic Connections: American Anti-Catholicism and the First Vatican Council (1869–1870)," *Catholic Historical Review* 100, no. 4 (autumn 2014): 695–720.

17. On the longer history of the concept of civilization and barbarism, see especially Raymond Williams, *Keywords: A Vocabulary of Culture and Society*, rev. ed. (New York: Oxford Univ. Press, 1985), 57–60; Gerrit W. Gong, *The Standard of "Civilization" in International Society* (New York: Oxford Univ. Press, 1984); Bruce Mazlish, *Civilization and Its Contents* (Stanford, Calif.: Stanford Univ. Press, 2004); and Brett Bowden, *The Empire of Civilization: The Evolution of an Imperial Idea* (Chicago: Univ. of Chicago Press, 2009). For the relationship between civilization and ideas about race, commerce, and technology, see

Ronald Takaki, "The Tempest in the Wilderness: The Racialization of Savagery," *Journal of American History* 79, no. 3 (December 1992): 892–912; Gregory D. Smithers, "The 'Pursuit of the Civilized Man': Race and the Meaning of Civilization in the United States and Australia, 1790s–1850s," *Journal of World History* 20, no. 2 (June 2009): 245–72; Philip Gould, *Barbaric Traffic: Commerce and Antislavery in the 18th Century Atlantic World* (Cambridge, Mass.: Harvard Univ. Press, 2003); Michael Adas, *Dominance by Design: Technological Imperatives and America's Civilizing Mission* (Cambridge, Mass.: Belknap Press of Harvard Univ. Press, 2006). The literature on the history of the concept of republicanism and these topics is too vast to cite here.

18. On protean nature of the concept of civilization, see Ninkovich, *Global Dawn*, 18–19; and Bowden, *Empire of Civilization*, 24–25, 26–34. On the broader history of contested keywords in politics in the United States, see Daniel T. Rodgers, *Contested Truths: Keywords in American Politics since Independence* (New York: Basic Books, 1987).

19. On civilization's meaning as both a stage and process of development, see Williams, *Keywords*, 57–60; Bowden, *Empire of Civilization*, 28. On the relation between progress and civilization, see Bowden, *Empire of Civilization*, 44–69. On the evolution of the idea of progress, see Charles Van Doren, *The Idea of Progress* (New York: Praeger, 1967), and Arthur Alphonse Ekirch, *The Idea of Progress in America, 1815–1860* (New York: Peter Smith, 1951).

20. On views of Native Americans, see Roy Harvey Pearce, *The Savages of North America: A Study of the Indian and the Idea of Civilization* (Baltimore: Johns Hopkins Univ. Press, 1965); and Walter L. Williams, "The United States Indian Policy and the Debate over Philippine Annexation: Implications for the Origins of American Imperialism," *Journal of American History* 66 (1980): 810–31. On the Gilded Age, see especially David Axeen, "'Heroes of the Engine Room': American 'Civilization' and the War with Spain," *American Quarterly* 36, no. 4 (autumn 1984): 481–502; Frank Ninkovich, "Theodore Roosevelt: Civilization as Ideology," *Diplomatic History* 10, no. 3 (July 1986): 221–45; Gail Bederman, *Manliness and Civilization: A Cultural History of Gender and Race in the United States, 1880–1917* (Chicago: Univ. of Chicago Press, 1995); Joseph Henning, *Outposts of Civilization: Race, Religion, and the Formative Years of American-Japanese Relations* (New York: New York Univ. Press, 2000); Matthew Frye Jacobson, *Barbarian Virtues: The United States Encounters Foreign Peoples at Home and Abroad, 1876–1917* (New York: Hill and Wang, 2000); Daniel E. Bender, *American Abyss: Savagery and Civilization in the Age of Industry* (Ithaca, N.Y.: Cornell Univ. Press, 2009); David Sehat, "The Civilizing Mission of Booker T. Washington," *Journal of Southern History* 73, no. 2 (May 2007): 289–323; Ninkovich, *Global Dawn*; and Allison L. Sneider, *Suffragists in an Imperial Age: U.S. Expansionism and the Woman Question, 1870–1929* (New York: Oxford Univ. Press, 2008).

21. The following works review the scholarship addressing republicanism as a specific political ideology: Joyce Appleby, "Republicanism and Ideology," *American Quarterly* 37, no. 4 (autumn 1985): 461–73; Gordon S. Wood, "Ideology and the Origins of Liberal America," *William and Mary Quarterly* 44, no. 3 (July 1987): 628–40; James T. Kloppenberg, "The Virtues of Liberalism: Christianity, Republicanism, and Ethics in Early American Political Discourse," *Journal of American History* 74, no. 1 (June 1987): 9–33; and Daniel T. Rodgers, "Republicanism: The Career of a Concept," *Journal of American History* 79, no. 1 (June 1992): 11–38.

22. On liberalism's meaning, particularly helpful is Leslie Butler, *Critical Americans: Victorian Intellectuals and Transatlantic Liberal Reform* (Chapel Hill: Univ. of North Carolina Press, 2007), 8–11, and J. M. Opal, "The Labors of Liberality: Christian Benevolence and National Prejudice in the American Founding," *Journal of American History* 94, no. 4 (March 2008): 1082–1107.

23. On the ideas of despotism and aristocracy in the broader Civil War–era United States, see especially: James L. Huston, "The American Revolutionaries, the Political Economy of Aristocracy, and the American Concept of the Distribution of Wealth, 1765–1900," *American Historical Review* 98, no. 4 (October 1993): 1079–1105; Andre M. Fleche, *The Revolutions of 1861: The American Civil War in the Age of Nationalist Conflict* (Chapel Hill: Univ. of North Carolina Press, 2012); W. Caleb McDaniel, *The Problem of Democracy in the Age of Slavery: Garrisonian Abolitionists and Transatlantic Reform* (Baton Rouge: Louisiana State Univ. Press, 2013); and Don H. Doyle, *The Cause of All Nations: An International History of the American Civil War* (New York: Basic Books, 2015).

24. See Robert Bonner's comments in David M. Prior et al., "Teaching the Civil War in Global Context," *Journal of the Civil War Era* 5, no. 1 (March 2015): 97–125, especially 141–42.

25. On these figures, see especially Evan C. Rothera, "Our South American Cousin: Domingo F. Sarmiento and Education in Argentina and the United States," in Prior, ed., *Reconstruction in a Globalizing World*, 21–49; Peggy Lamson, *The Glorious Failure: Black Congressman Robert Brown Elliott and the Reconstruction in South Carolina* (New York: Norton, 1973); and Mischa Honeck, *We Are the Revolutionists: German-Speaking Immigrants and American Abolitionists after 1848* (Athens: Univ. of Georgia Press, 2011). On transatlantic discussions of these keywords, see also Robert L. Kelley, *The Transatlantic Persuasion: The Liberal-Democratic Mind in the Age of Gladstone* (New York: Knopf, 1969; reprint, New Brunswick, N.J.: Transaction Publishers, 1989); Fleche, *The Revolution of 1861*; McDaniel, *The Problem of Democracy in the Age of Slavery*; and Doyle, *The Cause of All Nations*.

26. Mia Bay, *The White Image in the Black Mind: African-American Ideas about White People, 1830–1925* (New York: Oxford Univ. Press, 2000), part 2. There is of course a much broader literature that is relevant to this topic, including the works cited in chapter 4 of this volume. In addition to Bay's work, see especially Elsa Barkley Brown, "Negotiating and Transforming the Public Sphere: African American Political Life in the Transition from Slavery to Freedom," *Public Culture* 7, no. 1 (January 1994): 107–46, and Kathleen Ann Clark, *Defining Moments: African American Commemoration and Political Culture in the South, 1863–1913* (Chapel Hill: Univ. of North Carolina Press, 2005).

27. The historical literature on the various components of the broader debate over the nature of civilization and republicanism is too extensive to cite here, but see especially Eugene D. Genovese, *The Slaveholders' Dilemma: Freedom and Progress in Southern Conservative Thought, 1820–1860* (Columbia: Univ. of South Carolina Press, 1992); Elizabeth Fox-Genovese and Eugene D. Genovese, *The Mind of the Master Class: History and Faith in the Southern Slaveholders' Worldview* (New York: Cambridge Univ. Press, 2005); and Mitchell Snay, "Freedom and Progress: The Dilemma of Southern Republican Thought during Radical Reconstruction," *American Nineteenth Century History* 5, no. 1 (2004): 100–114.

28. As with the broader debates about the nature of civilization and savagery, the scholarship on the contested nature of nineteenth-century notions of peoplehood is too extensive to cite here. For the Civil War era, see especially the several relevant works that focus on the interplay of national identity, racism, and sectionalism, including: Susan-Mary Grant, *North over South: Northern Nationalism and American Identity in the Antebellum Era* (Lawrence: Univ. Press of Kansas, 2000); Melinda Lawson, *Patriot Fires: Forging a New American Nationalism in the Civil War North* (Lawrence: Univ. Press of Kansas, 2002); Edward J. Blum, *Reforging the White Republic: Race, Religion, and American Nationalism, 1865–1898* (Baton Rouge: Louisiana State Univ. Press, 2005); and Cecilia O'Leary, *To Die For: The Paradox of American Patriotism* (Princeton, N.J.: Princeton Univ. Press, 1999).

29. On the history of the blurred boundaries between these categories of difference, see,

for example, Nicholas Hudson, "From 'Nation' to 'Race': The Origin of Racial Classification in Eighteenth-Century Thought," *Eighteenth-Century Studies* 29, no. 3 (spring 1996): 247–64; Robert H. Wiebe, *Who We Are: A History of Popular Nationalism* (Princeton, N.J.: Princeton Univ. Press, 2002), chapter 3; Jacobson, *Barbarian Virtues,* 152–53.

30. A number of insightful works have noted the eagerness with which Civil War–era Americans made border-crossing analogies, but no work has yet provided an overarching explanation for why they did so. See, for example, Philip M. Katz, *From Appomattox to Montmartre: Americans and the Paris Commune* (Cambridge, Mass.: Harvard Univ. Press, 1998), 85–117, and Paola Gemme, *Domesticating Foreign Struggles: The Italian Risorgimento and Antebellum American Identity* (Athens: Univ. of Georgia Press, 2005), 116–24.

31. See Paddison, *American Heathens*; Linda K. Kerber, "The Abolitionist Perception of the Indian," *Journal of American History* 62, no. 2 (September 1975): 271–95, especially, 288–89, 290, 292–93, 294; Hannah Gourey, "Poetics of Memory and Marginality: Images of the Native American in African-American Newspapers, 1870–1900 and 1970–1990," in *The Black Press: New Literary and Historical Essays,* ed. Todd Vogel (New Brunswick, N.J.: Rutgers Univ. Press, 2001), 104–22.

32. As Ronald G. Walters pointed out in *The Antislavery Appeal: American Abolitionism after 1830* (Baltimore: Johns Hopkins Univ. Press, 1976), abolitionists and antebellum defenders of slavery shared more in common with each other, including notions of civilization and nationhood, than they do with people in the present.

33. See Amy M. Thomas, "Literacies, Readers, and Cultures of Print in the South," in *A History of the Book in America,* ed. Scott E. Casper et al. (Chapel Hill: Univ. of North Carolina Press, 2007), 3:379–85, 386–87; John Nerone, "Newspapers in the Public Sphere," in *A History of the Book in America,* ed. Scott E. Casper et al. (Chapel Hill: Univ. of North Carolina Press, 2007), 3:238; Mark Wahlgren Summers, *The Press Gang: Newspapers and Politics, 1865–1878* (Chapel Hill: Univ. of North Carolina Press, 1994), 207–8; Jeffrey D. Groves, "Introduction" to chapter 7 of *A History of the Book in America,* ed. Scott E. Casper et al. (Chapel Hill: Univ. of North Carolina Press, 2007), 3:226–27.

34. On the plight of southern Republicans in the press, see Eric Foner, *Reconstruction: America's Unfinished Revolution, 1863–1877* (New York: Harper and Row, 1988), 300; Richard Abbott, *For Free Press and Equal Rights: Republican Newspapers in the Reconstruction South* (Athens: Univ. of Georgia Press, 2004), especially 71, which notes the concentration of southern Republican newspapers in districts with substantial numbers of African Americans and in a few upcountry regions; and Summers, *The Press Gang,* especially 5, 209, 214–21.

35. Nerone, "Newspapers in the Public Sphere," 246; Donna Harrington-Lueker, "Finding a Market for Suffrage: Advertising and *The Revolution,* 1868–1870," *Journalism History* 33, no. 3 (fall 2007): 130–39.

36. Barbara Sicherman, "Ideologies and Practices of Reading," in *A History of the Book in America,* ed. Scott Casper et al. (Chapel Hill: Univ. of North Carolina Press, 2007), 3:279–81, 291, 294–300; Louise Stevenson, "Homes, Books, and Reading," in *A History of the Book in America,* ed. Scott Casper et al. (Chapel Hill: Univ. of North Carolina Press, 2007), 3:320; Ronald Zboray, *A Fictive People: Antebellum Economic Development and the American Reading Public* (New York: Oxford Univ. Press, 1993), 158, 162–73.

37. Patricia Okker, *Our Sister Editors: Sarah Hale and the Tradition of Nineteenth-Century American Women Editors* (Athens: Univ. of Georgia Press, 1995), 6–37; Summers, *The Press Gang,* 199; "Gynecocracy," *Clayton Herald,* August 17, 1867, 1.

38. Richard Kaplan, "From Partisanship to Professionalism: The Transformation of the

Daily Press," in *A History of the Book in America*, vol. 4, *Print in Motion: The Expansion of Publishing and Reading in the United States, 1880–1940*, ed. Carl F. Kaestle and Janice A. Radway (Chapel Hill: Univ. of North Carolina Press, 2009), 116–39, underestimates the broad reach of the mid-nineteenth-century partisan press, but provides a helpful overview of the financial restraints facing working-class Americans; see especially 116, 120. On literacy rates and reading habits among the northern working class, see Michael Denning, *Mechanic Accents: Dime Novels and Working-Class Culture in America* (New York: Verso, 1987), 30–45. For an argument for the oppositional culture of working-class reading, see Jan Goggans, "What Workers Were Reading, 1830–1890," in *A History of American Working-Class Literature*, ed. Nicholas Coles and Paul Lauter (New York: Cambridge Univ. Press, 2017), 163–76.

39. Sicherman, "Ideologies and Practices of Reading," 279, 283–93.

40. Summers, *The Press Gang*, 12–14.

41. Ibid., 10, 12–13, 18–20; Elmo Scott Watson, *A History of Newspaper Syndicates in the United States, 1865–1935* (Chicago: [Watson], 1936); Charles Johanningsmeier, "Newspaper Syndicates of the Late Nineteenth Century: Overlooked Forces in the American Literary Market-Place," *Publishing History* 37 (1995): 61–82; Michael McGerr, *The Decline of Popular Politics: The American North, 1865–1928* (New York: Oxford Univ. Press, 1986), 107–37; Kaplan, "From Partisanship to Professionalism," 116–39.

42. We need book-length studies on both of these topics, but see Nerone, "Newspapers in the Public Sphere," 232, 239, 240–41, 244–48, and Summers, *The Press Gang*, 11.

43. Summers, *The Press Gang*, 11; Richard L. Kaplan, "The Economics and Politics of Nineteenth-Century Newspapers," *American Journalism* 10, no. 1–2 (winter–spring 1993): 84–101, 93–96.

44. Summers, *The Press Gang*, 9–10, 12.

45. Eric Lupfer, "The Business of American Magazines," in *A History of the Book in America*, ed. Scott E. Casper et al. (Chapel Hill: Univ. of North Carolina Press, 2007), 3:249–50; Susan Belasco, "The Cultural Work of National Magazines," in *A History of the Book in America*, ed. Scott E. Casper et al. (Chapel Hill: Univ. of North Carolina Press, 2007), 3:259–60; Ninkovich, *Global Dawn*, 16.

46. Zboray, *Fictive People*, 156–57, 173–78.

47. John McKivigan, *Forgotten Firebrand: James Redpath and the Making of Nineteenth-Century America* (Ithaca, N.Y.: Cornell Univ. Press, 2008), 118–27.

48. Scott E. Casper, "The Census, the Post Office, and Governmental Publishing," in *A History of the Book in America*, ed. Scott Casper et al. (Chapel Hill: Univ. of North Carolina Press, 2007), 3:178–79, 188, 191–92.

49. Michael Winship, "Distribution and the Trade," in *A History of the Book in America*, ed. Scott E. Casper et al. (Chapel Hill: Univ. of North Carolina Press, 2007), 3:117–18, 120–30; Casper, "The Census, the Post Office, and Governmental Publishing," 187; David M. Henkin, "City Streets and the Urban World of Print," in *A History of the Book in America*, ed. Scott E. Casper et al. (Chapel Hill: Univ. of North Carolina Press, 2007), 3:331–32, 334–35, 336–41; Zboray, *Fictive People*, 56, 58–59, 62–67.

50. Richard John, *Spreading the News: The American Postal System from Franklin to Morse* (Cambridge, Mass.: Harvard Univ. Press, 1995), 37–38; Casper, "The Census, the Post Office, and Governmental Publishing," 182–87; Summers, *The Press Gang*, 20; Ryan Cordell and David A. Smith, "Viral Texts: Mapping Networks of Reprinting in 19th-Century Newspapers and Magazines," http://viraltexts.org/ (accessed January 3, 2016); Ryan Cordell, "Reprinting, Circulation, and the Network Author in Antebellum Newspapers," *American Literary History* 27, no. 3 (fall 2015): 417–45.

51. Sicherman, "Ideologies and Practices of Reading," 296; Zboray, *Fictive People,* 72–75, 160; Summers, *The Press Gang,* 13; Stevenson, "Homes, Books, and Reading," 320, 324–29; Winship, "Distribution and the Trade," 129.

52. Kenneth E. Carpenter, "Libraries," in *A History of the Book in America,* ed. Scott E. Casper et al. (Chapel Hill: Univ. of North Carolina Press, 2007), 3:305–9, 311.

53. Lupfer, "The Business of American Magazines," 250–53, 256–57; Belasco, "The Cultural Work of National Magazines," 260; Winship, "Distribution and the Trade," 119–20; Stevenson, "Homes, Books, and Reading," 322–23.

54. Consider Sicherman, "Ideologies and Practices of Reading," 297.

55. For helpful introductions to and assessments of these developments as they pertain to scholarship on the United States, see Thomas Bender, ed., *Rethinking American History in a Global Age* (Berkeley: Univ. of California Press, 2002); Thomas Bender, *A Nation among Nations: America's Place in World History* (New York: Hill and Wang, 2006); Robert Gross, "The Transnational Turn: Rediscovering American Studies in a Wider World," *Journal of American Studies* 34, no. 3 (December 2000): 373–93; Peter Kolchin, "The South and the World," *Journal of Southern History* 75, no. 3 (August 2009): 565–80; Ian Tyrrell, "Reflections on the Transnational Turn in United States History: Theory and Practice," *Journal of Global History* 4, no. 3 (November 2009), 453–74; Rosemarie Zagarri, "The Significance of the 'Global Turn' for the Early American Republic: Globalization in the Age of Nation-Building," *Journal of the Early Republic* 31 (spring 2011): 1–37; Paul Kramer, "Power and Connection: Imperial Histories of the United States in the World," *American Historical Review* 116 (December 2011): 1348–91; David Prior, "After the Revolution: An Alternative Future for Atlantic History," *History Compass* 12, no. 3 (March 2014): 300–309.

56. For overviews of this literature, see David Armitage et al., "Interchange: Nationalism and Internationalism in the Era of the Civil War," *Journal of American History* 98, no. 2 (September 2011): 455–89; Don H. Doyle, "The Global Civil War," in *A Companion to the U.S. Civil War,* ed. Aaron Sheehan-Dean, 2 vols. (Malden, Mass.: Wiley-Blackwell, 2014), 2:1103–20; Emily Conroy-Kurtz et al., "Interchange: Globalization and Its Limits between the American Revolution and the Civil War," *Journal of American History* 103, no. 2 (September 2016): 400–433; Douglas Egerton, "Rethinking Atlantic Historiography in a Postcolonial Era: The Civil War in Global Perspective," *Journal of the Civil War Era* 1, no. 1 (2011): 79–95; David Quigley, "Emancipations, Empires, and Democracies," in *Globalizing American History: The AHA Guide to Re-Imagining the U.S. Survey Course,* ed. Peter Stearns and Noralee Frankel (Washington, D.C.: American Historical Association, 2008), 73–92; Jay Sexton, "Toward a Synthesis of Foreign Relations in the Civil War Era, 1848–1877," *American Nineteenth Century History* 5, no. 3 (2004): 50–77; Mark M. Smith, "The Past as a Foreign Country: Reconstruction, Inside and Out," in *Reconstructions: New Perspectives on the Postbellum United States,* ed. Thomas J. Brown (New York: Oxford Univ. Press, 2006), 117–40; David Prior, "Introduction," in Prior, ed., *Reconstruction in a Globalizing World,* 1–20. In addition to those works cited immediately below, the following exemplify this modern drive to "internationalize" the Civil War era: Chang, "Whose 'Barbarism'? Whose 'Treachery'?"; Jay Sexton, "The United States, the Cuban Rebellion, and the Multilateral Initiative of 1875," *Diplomatic History* 30, no. 3 (June 2006): 335–65; Moon-Ho Jung, *Coolies and Cane: Race, Labor, and Sugar in the Age of Emancipation* (Baltimore: Johns Hopkins Univ. Press, 2006); Gregory P. Downs, "The Mexicanization of American Politics: The United States' Transnational Path from Civil War to Stabilization," *American Historical Review* 117, no. 2 (April 2012): 387–409; Alison Efford, *German Immigrants, Race, and Citizenship in the Civil War Era* (New York: Cambridge Univ. Press, 2013); and Sexton, "William Seward in the World."

57. See, for example, these excellent studies: Katz, *From Appomattox to Montmartre*;

Gemme, *Domesticating Foreign Struggles*; Edward Bartlett Rugemer, *The Problem of Emancipation: The Caribbean Roots of the American Civil War* (Baton Rouge: Louisiana State Univ. Press, 2008); Timothy Mason Roberts, *Distant Revolutions: 1848 and the Challenge to American Exceptionalism* (Charlottesville: Univ. of Virginia Press, 2009).

58. Ninkovich, *Global Dawn*, for example, largely confines international interest to the elite. See 2–3, 7–8, 15–16, 48, 57, and 77.

59. The literature on the federal politics surrounding Reconstruction, including its racial, sectional, and partisan dimensions, is vast, but see especially Michael W. Fitzgerald, "Reconstruction Politics and the Politics of Reconstruction," in *Reconstructions: New Perspectives on the Postbellum United States*, ed. Thomas J. Brown (New York: Oxford Univ. Press, 2006), 91–116, and Michael Perman, "The Politics of Reconstruction," in *A Companion to the Civil War and Reconstruction*, ed. Lacy K. Ford (Malden, Mass.: Blackwell, 2005), 322–41; Foner, *Reconstruction*; Heather Cox Richardson, *The Death of Reconstruction: Race, Labor, and Politics in the Post-Civil War North, 1865–1901* (Cambridge, Mass.: Harvard Univ. Press, 2001); Richardson, *West from Appomattox*; Slap, *The Doom of Reconstruction*; Xi Wang, *The Trial of Democracy: Black Suffrage and Northern Republicans, 1860–1910* (Athens: Univ. of Georgia Press, 1997); Calhoun, *Conceiving a New Republic*; Joel H. Silbey, *A Respectable Minority: The Democratic Party in the Civil War Era, 1860–1868* (New York: Norton, 1977); Faye E. Dudden, *Fighting Chance: The Struggle over Woman Suffrage and Black Suffrage in Reconstruction America* (New York: Oxford Univ. Press, 2011).

1. Contested Sympathy for the Cretans

1. The American interest in the insurrection has garnered some interest within specialized subfields of U.S. diplomatic history and in a handful of biographies, but has yet to be studied in relation to Reconstruction. See especially Emmanuel E. Marcoglou, *The American Interest in the Cretan Revolution, 1866–69* (Athens: National Center of Social Research, 1971), which offers helpful comparisons of American and British responses to the insurrection but otherwise explores a limited stock of writings and has but a slight grasp on the cultural and political currents shaping American perceptions. Early diplomatic studies include A. J. May, "Crete and the United States, 1866–1869," *Journal of Modern History* 16, no. 4 (December 1944): 286–93; and James A. Field, Jr., *America and the Mediterranean World, 1776–1882* (Princeton, N.J.: Princeton Univ. Press, 1969), 317–23. More recently, see especially Angelo Repousis, *Greek-American Relations from Monroe to Truman* (Kent, Ohio: Kent State Univ. Press, 2013), 92–112. For biographies, see Harold Schwartz, *Samuel Gridley Howe: Social Reformer, 1801–1876* (Cambridge, Mass.: Harvard Univ. Press, 1956), 282–87; and Stephen L. Dyson, *The Last Amateur: The Life of William J. Stillman* (Albany: State Univ. of New York Press, 2014), 125–40.

2. On the diplomacy surrounding the insurrection, see A. J. May, "Crete and the United States"; William Hale, *Turkish Foreign Policy, 1774–2000* (London: Frank Cass, 2000), 13–21; and M. S. Anderson, *The Eastern Question, 1774–1923: A Study in International Relations* (New York: St. Martin's Press, 1966), 149–77.

3. On western European views of "the East" from the eighteenth century to the late twentieth, see of course Edward Said, *Orientalism* (1979; reprint, New York: Vintage, 1994). For an overview of Said's Orientalism thesis and American diplomatic history, see Andrew J. Rotter, "Saidism without Said: Orientalism and U.S. Diplomatic History," *American Historical Review* 105, no. 4 (October 2000): 1205–17.

4. Repousis, *Greek-American Relations from Monroe to Truman*, especially 95–96.

5. Karine V. Walther, *Sacred Interests: The United States and the Islamic World, 1821–1921* (Chapel Hill: Univ. of North Carolina Press, 2015), 57–67.

6. Of the voluminous literature on this topic, see most recently Gemme, *Domesticating Foreign Struggles*; Fox-Genovese and Genovese, *The Mind of the Master Class,* chapter 2; Roberts, *Distant Revolutions*; Fleche, *The Revolutions of 1861*; Paul D. Quigley, "Secessionists in an Age of Secession: The Slave South in Transatlantic Perspective," in *Secession as an International Phenomenon: From America's Civil War to Contemporary Separatist Movements,* ed. Don H. Doyle (Athens: Univ. of Georgia Press, 2012), 151–73; Paul D. Quigley, *Shifting Grounds: Nationalism and the American South, 1848–1865* (New York: Oxford Univ. Press, 2012); Doyle, *The Cause of All Nations.*

7. Dyson, *The Last Amateur,* 125.

8. Paul Bergeron, *Andrew Johnson's Civil War and Reconstruction* (Knoxville: Univ. of Tennessee Press, 2014), 74–77, 91, 93; Foner, *Reconstruction,* 184–85, 216.

9. Bergeron, *Andrew Johnson's Civil War and Reconstruction,* 80–83, 86–89, 95–97, 106–18; Foner, *Reconstruction,* 190–91, 193–94, 196, 199–201, 208–9, 224–80, 333–45.

10. See, for example, "Telegraphic Summary," *Elevator,* October 25, 1867, 4; and "News of the Week," *Christian Recorder,* April 6, 1867.

11. Theocharis E. Detorakis, *History of Crete,* trans. John C. Davis (Iraklion, Crete, Greece: Detorakis, 1994), 291–329, 396.

12. Ibid., 328; James Reid, *Crisis of the Ottoman Empire: Prelude to Collapse, 1839–1878* (Stuttgart: Franz Steiner Verlag, 2000), 212; Leonidas Kallivretakis, "A Century of Revolutions: The Cretan Question between European and Near Eastern Politics," in *Eleftherios Venizelos: The Trials of Statesmanship,* ed. Paschalis M. Kitromilides (Edinburgh, UK: Edinburgh Univ. Press, 2006), 12–13, 15, 16, 18.

13. Reid, *Crisis of the Ottoman Empire,* 212; Davide Rodogno, *Against Massacre: Humanitarian Interventions in the Ottoman Empire, 1815–1914* (Princeton, N.J.: Princeton Univ. Press, 2015), 119–20; Kallivretakis, "A Century of Revolutions," 11, 13–15; Douglas Dakin, *The Unification of Greece, 1770–1923* (London: Ernest Benn, 1972), 107; Manos Perakis, "Muslim Exodus and Land Redistribution in Autonomous Crete," *Mediterranean Historical Review* 26, no. 2 (December 2011): 135–50, 136.

14. William J. Stillman, *The Cretan Insurrection of 1866–7–8* (New York: Holt, 1874), 48; J.E.H. Skinner, *Roughing It in Crete in 1867* (London: R. Bentley, 1868), xxii; Kallivretakis, "A Century of Revolutions," 19; Reid, *Crisis of the Ottoman Empire,* 221; Dakin, *The Unification of Greece,* 108–9, 110.

15. Stillman's account still informs scholarship on the insurrection's origins and development, as is especially apparent in Reid, *Crisis of the Ottoman Empire,* 212–25. Scholarship on the insurrection sorely needs an assessment of the reliability of Stillman's account, which at points draws heavily on secondhand information.

16. Kallivretakis, "A Century of Revolutions," 19–20; Reid, *Crisis of the Ottoman Empire,* 213–15; Stillman, *Cretan Insurrection,* 40–66; Dakin, *The Unification of Greece,* 109, 110–11.

17. Reid, *Crisis of the Ottoman Empire,* 222; Kallivretakis, "A Century of Revolutions," 20–21; Dakin, *The Unification of Greece,* 111.

18. Reid, *Crisis of the Ottoman Empire,* for example, finds Stillman's account credible and sees the Ottoman government as attempting to cover up atrocities in diplomatic discussion (218, 219–20, 222–25). On Omer Pasha, the Crimean War, and other instances of civilian atrocities under his command, see Orlando Figes, *The Crimean War: A History* (New York: Metropolitan Books, 2010), 119–21, 137, 138, 186, 194, 321, 398.

19. Reid, *Crisis of the Ottoman Empire,* 224; Rodogno, *Against Massacre,* 126–35, 137–38.

20. Dakin, *The Unification of Greece,* 116.

21. William N. Jeffers to Admiral D. G. Farragut, August 30, 1867, in *Report of the Secretary of the Navy,* December 1867 (Washington, D.C.: Government Printing Office, 1867), 43–44.

22. Reid, *Crisis of the Ottoman Empire,* 215–22; Maizie Harrison Johnson, "European Reaction to the Cretan Insurrection, 1866–1869" (Master's thesis, George Washington University, 1961), 9–13, 16; Detorakis, *History of Crete,* 332–42, 334–45.

23. Rodogno, *Against Massacre,* 129; Reid, *Crisis of the Ottoman Empire,* 217.

24. Kallivretakis, "A Century of Revolutions," 20; Johnson, "European Reaction to the Cretan Insurrection," 23–24; Roderic H. Davison, *Nineteenth Century Ottoman Diplomacy and Reforms* (Istanbul: Isis Press, 1999), 230; William Michael Rossetti, *Rossetti Papers, 1862–1870* (New York: Charles Scribner's Sons, 1903), 377, 419; Reid, *Crisis of the Ottoman Empire,* 219; Dakin, *The Unification of Greece,* 117.

25. Dakin, *The Unification of Greece,* 118–20.

26. "The Cretan War," *New York Times,* June 11, 1867, 1; "Foreign News," *Harper's Weekly,* August 17, 1867, 515; "Cretan War Ended!" *Cretan,* December 1868, 3. With no telegraph lines running to Crete, news often trickled in through the mail; see, for example, *Chicago Tribune,* February 18, 1868; April 3, 1868; May 26 and 29, 1868; and June 10, 1868, all on the front page.

27. Mark Twain, *The Innocents Abroad, or the New Pilgrim's Progress* (San Francisco: Bancroft, 1869), 374–75.

28. Dyson, *The Last Amateur,* 132; see also Detorakis, *History of Crete,* 338, for a short list of journalists who reached the island.

29. M. D. Kalipothakes to Hermann J. Warner, August 27, 1867, #148, and Phillips Brooks to Greek Relief Committee, October 27, 1867, #153, in The Cretan Letterbook, Samuel Gridley Howe Collection, Samuel P. Hayes Research Library, Perkins School for the Blind, Watertown, Mass.; George Mountfort to Frederick William Seward, February 11, 1868, William Henry Seward Papers, University of Rochester, Rush Rhees Library; "Foreign," *Frank Leslie's Illustrated Newspaper,* January 19, 1867, 275; "The East," *New York Times,* February 5, 1867, 8; "The Candian Revolution," *Cleveland Leader,* May 21, 1867, 2; and E. Joy Morris to Secretary of State Seward, 28 November 1866, in U.S. Congress, House of Representatives Executive Documents, no. 38, *Revolution in Candia,* 39th Cong., 2nd sess., 17.

30. See William J. Stillman, *Autobiography of a Journalist,* 2 vols. (London: G. Richards, 1901), 1:142–62, 331–32, 372–74; 2:377–81, 383–86; David Howard Dickason, *The Daring Young Men: The Story of the American Pre-Raphaelites* (Bloomington: Indiana Univ. Press, 1953), 40–41. Stillman's stance on southern slavery is difficult to ascertain, but by the time he wrote his autobiography he oscillated between romanticizing it and condemning it; see Stillman, *Autobiography of a Journalist,* 1:284, 288–89.

31. Stillman, *Autobiography of a Journalist,* 2:449–50, 454–56, 457–58; Stillman to Seward, September 22, November 16, December 6 and 31, 1868, and March 6, June 10, and July 11 and 19, 1869, all available in George Georgiades Arnakis, *Articles and Despatches from Crete* (Austin, Tex.: Center for Neo-Hellenic Studies, 1976); and Stillman, *Cretan Insurrection,* 59–60. On his views of southern Europeans, see Stillman, *Autobiography of a Journalist,* 2:431–32, and Gemme, *Domesticating Foreign Struggles,* 156–62.

32. See Schwartz, *Samuel Gridley Howe,* 43–48, and chapters 2, 3, 5, and 6.

33. George Fredrickson, *The Black Image in the White Mind: The Debate on Afro-American Character and Destiny, 1817–1914* (New York: Harper Row, 1971; reprint, Hanover, N.H.: Wesleyan Univ. Press, 1987), 160–64.

34. Julia Howe, *Reminiscences, 1819–1899* (Boston: Houghton, Mifflin, 1899), 218–19, 228–30, 252–59, 261–63, 264–67, 269–77.

35. On the initial fundraising, see "Aid for the Cretans," *New York Times,* January 27, 1867, 8; "The Cretan Refugees and Their American Helpers," *Cretan,* April 1868, 2; Julia Ward Howe, *Reminiscences,* 312–13. On the rifles, see Amos A. Lawrence to S. G. Howe, February 23, 1867, #86, The Cretan Letterbook; S. G. Howe to A. A. Lawrence, February 20, 1867 (two letters) and March 1, 4, 6, 1867, and A. A. Lawrence to the Subscribers of the Greene Rifles, February 22, 1867, all in box 21, Papers of Amos A. Lawrence, Massachusetts Historical Society, Boston.

36. On the distribution of the aid in Greece, see, S. G. Howe to Peter Ralli and Co., May 11, 1867, Autograph Notes on a Journey to Greece: Rome, 17 Apr 1867–Boston, 11 Feb 1868, vol. 1, Howe Family Manuscripts, Houghton Library, Harvard University, Cambridge, Massachusetts; and Michael Contopolous, *The Greek Community of New York City: Early Years to 1910* (New Rochelle, N.Y.: Aristide D. Caratzas, 1992), 5–8, 11–13, 26–27, and chapter 3.

37. Julia Howe's poems are available in Laura F. Richards and Maud Howe Elliot, *Julia Ward Howe, 1819–1910* (Boston: Houghton Mifflin, 1916), 1:281–82; and "At Sea—Homeward," no date, box 16 of 21, Poems, Julia Ward Howe Papers, Houghton Library, Harvard University, Cambridge, Massachusetts. On Julia Howe's charity fair, see her *Reminiscences,* 320–21; "Appeal for the Cretan Fair," *Cretan,* May 1868, 4; and Julia Ward Howe diary, October 30, 1867, November 20, 29, 1867, December 7, 31, 1867 (vol. 4), and January 24, February 14–16, 21, 24, March 1, 17, and April 6, 11, 14, 18, 1868 (vol. 5), Howe Family Papers, Houghton Library, Harvard University, Cambridge, Massachusetts. On the smuggling of the Howes's supplies into Crete, see, "The Insurrection in Crete," *National Anti-Slavery Standard,* September 19, 1868, 4.

38. There is little on the production of the *Cretan,* but see Julia Ward Howe diary, February 21, 1868 (vol. 5); "Cretan Provisional Government," *National Anti-Slavery Standard,* November 28, 1868, 2.

39. On the geography and social foundation of Republican Party strength, see Eric Foner, *Free Soil, Free Labor, Free Men: The Ideology of the Republican Party before the Civil War* (New York: Oxford Univ. Press, 1970), 11–39, 106–7; and William R. Brock, *An American Crisis: Congress and Reconstruction, 1865–1867* (New York: St. Martin's Press, 1963), 242–48.

40. Data on donations to the London relief fund are available in "Candian Refugees Relief Fund," #74, Cretan Letterbook. Even a conservative estimate of Greek donations to the London fund, based on the donors' names, has the Greek share of the total revenue (in pounds) at 51 percent (3,669/7,172), with non-Greek business donations constituting another 24 percent of the total (1,713/7,172). Samuel Gridley Howe commented on the predominance of Greek merchants in the London relief fund; see his *The Cretan Refugees and Their American Helpers* (Boston: Lee and Shepard, 1868), 12. Data on donations to the Boston and New York City relief funds, discussed below, are available in Howe, *The Cretan Refugees and Their American Helpers,* 53–64. On the rise of the Greek merchant community in England, including the Ralli and Rodocanachi families, see Maria Christina Chatziioannou, "Greek Merchants in Victorian England," in *Greek Diaspora and Migration since 1700: Society, Politics and Culture,* ed. Dimitris Tziovas (Abingdon, UK: Ashgate, 2009), 45–60; Timotheos Catsiyannis, *The Greek Community in London* (London: Zeno, 1993), 37, 39, 45–46, 52.

41. Henry W. Bellows to S. G. Howe, January 11, 1867, #45, Cretan Letterbook; "The Cretans' Appeal," *National Anti-Slavery Standard,* January 30, 1869, 3. Bellows traveled to Europe and the eastern Mediterranean in 1867 and 1868, but appears not to have concerned

himself with the Cretan Insurrection during his travels except through some brief comments about Greece's difficulties with the Eastern Question. See Henry W. Bellows, *The Old World in Its New Face: Impressions of Europe in 1867–1868*, vol. 2 (New York: Harper and Brothers, 1869), 467–70; and Walter Donald Kring, *Henry Whitney Bellows* (Boston: Skinner House, 1979), 347–54.

42. Repousis, *Greek-American Relations from Monroe to Truman*, 101; Lilian Handlin, *George Bancroft: The Intellectual as Democrat* (New York: Harper and Row, 1984), 268–81; and "Help for the Cretans," *New York Times*, January 20, 1867, 8.

43. [Henry Wadsworth Longfellow], "Crete," in Samuel Gridley Howe, "An Appeal to the People of the United States to Relieve from Starvation the Women and Children of the Greeks of the Island of Crete" (Boston: N.p., 1867). The Brown University Library notes that Henry Wadsworth Longfellow donated the pamphlet, but he is unmentioned in the document itself; see Brown University Library, Hay Harris Broadsides, database entry, available at https://search.library.brown.edu/catalog/b2375169 (accessed March 10, 2016).

44. "Concert for the Cretans," *Dwight's Journal of Music*, March 2, 1867, 406, 416.

45. Nearly 70 percent of the $12,364.01 came from sixty different businesses, a small number of which appear to have been Greek.

46. "The Cretans' Appeal," *National Anti-Slavery Standard*, January 30, 1869, 3; see also Repousis, *Greek-American Relations from Monroe to Truman*, 111.

47. Julie Roy Jeffrey, *The Great Silent Army of Abolitionism: Ordinary Women in the Antislavery Movement* (Chapel Hill: Univ. of North Carolina Press, 1998). Even if one presumes all anonymous or initialized donations came from males, roughly one out of seven (79/571) donations to the Boston committee came from women or groups of women, compared to one out of seventeen (12/204) for the London committee.

48. Howe, *The Cretan Refugees and Their American Helpers*, 41.

49. Repousis, *Greek-American Relations from Monroe to Truman*, 108–9.

50. The *Union*'s politics are difficult to describe in brief, in part because its opposition to the power of the Central Pacific Railroad led it to occasionally support Democratic tickets. On Reconstruction policies, however, its political editor, Henry Clay Watson, supported Republican measures; Dorothy Gile Firebaugh, "The Sacramento Union: Voice of California, 1851–1875," *Journalism and Mass Communication Quarterly* 30, no. 3 (1953): 321–30.

51. "The Cretan Refugees and Their American Helpers," *Cretan*, April 1868, 2–3; "Intervention," *Cretan*, May 1868, 2; Richards and Elliot, *Julia Ward Howe*, 260–61; Howe, "An Appeal"; "Aid for the Cretans," *New York Times*, January 27, 1867, 8. The Howes also spoke at the Cooper Institute in New York on January 26, 1867. See "The Cretan Meeting" *New York World*, January 26, 1867, 4.

52. "The Island of Crete," *Chicago Tribune*, April 18, 1868, 2.

53. "Crete," *New York Times*, April 24, 1868, 5; Stewart L. Woodford, *Crete: An Address* (Albany, N.Y.: Weed, Parsons, 1868); "Woodford, Stewart Lyndon," in *Appleton's Cyclopædia of American Biography*, 6 vols., ed. James Grant Wilson and John Fiske (New York: Appleton, 1899), 6:601–2.

54. William J. Stillman to William Seward, August 18, 1866, available in Arnakis, *Articles and Despatches from Crete*, 35–37.

55. William J. Stillman to William Seward, December 29, 1866, no. 35, 3, 5, Despatches from Crete, General Records of the Department of State, RG 59, National Archives, Washington, D.C. See also "Letter from Dr. Howe," *Cretan*, April 1868, 8.

56. Morris to Seward, August 28, 1866, and November 2, 1866, House of Representatives Executive Document, *Revolution in Candia*, 7–8, 13; A. S. York to William Seward, January

11, 1867, Despatches from Zante, General Records of the State Department, RG 59; and "Foreign," *Memphis Daily Avalanche,* January 17, 1867, 2; Repousis, *Greek-American Foreign Relations from Monroe to Truman,* chapter 6; May, "Crete and the United States," 289–91.

57. John Hay, Wednesday, November 13 [1867], Diaries and Notebooks, 1861–1908, Notebooks, 1866–1868, 1878, n.d., Papers of John Hay, Library of Congress; James E. Montgomery, *Our Admiral's Flag Abroad: The Cruise of Admiral D. G. Farragut, Commanding the European Squadron in 1867–68, in the Flag-Ship Franklin* (New York: G. P. Putnam and Son, 1869), 412–14, 432–33; and May, "Crete and the United States, 1866–1869," 292.

58. "Cretan Days, I," *Atlantic Monthly,* November 1867, 533–39; "Cretan Days, III," *Atlantic Monthly,* March 1868, 326–27; see also "Cretan Days, IV," *Atlantic Monthly,* August 1868, 226; "The Subjugated Nationalities of European Turkey," *Cretan,* August 1868, 1–2; and "The Cretan Refugees and Their American Helpers," *Cretan,* April 1868, 2–3.

59. "Cretan Days, I," *Atlantic Monthly,* November 1867, 533–35, 538–39. See also "Cretan Days, IV," *Atlantic Monthly,* August 1868, 222; and "Cretan Liberty and Cretan Commerce," *Cretan,* May 1868, 7.

60. "The Clouds Accumulating—Turkey About to Fall to Pieces," *New York Times,* January 31, 1867, 4; "Cretan Days, IV," *Atlantic Monthly,* August 1868, 224. For a more critical view, see Karl Blind, "Hellenic Nationality in the East," *Putnam's Magazine,* November 1869, 568.

61. "Letter from Dr. Howe," 8; see also "The Subjugated Nationalities of European Turkey," 2–3; "The Turks and the Cretans," *New York Times,* August 11, 1867, 4; "The Cretan War," *New York Tribune,* reprinted in the *Sacramento Daily Union,* October 1, 1867, 3.

62. The number of civilians and soldiers vary across sources; these are from Detorakis, *History of Crete,* 336.

63. "The War in Crete," *Harper's Weekly,* February 2, 1867, 68–69; see also "Home and Foreign Gossip," *Harper's Weekly,* June 6, 1868, 363. For a brief statement that describes the decision as more impulsive, see "A Cretan Blockade-Runner," *New York Times,* January 6, 1867, 4.

64. Theocharēs M. Provatakēs, *Monastery of Arkadi: History, Art, Traditions* (Athens: Graphic Arts of Michalis Toubis, 1980), 71, 75, identifies at least two survivors based on unattributed sources. Stillman mentions several captives based on secondhand information; Stillman, *Cretan Insurrection,* 86.

65. See Reid, *Crisis of the Ottoman Empire,* 216; Stillman, *Cretan Insurrection,* 85. On the presence of Coptic Christians in the Egyptian ranks, see Provatakēs, *Monastery of Arkadi,* 76.

66. Provatakēs, *Monastery of Arkadi,* 32, 65–66.

67. Skinner, *Roughing It in Crete,* 77.

68. Provatakēs, *Monastery of Arkadi,* 25–27.

69. U.S. Congress, House of Representatives, Miscellaneous Documents, *Sympathy for the Greeks: Concurrent Resolution of the Legislature of New York, expressive of Sympathy for the Greeks, who are now struggling for freedom,* no. 58, 39th Cong., 2nd sess. The legislature of Maine passed a similar statement in December 1867; see also U.S. Congress, House of Representatives, Miscellaneous Documents, *Resolutions of the legislature of Maine expressing sympathy for the Cretans in their struggle for independence,* no. 9, 40th Cong., 2nd sess.

70. Woodford, *Crete,* 18.

71. "Our Interest in the Levant," *Frank Leslie's Illustrated Newspaper,* October 20, 1866, 66; Joshua Brown, *Beyond the Lines: Pictorial Reporting, Everyday Life, and the Crisis of Gilded-Age America* (Berkeley: Univ. of California Press, 2003).

72. "Attack upon the Convent of Arkadi, Crete," *Frank Leslie's Illustrated Newspaper,*

March 2, 1867, 372; see also "The Convent of Arkadi, Crete, at the Moment of the Assault and Explosion," *Frank Leslie's Illustrated Newspaper,* February 16, 1867, 340–41.

73. "The Cretan Question," *Frank Leslie's Illustrated Newspaper,* October 12, 1867, 50; see also "Mexico and the United States," *Putnam's Magazine,* May 1869, 618–21.

74. Groups in Cincinnati, Milwaukee, and Lowell, Massachusetts, for example, politely declined invitations to start fundraising committees to aid Cretan refugees; see S. Davis Soles to N. G. Chapin, February 8, 1867, #17; Isley to N. G. Chapin, February 8, 1867, #16; and Richardson to Warner, February 7, 1867, #12, all in the Cretan Letterbook.

75. William M. Armstrong, *E. L. Godkin: A Biography* (Albany: State Univ. of New York Press, 1978), 111.

76. "The Eastern Question—Crete the Opening Wedge," *New York Times,* October 16, 1866, 4.

77. "The Clouds Accumulating—Turkey About to Fall to Pieces," 4. See also "Foreign News," *Harper's Weekly,* April 20, 1867, 243, and "The Eastern Question," *Harper's Weekly,* January 18, 1868, 35.

78. "Our Foreign Correspondents," *New York Tribune,* October 16 1866, 4.

79. J.S.C. Abbott, "The Eastern Question," *Putnam's Magazine,* April 1869, 456–65; "The Appeal of Crete," *Harper's Weekly,* February 2, 1867, 66–67, and "Europe Ready for an Explosion," *Sacramento Daily Union,* October 7, 1867, 4.

80. "The Cretan Refugees and Their American Helpers," *Cretan,* April 1868, 2–3; see also "The Clouds Accumulating—Turkey About to Fall to Pieces," 4; "Recognition of Crete," *Congressional Globe,* 40th Cong., 3rd sess., January 7, 1869, 244.

81. William Brock "The Image of England and American Nationalism," *Journal of American Studies* 5 (1971): 225–45; Mitchell Snay, "Transatlantic Liberalism: Radical Republicans and the British Reform Act of 1867," in *Reconstruction in a Globalizing World,* ed. David Prior (New York: Fordham Univ. Press, 2018), 74–93.

82. "The Eastern Question," *Sacramento Daily Union,* November 3, 1866, 2; Roderic Davison, "Ottoman Public Relations in the Nineteenth Century: How the Sublime Porte Tried to Influence European Public Opinion," in *Historie Économique et Sociale de l'Empire Ottoman et de la Turquie (1326-1960),* ed. Daniel Panzac (Paris: Peeters, 1995), 593–603, 597.

83. "The Cretan War," republished in the *Sacramento Daily Union,* October 1, 1867, 3.

84. "Which Is the Infidel," *Harper's Weekly,* August 17, 1867, 528; see also "The Tragedy of Crete," *Harper's Weekly,* August 31, 1867, 547.

85. Reid, *Crisis of the Ottoman Empire,* 218–19; Rodogno, *Against Massacre,* 124, 125–26, 135. On British stances, see also Maureen M. Robson, "Lord Clarendon and the Cretan Question, 1868–9," *Historical Journal* 3, no. 1 (1960): 38–55; Ann Pottinger Saab, "The Doctors' Dilemma: Britain and the Cretan Crisis, 1866–1869," *Journal of Modern History* 49, no. 4. supplement (December 1977): D1383–D1407. In 1876, British statesmen, especially William Gladstone, would be much more openly critical of Ottoman actions in Bulgaria; see Robert Kelley, *The Transatlantic Persuasion: The Liberal-Democratic Mind in the Age of Gladstone* (New York: Knopf, 1969; reprint, New Brunswick, N.J.: Transaction Publishers, 1989), 218–20. French policy toward the insurrection, moreover, changed from supporting the Ottoman Empire, to intriguing with Russia on behalf of Crete, to helping arbitrate the conflict in favor of the Ottoman Empire; Johnson, "European Reaction to the Cretan Insurrection," 26–27, 32–34, 39–42, 45–55, 61–67, 76–81, 83–96, 101–7, 109–10, 116–19.

86. Rodogno, *Against Massacre,* 124–25; Repousis, *Greek-American Relations from Monroe to Truman,* 100, 108.

87. "The Eastern Question," *Cleveland Leader,* October 19, 1866, 2. See also "The Prayer

of the Greeks," *Sacramento Daily Union,* October 2, 1866, 2; "The Aggressive Powers," *Sacramento Daily Union,* October 18, 1866, 2; and "What May Happen in Europe," *Sacramento Daily Union,* October 10, 1867, 2.

88. On Russian sympathy for the Cretans, see Johnson, "European Reactions to the Cretan Insurrection," 10, 12, 14, 21–23, 24, 27–32, 80, 85.

89. Robert de la Sizeranne, *The Pre-Raphaelites* (New York: Parkstone International, 2012), 7–76. On Stillman's pre-insurrection ties, see Dickason, *Daring Young Men,* chapter 4; Rossetti, comp., *Rossetti Papers,* 299; William Michael Rossetti, *Some Reminiscences of William Michael Rossetti,* 2 vols. (New York: Charles Scribner's Sons, 1906), 1:180, 267, 2:348; Aris Sarafianos, "The Diaspora of Greek Painting in the Nineteenth Century: Christou's Model and the Case of Marie Spartali-Stillman," *Historein* 6 (2006): 150–69, especially 160; and Dante Rossetti to John Lucas Tupper, January 17, 1856, in William E. Fredeman, ed., *The Correspondence of Dante Gabriel Rossetti,* vol. 7, *The Formative Years, 1835–1862,* part 2, *1855–1862* (Cambridge, UK: D. S. Brewer, 2002), 90 and 90n2.

90. Dante Rossetti's father, the exiled Italian radical, had married the sister of one of the friends of Lord Byron, the most famous British philhellene from the Greek War of Independence; Sizeranne, *The Pre-Raphaelites,* 16. On Rossetti and Stillman's writings, see Rossetti, *Rossetti Papers,* 377–78; on Britain's Greek community and the arts, see Maria Christina Chatziioannou, "Greek Merchants in Victorian England," 50; Sarafianos, "The Diaspora of Greek Painting in the Nineteenth Century," 157–58.

91. Dyson, *The Last Amateur,* 134–35; Rossetti, comp., *Rossetti Papers,* 331, 333, 337, 338, 340, 419. On Dilberoglue and his relationship with the Rossetti family, see William Michael Rossetti, ed., *The Family Letters of Christina Georgina Rossetti* (New York: Charles Scribner's Sons, 1908), 37; Rossetti, *Rossetti Papers,* 274, 336, 359; Rossetti, *Some Reminiscences of William Michael Rossetti,* 2:342. On Dilberoglue and the Greek community in Britain, see Catsiyannis, *The Greek Community of London,* 487, 488, 489, 491.

92. On Stillman's visit after the insurrection, see Rossetti, *Rossetti Papers,* 412.

93. On Marie Spartali-Stillman, see Rossetti, *Some Reminiscences of William Michael Rossetti,* 1:267, 2:342; Sarafianos, "The Diaspora of Greek Painting in the Nineteenth Century," 153, 156, 158–61, 162–63. On Michael Spartali, see Sarafianos, "The Diaspora of Greek Painting in the Nineteenth Century," 157–58.

94. Algernon Swinburne, "Ode on the Insurrection in Candia," *Fortnightly Review,* March 1867, 284–89; Rossetti, *Rossetti Papers,* 221; A. C. Swinburne to Edmund Gosse, November 8, 1880, in Edmund Gosse and Thomas James Wise, eds., *The Letters of Algernon Charles Swinburne,* 2 vols. (New York: John Lane, 1919), 2:73–74.

95. "The Candian Revolution," *Cleveland Leader,* May 21, 1867, 2; Rossetti, *Rossetti Papers,* 226.

96. Paul Maurice, ed., *The Letters of Victor Hugo from Exile, and After the Fall of the Empire* (Boston: Houghton Mifflin, 1898), 222–23; "Victor Hugo on Crete," *National Anti-Slavery Standard,* February 13, 1869, 4.

97. On Garibaldians and the Cretan Insurrection, see Eric Terzuolo, "The Garibaldini in the Balkans, 1875–1876," *International History Review* 4, no. 1 (February 1982): 111–26, especially 112, 115, 124, 126; Gilles Pécout, "Philhellenism in Italy: Political Friendship and the Italian Volunteers in the Mediterranean in the Nineteenth Century," *Journal of Modern Italian Studies* 9, no. 4 (2004): 405–27, especially 412–14; Johnson, "European Reaction to the Cretan Insurrection," 123; William Miller, "George Finlay as a Journalist," *English Historical Review* 39, no. 156 (October 1924): 552–67, 560; Rodogno, *Against Massacre,* 126–27.

98. Leonidas Kallivretakis, "Jules Verne's Captain Nemo and French Revolutionary Gus-

tave Flourens: A Hidden Character Model?" *Historical Review/La Revue Historique* 1 (2004): 207–43, especially 221–24, 226–28, 231, 234–42.

99. William J. Stillman to Seward, December 29, 1866, Despatches from Crete, General Records of the Department of State.

100. "Cretan Liberty and Cretan Commerce," 6.

101. "American Diplomacy," *New York Times*, September 19, 1868, 4.

102. Repousis, *Greek-American Relations from Monroe to Truman*, 98–99.

103. "The Prayer of the Greeks," 2.

104. "To Members of Congress," *Cretan*, April 1868, 1.

105. On Seward, see Field, *America and the Mediterranean World*, 318; "Our Government and the Cretans," *New York Times*, February 6, 1867, 4. On the *Cretan*'s criticism, see also "Policy vs. Statesmanship.—Diplomacy vs. Wisdom.—Government vs. Justice," May 1868, 1; "The Subjugated Nationalities of European Turkey," 2; "Crete and Spain," *Cretan*, December 1868, 2.

106. "Crete and Spain," 2; see also "American Influences Abroad," *Cretan*, November 1868, 3.

107. "The Cretan Refugees and Their American Helpers," *Cretan*, April 1868, 2–3.

108. Repousis, *Greek-American Relations from Monroe to Truman*, 106–7; "Sympathy with Crete," *Congressional Globe*, 40th Cong., 1st sess., July 19, 1867, 727; "Cretan Independence," *Congressional Globe*, 40th Cong., 2nd sess., July 20, 1868, 4253; "Sympathy for Crete," *Congressional Globe*, 40th Cong., 2nd sess., July 21, 1868, 4283; "Sympathy with Crete," *Congressional Globe*, 40th Cong., 2nd sess., July 25, 1868, 4488; and May, "Crete and the United States, 1866–1869," 290–92. For criticism of the limited congressional support, see "Crete and Congress," *Cretan*, July 1868, 1; "The Subjugated Nationalities of European Turkey," 2; and "The Senate Cretan Resolution," *Cretan*, August 1868, 2–3.

109. See July 23, 1867, in Gideon Welles and Edgar Thaddeus Welles, *Diary of Gideon Welles: Secretary of the Navy under Lincoln and Johnson*, 3 vols. (Boston: Houghton Mifflin, 1911), 3:138–39, and September 1, 1868, 3:425.

110. Repousis, *Greek-American Relations from Monroe to Truman*, 109.

111. Glyndon Van Deusen, *William Henry Seward* (New York: Oxford Univ. Press, 1967), 489–91, 496; Thomas A. Bailey, *A Diplomatic History of the American People*, 8th ed. (New York: Appleton-Century-Crofts, 1969), 351–55; Sexton, "The United States, the Cuban Rebellion, and the Multilateral Initiative of 1875," 338–45.

112. Repousis, *Greek-American Relations from Monroe to Truman*, 94, 95.

113. Ibid., 108.

114. Skinner, *Roughing It in Crete*, 207–11, 212–15; Field, *America and the Mediterranean World*, 319. DeKay was accompanied by L. D. Rodokanachis, a Greek-American who had served in the Union navy.

115. "An American Officer Fallen in Crete," *New York Times*, October 7, 1867, 4; Jeffers to Farragut, August 30, 1867, in *Report of the Secretary of the Navy*, 43.

116. Repousis, *Greek-American Relations from Monroe to Truman*, 99.

117. Syed Tanvir Wasti, "Ahmed Rüstem Bey and the End of an Era," *Middle Eastern Studies* 48, no. 5 (September 2012): 781–96, 790ff5; Davison, "Ottoman Public Relations in the Nineteenth Century," 594.

118. Repousis, *Greek-American Relations from Monroe to Truman*, 106.

119. "Washington," *New York Times*, October 9, 1868, 3; J.M.R., "The Provisional Government of Crete," *New York Times*, October 20, 1869, 2; "Cretan Provisional Government," *National Anti-Slavery Standard*, November 28, 1868, 2.

120. Repousis, *Greek-American Relations from Monroe to Truman*, 110.

121. "The Cretans' Appeal," *National Anti-Slavery Standard,* January 30, 1869, 3.

122. Charles Keating Tuckerman, *Personal Recollections of Notable People at Home and Abroad,* 2 vols. (London: Richard Bentley and Sons, 1895) 2:126–31, 139–40.

123. "Crete," *Evening Telegraph,* September 7, 1868, 1; Repousis, *Greek-American Relations from Monroe to Truman,* 110.

124. "Tuckerman, Charles Keating," *The National Cyclopedia of American Biography* (New York: J. T. White, 1910), 24:426; Stillman, *The Cretan Insurrection,* iv–v; Dyson, *The Last Amateur,* 133.

125. John Dean Ward, *Biographical Sketch of George Mountfort, Esq.* (Boston: N.p., 1886), 4; Dyson, *Last Amateur,* 126.

126. Dyson, *Last Amateur,* 138–39.

127. On border-crossing analogies, see also Katz, *From Appomattox to Montmartre,* 85–117; Gemme, *Domesticating Foreign Struggles,* 116–24; Repousis, *Greek-American Relations from Monroe to Truman,* 101–3.

128. William J. Stillman to Seward, December 29, 1866, Despatches from Crete, General Records of the Department of State; see also A. A. Lawrence to the Subscribers of the Green Rifles, February 22, 1867, box 21, 1867, Papers of Amos A. Lawrence.

129. Repousis, *Greek-American Relations from Monroe to Truman,* 101–2.

130. Woodford, *Crete,* 14.

131. "Cretan War Ended!" 3; see also "The Turks and the Copperheads," *New York Times,* January 23, 1867, 4. The "copper-headed employee" was likely John P. Brown; see Dyson, *Last Amateur,* 133.

132. "The Turks and the Cretans," 4; see also "Crete," *Harper's Weekly,* January 23, 1869, 51.

133. "The Subjugated Nationalities of European Turkey," 1, 2.

134. Dyson, *Last Amateur,* 137.

135. "Crete," *Harper's Weekly,* January 23, 1869, 51.

136. "Cretan Days," *Atlantic Monthly,* August 1868, 222; see also "Cretan Liberty and Cretan Commerce," *Cretan,* May 1868, 7; and "The Clouds Accumulating—Turkey About to Fall to Pieces," 4.

137. "The Situation in Crete," *Cretan,* May 1868, 7; see also "The Cretan Cause," *Cretan,* July 1868, 4; "Mormonism in Turkey," *Cretan,* July 1868, 5; "The Pursuit of a Fair Under Difficulties," *Cretan,* July 1868, 6; "Turkish Massacres.—Official Statistics," *Cretan,* October 1868, 2; and "Recognition of Crete," *Congressional Globe,* 40th Cong., 3rd sess., January 7, 1869, 246.

138. "Prospectus of the Cretan," *Cretan,* August 1868, 4.

139. Quoted in Repousis, *Greek-American Relations from Monroe to Truman,* 102.

140. "The Cretan Refugees and Their American Helpers," *Cretan,* April 1868, 3; see also "Schuyler Colfax and His Fenian Friends," *New York Times,* May 8, 1867, 5.

141. "Recognition of Crete," *Congressional Globe,* 40th Cong., 3rd sess., January 7, 1869, 244.

142. Repousis, *Greek-American Relations from Monroe to Truman,* 94; "Letters to the Editor," *The Round Table,* January 4, 1868, 7–8.

143. "Cretan Days," *Atlantic Monthly,* August 1868, 224; "The Subjugated Nationalities of European Turkey," 1; Edward J. Morris to Secretary of State Seward, September 29, 1866, House of Representatives Executive Documents, *Revolution in Candia,* 10–11.

144. "Crete," *Harper's Weekly,* January 23, 1869, 51; Lewis R. Packard, "Observations on the Modern Greeks," *New Englander* (October 1867): 656–71, especially 659–60. On Packard,

see T.D.S., "Lewis R. Packard," *American Journal of Philology,* 5, no. 3 (1884): 403–6, especially 403.

145. Rodogno, *Against Massacre,* 123, 134.

146. "Intervention," 2. See also "Actual Condition of the Cretan Struggle," *Cretan,* May 1868, 3; "The Greek Race," *Cretan,* July 1868, 3; Edward Morris to Secretary of State Seward, September 29, 1866, House of Representatives Executive Documents, *Revolution in Candia,* 10–11.

147. Julia Howe, *From the Oak to the Olive: A Plan of a Pleasant Journey* (Boston: Lee and Shepard, 1868), 173–74, 222–33; see also Julia Ward Howe diary, February 7, 1868 (vol. 5); "Religion of the Greeks and the Greek Church," *National Anti-Slavery Standard,* July 11, 1868, 4; and S.G.W. Benjamin, "Historical Sketch of Crete," *Harper's New Monthly Magazine,* May 1867, 758–64.

148. Excerpt from an untitled, undated poem by Julia Ward Howe, available in Richards and Elliot, *Julia Ward Howe,* 281–82.

149. "The Cretan Refugees and Their American Helpers," *Cretan,* April 1868, 3–4; "The Cretan Industrial Schools at Athens," *Cretan,* July 1868, 7; "Our Schools in Athens," *Cretan,* August 1868, 5–6.

150. "American Influences Abroad," 3.

151. Available in Charles Keating Tuckerman to Frederick William Seward, July 1, 1867, William Henry Seward Papers, Rush Rhees Library, University of Rochester, Rochester, New York. On postbellum Republican expansionism, see Foner, *Reconstruction,* 495.

152. "Canting Sympathies," *Constitution,* July 31, 1868, 2. See also "Foreign versus Home Philanthropy," *Constitution,* June 19, 1868, 2. On the antebellum origins of such accusations, see Joel H. Silbey, *The Partisan Imperative: The Dynamics of American Politics before the Civil War* (New York: Oxford Univ. Press, 1985), 166–89.

153. "Foreign versus Home Philanthropy," 2.

154. Ibid.

155. "Canting Sympathies," 2.

156. "Work for the Cretan Committee," *New York World,* February 1, 1867, 4.

157. "A Bostonian War in the East," *New York World,* June 10, 1868, 4.

158. "Foreign versus Home Philanthropy," 2. The Howes and others countered that such accusations were superficial; see "Cretan Liberty and Cretan Commerce," 6; and "Recognition of Crete," *Congressional Globe,* 40th Cong., 3rd sess., January 7, 1869, 244.

159. "The Cretan Meeting," 4.

160. "Editorial," *Memphis Daily Avalanche,* February 21, 1867, 2.

161. "The Cretan Meeting," 4.

162. "Unparalleled Cruelty," *Richmond Enquirer and Sentinel,* November 18, 1867, 2; see also "The Effects of Reconstruction," *Richmond Enquirer and Sentinel,* December 17, 1867, 2.

163. "Foreign versus Home Philanthropy," 2. See also "The Cretan Meeting," 4. Southern whites continued to refer to the insurrection months after its collapse; see "Editorial," *Memphis Daily Avalanche,* November 20, 1869, 2.

164. "Canting Sympathies," 2.

165. "Turk or Christian," *New York World,* May 9, 1868, 4.

166. See also Anne Sarah Rubin, *A Shattered Nation: The Rise and Fall of the Confederacy, 1861–1868* (Chapel Hill: Univ. of North Carolina Press, 2005), 162–63.

167. "Foreign versus Home Philanthropy," 2.

168. "Canting Sympathies," 2.

169. Ibid.

170. "Editorial," *Memphis Daily Avalanche,* February 21, 1867, 2. See also "Editorial," *Memphis Daily Avalanche,* February 22, 1867, 2.

171. "Work for the Cretan Committee," 4.

172. "Foreign versus Home Philanthropy," 2.

173. Kallivretakis, "A Century of Revolutions," 21–31.

174. Perakis, "Muslim Exodus and Land Redistribution in Autonomous Crete," 137–38, 145.

175. Repousis, *Greek-American Relations from Monroe to Truman,* 111–12.

176. L.B.C., "The Fifteenth Versus the Sixteenth Amendment," *Woman's Advocate,* July 1869, 39–42, 40.

2. Paul Du Chaillu, a White Supremacist in Passing

1. Literature on southern white supremacist violence in the decade following the Civil War is too extensive to cite in full, but see especially Allen Trelease, *White Terror: The Ku Klux Klan Conspiracy and Southern Reconstruction* (Westport, Conn.: Greenwood, 1971); Lisa Cardyn, "Sexual Terror in the Reconstruction South," in *Gender and Sexuality in the American Civil War,* ed. Catherine Clinton and Nina Silber (New York: Oxford Univ. Press, 2006), 140–67; and Ash, *A Massacre in Memphis.*

2. Forrest G. Wood, *Black Scare: The Racist Response to Emancipation and Reconstruction* (Berkeley: Univ. of California Press, 1968), 25–29, 120–23; Joel Williamson, *After Slavery: The Negro in South Carolina during Reconstruction, 1861-1877,* (New York: Norton, 1965) 246–52; Silbey, *A Respectable Minority,* 80–83. For the earlier history of the idea of black racial menace, see Alfred N. Hunt, *Haiti's Influence on Antebellum America* (Baton Rouge: Louisiana State Univ. Press, 1988), chapter 4, and Charles B. Dew, *Apostles of Disunion: Southern Secession Commissioners and the Causes of the Civil War* (Charlottesville: Univ. Press of Virginia, 2001).

3. See especially Foner, *Reconstruction,* 25–28; Summers, *The Ordeal of the Reunion*; Chandra Manning, *What This Cruel War Was Over: Soldiers, Slavery, and the Civil War* (New York: Knopf, 2007); David W. Blight, *Race and Reunion: The American Civil War in American Memory* (Cambridge, Mass.: Belknap Press of Harvard Univ. Press, 2001); Fredrickson, *The Black Image in the White Mind*; Kate Masur, "'A Rare Phenomenon of Philological Vegetation': The Word 'Contraband' and the Meanings of Emancipation in the United States," *Journal of American History* 93, no. 4 (March 2007): 1050–84.

4. For evidence of the uncertainty over Du Chaillu's place and date of birth, see Michel Vaucaire, *Paul Du Chaillu: Gorilla Hunter* (New York: Harper and Brothers, 1930), 1–5; "Paul Du Chaillu Dead," *New York Times,* 1 May 1903, 9. For evidence that Du Chaillu encouraged these various beliefs, see Edward Clodd, *Memories* (New York: G. P. Putnam's Sons, 1916), 71. On both topics, see Lysle E. Meyer, *The Farther Frontier: Six Case Studies of Americans and Africa, 1848–1936* (Selinsgrove, Pa.: Susquehanna Univ. Press, 1992), 33–34.

5. Henry Bucher Jr., "Canonization by Repetition: Paul Du Chaillu in Historiography," *Revue Française d'Historie d'Outre-Mer* 66 (1979): 15–32, 16–17; Monte Reel, *Between Man and Beast: An Unlikely Explorer, the Evolution Debate, and the African Adventure that Took the Victorian World by Storm* (New York: Doubleday, 2013), 10; K. David Patterson, "Paul B. Du Chaillu and the Exploration of Gabon, 1855–1865," *International Journal of African Historical Studies* 7 (1974): 647–67, 649.

6. Bucher, "Canonization by Repetition," 17; Reel, *Between Man and Beast,* 8–12.

7. Patterson, "Paul B. Du Chaillu and the Exploration of Gabon," 649; Bucher, "Canonization by Repetition," 18; Reel, *Between Man and Beast,* 20–21.

8. Paul Du Chaillu, *Explorations and Adventures in Equatorial Africa* (New York: Harper and Brothers, 1861), 25; Bucher, "Canonization by Repetition," 18 (Bucher incorrectly lists Du Chaillu's departure date as 1856); Reel, *Between Man and Beast,* 26–29.

9. Patrick Brantlinger, "Victorians and Africans: The Genealogy of the Myth of the Dark Continent," *Critical Inquiry* 12, no. 1 (autumn 1985): 166–203, 177–78; Dane Kennedy, *The Highly Civilized Man: Richard Burton and the Victorian World* (Cambridge, Mass.: Harvard Univ. Press, 2005), 93, 128–30.

10. Philip D. Curtin, *The Image of Africa: British Ideas and Action, 1780–1850* (Madison: Univ. of Wisconsin Press, 1964), 9; Kennedy, *The Highly Civilized Man,* 96–99.

11. Reel, *Between Man and Beast,* 7, 73–75; Patterson, "Paul B. Du Chaillu and the Exploration of Gabon," 651, 663–64; Meyer, *Farther Frontier,* 35–37.

12. See "New Publications," *Burlington Free Press,* August 9, 1861, 2.

13. Reel, *Between Man and Beast,* 28, 63; Meyer, *Farther Frontier,* 53. Burton even believed the scientific bent of recent exploratory writing made it boring; Kennedy, *The Highly Civilized Man,* 101, 121. Speke was a hunter more than an explorer, and might have crafted a tail for popular tastes, but he hated writing; Kennedy, *The Highly Civilized Man,* 113.

14. Reel, *Between Man and Beast,* 5–6, 12, 15–19; Toby A. Appel, "Jeffries Wyman, Philosophical Anatomy, and the Scientific Reception of Darwin in America," *Journal of the History of Biology* 21 (1988): 69–94, 73–75, 76.

15. Reel, *Between Man and Beast,* 19–20, 186; Ted Gott and Kathryn Weir, *Gorilla* (London; Reaktion, 2013), 36–39. John Leighton Wilson also described the gorilla as a ferocious and terrifying animal, and his descriptions likely influenced Du Chaillu's perspective; see Meyer, *Farther Frontier,* 45. On the accuracy of Du Chaillu's descriptions, see Meyer, *Farther Frontier,* 44–47.

16. Patterson, "Paul B. Du Chaillu and the Exploration of Gabon," 654; Reel, *Between Man and Beast,* 56–57, 88–90.

17. On Kneeland and Du Chaillu, see Meyer, *Farther Frontier,* 42–43. Kneeland was an active member of the Boston Society for Natural History, which Wyman was the president of from 1856 to 1870, and worked with Wyman on occasion; see George Adams, "Society of Natural History," *Massachusetts Register* 91 (1857): 203–4; Boston Natural History Society, *Anniversary Memoirs of the Boston Society of Natural History, 1830–1880* (Boston: Boston Natural History Society, 1880), 63, 80–81; Toby A. Appel, "A Scientific Career in the Age of Character: Jeffries Wyman and Natural History at Harvard," in *Science at Harvard: Historical Perspectives,* ed. Clark A. Elliott and Margaret W. Rossiter (Bethlehem, Pa.: Lehigh Univ. Press, 1992), 96–120, especially 96–98, 109–10.

18. Reel, *Between Man and Beast,* 137; Meyer, *Farther Frontier,* 33; David M. Wrobel, *Global West, American Frontier: Travel, Empire, and Exceptionalism from Manifest Destiny to the Great Depression* (Albuquerque: Univ. of New Mexico Press, 2013), 29.

19. Du Chaillu also noted that gorillas were herbivores and that they could sound eerily human when under duress, but the overall picture that emerged was one of an intimidating beast. Reel, *Between Man and Beast,* 51, 58–59, 61, 62–63, 76–78, 125.

20. Gott and Weir, *Gorilla,* 172–74; Reel, *Between Man and Beast,* 268–69.

21. Nicholaas A. Rupke, *Richard Owen: Biology without Darwin* (Chicago: Univ. of Chicago Press, 2009), 192–208, 209–20; see 200 and 212 for early references to Du Chaillu and the gorilla. See also Gott and Weir, *Gorilla,* 158–65; Bucher, "Canonization by Repetition," 25; and Reel, *Between Man and Beast,* 104.

22. Bucher, "Canonization by Repetition," 29; Reel, *Between Man and Beast,* 81–83, 96–99, 109, 125–26; Rupke, *Richard Owen,* 236, 243.

23. Reel, *Between Man and Beast,* 109–12, 114–25; Richard Owen, *The Life of Richard Owen,* 2 vols. (London: John Murray, 1894), 2:115, 116; Meyer, *Farther Frontier,* 205n1.

24. Reel, *Between Man and Beast,* 126; Du Chaillu, *Explorations and Adventures in Equatorial Africa,* 424.

25. Meyer, *Farther Frontier,* 43; Rupke, *Richard Owen,* 238, 240–41; Bucher, "Canonization by Repetition," 19–20; Reel, *Between Man and Beast,* 143–45.

26. Bucher, "Canonization by Repetition," 22–23; Meyer, *Farther Frontier,* 44, 47; Reel, *Between Man and Beast,* 147, 175–77.

27. Meyer, *Farther Frontier,* 47–48; Patterson, "Paul B. Du Chaillu and the Exploration of Gabon," 662–63, 664–65.

28. Patterson, "Paul B. Du Chaillu and the Exploration of Gabon," 659, 663–64; Bucher, "Canonization by Repetition," 20–21; Reel, *Between Man and Beast,* 148, 191, 195–202.

29. Bucher, "Canonization by Repetition," 21–22; Meyer, *Farther Frontier,* 45–47; Reel, *Between Man and Beast,* 203–7.

30. Reel, *Between Man and Beast,* 208–10, 213–14, 215, 216–49, 254–56, 258–59; Patterson, "Paul B. Du Chaillu and the Exploration of Gabon," 654–55; Meyer, *Farther Frontier,* 49; John Dickenson, "The Naturalist on the River Amazons and a Wider World: Reflections on the Centenary of Henry Walter Bates," *Geographical Journal* 158, no. 2 (July 1992): 207–14.

31. On the origins of the association of "Negroes" with apes, see Winthrop D. Jordan, *White over Black: American Attitudes Toward the Negro, 1550–1812* (Chapel Hill: Univ. of North Carolina Press, 1968; reprint, Baltimore: Pelican, 1969), 29–32, 235–39, 490–97.

32. Reel, *Between Man and Beast,* 190–92.

33. Ibid., 91–94.

34. No title, *Highland Weekly News,* February 28, 1861, 1; *Green-Mountain Freeman,* March 7, 1861, 2.

35. "Negro Immigration," *Memphis Daily Appeal,* October 2, 1861, 1.

36. "Just Published," *Cleveland Morning Leader,* September 10, 1861, 2; "Juvenile Books for the Boys," *Cleveland Morning Leader,* December 24, 1862, 3. For excerpts, see "The Gorilla in His Native Wilds," *Civilian and Telegraph,* August 29, 1861, 1; "The Gorilla in His Native Wilds," *Evening Star,* June 20, 1861, 1; "The Gorilla in His Native Wilds," *Indiana State Sentinel,* July 3, 1861, 1; "The Gorilla in His Native Wilds," *Cincinnati Daily Press,* June 27, 1861, 4; "The King of the African Forest," *Columbia Democrat and Bloomsburg General Advertiser,* July 20, 1861, 1; "Killing a Gorilla," *Star of the North,* October 16, 1861, 1; "My First Gorilla," *Orleans Independent Standard,* August 9, 1861, 1; "Capture of a Young Gorilla," *Orleans Independent Standard,* September 6, 1861, 4; "The Gorilla," *New York Sun,* June 10, 1861, 1; "The Gorilla," *New York Sun,* June 15, 1861, 1; "Adventures in Africa," *Pacific Commercial Advertiser,* October 10, 1861, 4; "Strength and Ferocity of the African Gorillas," *Gazette and Sentinel,* January 5, 1861, 1; "The Wild Man of the Woods," *Ottawa Free Trader* August 31, 1861, 1; "The Gorilla," *Daily Exchange,* June 21, 1861, 2; no title, *New York Daily Tribune,* August 11, 1861, 2; "Gorillas and Their Ferocity," *Weekly Lancaster Gazette,* April 4, 1861, 1.

37. No title, *Caledonian,* August 23, 1861, 2; no title, *Burlington Free Press,* August 30, 1861, 2; no title, *Lamoille New Dealer,* August 30, 1861, 2; no title, *Daily Nashville Patriot,* August 31, 1861, 3; no title, *Gallipolis Journal,* August 29, 1861, 3.

38. "The Step-Children of Science," *Sun,* January 13, 1862, 1; no title, *Evening Star,*

October 24, 1861, 1; no title, *Evening Star,* November 6, 1861, 1; no title, *Evening Star,* November 26, 1861, 2; no title, *Daily Intelligencer,* December 24, 1861, 2; Reel, *Between Man and Beast,* 161–67.

39. Reel, *Between Man and Beast,* 191.

40. "The News of the Week," *Camden Confederate,* February 28, 1862, 2; "Our Acknowledgement as a Belligerent Power," *Daily Nashville Patriot,* September 8, 1861, 2.

41. "The Imbroglio," *New Orleans Daily Crescent,* December 16, 1861, 1; "Can't Stand It," *Clarksville Chronicle,* December 20, 1861, 2; no title, *Daily Nashville Patriot,* November 21, 1861, 2.

42. "Our Richmond Correspondence," *Charleston Mercury,* October 15, 1861, 1; "From Alexandria," *New Orleans Daily Crescent,* June 4, 1861, 1; "Trouble in the Camp," *New Orleans Daily Crescent,* December 6, 1861, 2; "Report of U.S. Secretary of War," *New Orleans Daily Crescent,* December 17, 1861, 1; "Getting Less Bloodthirsty," *New Orleans Daily Crescent,* June 28, 1861, 2; "News Extraordinary by Way of the Southern Confederacy," *Pomeroy Weekly Telegraph,* November 8, 1861, 3; "Mene, Mene, Tekel," *Memphis Daily Appeal,* September 6, 1861, 2; "The Fall of Scott," *Daily Nashville Patriot,* November 8, 1861, 3; "Impudence," *New Orleans Daily Crescent,* May 24, 1861, 2.

43. Malou, "Washington Correspondence," *New Orleans Daily Crescent,* March 18, 1861, 3; "Our Richmond Correspondence," *Charleston Mercury,* December 4, 1861, 1; "Our Richmond Correspondence," *Charleston Mercury,* December 17, 1861, 1; "Richmond News and Gossip: Our Own Correspondent," *Charleston Mercury,* February 3, 1862, 1; "Letters from Richmond," *Charleston Mercury,* January 22, 1863, 1.

44. No title, *Chattanooga Daily Rebel,* November 20, 1862, 2; "Fears for the Personal Safety of the President," *Memphis Daily Appeal,* October 15, 1862, 2; no title, *Memphis Daily Appeal,* December 20, 1862, 1; "A Demon English Press," *Memphis Daily Appeal,* November 1, 1862, 2; "Feeling at the North," *Memphis Daily Appeal,* October 4, 1862, 2; "Retaliation a Duty," *Memphis Daily Appeal,* October 10, 1862, 2; "Return of Lincoln to Washington—His Speeches in Maryland," *Daily Dispatch,* October 9, 1862, 1.

45. "The Pupil and His Teacher," *Liberator,* May 12, 1865, 1. On Burr, see Jay B. Hubbell, "Charles Chauncey Burr: Friend of Poe," *PMLA* 69, no. 4 (September 1954): 833–40, 834.

46. "The Federal Flotilla—Its Design," *Memphis Daily Appeal,* November 15, 1861, 2.

47. "More High-Toned Southern Journalism," *Cincinnati Daily Press,* April 2, 1861, 1; "Elegant Literature," *Cleveland Morning Leader,* March 30, 1861, 2; "Elegant Literature," *Holmes County Republican,* April 4, 1861, 2; no title, *Cleveland Morning Leader,* July 1, 1861, 1; no title, *Burlington Free Press,* April 5, 1861, 2; no title, *White Cloud Kansas Chief,* August 8, 1861, 2.

48. "A Lincoln Mayor Forced to Hurrah for Jeff Davis," *Daily Chronicle and Sentinel* (Augusta, Georgia), January 11, 1865, 4.

49. "The Murder, Wholesale and Hellish, of Union Men," *New York Tribune,* October 29, 1862, 4; Henry Louis Stephens and James Fuller Queen, *The Adventures of a Conscript as Told by Himself,* circa 1863, Library of Congress, Washington, D.C.; "The Newest Thing Out. Stephen's Album Cards," *Nashville Daily Union,* May 21, 1864, 4.

50. Searching the Library of Congress's newspaper database *Chronicling America* for the term "gorilla" renders 158 pages with the word in 1861, one hundred for 1862, fifty for 1863, a spike to ninety-six in 1864, and then a decline back to thirty-four in 1865. In 1866, by which time news of the completion of Du Chaillu's second expedition reached the United States, the number was sixty-one. In 1867, by which time Du Chaillu was speaking in the United States, the number climbed to 286. Google's Ngram viewer similarly illustrates a spike in the

occurrence of the word "gorilla" in American publications in 1861, but then a rapid drop off in its usage, interrupted by a minor spike in 1864. The 1861 spike no doubt reflects the publication of Du Chaillu's *Explorations and Adventures,* both because it itself adds to the total number of occurrences measured by the Ngram and because it was so widely reviewed and discussed. The spike in the number of references to the gorilla in 1864 likely stems from the use of the term as an epithet for the Lincoln administration in the 1864 campaign, excerpts from W. Winwood Reade's recently published *Savage Africa* (Harper and Brothers, 1864), and the publication of "A Club-Man in Africa," *Harper's New Monthly Magazine,* August 1864, 281–92. The latter reviewed Reade's *Savage Africa* and defended Du Chaillu's first volume, which was also published by Harper and Brother's; see "A Club-Man in Africa," 284–85; Bucher, "Canonization by Repetition," 21.

51. "New Publications," *Albany Journal,* April 22, 1867, 2. See also the slightly more restrained "Du Chaillu's African Explorations," *New York Times,* April 28, 1867, 3.

52. "New Publications," *San Francisco Bulletin,* May 11, 1867, 1.

53. "Explorers in Africa," *Mobile Nationalist,* March 28, 1867, 1. Some newspapers in the United States reported on Du Chaillu's lecture before the Royal Geographical Society in London after his second expedition, noting that it had bolstered his legitimacy as an explorer; see "M. Du Chaillu, the Great Explorer," *Philadelphia Enquirer,* January 29, 1866, 2; "M. Du Chaillu's Last Expedition," *San Francisco Bulletin,* March 6, 1866, 3; and "Central Africa and Its Inhabitants," *Enquirer* (Columbus, Georgia), September 19, 1866, 4.

54. James Redpath, "Du Chaillu," *Boston Daily Advertiser,* July 9, 1868, 2; McKivigan, *Forgotten Firebrand,* 124; Charles F. Horner, *The Life of James Redpath and the Development of the Modern Lyceum* (New York: Barse and Hopkins, 1926), 152.

55. For advertisements of Du Chaillu's books and lectures, see, for example, "M. Du Chaillu's Second Expedition," *New York Times,* April 6, 1867, 5; and "From Dayton," *Cincinnati Daily Gazette,* December 12, 1868, 3.

56. "Equatorial Africa," *New York Times,* May 9, 1867, 8; "African Explorations," *New York Times,* May 15, 1867, 5; "The Gorilla," *New York Times,* May 18, 1867, 8; no title, *Public Ledger* (Philadelphia), December 10, 1867, 2.

57. "Mons. Du Chaillu's Lecture," *Daily Press* (St. Paul, Minnesota), December 19, 1868, 4.

58. Excerpted in the *Daily State Register* (Des Moines, Iowa); "Cannibals—Narrative by M. Du Chaillu," March 6, 1868, 3.

59. Meyer, *Farther Frontier,* 52.

60. William Rideing, "Two Explorers and a Literary Parson," *McClure's Magazine,* December 1909, 214–20, 217.

61. "Local Notices," republished in *Watertown Times,* January 6, 1871, 3; "Young Men's Association," *Essex County Republican,* February 23, 1871, 3; see also "Du Chaillu Last Lectures," *New York Herald,* June 7, 1869, 5.

62. "Our Traveler," *Troy Weekly Times,* August 1, 1868, 4.

63. "Du Chaillu as Prophet," *Zion's Herald* (Boston), March 18, 1869, 126; "The Lecture Season," *New York Herald,* November 7, 1870, 7.

64. Clodd, *Memories,* 72–73.

65. "Among the Gorillas," *Cleveland Plain Dealer,* February 18, 1870, 3.

66. Meyer, *The Farther Frontier,* 56–58, 61–62; Donnarae MacCann, *White Supremacy in Children's Literature: Characterizations of African Americans, 1830–1900* (New York: Garland, 1998), 197–98.

67. "Du Chaillu," *Watertown Times,* March 3, 1871, 3; "Du Chaillu on the Gorilla," reprinted in *Daily Alta California,* March 15, 1868, 3; "African Exploration," *Ithaca Journal,* January 9, 1872, 1.

68. Clodd, *Memories,* 72–73.

69. For newspaper coverage of in-town talks, see "Mons. Du Chaillu's Lecture," *Daily Press* (St. Paul, Minnesota), December 19, 1868, 4; for excerpts from other papers, see "Du Chaillu on Africa and the Gorilla," *Cincinnati Gazette,* May 15, 1867, 4; "Equatorial Africa," *Daily Columbus Enquirer,* May 16, 1867, 2; "Cannibals—Narrative by M. Du Chaillu," *Daily State Register* (Des Moines, Iowa) March 6, 1868, 3; "The Gorilla," *Baltimore Sun,* May 28, 1867, 5.

70. "For Gentlemen Only," *Daily Alta California,* May 12, 1868, 4.

71. No title, *Marysville Daily Appeal,* July 30, 1868, 2; on McConnell, see William H. Rhodes, "John R. McConnell," in Oscar T. Shuck, *Representative and Leading Men of the Pacific* (San Francisco: Bacon, 1870), 529–33.

72. Emanuel Herzberg, *Gorilla Catechism* (New York: American News Company, 1869).

73. No title, *San Francisco Bulletin,* April 19, 1871, 1.

74. Reel, *Between Man and Beast,* 102, 125–26, 193; see also "The News," *New York Herald,* January 4, 1861, 1.

75. Reel, *Between Man and Beast,* 223, 251–53; Rupke, *Richard Owen,* 242; Richard Owen, Appendix I, in Paul Du Chaillu, *A Journey to Ashango-Land* (New York: Appleton, 1867), 439–60.

76. No title, *Tarboro' Southerner,* April 2, 1868, 2.

77. "Editorial News Items," *Patriot,* October 23, 1867, 2.

78. "Arrival of a Live Gorilla from Africa," *New-York Daily Reformer,* October 4, 1867, 1; "Editor's Table," *Old Guard,* January 1868, 78–79.

79. "Mr. Gorilla or Mr. Baboon," *Round Table,* October 5, 1867, 224–25.

80. "Death of a Distinguished African," *Richmond Enquirer and Examiner,* March 5, 1868, 2.

81. "Gen. Rowe in His Sphere," *Marysville Daily Appeal,* October 6, 1868, 3.

82. Georges Clemenceau, *American Reconstruction, 1865–1870,* ed. Fernand Baldensperger, trans. Margaret MacVeagh (New York: L. MacVeagh, Dial Press, 1928), 131.

83. Foner, *Reconstruction,* 340–41; "Speech of General F. P. Blair," *Ohio Statesman* September 25, 1868, 1.

84. "What to Do with the South," *New York Tribune,* June 6, 1867, 4; "What to Do with the South," *Evening Telegraph,* June 7, 1867, 2.

85. "Democracy Courting the Colored Vote," *New Orleans Republican,* June 4, 1868, 2.

86. A., "Letter from Washington," *New Orleans Tribune,* October 27, 1867, 4. On the papers' rivalry, see F. Wayne Binning, "Carpetbaggers' Triumph: The Louisiana State Election of 1868," *Louisiana History* 14, no. 1 (winter 1973): 21–39, 26–27, 32, 34, 35–36, 38–39.

87. Representative James Mullins on June 24, 1868, 40th Cong., 2nd sess., *Congressional Globe,* part 4, 3452.

88. L. Perry Curtis Jr., *Apes and Angels: The Irishman in Victorian Culture,* rev. ed. (Washington, D.C.: Smithsonian Institution Press, 1997), 58–60. On the broader career of the gorilla as a symbol for barbarism, see Gott and Weir, *Gorilla,* 165–72.

89. "Seventh Ward Republican Club," *Evening Star,* June 6, 1867, 1.

90. "Liberia," *Weekly Louisianian,* February 18, 1872, 1. On Roye's overthrow, which was not entirely peaceful, see James Ciment, *Another America: The Story of Liberia and the Former Slaves Who Ruled It* (New York: Hill and Wang, 2013), 117–19.

91. The description offered exactly the type of sensationalistic accounts associated with Du Chaillu's first voyage that he was disavowing by 1867. On the specific claim here, that gorillas carried off African women, see Du Chaillu's dismissal of such claims in "Du Chaillu on the Gorilla," *Massachusetts Spy,* May 24, 1867, 3.

92. No title, *San Antonio Express,* October 22, 1867, 2.

93. Meyer, *Farther Frontier,* 37.

94. Du Chaillu, *Explorations and Adventures in Equatorial Africa,* 102; Du Chaillu, *A Journey to Ashango-Land,* 149.

95. Reel, *Between Man and Beast,* 7–8.

96. Bucher, "Canonization by Repetition," 17.

97. Rupke, *Richard Owen,* 201, 213.

98. Du Chaillu, *A Journey to Ashango-Land,* 12, 17, 18, 27–28, 31, 32–35, 36, 38, 72, 79, 86, 89, 101–2, 115, 121–22, 131–32, 149–51, 167, 169, 170–71, 173–77, 186, 192, 199–201, 231, 232, 238–39, 273, 283, 293, 294–95, 309–10, 313–14, 370, 384.

99. Ibid., 22, 26, 41–42 51–53, 99–100, 110; quotation from 51.

100. Ibid., 42.

101. Ibid., 23, 27, 119, 125–26, 127, 157–58, 230, 258, 285, 288–90, 361–62, 379, 404–5.

102. Ibid., 132, 134, 143–44, 164–65.

103. Ibid., 16, 18, 31.

104. Reel, *Between Man and Beast,* 189–90; Meyer, *Farther Frontier,* 54–56.

105. "African Women," *San Francisco Elevator,* August 21, 1868, 4.

106. Patterson, "Paul B. Du Chaillu and the Exploration of Gabon," 659–61, 664–65, 666; Meyer, *Farther Frontier,* 59; Norman Robert Bennett, "David Livingstone: Exploration for Christianity," in *Africa and Its Explorers: Motives, Methods, and Impact,* ed Robert I. Rotberg (Cambridge, Mass.: Harvard Univ. Press, 1970), 39–61, especially 51–52, 56–57; Kennedy, *The Highly Civilized Man,* 150–55. For Du Chaillu's interest in local African customs and beliefs relative to other explorers, see Du Chaillu, *A Journey to Ashango-Land,* xiii.

107. Du Chaillu's contact with scientific racists began as early as 1859 when Samuel Kneeland helped Du Chaillu write *Explorations and Adventures.* Kneeland was a leading proponent of polygenism and scientific racism, and working with him may have exposed Du Chaillu to his ideas. Kneeland's landmark contribution to scientific racism was an eighty-page introduction to the 1851 American edition of British traveler Charles Hamilton Smith's *The Natural History of the Human Species.* It began with a respectful and detailed fifty-two-page overview of competing scientific theories of race ranging from Johann Blumenbach to James Prichard to Samuel G. Morton. It then drew on the work of William Frederick Van Amringe and Louis Agassiz to argue for a variant of polygenism that held that God created human races as physiologically distinctive species in their own environments. He held as well that while these separate races could produce offspring with each other, these would tend to either die off over several generations or melt back into a racially pure population around them. His "Introduction" closed with an assessment of racial inequality that looked down on "the dark races" and esteemed whites to be "the most perfect type of humanity." Samuel Kneeland, "Introduction," in Charles Hamilton Smith and Samuel Kneeland, *The Natural History of the Human Species* (1851; reprint, Boston: Gould and Lincoln, 1859), 15–98, quotations from 95, 96; David N. Livingstone, *Adam's Ancestors: Race, Religion, and the Politics of Human Origins* (Baltimore: Johns Hopkins Univ. Press, 2008), 94–99. See also Samuel Kneeland, "The Hybrid Races of Animals and Men," *De Bow's Review* (November 1855): 535–39.

108. Reel, *Between Man and Beast,* 168–75.

109. Kennedy, *The Highly Civilized Man,* 132–34, 137–39; Thomas Sebrell II, *Persuading John Bull: Union and Confederate Propaganda in Britain, 1860-1865* (Lanham, Md.: Lexington, 2014), 58; Doyle, *The Cause of All Nations,* 36–37.

110. Kennedy, *The Highly Civilized Man,* 140–41, 151; Ter Ellingson, *The Myth of the Noble Savage* (Berkeley: Univ. of California Press, 2001), 212, 252–53, 308–9; Reel, *Between*

Man and Beast, 174–76; James Hunt, *On the Negro's Place in Nature* (London: Trübner, 1863), 31, 48; James Hunt, *On the Negro's Place in Nature* (New York: Van Evrie, Horton, 1864).

111. Du Chaillu, *A Journey to Ashango-Land,* 424, see also xiii.

112. Du Chaillu provided no citations to indicate who his disagreement was with, but it may have been his friend and colleague Richard F. Burton; see Kennedy, *The Highly Civilized Man,* 146–47.

113. Du Chaillu, *A Journey to Ashango-Land,* 434–35.

114. Ibid., 436–37.

115. "African Explorations," *New York Times,* May 15, 1867, 5; "The Gorilla and the Negro—Mr. Du Chaillu's Lectures," *New York Herald,* January 22, 1868, 4; "Du Chaillu's Lectures for Young Folks," *Harper's Weekly,* 148; Reel, *Between Man and Beast,* 194.

116. "Du Chaillu's Lectures," *New York Times,* February 29, 1868, 5.

117. Fredrickson, *The Black Image in the White Mind,* 160–64.

118. "Du Chaillu's Lectures for Young Folks," *Harper's Weekly,* 148.

119. "Du Chaillu's African Explorations," *New York Times,* April 28, 1867, 3.

120. "Du Chaillu's Travels in Equatorial Africa," *African Repository,* May 1867, 143–46.

121. "Researches in Equatorial Africa," *African Repository,* August 1867, 231–36, quotations from 236.

122. "Du Chaillu as Prophet," *Zion's Herald,* March 18, 1869, 126–27. For the political viewpoints of *Zion's Herald,* see Victor B. Howard, *Religion and the Radical Republican Movement, 1860–1870* (Lexington: Univ. Press of Kentucky, 1990), 25, 54, 82, 91, 93, 96, 108, 143, 156, 160, 161, 183, 197, 198, and 205.

123. "Du Chaillu's African Explorations," *Hours at Home,* June 1867, 179–86; quotations from 186. On *Hours at Home,* see Frank Luther Mott, *A History of American Magazines, 1865–1885* (Cambridge, Mass.: Harvard Univ. Press, 1957), 32–33.

124. "Du Chaillu on the Negro's Destiny," *New York Tribune,* May 18, 1867, 4.

125. Editorial, *Daily Enquirer* (Columbus, Georgia), May 24, 1867, 3.

126. "Du Chaillu, the Negroes and the 'Tribun,'" *Brooklyn Daily Eagle,* May 18, 1867, 2.

127. "Africa," *Richmond Enquirer and Sentinel,* May 11, 1867, 1.

128. "Equatorial Africa," *Richmond Enquirer and Sentinel,* May 17, 1867, 1.

129. "Negro Supremacy in Hayti—Salnave a Specimen Brick," *Richmond Enquirer and Sentinel,* December 28, 1867, 1; see also "Negro Barbarism—Experience of the West Indies," reprinted in *Richmond Enquirer and Sentinel,* November 22, 1867, 2.

130. On the *Herald's* circulation, see Summers, *The Press Gang,* 16.

131. "The Gorilla and the Negro—Mr. Du Chaillu's Lectures," *New York Herald,* January 22, 1868, 4.

132. "From the New York Herald," *Clarksville Chronicle,* February 7, 1868, 1.

133. John Codman, *Ten Months in Brazil* (Boston: Lee and Shepard, 1867). For his travel dates, see 11 and 42; on race, see, passim and 190, 195.

134. Ibid., 187–88, 195–200, 203–4.

135. "Du Chaillu's Account of the African," *Cultivator and Country Gentleman,* June 20, 1867, 402.

136. "Barbaric Economy," *Marysville Daily Appeal,* May 7, 1868, 2.

137. "Africa and the Africans," *Crisis,* May 15, 1867, 121.

138. Clodd, *Memories,* 71.

139. Bucher, "Canonization by Repetition," 16–18; Reel, *Between Man and Beast,* 186.

3. From North and South to East and West

1. I refrain from placing the terms *East* and *West* in quotation marks throughout this chapter because doing so becomes too obtrusive in some passages. Readers should of course understand them as terms from the past, not enduring frames of analysis.

2. On Reconstruction as a success, see Summers, *The Ordeal of the Reunion.*

3. See Eric Hobsbawm, *The Age of Capital: 1848–1875* (London: Weidenfeld and Nicolson, 1995), chapter 3.

4. Maury Klein, *The Power Makers: Steam, Electricity, and the Men Who Invented Modern America* (New York: Bloomsbury Press, 2008), 69.

5. Michael S. Green, *Freedom, Union, and Power: Lincoln and His Party during the Civil War* (New York: Fordham Univ. Press, 2004), 46–48, 301–7.

6. E. Fletcher, "The Suez Canal and World Shipping, 1869–1914," *Journal of Economic History* 18, no. 4 (December 1958): 556–73, especially, 556–63, 567–68, 569–70, 572; D. A. Farnie, *East and West of Suez: The Suez Canal in History, 1854–1956* (Oxford: Clarendon Press, 1969), 7–8, 12–13, 14–15, 18, 27, 55–80, 81, 90–91, 97–108; Joyce E. Chaplin, *Round About the Earth: Circumnavigation from Magellan to Orbit* (New York: Simon and Schuster, 2012), 205–7.

7. Sexton, "William H. Seward in the World," 398–430, 405–6.

8. John Hurd and Ian J. Kerr, *India's Railway History: A Research Handbook* (Leiden, The Netherlands: Brill, 2012), 5–12.

9. Cara Murray, "Imperial Ways: The Victorians, the Suez Canal, and Narrative" (Ph.D. diss., City University of New York, 2005), 173–200; Chaplin, *Round About the Earth,* 193–200, 214–15, 235; Sexton, "William Seward in the World," 402–3.

10. In fact, as Train commented later in life, after having made two other record-setting trips around the globe, one saw little of interest when traveling at such speeds; see George Francis Train, *My Life in Many States and in Foreign Lands* (New York: Appleton, 1902), 336. Train actually spent about one month in France, where he attempted to aid the Communards in their struggles against French Republicans and Prussian occupiers, but excluded this period when calculating his travel time; see Willis Thornton, *The Nine Lives of Citizen Train* (New York: Greenberg, 1948), 197–211.

11. On the relationship between George Francis Train, William Fogg, and the character Phileas Fogg in Jules Verne's *Around the World in 80 Days,* see Chaplin, *Round About the Earth,* 214–15; Murray, "Imperial Ways," 200–201.

12. Lynne Withey, *Grand Tours and Cook's Tours: A History of Leisure Travel, 1750 to 1915* (New York: William Morrow, 1997), 270–72.

13. William Elliott Griffis, *Charles Carleton Coffin: War Correspondent, Traveller, Author, and Statesman* (Boston: Estes and Lauriat, 1898), 34–37.

14. Charles Carleton Coffin, *Our New Way Round the World* (Boston: Fields, Osgood, 1869), preface, 1, 4, 506–7. Chaplin, *Round About the Earth,* 207, offers a brief discussion of Carleton's voyage.

15. See Coffin, *Our New Way Round the World,* dedication, 1, 195, 250–51.

16. We know less about William Fogg's life, but the following encyclopedia entry does help with some of the details: "Fogg, William Perry," *Encyclopedia of Cleveland History,* Case Western University, http://ech.case.edu/cgi/article.pl?id=FWP (accessed February 8, 2014). That Fogg was a Republican can be inferred from his employment with the *Leader,* Cleveland's radical Republican paper, and his statements in William Fogg, *"Round the World": Letters from Japan, China, India, and Egypt* (Cleveland: *Cleveland Leader,* 1872), especially

7, 10, 18, 24, and 130. For the travel dates and route, see Fogg, *"Round the World,"* 7, 21, 229. That Fogg was traveling alone is evident periodically in the narrative; see for example Fogg, *"Round the World,"* 191.

17. For Fogg's mention of Carleton's volume, see Fogg, *"Round the World,"* 76. For the lifted passages, compare his and Carleton's descriptions of the port of Aden and the British capture of the Island of Perim (Fogg, *"Round the World,"* 205, 208, and Coffin, *Our New Way Round the World,* 72–73, 74) and one portion of their descriptions of the Japanese civil war (Fogg, *"Round the World,"* 48, and Coffin, *Our New Way Round the World,* 454).

18. Fogg, *"Round the World,"* preface. On the *Cleveland Leader,* see The Cleveland Leader, *Then and Now: The Story of the Cleveland Leader and the Cleveland News* (Cleveland: Art Engraving and Electrotyping, 1913), 14–15.

19. Fogg did not bother including letters on the Levant and Europe in his work; Fogg, *"Round the World,"* preface. Carleton deliberately kept short his discussion of his time in Europe, explaining that "So much has been written in regard to Europe, that the lines of travel only have been indicated between London and Alexandria." Coffin, *Our New Way Round the World,* preface; see also 3. On antebellum American travel writing on Europe, see Alfred Bendixen, "American Travel Books about Europe before the Civil War," in *The Cambridge Companion to American Travel Writing,* ed. Alfred Bendixen and Judith Hamera (New York: Cambridge Univ. Press, 2009), 103–26.

20. On the Sewards' travels, see also Sexton, "William Seward in the World."

21. William H. Seward, *William H. Seward's Travels around the World,* ed. Olive Risley Seward (New York: Appleton, 1873), 17, 777; Sexton, "William Seward in the World," 402.

22. On his traveling companions, see Seward, *William H. Seward's Travels,* 4; Van Deusen, *William Henry Seward,* 558.

23. Little information survives about this William Freeman, who should not be confused with the deceased African American man William Seward had famously defended in court in the 1840s. Van Deusen's *William Henry Seward* and Walter Stahr's *Seward: Lincoln's Indispensable Man* (New York: Simon and Schuster, 2012) describe him only as William's servant, not even mentioning that Freeman was African American; see Van Deusen, *William Henry Seward,* 558, and Stahr, *Seward,* 540. That William Freeman was African American was evident from a few brief comments in *William H. Seward's Travels,* including a description of him as "the colored servant" and a reference to his receiving his political rights under the Fifteenth Amendment (see pages 10, 335, 466). One Indonesian observer speculated that Freeman was "the son of a slave," but the Sewards' narrative does not directly confirm this (see 335). The volume's index contains an entry for Freeman, but it neglects the following pages that reference him: 120, 128, 335, 455, 469, 561, 605, and 686. Part of the way through the voyage, William found that Freeman was overwhelmed by work, so he hired a second servant, an Englishman named Arthur Price. See Van Deusen, *William Henry Seward,* 560, and William Henry Seward to William Henry Seward Jr., December 19, 1870, 1–2, Seward Family Digital Archive (hereafter SFDA), https://sewardproject.org/. On the hiring of Freeman by William Henry Seward Jr., see William Henry Seward Jr. to William Henry Seward, April 15, 1871, 3–4, SFDA. On Freeman's difficulty hearing, see William Henry Seward to William Henry Seward Jr., April 10, 1871, 5–6, SFDA. In three instances *William H. Seward's Travels* refers to three employees, Freeman, Price, and a Jenny "Jeanie" Corell; Seward, *William H. Seward's Travels,* 455, 469, 686.

24. On Hanson and his relationship with William, see Seward, *William H. Seward's Travels,* 4; Van Deusen, *William Henry Seward,* 553–55, 557–58, 559; and Stahr, *Seward,* 540–41.

25. On William's and Olive's mutual attachment, see Van Deusen, *William Henry Seward,* 553–54, 558, 559–60; Sexton, "William Seward in the World," 402. Harriet Risley was six years younger than Olive; see Van Deusen, *William Henry Seward,* 553–54.

26. The deliberations about and the act of adoption go unmentioned in Seward's narrative, although the volume does begin by acknowledging Olive as his adopted daughter; see Seward, *William H. Seward's Travels,* 4. On the decision to adopt, see Van Deusen, *William Henry Seward,* 558–59; Stahr, *Seward,* 539–40; William Henry Seward to Frederick William Seward, December 7, 1870, 3, SFDA; William Henry Seward Jr. to William Henry Seward, February 12, 1871, 9–10, SFDA; William Henry Seward to William Henry Seward Jr., April 10, 1871, 4, 6–7.

27. On the intellectual component of their relationship, see Van Deusen, *William Henry Seward,* 554, 555, 558, 559–60, 561–62, and Stahr, *Seward,* 538. On Seward's injuries, see Van Deusen, *William Henry Seward,* 557, and Stahr, *Seward,* 537, 539, 541.

28. Olive Risley Seward to Lazette Miller Worden, February 1871, 2, SFDA.

29. Van Deusen, *William Henry Seward,* 562–63; Stahr, *Seward,* 540. Fogg, who crossed paths with Seward while in China, described Olive as William's private secretary; see Fogg, *"Round the World,"* 95. When William and Olive decided to try to publish Olive's notes of the journey, one of the men involved in the decision, James Derby, described Olive as "the fair authoress"; see Van Deusen, *William Henry Seward,* 562. Although it is outside of the chronological scope of this volume, Olive later published her own volume, *Around the World Stories* (Boston: D. Lothrop, 1889), based on her travels. On the title page of that volume, she described herself as the "editor" of William's book.

30. Coffin, *Our New Way Round the World,* 405. The Sewards did at one point describe their work as a "study," and if we understand this in the sense of portraying a scene, it also captures the spirit of these volumes; Seward, *William H. Seward's Travels,* 3, and see also 278, 502.

31. Fogg, *"Round the World,"* preface. On the idea of a nineteenth-century global technological frontier, see Hobsbawm, *Age of Capital,* 61.

32. Coffin, *Our New Way Round the World,* 3.

33. On William Seward's expectation that technology and commerce would bring about cultural change, see Sexton, "William Seward in the World," 417–18. On the tendency of Americans, especially during the mid-nineteenth century, to believe that advanced technology in the United States would yield influence over the non-Western world, see Adas, *Dominance by Design,* 12, 74–75. For the place of technology (including especially the railroad) in mid-nineteenth-century American notions of national identity, see Adas, *Dominance by Design,* 79–85, 125.

34. See David E. Nye, *The American Technological Sublime* (Cambridge, Mass.: MIT Press, 1994).

35. Seward, *William H. Seward's Travels,* 32–33.

36. Fogg, *"Round the World,"* 26.

37. Coffin, *Our New Way Round the World,* 504.

38. Seward, *William H. Seward's Travels,* 528.

39. Coffin, *Our New Way Round the World,* 507.

40. Fogg, *"Round the World,"* 61–66; Seward, *William H. Seward's Travels,* 48–50, 74, 76. Carleton also praised the Tokaido, but did not travel it extensively because he arrived during the Japanese civil war; see Coffin, *Our New Way Round the World,* 436, 458.

41. Coffin, *Our New Way Round the World,* chapter 13. See also Fogg's discussion of his trip into the Himalayas in *"Round the World,"* chapters 24–25.

42. Seward, *William H. Seward's Travels,* 124–37, quotation on 124.
43. Fogg, *"Round the World,"* 123.
44. Ibid., 119–20.
45. Seward, *William H. Seward's Travels,* 181–82.
46. Ibid., 226. On Seward's encounters with and celebration of "American" technology and commerce during his travels, see Sexton, "William Seward in the World," 405. On American ideas about the rebirth of China and the East more generally, see also Adas, *Dominance by Design,* 107, 109–10, 116.
47. Seward, *William H. Seward's Travels,* 483.
48. Fogg, *"Round the World,"* 143.
49. Coffin, *Our New Way Round the World,* 36.
50. Ibid., 107; see also 166. For Seward, see Sexton, "William Seward in the World," 417.
51. Coffin, *Our New Way Round the World,* 176.
52. Fogg, *"Round the World,"* 164.
53. Ibid., 200.
54. Seward, *William H. Seward's Travels,* 278; Sexton, "William Seward in the World," 417.
55. Seward, *William H. Seward's Travels,* 71.
56. Fogg, *"Round the World,"* 151–52.
57. Coffin, *Our New Way Round the World,* 149–50.
58. Fogg said little about Ismael Pasha in his letters on Egypt, focusing instead on his excursions as a tourist and his time in Cairo.
59. Coffin, *Our New Way Round the World,* 29.
60. Seward, *William H. Seward's Travels,* 533; Sexton, "William Seward in the World," 416; William Henry Seward to Frederick William Seward, May 11, 1871, 3, SFDA. On the ambitious nature of the viceroy's economic agenda, see F. Robert Hunter, "Egypt under the Successors of Muhammad 'Ali," in *The Cambridge History of Egypt,* vol. 2, *Modern Egypt from 1517 to the End of the 20th Century,* ed. M. W. Daly (New York: Cambridge Univ. Press, 1998), 180–97, especially 186–87.
61. Coffin, *Our New Way Round the World,* 28.
62. On the tensions between universalism and racism in William Seward's observations, see also Sexton, "William Seward in the World," 403.
63. Fogg, *"Round the World,"* 40.
64. Ibid., 68–69.
65. Coffin, *Our New Way Round the World,* 454, 456.
66. Ibid., 186.
67. See Christopher Munn, *Anglo-China: Chinese People and British Rule in Hong Kong, 1841–1880* (Richmond, Surrey, UK: Curzon, 2001), 1–4, 330–31, 341–57.
68. Fogg, *"Round the World,"* 110.
69. Ibid., 185.
70. In addition to the quotations below, see also Sexton, "William Seward in the World," 415–16.
71. Seward, *William H. Seward's Travels,* 100, 103–4.
72. Carleton, *Our New Way Round the World,* 133–36.
73. Fogg, *"Round the World,"* 187–88, quotations from 188.
74. Ibid., 190–91.
75. Fogg, *"Round the World,"* 109. The original text contains a misplaced quotation mark at the end of the sentence.

76. Coffin, *Our New Way Round the World*, 43.

77. Ibid., 454.

78. In addition to the moments mentioned below, the following scenes from Seward, *William H. Seward's Travels*, offer some clues about these relationships, albeit only faint ones: 120 (Freeman mentions to an American admiral that one of his marines aboard ship has previously met Seward); 128 (the "faithful Freeman" bunks with Seward as they make their way up the Pei-ho [Hai] River); 140 (Freeman, watching over the luggage, brings up the rear of their party); 144 (the party gets separated from each other in Beijing, with the "trusty Freeman" the most concerned for the missing members); 224–25 (Freeman has learned some pigeon-English in hopes of being able to dismiss the Sewards' Chinese servants); 455 (Freeman and the group's other two servants enter an Indian town behind William, the local maharaja, Olive, Harriet, and a British captain, but ahead of the minister of justice); 465 (in a second trip riding elephants, the group temporarily fails to notice that Freeman's elephant was left behind); 469 (Freeman and the other two servants watch with wonder as the prince of Putteeala bestows gifts on the party, and then becomes "suddenly perplexed" about how to fit it all in the group's railway car); 480 (William, Olive, and Harriet travel by carriage while "the servants," including Freeman, follow behind on elephants); 561 (the group enters a series of caves in Upper Egypt and Freeman falls four or five feet—while he lands unhurt, the group decides to leave); 605 (Freeman, as many travelers did, carves his name into the granite rocks at Philae, the farthest navigable point up the Nile); and 686 (in Istanbul an official guard of honor "with due solemnity and respect" escorts the servants to the entrance of the hotel the group was staying at). Olive's and William's private correspondence during the voyage conform with the tone of the narrative, addressing Freeman as a servant but typically on cordial terms. From the SFDA, see William Henry Seward to Frederick William Seward, March 10, 1871, 4; William Henry Seward to William Henry Seward Jr., April 10, 1871, 5–6; William Henry Seward Jr. to William Henry Seward, April 15, 1871, 3–4; William Henry Seward to Frederick William Seward, June 7, 1871, 1–2.

79. Seward, *William H. Seward's Travels*, 10.

80. Ibid., 466.

81. Ibid., 114. The interpretation here differs slightly from that offered in Sexton, "William Seward in the World," 413. It concurs with Sexton's emphasis on Seward's lack of attention to black agency, but does not go so far as to argue that Seward was advancing a distinctively conservative interpretation of Reconstruction. Rather, he was being inconsistent in both celebrating the cause of equality and failing to attend to the actual opinions of African Americans.

82. Seward, *William H. Seward's Travels*, 300.

83. Ibid., 339; on "the Malays" and irrigation, see also 319, 333. For the Sewards' other comments on "the Malays," see 307, 308, 323.

84. Ibid., 602–3.

85. Ibid., 520–21.

86. Coffin, *Our New Way Round the World*, 113.

87. Seward, *William H. Seward's Travels*, 555. Fogg also compared dervishes with the Shakers, although without the emphasis on human nature; see Fogg, *"Round the World,"* 228.

88. Seward, *William H. Seward's Travels*, 573, 575.

89. William Henry Seward to Frederick William Seward, June 7, 1871, 3, SFDA.

90. On earlier American discussions of the British Empire and India, see Elizabeth Kelly Gray, "'Whisper to Him the Word 'India': Trans-Atlantic Critics and American Slavery, 1830–1860," *Journal of the Early Republic* 28, no. 3 (fall 2018): 379–406.

91. Wrobel, *Global West, American Frontier.*

92. Fogg, *"Round the World,"* 194–95; all quotations from 195. William Seward, in private correspondence, also noted the British fear of a Russian-American alliance; William Henry Seward to Frederick William Seward, March 10, 1871, 5, SFDA.

93. Coffin, *Our New Way Round the World,* 129–32.

94. Ibid., 184–86.

95. Ibid., 186.

96. Seward, *William H. Seward's Travels,* 309, 311, 314, 318, 353–76; Sexton, "William Seward in the World," 408–9.

97. William Henry Seward to Frederick William Seward, April 19, 1871, 1–2, SFDA. On the Sewards' privileged treatment when traveling, see Sexton, "William Seward in the World," and, from the SFDA: William Henry Seward to William Henry Seward Jr., January 29, 1871, 4; William Henry Seward to William Henry Seward Jr., February 21, 1871, 2–3; William Henry Seward to William Henry Seward Jr., March 1, 1871, 3–4; William Henry Seward to Frederick William Seward, March 10, 1871, 2; William Henry Seward to William Henry Seward Jr., April 3, 1871, 1–2; William Henry Seward to William Henry Seward Jr., April 10, 1871, 3; William Henry Seward to Frederick William Seward, May 4, 1871, 1; William Henry Seward to Frederick William Seward, May 11, 1871, 1–3; William Henry Seward to William Henry Seward Jr., June 1, 1871, 1; William Henry Seward to Frederick William Seward, June 7, 1871, 5–7; William Henry Seward to William Henry Seward Jr., June 28, 1871, 1, 2, 3.

98. Sexton, "William Seward in the World," 407–11.

99. Seward, *William H. Seward's Travels,* 302, 311, 322–23, quotation from 322; William Henry Seward to William Henry Seward Jr., January 29, 1871, 2–3. For an overview of Java's economy at this time, see M. C. Ricklefs, *A History of Modern Indonesia Since c. 1200,* 4th ed. (New York: Palgrave, 2008), 146–50.

100. Seward, *William H. Seward's Travels,* 338–39; on the troop ship, see 304; on violence and Dutch rule, see also 313; on Dutch tyranny, see also 311. The chronological scope of the Sewards' comparison here is confusing since Spanish rule in the Americas ended around the same time that the Dutch government assumed control of colonial Indonesia from the Dutch East India Company (VOC). If the Sewards meant the comparison to address the long arc of European maritime imperialism, then their favorable views of the Dutch were misplaced. The VOC practiced slavery and campaigns of extermination in the archipelago. See Ricklefs, *A History of Modern Indonesia,* 4th ed.

101. Seward, *William H. Seward's Travels,* 324–26.

102. Ibid., 335; on the Dutch fellow traveler, see also 329.

103. Ibid., 331, 335.

104. Ibid., 339.

105. Seward, *William H. Seward's Travels,* 504–5. Seward's visit was significant enough to warrant mention in one member's history of the club, although the author offered no substantive commentary on how the audience received the speech; see Samuel T. Sheppard, *The Byculla Club, 1833–1916, A History* (Bombay: Bennett, Coleman, 1916), 78–79.

106. Seward, *William H. Seward's Travels,* 503–4.

107. Ibid., 647; Fogg, *"Round the World,"* 126; Coffin, *Our New Way Round the World,* 82.

108. Seward, *William H. Seward's Travels,* 404.

109. Coffin, *Our New Way Round the World,* 45, 415; see also Seward, *William H. Seward's Travels,* 148.

110. Kevin C. Murphy, *The American Merchant Experience in Nineteenth-Century Japan* (London: RoutledgeCurzon, 2003), 61, 70–71, 85–91; James Hoare, *Japan's Treaty Ports and*

Foreign Settlements: The Uninvited Guests, 1858–1899 (Folkestone, Kent, UK: Japan Press, 1994), 6–8, 14–15, 20–24, 26–27, 28. Murphy points out that American merchants did have regular contact with Japanese servants, employees, and prostitutes.

111. Seward, *William H. Seward's Travels*, 40; Murphy, *The American Merchant Experience in Nineteenth-Century Japan*, 59, 63–66.

112. Seward, *William H. Seward's Travels*, 79. On the gender disparity in Yokohama, see Hoare, *Japan's Treaty Ports and Foreign Settlements*, 23, and Murphy, *The American Merchant Experience in Nineteenth-Century Japan*, 5.

113. Seward, *William H. Seward's Travels*, 288–89. On French conquests, see Mark W. McLeod, *The Vietnamese Response to the French Intervention, 1862–1874* (New York: Praeger, 1990), chapters 2–3.

114. Fogg, *"Round the World Letters,"* 46.

115. Ibid., 130.

116. Seward, *William H. Seward's Travels*, 340.

117. Ibid., 296; see also, 278. On the influence of Chinese migration to and trade with Singapore, see Stephen Dobbs, "The Singapore River/Port in Global Context," in *Singapore in Global History*, ed. Derek Heng and Syed Muhd Khairudin Aljunied (Amsterdam: Amsterdam Univ. Press, 2011): 51–65, especially 60–61; Catherine Paix, "Singapore as a Central Place between the West, Asia and China: From the 19th to the 21st Centuries," in *Singapore from Temasek to the 21st Century: Reinventing the Global City*, ed. Karl Hack and Jean-Louis Margolin, with Karine Delaye (Singapore: National Univ. of Singapore Press, 2010), 210–42, especially 211–14; and Mark Ravinder Frost and Yu-Mei Balasingamchow, *Singapore: A Biography* (Hong Kong: Hong Kong Univ. Press, 2009), 91–93. According to Frost and Balasingamchow, the Chinese share of Singapore's population was closer to two-thirds (*Singapore*, 91). Some influential Chinese merchants in Singapore were native to and/or arrived from other parts of the Malaysian peninsula, not China; see Frost and Balasingamchow, *Singapore*, 93–98.

118. Sexton, "William Seward in the World," 418.

119. See, for example, William Henry Seward to Janet Watson Seward, September 16, 1870, 5, SFDA.

120. Seward, *William H. Seward's Travels*, 557–58.

121. Coffin, *Our New Way Round the World*, 60.

122. Fogg, *"Round the World,"* 109.

123. Ibid.,125; see also Seward, *William H. Seward's Travels*, 296–97, 297–98. On Singapore's diversity, which was a function of its rapid growth and open commerce during the nineteenth century, see Dobbs, "The Singapore River/Port in Global Context," 57–63; and Karine Delaye, "Singapore: A Model for Indochina? (1860s–1920s)," in *Singapore from Temasek to the 21st Century: Reinventing the Global City*, ed. Karl Hack and Jean-Louis Margolin, with Karine Delaye (Singapore: National Univ. of Singapore Press, 2010), 185–209, especially 187–88.

124. Seward, *William H. Seward's Travels*, 617; see also their similar statement about Batavia, 305.

125. Coffin, *Our New Way Round the World*, 24–25. On Egypt and the Suez Canal as a meeting point between East and West, see also Murray, "Imperial Ways," 193.

126. Coffin, *Our New Way Round the World*, 79.

127. Fogg, *"Round the World,"* 139.

128. Coffin, *Our New Way Round the World*, 69.

129. Fogg, *"Round the World,"* 124. According to Mark Ravinder Frost and Yu-Mei Bal-

asingamchow, the majority of Chinese immigrants, at least in the 1830s, worked in tin mines and local plantations; see Frost and Balasingamchow, *Singapore,* 87. Chinese migration to Malaysia to work in tin mines dated to the first half of the eighteenth century; see Ricklefs, *A History of Modern Indonesia,* 4th ed., 85. By one account, the rise of canned food technology in the United States led to "a veritable 'tin rush' in Malaya," roughly during the period these travelers visited Singapore; see Jim Baker, *The Eagle in the Lion City: America, Americans and Singapore* (Singapore: Landmark Books, 2005), 82. On the eastern appropriation of western technology alluded to in Fogg's passage, see also Adas, *Dominance by Design,* 126–27.

130. Fogg, *"Round the World,"* 127. Mr. Whampoah, originally Hoo Ah Kay, was a leading merchant who had close ties to the British, was a prominent member of Singapore's social elite, had done business with Americans, and had feted Commodore Matthew Perry years earlier when Perry was en route to Japan. He was the first Chinese consul-general to Singapore. In 1869 he became the first Asian to serve on Singapore's Legislative Council. In 1876 he was decorated by the queen of England. See "China, relations with," and "Hoo Ah Kay (1816–1880)," *Historical Dictionary of Singapore,* new ed., ed. Justin Corfield (Lanham, Md.: Scarecrow Press, 2011), 57, 108; "Hoo Ah Kay (1814–1880)," *Historical Dictionary of Singapore,* ed., K. Mulliner and Lian The-Mulliner (Metuchen, N.J.: Scarecrow Press, 1991), 67; and Baker, *Eagle in the Lion City,* 45, 103. Fogg was introduced to Kay by the local American consul, James Jewell. On Jewell, see Baker, *Eagle in the Lion City,* 103–4, 105. On the importance of Chinese merchants to British rule in mid-century Singapore, see Paix, "Singapore as a Central Place between the West, Asia and China," 211–18.

131. Fogg, *"Round the World,"* 127.

132. That Carleton was visiting Whampoah is based on the description of the latter's house available in Charles Burton Buckley, *An Anecdotal History of Old Times in Singapore,* 2 vols. (Singapore: Fraser and Neave, 1902), 2:658–59, 710.

133. Coffin, *Our New Way Round the World,* 240.

134. Ibid., 157.

135. Fogg, *"Round the World,"* 149–50.

136. Seward, *William H. Seward's Travels,* 356.

137. Carleton, *Our New Way Round the World,* 64.

138. On this dynamic, consider John Higham, *Strangers in the Land: Patterns of American Nativism, 1860–1925* (New Brunswick, N.J.: Rutgers Univ. Press, 1955).

139. Seward, *William H. Seward's Travels,* 204.

4. "Our Papers"

1. Benjamin J. K. Anderson, *Narrative of a Journey to Musardu, the Capital of the Western Mandingoes* (New York: S. W. Green, 1870), 3, 72, 114–16; Humphrey Fisher, "New Introduction," in Benjamin J. K. Anderson, *Journeys to Musadu,* ed. Humphrey Fisher (1870 and 1912; reprint, London: Frank Cass, 1971), v; See James Fairhead et al., eds., *African-American Exploration in West Africa: Four Nineteenth-Century Diaries* (Bloomington: Indiana Univ. Press, 2003), 41–46.

2. Fisher, "Introduction," vii–xi; M. B. Akpan, "Black Imperialism: Americo-Liberian Rule over the African Peoples of Liberia, 1841–1964," *Canadian Journal of African Studies* 7, no. 2 (1973): 217–36, 220–25; Ciment, *Another America,* 132; Anderson, *Narrative of a Journey to Musardu,* 5–6, 20, 67, 100–103.

3. For information on Anderson, see Fairhead, *African-American Exploration in West Africa,* 51–55, 56–57. On Liberia's politics, see Ciment, *Another America,* chapter 5.

4. Fisher, "New Introduction," i; Fairhead, *African-American Exploration in West Africa,* 55–56.

5. Anderson, *Narrative of a Journey to Musardu,* 5.

6. Fairhead, *African-American Exploration in West Africa,* 42, 55–56; Anderson, *Narrative of a Journey to Musardu,* 48.

7. Anderson, *Narrative of a Journey to Musardu,* 7, 51, 53–54, 61–62, 79–80, 110.

8. Ibid., 91–92.

9. Ibid., 29–30, 32, 40, 57–58, 62–63, 64–65, 106–7, 110.

10. Ibid., 16–18, 86.

11. Ibid., 10, 18, 30, 44, 55, 56, 74, 100, 103–4, 114–15.

12. Ibid., 10, 20–21, 23–25, 27, 32–33, 47, 48, 50, 60–61, 70, 71–72, 75, 76, 113–14.

13. Ibid., 21–22, 25, 39, 41–44, 79, 95, 103, 109.

14. Ibid., 7–9; Fairhead, *African-American Exploration in West Africa,* 57.

15. Anderson, *Narrative of a Journey to Musardu,* 71.

16. "Missionaries Wanted," *American Union,* July 30, 1869, 2; "Editor's Literary Record," *Harper's Monthly,* October 1870, 783–84.

17. Anderson, *Narrative of a Journey to Musardu,* 3; See Khalil Mahmud, "Introduction," in *The People of Africa: A Series of Papers on Their Character, Condition, and Future Prospects,* comp. Henry Schieffelin, ed. Khalil Mahmud, v–xxiii (1871; reprint, Ibadan, Nigeria: Ibadan Univ. Press, 1974), viii.

18. Joseph Henry to Asa Gray, December 7, 1860, in *The Papers of Joseph Henry,* 12 vols., ed. Marc Rothenberg (Washington, D.C.: Smithsonian Institution Press, 1972–2008), 10:183–84; see also Joseph Henry to John Torrey, November 27, 1860, in *The Papers of Joseph Henry,* 10:178–79; Marc Rothenberg, "Introduction," in *The Papers of Joseph Henry,* 10:xv–xlviii, especially xxiv–xxvi.

19. Fisher, "Introduction," viii; Anderson, *A Journey to Musardu,* 3; and Fairhead et al., *African-American Exploration in West Africa,* 57.

20. For the broader history of these factors, see especially Manisha Sinha, *The Slave's Cause: A History of Abolition* (New Haven, Conn.: Yale Univ. Press, 2016); Douglas R. Egerton, *The Wars of Reconstruction: The Brief, Violent History of America's Most Progressive Era* (New York: Bloomsbury Press, 2014); and Steven H. Hahn, *A Nation under Our Feet: Black Political Struggles in the Rural South, from Slavery to the Great Migration* (Cambridge, Mass.: Belknap Press of Harvard Univ. Press, 2003).

21. On the antebellum African American editorial tradition, see Ivy G. Wilson, "The Brief and Wondrous Life of the *Anglo-African Magazine*; Or, Antebellum African American Editorial Practice and Its Afterlives," in *Publishing Blackness: Textual Constructions of Race since 1850,* ed. George Hutchinson and John K. Young (Ann Arbor: Univ. of Michigan Press, 2013), 18–38. On Douglass's views on race and the press, see Robert Fanuzzi, "Frederick Doulgass's 'Colored Newspaper': Identity Politics in Black and White," in *The Black Press: New Literary and Historical Essays,* ed. Todd Vogel (New Brunswick, N.J.: Rutgers Univ. Press, 2001), 55–70. Fanuzzi overstates the role of Douglass's editorial ambitions in his break with William Lloyd Garrison; see Sinha, *The Slave's Cause,* 492.

22. On the name changes, see "The Change in Our Name," *New National Era,* September 8, 1870, 2, and "The New National Era and Citizen," *New National Era and Citizen,* June 12, 1873, 2. On Frederick Douglass's ownership and control of the paper, see Frederick Douglass, "Another Change," *New National Era,* December 15, 1870, 2.

23. L. Diane Barnes, *Frederick Douglass: Reformer and Statesman* (New York: Routledge, 2013), 104, 107, 109–10; Benjamin Quarles, *Frederick Douglass* (New York: Da Capo Press, 1997), 110, 271.

24. Quarles, *Frederick Douglass,* 281.

25. [J.] Sella Martin to Frederick Douglass, March 29, 1869, General Correspondence, Frederick Douglass Papers, Library of Congress; Frederick Douglass to J. Sella Martin, April 5, 1869, General Correspondence, Frederick Douglass Papers, Library of Congress; Barnes, *Frederick Douglass,* 109–10; David W. Blight, *Frederick Douglass: Prophet of Freedom* (New York: Simon and Schuster, 2018), 524–25.

26. Barnes, *Frederick Douglass,* 107–8, 110–14; David Blight, *Frederick Douglass' Civil War: Keeping Faith in Jubilee* (Baton Rouge: Louisiana State Univ. Press, 1989), 204–5, 216–18.

27. On the importance of these ideas to Frederick Douglass, see Barnes, *Frederick Douglass,* 110; Blight, *Frederick Douglass' Civil War,* 196, 203–4, 208; Dorothy Ross, "'Are We a Nation?': The Conjuncture of Nationhood and Race in the United States, 1850–1876," *Modern Intellectual History* 2, no. 3 (November 2005): 327–60.

28. "The *New Era,*" *Elevator,* February 25, 1870, 3.

29. Reginald F. Hildebrand, *The Times Were Strange and Stirring: Methodist Preachers and the Crisis of Emancipation* (Durham, N.C.: Duke Univ. Press, 1995); Joe M. Richardson, *Christian Reconstruction: The American Missionary Association and Southern Blacks, 1861–1890* (Tuscaloosa: Univ. of Alabama Press, 1986); Ronald E. Butchart, *Schooling the Freedpeople: Teaching, Learning, and the Struggle for Black Freedom, 1861–1876* (Chapel Hill: Univ. of North Carolina Press, 2010); Michael W. Fitzgerald, *The Union League Club Movement in the Deep South: Politics and Agricultural Change during Reconstruction* (Baton Rouge: Louisiana State Univ. Press, 1989); P. Gabrielle Foreman et al., "Colored Conventions: Bringing Nineteenth-Century Black Organizing to Digital Life," http://coloredconventions.org/. On the processes of southern black political mobilization, see Foner, *Reconstruction,* and Hahn, *A Nation under Our Feet.*

30. Donna L. Dickerson, "George T. Ruby: Reconstruction Politician/Journalist," *American Journalism* 15, no. 1 (winter 1998): 51–68, 62.

31. See, for example, Eric Gardner, *Unexpected Places: Relocating Nineteenth-Century African American Literature* (Jackson: Univ. Press of Mississippi, 2009), 113.

32. Penelope L. Bullock, *The Afro-American Periodical Press, 1839–1909* (Baton Rouge: Louisiana State Univ. Press, 1981), 64; Wilson, "The Brief and Wondrous Life of the *Anglo-African Magazine,*" 26–27; Carla Peterson, *"Doers of the Word": African-American Women Speakers and Writers in the North (1830–1880)* (New Brunswick, N.J.: Rutgers Univ. Press, 1998), 208–9, 216, 233–35.

33. On intellectual autonomy, see Wilson, "The Brief and Wondrous Life of the *Anglo-African Magazine,*" 23–25.

34. Summers, *The Press Gang,* 12, 210, 221; Dickerson, "George T. Ruby," 52–54; Abbott, *For Free Press and Equal Rights,* 45–46, 60.

35. Sicherman, "Ideologies and Practices of Reading," 3:281; Jeannine Marie DeLombard, "African American Cultures of Print," in *A History of the Book in America,* ed. Scott Casper et al. (Chapel Hill: Univ. of North Carolina Press, 2007), 3:367–68, 369–72; Amy M. Thomas, "Literacies, Readers, and Cultures of Print in the South," in *A History of the Book in America,* ed. Scott Casper et al. (Chapel Hill: Univ. of North Carolina Press, 2007), 3:374; Janet Cornelius, "'We Slipped and Learned to Read': Slave Accounts of the Literacy Process, 1830–1865," in *Literacy and Historical Development: A Reader,* ed. Harvey J. Graff (Carbon-

dale: Southern Illinois Univ. Press, 2007), 315–33, 325–26; Foner, *Reconstruction*, 97–100, 284; Dickerson, "George T. Ruby," 51–68, 52–53; Julius E. Thompson, *The Black Press in Mississippi, 1865–1985* (Gainesville: Univ. Press of Florida, 1993), 5; Christopher Hager, *Word by Word: Emancipation and the Act of Writing* (Cambridge, Mass.: Harvard Univ. Press, 2013), 181–88.

36. Abbott, *For Free Press and Equal Rights*, 71; Dickerson, "George T. Ruby," 53.

37. On the history of black abolitionist publishing, see Carter R. Bryan, "Negro Journalism in America before Emancipation," *Journalism Monographs* 12 (September 1969): 1–29; Sinha, *The Slave's Cause*; and Wilson, "The Brief and Wondrous Life of the *Anglo-African Magazine*."

38. Bryan, "Negro Journalism in America before Emancipation," 2.

39. For an overview of southern African American papers, including their generally short life spans during Reconstruction, see Armistead Scott Pride, "A Register and History of Negro Newspapers in the United States: 1827–1950" (Ph.D. diss., Northwestern University, 1950), 18–32, 47–52, 54–58, 65–80, 95–104, 111–14, 132–34, 145–55, 157–62, 164–65. Also helpful are I. Garland Penn, *The Afro-American Press and Its Editors* (Springfield, Mass.: Willey, 1891; reprint, New York: Arno Press and the New York Times, 1969) 100–115; and Frederick G. Detweiler, *The Negro Press in the United States* (Chicago: Univ. of Chicago Press, 1922), 44–46.

40. Debra Jackson, "'A Cultural Stronghold': The 'Anglo-African' Newspaper and the Black Community of New York," *New York History* 85, no. 4 (fall 2004): 331–57; Wilson, "The Brief and Wondrous Life of the *Anglo-African Magazine*," 20–27; Bullock, *The Afro-American Periodical Press*, 72.

41. Felecia G. Jones Ross, "Democracy's Textbook: A History of the Black Press in Ohio, 1865–1985," in *The Black Press in the Middle West, 1865–1985*, ed. Henry Lewis Suggs (Westport, Conn.: Greenwood, 1996), 243–66, 245–46.

42. See Frank H. Goodyear, "'Beneath the Shadow of Her Flag': Philip A. Bell's *The Elevator* and the Struggle for Enfranchisement, 1865–1870," *California History* 78, no. 1 (spring 1999): 26–39; Gardner, *Unexpected Places*, 104–13; Roland E. Wolseley, *The Black Press, U.S.A.*, 2nd ed. (Ames: Iowa State Univ. Press, 1990), 26–27.

43. "Prospectus of the Colored Citizen," *Colored Citizen*, 19 May 1866, 2.

44. See, "Our Name," "Our Motto," and "Our Position," *Elevator*, April 14, 1865, 3.

45. Gilbert Anthony Williams, "The 'A.M.E. Christian Recorder': Forum for the Social Ideas of Black Americans, 1854–1902," Ph.D. diss., University of Illinois at Urbana-Champaign, 1979, 9–10, 28–29, 33, 40–45; Mitch Kachun, "Interrogating the Silences: Julia C. Collins, 19th-Century Black Readers and Writers, and the *Christian Recorder*," *African American Review* 40, no. 4 (winter 2006): 649–59; Hager, *Word by Word*, 182–83.

46. Heather Andrea Williams, *Help Me Find My People: The African American Search for Family Lost in Slavery* (Chapel Hill: Univ. of North Carolina Press, 2012), 140–68; Hager, *Word by Word*, 183.

47. For an at times imaginative rendering of Pinchback's life, see James Haskins, *Pinckney Benton Stewart Pinchback* (New York: Macmillan, 1973).

48. Paul H. Gates Jr., "Toward a Common Goal: Jean-Charles Houzeau, P.B.S. Pinchback and New Orleans' Black Press, 1862–1882," in *Proceedings of the American Journalism Historians' Association Conference (Salt Lake City, Utah, October 5–7, 1993)*, part 2, *Issues of Race* (Salt Lake City: N.p., 1993), 181–82, 186, 191.

49. Lamson, *The Glorious Failure*, 34.

50. Dickerson, "George T. Ruby," 54; Thompson, *The Black Press in Mississippi*, 5–6.

51. Dickerson, "George T. Ruby," 54, 55.

52. Ibid., 59–60, 62, 64.

53. Gates Jr., "Toward a Common Goal," 185, 189–90.

54. Dickerson, "George T. Ruby," 59.

55. Peter J. Breaux, "William G. Brown and the Development of Education: A Retrospective on the Career of a State Superintendent of Public Education of African Descent in Louisiana," Ph.D. diss., Florida State University, 2006, 1–2.

56. Lamson, *The Glorious Failure,* 22, 23–30.

57. See, for example, Breaux, "William G. Brown and the Development of Education," 2; "Is the Negro a Man?" *Mobile Nationalist,* December 27, 1866, 1.

58. David E. Rankin, "Introduction," in Jean-Charles Houzeau, *My Passage at the New Orleans* Tribune*: A Memoirof the Civil War Era,* ed., David E. Rankin, trans. Gerard F. Denault (Baton Rouge: Louisiana State Univ. Press, 1984), 1–67, 24; William P. Connor, "Reconstruction Rebels: The *New Orleans Tribune* in Post-War Louisiana," *Louisiana History* 21, no. 2 (spring 1980): 159–81 160–62, 163–64, 169–70, 172–76, 177ff77; Gates Jr., "Toward a Common Goal," 178.

59. Rankin, "Introduction," 47–57; Gates Jr., "Toward a Common Goal," 176–81; Binning, "Carpetbaggers' Triumph," 21–39, especially 34–35; Connor, "Reconstruction Rebels," 159–81, 179.

60. Michael W. Fitzgerald, *Urban Emancipation: Popular Politics in Reconstruction Mobile, 1860–1890* (Baton Rouge: Louisiana State Univ. Press, 2002), 49–86, 109, 129–30, 139–40, 146–47.

61. See, for example, the fourth page of the following issues of the *New National Era/New National Era and Citizen*: December 29, 1870; January 12, 1871; July 20, 1871; December 21, 1871; June 20, 1872; December 12, 1872; July 10, 1873; December 4, 1873; February 12, 1874; June 18, 1874; and October 8, 1874.

62. "Our Premiums," *New National Era,* November 16, 1871, 4; "Prospectus of the New National Era," *New National Era and Citizen,* February 19, 1874, 3.

63. "Official," *New National Era,* October 12, 1871, 4.

64. Peterson, *"Doers of the Word,"* 233.

65. Douglass, "Another Change."

66. "The New National Era and Citizen," *New National Era and Citizen,* June 12, 1873, 2.

67. Blight, *Frederick Douglass,* 532–34.

68. See "Our Journal" and "A Few Words to Our Friends," *New Era,* January 13, 1870, 2; "Salutatory of the Corresponding Editor," *New Era,* January 27, 1870, 2; "The Place We Fill," *New Era,* February 10, 1870, 2; "The Change in Our Name" and "Salutatory," *New National Era,* September 8, 1870, 2.

69. "The Progressive American," *New National Era,* July 30, 1874, 2; "The Progressive American Again," *New National Era,* August 20, 1874, 2; "Reply to the 'Era,'" *New National Era,* August 20, 1874, 2; "A Controversy," *Elevator,* September 19, 1874, 2; "The 'Elevator,'" *New National Era,* October 1, 1874, 2; "Let Us Be Friends," *Elevator,* October 24, 1874, 3.

70. "The Christian(?) Recorder," *New National Era,* January 26, 1871, 2; "The Christian Recorder," *New National Era,* November 28, 1872, 2; no title, *New National Era and Citizen,* June 12, 1873, 2.

71. "The New Era," *New Era,* March 31, 1870, 1; George Washington Jr., "The Near Future," *New Era,* April 28, 1870, 1; "Barbarism in Kentucky," *New Era,* June 23, 1870, 1; "Barbarism against Civilization," *New National Era,* April 6, 1871, 2; "The Black Man's Progress on This Continent," *New National Era,* July 27, 1871, 2; "Progress," *New National Era,* Sep-

tember 14, 1871, 3; "A Barbarous Virginian," *New National Era*, May 2, 1872, 3; "Barbarism of White America," *New National Era and Citizen*, July 17, 1873, 1; "American Civilization," *New National Era and Citizen*, July 17, 1873, 2; "The 'Barbarism of Slavery,'" *New National Era*, April 2, 1874, 2; and "Southern Brutality," *New National Era*, July 30, 1874, 2; Blight, *Frederick Douglass' Civil War*, 211–12.

72. See for example, "The United States and Hayti," *New Era*, March 17, 1870, 3; "Hon. E. D. Bassett," *New National Era*, September 15, 1870, 2; "The Testimony of an Ex-Haytien Minister," *New National Era*, September 12, 1872, 2; "From Pennsylvania," *New National Era*, July 23, 1874, 1; Christopher Teal, *Hero of Hispaniola: America's First Black Diplomat, Ebenezer D. Bassett* (Santa Barbara, Calif.: Praeger, 2008). On postbellum African American interpretations of Haiti, see Brandon Byrd, "Black Republicans, Black Republic: African-Americans, Haiti, and the Promise of Reconstruction," *Slavery and Abolition* 36 (December 2015): 545–67.

73. On the politics surrounding Grant's annexation scheme, see Eric T. Love, *Race over Empire: Racism and U.S. Imperialism, 1865-1900* (Chapel Hill: Univ. of North Carolina Press, 2004), chapter 2; Allison L. Sneider, *Suffragists in an Imperial Age: U.S. Expansion and the Woman Question, 1870–1929* (New York: Oxford Univ. Press, 2008), chapter 2; and Nicholas Guyatt, "America's Conservatory: Race, Reconstruction, and the Santo Domingo Debate," *Journal of American History* 97, no. 4 (March 2011): 974–1000.

74. Merline Pitre, "Frederick Douglass and American Diplomacy in the Caribbean," *Journal of Black Studies* 13, no. 4 (June 1983): 457–75, especially 457–68; Christopher Wilkins "'They had heard of emancipation and the enfranchisement of their race': The African American Colonists of Samaná, Reconstruction, and the State of Santo Domingo," in *The Civil War as Global Conflict: Transnational Meanings of the American Civil War*, ed. David T. Gleeson and Simon Lewis (Columbia: Univ. of South Carolina Press, 2014), 211–34; and Blight, *Frederick Douglass' Civil War*, 210.

75. See the following from the *New National Era*: [1] "The San Domingo Flurry," December 29, 1870, 2; [2] "'Let Us Have Peace,'" January 5, 1871, 2; [3] "Annexation of San Domingo," January 12, 1871, 2; [4 and 5] "The Commissioners to San Domingo" and "San Domingo," January 19, 1871, 2; [6] "Imaginary Danger of Annexation," February 2, 1871, 2; [7] "Important Communication Relative to San Domingo," February 16, 1871, 1; [8] Charles R. Douglas, "Correspondence from Santo Domingo," March 2, 1871, 2; [9 and 10] "The Dominican Expedition" and "Hayti and Santo Domingo," March 9, 1871, 1; [11] "San Domingo Amusements," March 9, 1871, 3; [12] "Santo Domingo," March 23, 1871, 3; [13] "San Domingo," March 30, 1871, 3; [14 and 15] "Dear Readers" and "Mr. Douglass' View," April 6, 1871, 2; [16] "San Domingo," April 13, 1871, 1; [17 and 18] "Letter on Santo Domingo, No. 2" and "The President's Message on Santo Domingo," April 13, 1871, 2; [19] "Santo Domingo, No. 3," April 20, 1871, 2; [20] "What Jamaica Thinks of Annexation," April 20, 1871, 3; [21] Henry B. Blackwell, "Santo Domingo—The Case Stated," April 27, 1871, 1; [22] "Santo Domingo, No. 4," April 27, 1871, 2; [23] "Santo Domingo—No. 5," May 4, 1871, 2; [24] "Santo Domingo," May 4, 1871, 3; [25] "Sherman on Sumner," May 11, 1871, 1; [26] "Santo Domingo—No. 7," May 18, 1871, 2; [27] "What Is the 'Toe Disease'?" May 25, 1871, 1; [28] "San Domingo," May 25, 1871, 3; [29] "San Domingo," June 1, 1871, 1; [30] "Santo Domingo," June 8, 1871, 1; [31] "Santo Domingo—No. 8," June 15, 1871, 2; and [32] "The Discussion with Mr. Downing Ended," July 13, 1871, 2. Coverage continued thereafter, with subsequent upticks in discussion activity in April of 1872 and the winter of 1873–1874.

76. With the Franco-Prussian War, for instance, the paper ran articles about every other

issue from July 1870 until May 1871. See, for example, in the *New National Era*: "The War in Europe," September 8, 1870, 2; "A Sign of Peace" and "Progress of the War," September 15, 1870, 2; "Adulterated Republicanism," April 6, 1871, 2.

77. No title, *New National Era,* June 15, 1871, 1.

78. Frank J. Webb, "International Exhibition," *New Era,* January 20, 1870, 1.

79. M. R. Delany, "Civil Rights," *New Era,* February 24, 1870, 1.

80. George B. Vashon, "The Nile," *New Era,* April 14, 1870, 1.

81. On these points, see Blight, *Frederick Douglass,* 525, 529–30, 539; Peterson, *"Doers of the Word,"* 109–10, 233–34; and Sneider, *Suffragists in an Imperial Age,* 29, 53.

82. "Letter from St. Thomas," *New National Era,* September 28, 1871, 1.

83. David T. S. Fuller, "An Evening at the House of Melvil Bloncourt, Deputy from Guadalupe," *New National Era,* February 29, 1872, 1, and Fuller, "Letter from Paris," *New National Era and Citizen,* June 5, 1873, 1. See also Fuller, "Letter from Paris," *New National Era,* May 30, 1872, 1; Fuller, "Baudin Monument," *New National Era,* January 9, 1873, 1; Thomas Scott, "Letter from Paris," *New National Era and Citizen,* June 19, 1873, 3; Fuller, "From France," *New National Era,* June 18, 1874, 1; Blight, Frederick Douglass, 539; "Melvil-Bloncourt, Sainte Suzanne," in *Appleton's Cyclopædia of American Biography,* vol. 4, ed. James Grant Wilson and John Fiske (New York: Appleton, 1888), 293.

84. H., "Letter from England," *New National Era and Citizen,* August 14, 1873, 1.

85. "Items from the Monrovia New Era," *New National Era and Citizen,* September 11, 1873, 3; "The Sons of Ham," *New National Era and Citizen,* July 17, 1873, 1; "Khiva," *New National Era,* November 28, 1872, 3.

86. The *New National Era* also defend the principle of religious freedom in its pages, including for Catholics and free thinkers. See "The Bible in School," *New National Era,* January 4, 1872, 2; and "Erroneous Notions about Religious Liberty," *New National Era,* December 27, 1872, 2.

87. On the Irish and African Americans, see Christian G. Samito, *Becoming American under Fire: Irish Americans, African Americans, and the Politics of Citizenship during the Civil War Era* (Ithaca, N.Y.: Cornell Univ. Press, 2009).

88. Ward M. McAfee, *Religion, Race, and Reconstruction: The Public School in the Politics of the 1870s* (Albany: State Univ. of New York Press, 1988); Verhoeven, "Transatlantic Connections," 695–720. On the transatlantic dimensions of anti-Catholic thinking, see also Evan C. Rothera, "Our South American Cousin: Domingo F. Sarmiento and Education in Argentina and the United States," in *Reconstruction in a Globalizing World,* ed. David Prior (New York: Fordham Univ. Press, 2018), 21–49.

89. Rev. J. E. Rankin, "Bible Civilization," *New Era,* January 13, 1870, 2.

90. "Papist Self-Righteousness," *New National Era,* January 5, 1871, 2.

91. "What Roman Catholics Propose," *New National Era,* September 15, 1870, 3.

92. "'Let Us Have Peace,'" *New National Era,* January 5, 1871, 2.

93. Verhoeven, "Transatlantic Connections," 702–17.

94. "Progress of the Infallibility Discussion," *New Era,* June 16, 1870, 1; "The Infallibility Dogma," *New Era,* June 23, 1870, 2.

95. "anathema," *New Era,* July 7, 1870, 2.

96. "Frederick the Great on Papal Infallibility and the French Nation," *New National Era,* August 24, 1871, 3.

97. "Living Mummies," *New National Era,* April 27, 1871, 2; Verhoeven, "Transatlantic Connections," 709.

98. "Bayonets a Better Protection than Infallibility," *New Era*, August 4, 1870, 2.

99. See "Italian Unity Secured," *New National Era*, September 29, 1870, 3; and "Rome-Sketch of the Papal Territory," *New National Era*, October 6, 1870, 1.

100. "The Temporal Power of the Pope Overthrown," *New National Era*, October 6, 1870, 2.

101. "Too Late for the Past and Not Quite Fit for the Future," *New National Era*, July 20, 1871, 2.

102. "Imported Patriotism," *New National Era*, November 2, 1871, 2.

103. "Ultramontane Plots," *New National Era*, April 18, 1872, 2. See also "The Clerical War in Germany," *New National Era*, May 2, 1872, 1.

104. "Machinations of the Jesuits," *New National Era*, June 27, 1872, 2. For anti-Jesuit sentiment in the paper, see also "A Miracle in Alsace," *New National Era*, October 10, 1872, 1; and "The Jesuit Oath," *New National Era*, October 24, 1872, 1.

105. On these emancipations, see Seymour Drescher, *Abolition: A History of Slavery and Antislavery* (New York: Cambridge Univ. Press, 2009), chapters 10–12.

106. "Emancipation of Slaves and Serfs," *Elevator*, April 14, 1865, 4; "Serfdom and Slavery," *Elevator*, April 14, 1865, 2. On the political views of the *Philadelphia Press*, see Brayton Harris, *Blue and Gray in Black and White: Newspapers in the Civil War* (Washington, D.C.: Brassey's, 1999), 308.

107. A Reader, "The American Colored Man as a Civilizer Abroad," *Black Republican*, May 13, 1865, 3.

108. "An Englishman in Hayti," *Colored Citizen*, May 19, 1866, 2.

109. Ada Ferrer, *Insurgent Cuba: Race, Nation, and Revolution, 1868–1898* (Chapel Hill: Univ. of North Carolina Press, 1999), chapters 1–2; Drescher, *Abolition*, 343–46.

110. Walter Johnson, *River of Dark Dreams: Slavery and Empire in the Cotton Kingdom* (Cambridge, Mass.: Belknap Press of Harvard Univ. Press, 2013), chapters 11–12; Wong, *Racial Reconstruction*, chapter 1.

111. Lisa Brock, "Back to the Future: African-Americans and Cuba in Time(s) of Race," *Contributions in Black Studies* 12 (1994): 9–32; Andrew Priest, "Thinking about Empire: The Administration of Ulysses S. Grant, Spanish Colonialism and the Ten Years' War in Cuba," *Journal of American Studies* 48, no. 2 (May 2014): 541–58; Sexton, "The United States, the Cuban Rebellion, and the Multilateral Initiative of 1875," 335–65; James Burke Chapin, "Hamilton Fish and American Expansion," Ph.D. diss., Cornell University, 1971.

112. Paul Gerrard, "Cuba Not to Be Annexed," *New Era*, March 24, 1870, 1.

113. John A. Frith, "Sunday in Cuba," *New Era*, April 14, 1870, 2; John A. Frith, "A Trip to Cuba," *New Era*, April 21, 1870, 1.

114. "Another Cuban Failure" and "The President's Message on Cuba," *New Era*, June 23, 1870, 2.

115. "Gradual Abolition of Slavery in Cuba," *New National Era*, October 6, 1870, 2.

116. "Spain and Cuba," *New National Era*, October 31, 1872, 2.

117. "Cuba for Sale," *New National Era*, March 23, 1871, 1.

118. "Abolition of Slavery in Cuba and Porto Rico," *New National Era*, May 4, 1871, 1.

119. "Freedom and Slavery in Cuba," *New National Era*, July 6, 1871, 1; "Chinese Labor in Cuba," *New National Era*, August 3, 1871, 3; "Letter from Havana," *New National Era*, October 5, 1871, 1.

120. "An Appeal for Cuba," *New National Era*, February 15, 1872, 4. On Vidal, see Anne Marie Davis, Gabrielle Foreman, and Samantha de Vera, "Ulysses B. Vidal," *Colored Conventions: Bringing Nineteenth-Century Black Organizing to Digital Life*, http://coloredconven

tions.org/exhibits/show/mobilitymigration1855/delegates/ulysses-b--vidal (accessed August 25, 2018).

121. "Spain and Cuba," 2. For the paper's coverage of Spanish debates, see also "Cuba in the Cortes," *New National Era,* December 19, 1872, 1.

122. On Ryan's career and politics, see [John George Ryan], *Life and Adventures of Gen. Ryan, the Cuban Martyr* (Chicago: Scully, 1876), 57–58, 71, 84–86, 237–41; on his letters to the *New National Era,* see 216.

123. W.A.C. Ryan, "To the Colored People of Washington City," *New National Era,* January 23, 1873, 3; "The Revolution in Cuba," *New National Era,* February 6, 1873. On Ryan and Cuban belligerency, see also [Ryan], *Life and Adventures of Gen. Ryan,* 200–201, 203–5.

124. "Cuba," *New National Era,* January 23, 1873, 2; "Our Cuban Policy," *New National Era,* 3.

125. D. A. Straker, "Non-Interference with Cuba," *New National Era,* January 30, 1873, 1; Straker, "Cuban Belligerency Recognized," *New National Era,* February 13, 1873, 1. On Straker, see Dorothy Drinkard Hawkshawe, "David Augustus Straker, Black Lawyer and Reconstruction Politician, 1842–1908" (Ph.D. diss., Catholic University of America, 1974), 1–18.

126. "The Cuban Republic," *New National Era,* February 13, 1873, 2.

127. "The Cuban Conference," *New National Era,* March 13, 1873, 2.

128. "Cuba," *New National Era,* February 27, 1873, 2.

129. "Our Cuban Policy Censured," *New National Era and Citizen,* June 5, 1873, 2.

130. P. Gabrielle Foreman et al., "National Convention at New Orleans, LA," *Colored Conventions: Bringing Nineteenth-Century Black Organizing to Digital Life,* http://coloredconventions.org/items/show/544 (last accessed November 4, 2018).

131. Cuban Anti-Slavery Committee, *Slavery in Cuba: A Report of the Proceedings of the Meeting Held at Cooper Institute* (New York: Powers, MacGowan and Slipper, 1872), available at http://coloredconventions.org/items/show/322.

132. Wm. Lawson, "Cuba," *New National Era,* February 20, 1873, 1; "Cuba," *New National Era,* March 13, 1873, 2; Ulysses B. Vidal, "The Right of Cuban Independence," *New National Era,* March 20, 1873, 1; Grotius, "Views on the Cuban Question and Civil Rights," *New National Era,* March 20, 1873, 1; "Slavery in Cuba," *New National Era,* April 10, 1873, 1.

133. In addition to the sources cited in note 4.75, see also Blight, *Frederick Douglass,* 545.

134. "The New Orleans Semi-Weekly Louisianian," *New National Era,* June 8, 1871, 2; see also "A New Volume," *San Francisco Elevator,* September 19, 1874, 2.

135. "Our Papers," *Elevator,* December 12, 1874, 2; Barnes, *Frederick Douglass,* 114; Blight, *Frederick Douglass,* 549–50. On the number of papers, see Summers, *The Press Gang,* 10.

136. *Convention of Colored Newspaper Men,* (Cincinnati: N.p., August 4, 1875), 1, 2.

137. Ibid., 5, 6.

138. Ibid., 4.

139. Ibid., 6.

140. See P. Gabrielle Foreman et al., "Conventions by Year," *Colored Conventions: Bringing Nineteenth-Century Black Organizing to Digital Life,* http://coloredconventions.org/convention-by-year (last accessed November 3, 2018), and *Proceedings of the National Conference of Colored Men of the United States* (Washington, D.C.: Rufus H. Darby, 1879), 5–6, available also at http://coloredconventions.org/files/original/7135bd2d59c9a3b7acb8c56c020b4bbd.pdf.

141. Philip S. Foner, "Black Participation in the Centennial of 1876," *Phylon* 39, no. 4 (1978): 283–96, 283–84, 285–86.

142. James P. Danky, "Reading, Writing, and Resisting: African American Print Culture," in *A History of the Book in America*, vol. 4, *Print in Motion: The Expansion of Publishing and Reading in the United States, 1880–1940*, ed. Carl F. Kaestle and Janice A. Radway (Chapel Hill: Univ. of North Carolina Press, 2009), 339–58; Bullock, *The Afro-American Periodical Press*, chapters 3 and 4.

143. Blight, *Frederick Douglass*, 721–22, 733–35, 737, 739–40.

144. M. Giulia Fabi, "Reconstructing Race: The Novel after Slavery," in *The Cambridge Companion to the African American Novel*, ed. Maryemma Graham (New York: Cambridge Univ. Press, 2004), 34–49; Isabel Wilkerson, *The Warmth of Other Suns: The Epic Story of America's Great Migration* (New York: Vintage, 2010), 191.

5. Mormon Utah, the Blossoming Plague-Spot

An earlier version of this chapter appeared in "Civilization, Republic, Nation: Contested Keywords, Northern Republicans, and the Forgotten Reconstruction of Mormon Utah," *Civil War History* 56, no. 3 (September 2010): 281–308, and is used here with the permission of Kent State University Press.

1. On this topic, see also Wrobel, *Global West, American Frontier.*

2. See especially Richardson, *West from Appomattox.*

3. Mormon Utah has largely escaped the attention of Reconstruction scholars until very recently. Foner, *Reconstruction*, to offer but one example, touches on the subject indirectly and in passing, though it also helpfully points to one instance in which the racist *New York World* attempted to slander southern freedmen by equating them with Mormons; see 217, 474. In her excellent study exploring the connections between the North-South sectional conflict, the Gilded Age, and the conquest of the American West, Heather Richardson treats Mormon Utah with similar brevity (*West from Appomattox*, 106, 128). Historians of Mormon Utah have, of course, written about the territory's Reconstruction, often using that term, if not expanding on it in much detail. See especially Robert Dwyer, "The Gentile Comes to Utah: A Study in Religious and Social Conflict" (Ph.D. diss., Catholic University of America, 1941); Richard D. Poll, "The Political Reconstruction of Utah Territory, 1866–1890," *Pacific Historical Review* 27, no. 2 (May 1958): 111–26; Everett L. Cooley, "Carpet-bag Rule—Territorial Government in Utah," *Utah Historical Quarterly* 26, no. 2 (April 1958): 107–29; Mark W. Cannon, "The Mormon Issue in Congress 1872–1882: Drawing on the Experience of Territorial Delegate George Q. Cannon" (Ph.D. diss., Harvard University, 1960); Thomas G. Alexander, "Federal Authority versus Polygamic Theocracy: James B. McKean and the Mormons, 1870–1875," *Dialogue: A Journal of Mormon Thought* 1, no. 3 (1966): 85–100; Alan Haynes, "The Federal Government and Its Policies Regarding the Frontier Era of Utah Territory, 1850–1877" (Ph.D. diss., Catholic University of America, 1968); Gustive O. Larson, *The "Americanization" of Utah for Statehood* (San Marino, Calif.: Huntington Library, 1971); Richard D. Poll, ed., *Utah's History* (Provo, Utah: Brigham Young Univ. Press, 1978), chapters 13, 14, and 21; Leonard J. Arrington and Davis Bitton, *The Mormon Experience: A History of the Latter-day Saints*, 2nd ed. (Urbana: Univ. of Illinois Press, 1992), chapter 9; Stephen Cresswell, *Mormons and Cowboys, Moonshiners and Klansmen: Federal Law Enforcement in the South and West, 1870–1893* (Tuscaloosa: Univ. of Alabama Press, 1991),

chapters 1 and 3; B. Carmon Hardy, *Solemn Covenant: The Mormon Polygamous Passage* (Urbana: Univ. of Illinois Press, 1992), chapter 3; Sarah Barringer Gordon, *The Mormon Question: Polygamy and Constitutional Conflict in Nineteenth Century America* (Chapel Hill: Univ. of North Carolina Press, 2002).

4. W. Paul Reeve, *Religion of a Different Color: Race and the Mormon Struggle for Whiteness* (New York: Oxford Univ. Press, 2015), offers extensive discussion of the relationship between racial thinking and Mormon polygamy, although it neglects Reconstruction and differences in political persuasion among Americans more generally. On southern white attitudes toward Mormons and polygamy, see Hardy, *Solemn Covenant,* 39–40; and Fox-Genovese and Genovese, *The Mind of the Master Class,* 764–65. On the lynchings, see Patrick Q. Mason, *The Mormon Menace: Violence and Anti-Mormonism in the Postbellum South* (New York: Oxford Univ. Press, 2011).

5. As is often noted, the more precise designation for Mormon marriage practices is polygyny, which refers to the marriage of one man to multiple wives, as opposed to polygamy, which indicates marriages involving multiple spouses. It is important to note, moreover, that condemnations of what the Mormons often called "celestial marriage" routinely failed to understand the practice, or its theological and social underpinnings. For a concise discussion and leads to further readings, see Larson, *The "Americanization" of Utah for Statehood,* chapter 2; and O. Kendall White Jr. and Daryl White, "Polygamy and Mormon Identity," *Journal of American Culture* 28, no. 2 (2005): 165–77.

6. Hardy, *Solemn Covenant,* 41–42; on manliness, masculinity, and Civil War–era political parties, see Amy S. Greenberg, *Manifest Manhood and Antebellum American Expansion* (New York: Cambridge Univ. Press, 2005), 11–13, 161.

7. Cannon, "The Mormon Issue in Congress," 123–24, 307–8; on the role of gendered notions of domesticity in the process of othering, see Amy Kaplan, *The Anarchy of Empire in the Making of U.S. Culture* (Cambridge, Mass.: Harvard Univ. Press, 2002), chapter 1.

8. Nancy Bentley, "Marriage as Treason: Polygamy, Nation, and the Novel," in *The Futures of American Studies,* ed. Donald E. Pease and Robyn Wiegman, 341–70, especially, 345–47 (Durham, N.C.: Duke Univ. Press, 2002); Bruce Burgett, "On the Mormon Question: Race, Sex, and Polygamy in the 1850s and the 1990s," *American Quarterly* 57, no. 1 (March 2005): 75–102, especially 76–77; Leonard J. Arrington and John Haupt, "Intolerable Zion: The Image of Mormonism in Nineteenth Century American Literature," *Western Humanities Review* 22 (1968): 246, 248; Gordon, *The Mormon Question,* 47–49.

9. See Kirk H. Porter and Donald Bruce Johnson, comp., *National Party Platforms, 1840–1956* (Urbana: Univ. of Illinois Press, 1956), 27; Foner, *Free Soil, Free Labor, Free Men,* 130, 132–33.

10. J. Spencer Fluhman, *"A Peculiar People": Anti-Mormonism and the Making of Religion in Nineteenth-Century America* (Chapel Hill: Univ. of North Carolina Press, 2012), chapter 4. On anti-Mormonism, see also David Brion Davis, "Some Themes of Counter-Subversion: An Analysis of Anti-Mason, Anti-Catholic, and Anti-Mormon Literature," *Mississippi Valley Historical Review* 47, no. 2 (September 1960): 205–24; Arrington and Haupt, "Intolerable Zion," 243–60; Leonard J. Arrington, "Kate Field and J. H. Beadle: Manipulators of the Mormon Past," American West Lecture, Salt Lake City, March 31, 1971; Charles A. Cannon, "The Awesome Power of Sex: The Polemical Campaign against Mormon Polygamy," *Pacific Historical Review* 43, no. 1 (February 1974): 61–82; Bentley, "Marriage as Treason."

11. Laurel Thatcher Ulrich, *A House Full of Females: Plural Marriage and Women's Rights in Early Mormonism, 1835–1870* (New York: Knopf, 2017).

12. Nicolay's novel manuscript is available in "Mormon Novel," Memoranda and Outline, John G. Nicolay Papers, Library of Congress. Extant secondary sources provide no information about Nicolay's decision to attempt to write the novel. For general background on Nicolay, see Michael Burlingame, "Introduction," in *With Lincoln in the White House: Letters, Memoranda, and Other Writings of John G. Nicolay, 1860–1865,* ed. Michael Burlingame (Carbondale: Southern Illinois Univ. Press, 2000), xi–xxi.

13. On Congressional debates concerning Mormon Utah, which generally revolved around northern Republican initiatives, see especially Cannon, "The Mormon Issue in Congress," especially, 38–106; B. H. Roberts, *A Comprehensive History of the Church of Jesus Christ of Latter-day Saints: Century I,* vol. 5 (Provo, Utah: Brigham Young Univ. Press, 1965), 225–31, 433–39; and Poll, ed., *Utah's History,* 250–51.

14. While Sarah Barringer Gordon has suggested that anti-Mormon campaigns accelerated after, and in part because of, the collapse of Reconstruction, it is also worth noting that attempts to reform Utah were active during the formative years of northern Republican policy-making concerning Reconstruction's two issues, that northern Republicans maintained at least some concern for southern freedpeople and contempt for southern whites after the conventional 1877 end date of Reconstruction, and that legislation concerning both the South and Utah were checked by the decline of Republican political power in the late 1870s. On these points, see Gordon, *The Mormon Question,* 119–20; Richardson, *Death of Reconstruction,* chapter 5; and Calhoun, *Conceiving a New Republic.*

15. Arrington, "Kate Field and J. H. Beadle," 16; John H. Beadle, *Brigham's Destroying Angel: Being the Life, Confession, and Startling Disclosures of the Notorious Bill Hickman, the Danite Chief of Utah* (New York: G. A. Crofutt, 1872). Because of the uncertain accuracy of Hickman's published confession, citations here refer to Beadle's introduction and appendixes. On Hickman, see Ronald W. Walker et al., *Mormon History* (Urbana: Univ. of Illinois Press, 2001), 13.

16. Beadle, *Brigham's Destroying Angel,* 13–14.

17. Harriet Beecher Stowe's "Preface" in T.B.H. Stenhouse, *"Tell It All": The Story of a Life's Experience in Mormonism* (Hartford, Conn.: A. D. Worthington, 1874), vi.

18. On Knox's controversial career during the Civil War and his politics, see J. Cutler Andrews, *The North Reports the Civil War* (1955; reprint, Pittsburgh, Pa.: Univ. of Pittsburgh Press, 1983), 380–83; and John F. Marszalek, *Sherman's Other War: The General and the Civil War Press* (Kent, Ohio: Kent State Univ. Press, 1999), 141–63.

19. Thomas W. Knox, "Across the Continent. Overland Scenes," *Frank Leslie's Illustrated Newspaper,* February 5, 1870, 353–54.

20. "A Mormon Nation—A Polygamic Polynesian Kingdom," *Frank Leslie's Illustrated Newspaper,* June 25, 1870, 226; "Monogamy v. Polygamy," *Frank Leslie's Illustrated Newspaper,* August 27, 1870, 371. During the Civil War, the Mormon leadership at times condemned both the North and the South, anticipated the final dissolution of the United States, but also claimed the Mormons to be the true defender of the Constitution, including the principle of freedom of religion. See Roberts, *A Comprehensive History,* 5:11–12; Poll, ed., *Utah's History,* 244–46.

21. On Bowles's travels, see George Merriam, *The Life and Times of Samuel Bowles,* 2 vols. (New York: Century, 1885), 2:1–3, 5, 15; On Bowles's later work with the Liberal Republican Party, see Slap, *The Doom of Reconstruction.* On Richardson's politics and journalistic career, see Michael Fuhlhage, "'To Limit the Spread of Slavery': A *Boston Journal* Correspondent's Multiple Roles in the Kansas Free State Movement," *Journalism History* 43, no. 3 (2017): 143–53.

22. Samuel Bowles, *Across the Continent: A Summer's Journey to the Rocky Mountains, the Mormons, and the Pacific States, with Speaker Colfax* (Springfield: Bowles, 1865), 107.

23. For James F. Rusling's politics, consider page 107 of his *The Great West and the Pacific Coast* (New York: Sheldon, 1877).

24. Miscellaneous House Documents, No. 153, *Affairs in Utah and the Territories*, 40th Cong., 2nd sess., 25, 27.

25. The *Boston Journal*, reprinted in "Home and Foreign Gossip," *Harper's Weekly*, March 6, 1869, 151. On the *Boston Journal*'s Republican politics, see Harris, *Blue and Gray in Black and White*, 15–16. See also Coffin, *Our New Way Around the World*, 491–500.

26. Schuyler Colfax, "Across the Continent by Overland Stage in 1865," digitized unpublished reminiscence, 1865, 34–35, Brigham Young University, Harold B. Lee Library, Special Collections VMSS 501, available at "Trails of Hope: Overland Diaries and Letters, 1846–1869," overlandtrails.lib.byu.edu; see also Albert D. Richardson, *Beyond the Mississippi: From the Great River to the Great Ocean* (Hartford: American Publishing, 1867), 344. For an earlier instance of similar rhetoric, see Reeve, *Religion of a Different Color*, 32. For one analysis of why Mormon polygamy sometimes entailed one man marrying multiple sisters, see Larson, *The "Americanization" of Utah for Statehood*, 45–46.

27. See James B. Pond, *Eccentricities of Genius: Memoirs of Famous Men and Women of the Platform and Stage* (New York: G. W. Dillingham, 1900), xvii–xxvi. *The Salt Lake Tribune* had been founded by a group of schismatic Mormons, but quickly came under the control of anti-Mormon gentiles; see O. N. Malmquist, *The First Hundred Years: A History of the* Salt Lake Tribune, 1871–1971 (Salt Lake City: Utah State Historical Society, 1971), 8–33.

28. "The Mormon Tabernacle," *Harper's Weekly*, September 30, 1871, 912–14.

29. William H. Seward, *William H. Seward's Travels Around the World*, ed. Olive Risley Seward (New York: Appleton, 1873), 23.

30. "Plurality of Wives," *Overland Monthly and Out West Magazine*, December 1871, 551–58, quotation from 552–53. On comparisons between Mormons and Turks, see Arrington and Haupt, "Intolerable Zion," 247–48.

31. Catherine V. Waite, *The Mormon Prophet and His Harem; or An Authentic History of Brigham Young, His Numerous Wives and Children* (Cambridge, Mass.: Riverside Press, 1866), 215–16, 224. On the Waites, see Dwyer, "The Gentile Comes to Utah," 8, 17–18.

32. See Reeve, *Religion of a Different Color*, 224–25.

33. John H. Beadle, *Life in Utah; or the Mysteries and Crimes of Mormonism: Being an Exposé of the Secret Rites and Ceremonies of the Latter-Day Saints, with a Full and Authentic History of Polygamy and the Mormon Sect from Its Origins to the Present Time* (Philadelphia: National Publishing Company, 1870), 355–57. See also Bowles, *Across the Continent*, 115; and William Elkanah Waters, *Life among the Mormons, and a March to Their Zion: To Which Is Added a Chapter on the Indians of the Plains and Mountains of the West* (New York: Moorhead, Simpson and Bond, 1868), 133–34, 143.

34. Beadle, *Life in Utah*, 357, 358, 365, see also 359; and Bowles, *Across the Continent*, 123–24. The belief that polygamists were weaker in spirit and body than monogamists also found expression in the antebellum writing of Samuel Cartwright; see Reeve, *Religion of a Different Color*, 17.

35. For other instances of Republican commentators invoking racial distinctions, consider William Hepworth Dixon, *New America* (Philadelphia: J. B. Lippincott, 1867), 244 and "The Mormon Tabernacle," *Harper's Weekly*, September 30, 1871, 912–14.

36. Hardy, *Solemn Covenant*, 57–59.

37. Waite, *The Mormon Prophet and His Harem*, iv.

38. James B McKean, reported in the *Salt Lake Tribune,* October 8, 1874; quoted in Alexander, "Federal Authority versus Polygamic Theocracy," 99–100. See also Haynes, "The Federal Government and its Policies Regarding the Frontier Era of Utah Territory," 197–98. On McKean's judicial campaign against Young, see John G. Turner, *Brigham Young: Pioneer Prophet* (Cambridge, Mass.: Belknap Press of Harvard Univ. Press, 2012), 364–68.

39. Robert Baskin, *Reminiscences of Early Utah* (Salt Lake City: Tribune-Reporter, 1914), 23–24.

40. Beadle, *Life in Utah,* 382; Arrington, "Kate Field and J. H. Beadle," 17.

41. Beadle, *Brigham's Destroying Angel,* 204.

42. Charles Nordhoff, *California: For Health, Pleasure, and Residence* (New York: Harper and Brothers, 1874), 43.

43. "King Young," *New York Times,* August 29, 1870, 4.

44. Waters, *Life among the Mormons,* 97, 106–7, 121, 184–87; on his politics, consider, 109, 154, 172–73.

45. Ibid., 74–75, 79, 111, 131–33, 155, 159, 181, 183, 192, 195.

46. George L. Woods, "Recollections by George L. Woods," unpublished manuscript, Bancroft Library, Berkeley, 4–5, 10–11, 58–59, 67–68. On the broader significance of Utah's woman suffrage, see Sarah Barringer Gordon, "'The Liberty of Self-Degradation': Polygamy, Woman Suffrage, and Consent in Nineteenth-Century America," *Journal of American History* 83, no. 3 (December 1996): 815–47; and Allison L. Sneider, *Suffragists in an Imperial Age: U.S. Expansion and the Woman Question, 1870–1929* (New York: Oxford Univ. Press, 2008), 73–86.

47. "The Mormon Tabernacle," *Harper's Weekly,* September 30, 1871, 914.

48. "The Mormon Prophet's Tragedy," *Atlantic Monthly,* December 1869, 669–79; quotations from 679.

49. Selections of Boreman's reminiscences, likely written around 1895, are published with a biographical overview in Leonard J. Arrington, "Crusade against Theocracy: The Reminiscences of Judge Jacob Smith Boreman of Utah, 1872–1877," *The Huntington Library Quarterly* 24, no. 1 (November 1960): 1–46; for comments above, see 3–4; quotation from 8.

50. Colfax, "Across the Continent by Overland Stage in 1865," 31. For similar descriptions, see Bowles, *Across the Continent,* 86, 113.

51. "Marching through Zion" (undated), in "Political Parties," *Heart Throbs of the West,* vol. 10 (Salt Lake City: Daughters of the Utah Pioneers, 1949), 18. A small number of excommunicated Mormon businessmen also helped found the party, which lasted into the 1890s.

52. "Mormon Trials," *Harper's Weekly,* November 18, 1871, 1075.

53. "The Mormon Problem," *Morning Republican,* November 16, 1871, 2.

54. Fred W. Loring, "A Glimpse of Mormonism," *Appleton's Journal,* August 19, 1871, 214–15.

55. Miscellaneous House Documents, No. 75, *Utah Territory,* 39th Cong., 2nd sess., 4, 5. On Hazen and Garfield, see "William Hazen Babcock," in *Encyclopedia of the American Civil War: A Political, Social, and Military History,* ed. David S. Heidler and Jeanne T. Heidler (New York: Norton, 2000), 959–60.

56. Beadle, *Brigham's Destroying Angel,* 16.

57. Charles H. Brigham, "The Mormon Problem," *Old and New,* May 1870, 628–41.

58. On her popularity, see Angela G. Ray, *The Lyceum and Public Culture in the Nineteenth-Century United States* (East Lansing: Michigan State Univ. Press, 2005), 144.

59. Ibid., 146, 151–53, 162–63, and Anna Dickinson, "Whited Sepulchers," Appendix 6, in Ray, *The Lyceum and Public Culture in the Nineteenth-Century United States,* 221–38, esp. 222–26, 229–30, and 233.

60. Dickinson, "Whited Sepulchers," in Ray, *The Lyceum and Public Culture in the Nineteenth-Century United States,* 230–32; J. Matthew Gallman, *America's Joan of Arc: The Life of Anna Elizabeth Dickinson* (New York: Oxford Univ. Press, 2006), 5, 70, 127, and chapter 5; Gordon, "'The Liberty of Self-Degradation,'" 819.

61. See "Anna E. Dickinson in Boston," *Revolution,* October 21, 1869, 1–2; "'Whited Sepulchres,'" *National Anti-Slavery Standard,* October 23, 1869, 1; "'Whited Sepulchres,'" *National Anti-Slavery Standard,* December 25, 1869, 2; "Anna Dickinson—Equal Rights for Women," *National Anti-Slavery Standard,* January 1, 1870, 3.

62. "Wyoming's Noble Position," *New Northwestern,* July 12, 1872, reprinted in *"Yours for Liberty": Selections from Abigail Scott Duniway's Suffrage Newspaper,* ed. Jean M. Ward and Elaine A. Maveety (Corvallis: Oregon State Univ. Press, 2000), 76; see also 23, 138. On Duniway's support for Grant in 1872, see *"Yours for Liberty,"* 18.

63. "City and Valley of the Great Salt Lake," *Harper's Weekly,* August 18, 1866, 513–14, for illustration, see 520–21. *Harper's,* like many others, borrowed the phrase from Isaiah 35:1.

64. Bowles, *Across the Continent,* 80.

65. "The Mormon Question," *New York Times,* February 21, 1870, 4.

66. Nordhoff, *California,* 42–44.

67. Seward, *William Seward's Travels around the World,* 23.

68. Miscellaneous House Documents, No. 75, *Utah Territory,* 39th Cong., 2nd sess., 2, 3.

69. "The Pacific Railroad—open. II," *Atlantic Monthly,* May 1869, 617–25, quotation from 619.

70. Thomas W. Knox, "Across the Continent. Overland Scenes," *Frank Leslie's Illustrated Newspaper,* January 22, 1870, 326. In a later article of the same title, however, Knox briefly described Mormons as "an industrious and temperate people," without adding any qualifications; *Frank Leslie's Illustrated Newspaper,* February 12, 1870, 372.

71. See Ekirch, *The Idea of Progress in America,* chapter 7; Baskin, *Reminiscences of Early Utah,* 198–203; Bowles, *Across the Continent,* 115–16, 398; Waters, *Life among the Mormons,* 179–80; Cooley, "Carpet-bag Rule," 117–18; Dwyer, "The Gentile Comes to Utah," 40–41; Larson, *The "Americanization" of Utah for Statehood,* 54–55; and Cresswell, *Mormons and Cowboys, Moonshiners and Klansmen,* 131–32.

72. Beadle, *Life in Utah,* 466–67. See also Beadle, *Brigham's Destroying Angel,* 15.

73. "A Glimpse of Mormonism," *Appleton's Journal,* August 19, 1871, 214–15. See also the description of the Mormon Tabernacle in "The Mormon Tabernacle," *Harper's Weekly,* September 30, 1871, 914.

74. Waite, *The Mormon Prophet and His Harem,* 276–77.

75. "Don Quixote in Utah," *New York Times,* August 23, 1870, 4.

76. Colfax, "Across the Continent by Overland Stage in 1865," 29, 32.

77. Beadle, *Life in Utah,* 301. See also Beadle, *Brigham's Destroying Angel,* 24. Many Mormons were in fact immigrants from the laboring classes of Europe; see Gustive O. Larson, "The Mormon Gathering," in *Utah's History,* ed. Richard D. Poll (Provo, Utah: Brigham Young Univ. Press, 1978), 175–91. On Republican efforts to limit the immigration of Mormon polygamists, see William Mulder, "Immigration and the 'Mormon Question': An International Episode," *Western Political Quarterly* 9 (1956): 416–33.

78. Dickinson, "Whited Sepulchers," in Ray, *The Lyceum,* 224.

79. Bowles, *Across the Continent,* 117.

80. Colfax, "Across the Continent by Overland Stage in 1865," 38.

81. "Troublous Times in Utah," *Harper's Weekly,* November 25, 1871, 1108.

82. "A Glimpse of Mormonism," *Appleton's Journal,* August 19, 1871, 214–15.

83. "The Pacific Railroad—open. II," *Atlantic Monthly,* May 1869, 619.

84. E. T., "Communication," *Elevator,* April 28, 1865, 1.

85. See Cannon, "The Mormon Issue in Congress," especially, 38–106; Roberts, *A Comprehensive History of the Church of Jesus Christ of Latter-day Saints,* 5:225–31, 433–39; and Poll, ed., *Utah's History,* 250–51.

86. House Miscellaneous Documents, No. 153, *Affairs in Utah and the Territories,* 40th Congress, 2nd sess., 27.

87. Hazen, however, even while he noted that many Mormons were immigrants, pinned the foreignness of the Mormons on their disdain for American laws and their peculiar religion. Language, he argued, did not distinguish the Mormons from Americans.

88. House Miscellaneous Documents, *Utah Territory,* 39th Congress, 2nd sess., 4–5. See also, Cannon, "The Mormon Issue in Congress," 195–202.

89. Newman had also worked as a missionary in New Orleans earlier in Reconstruction; see Abbott, *For Free Press and Equal Rights,* 72.

90. The debates are available in Orson Pratt and John P. Newman, *Great Discussion! Does the Bible Sanction Polygamy!* (Milwaukee: N.p., 1875).

91. "Polygamy," *New National Era,* September 8, 1870, 2. See also "Fruit of Dr. Newman's Labors," *New National Era,* September 22, 1870, 2, which contains an excerpt from a letter by Newman to a Washington, D.C., newspaper on the trip's success.

92. "Don Quixote in Utah," *New York Times,* August 23, 1870, 4.

93. Waters, *Life among the Mormons,* 117–23.

94. Stowe, "Preface," in Stenhouse, *"Tell It All,"* vi.

95. Quotation from "The Mormon Question," *New York Times,* February 21, 1870, 4, but see also "Mr. Cullom's Utah Bill," *New York Times,* February 18, 1870, 4. The *New York Times* also suggested that gold prospecting and territorial reapportionment by Congress would resolve the Mormon problem. See "The Mormon Question—Its Easy and Peaceful Solution," *New York Times,* November 28, 1865, 4. On analogous debates over the necessity of federal action in ending slavery among antebellum Republicans, see Foner, *Free Soil, Free Labor, Free Men,* 207–8.

96. Beadle, *Brigham's Destroying Angel,* 11.

97. "A Mormon Nation—A Polygamic Polynesian Kingdom," *Frank Leslie's Illustrated Newspaper,* June 25, 1870, 226. On Mormon missionizing in the Pacific islands, see Matthew Kester, "Race, Religion, and Citizenship in Mormon Country: Native Hawaiians in Salt Lake City, 1869–1889," *Western Historical Quarterly* 40, no. 1 (spring 2009): 51–76, 54–56.

98. Waite, *The Mormon Prophet and His Harem,* 280.

99. Bowles, *Across the Continent,* 108.

100. Dixon, *New America,* 247.

101. Mark Twain, *Roughing It* (New York, 1872; reprint, New York: Oxford Univ. Press, 1996), 125–26. The Democratic *New York World* similarly derided Mormon women as those who had otherwise failed to find a spouse; see Editorial, *New York World,* 26 July 1867, 4. Republicans noted humor about the Mormons, as when *Harper's Weekly* published an account—from a southern paper—of Brigham Young interrogating one of his wives to determine what her name was and when he married her. See "Home and Foreign Gossip," *Harper's Weekly,* 11 August 1866, 510.

102. John Codman, *The Mormon Country: A Summer with the "Latter-Day Saints"* (New York: United States Publishing Company, 1874), 2.

103. Ibid., 152, 165–68.

104. Ibid., 96, 142, 145.

105. Ibid., 15–16, 73–74, 82–83, 84, 87–92, 116–17, 123–26, 130–31; some examples that run contrary to his general impression are, 18–19, 20–21, 64–65.

106. Ibid., 163, 168–69, 172–74.

107. Ibid., 66–67, 159, 164.

108. Ibid., 141–46.

109. Ibid., 13, 53, 90–91, 128, 145–46, 153–58.

110. Ibid., 215.

111. Ibid., dedication and 225.

112. On the sales of Codman's *The Mormon Country,* see "John Codman Again," *Salt Lake Weekly Tribune,* August 28, 1875, 6.

113. See "An Apology at Last," *Salt Lake Weekly Tribune,* August 7, 1875, 9; "John Codman," *Salt Lake Weekly Tribune,* August 12, 1876, 1; and "John Codman Again," *Salt Lake Weekly Tribune,* August 28, 1875, 6.

114. Editorial, *Memphis Daily Avalanche,* November 22, 1866, 2.

115. "Toleration and Indifference," *New National Era,* May 11, 1871, 2.

116. "Mormonism and Polygamy," *Memphis Daily Appeal,* June 10, 1874, 2.

117. "The Latter Day Saints," *Charleston Daily News,* January 4, 1868, 4.

118. No title, *The Star of the North,* June 21, 1865, 1.

119. James A. Bennett, "'Until this Curse of Polygamy Is Wiped Out': Black Methodism, White Mormons, and Constructions of Racial Identity in the Late Nineteenth Century," *Religion and American Culture* 21, no. 2 (summer 2011): 167–94, especially 175–76.

120. No title, *Memphis Daily Appeal,* July 2, 1869, 2.

121. "Lo! The Poor Negro!" *Public Ledger,* February 19, 1869, 3.

122. No title, *Columbia Herald,* September 9, 1870, 3.

123. "Colored Ku Klux in Fairfiled," *Fairfield Herald,* February 11, 1874, 3.

124. No title, *Stark County Democrat,* October 27, 1870, 2.

125. Foner, *Reconstruction,* 340–41; "Speech of General F. P. Blair," *Ohio Statesman,* September 25, 1868, 1.

126. "A Negro Mormon," *Nashville Union and Dispatch,* April 30, 1868, 3.

127. "Northern Views of the Qualification of Negroes to Vote," *Fayetteville Observer,* November 29, 1866, 2.

128. No title, *Chicago Tribune,* October 19, 1865, 2.

129. On the unwinding of northern Republican support for Reconstruction, see especially Summers, *The Ordeal of the Reunion*; Foner, *Reconstruction*; Richardson, *The Death of Reconstruction*; Slap, *The Doom of Reconstruction*; David Montgomery, *Beyond Equality: Labor and the Radical Republicans, 1862–1872* (Urbana: Univ. of Illinois Press, 1981); William Gillette, *Retreat from Reconstruction, 1869–1879* (Baton Rouge: Louisiana State Univ. Press, 1979).

Conclusion

1. Eunsun Celeste Han, "Making a Black Pacific: African Americans and the Formation of Transpacific Community Networks," *Journal of African American History* 101, no. 2 (winter–spring 2016): 23–48, 25. Gardner, *Unexpected Places,* 94–97. For Cole's comments on life in the merchant community in Yokohama, which include some brief comments about the social isolation of educated African Americans in East Asia, see Peter K. Cole, "Letter No.

6 from Japan," *Elevator,* February 21, 1868, 3; and Peter K. Cole, "Letter No. 7 from Japan," *Elevator,* April 10, 1868, 2.

2. On Cole's letters, see Gardner, *Unexpected Places,* 97–103.

3. Peter K. Cole, "Letter No. 2 from Japan" *Elevator,* September 20, 1867, 2.

4. Peter K. Cole, "Letter No. 3 from Japan" *Elevator,* November 29, 1867, 2.

5. Peter K. Cole, "Letter No. 4 from Japan," *Elevator,* January 10, 1868, 2.

6. Peter K. Cole, "Letter No. 8 from Japan," *Elevator,* May 22, 1868, 2–3.

7. Peter K. Cole, "Letter No. 2 from Japan," *Elevator,* September 20, 1867, 2–3.

8. See Jennifer Taylor's comment in David M. Prior et al., "Reconstruction in Public History and Memory," *Journal of the Civil War Era* 7, no. 1 (March 2017): 120.

Bibliography

Unpublished Primary Sources

Bancroft Library, University of California, Berkeley

George L. Woods, "Recollections by George L. Woods," unpublished manuscript

Houghton Library, Harvard University, Cambridge, Massachusetts

Howe Family Manuscripts
Julia Ward Howe Papers

Library of Congress, Washington, D.C.

Frederick Douglass Papers
Papers of Schuyler Colfax
Papers of John Hay
Papers of John G. Nicolay

Massachusetts Historical Society, Boston

Papers of Amos A. Lawrence

Samuel P. Hayes Research Library, Perkins School for the Blind, Watertown, Massachusetts

Samuel Gridley Howe Collection

Published Primary Sources

Periodicals

African Repository (Washington, D.C.)
Albany Journal (Albany, New York)
American Union (Griffin and Macon, Georgia)
American Whig Review (New York, New York)
Appleton's Journal (New York, New York)
Ashland Union (Ashland, Ohio)

Atlantic Monthly (Boston, Massachusetts)
Baltimore Sun (Baltimore, Maryland)
Black Republican (New Orleans, Louisiana)
Boston Daily Advertiser (Boston, Massachusetts)
Boston Journal (Boston, Massachusetts)
Brooklyn Daily Eagle (Brooklyn, New York)
Burlington Free Press (Burlington, Vermont)
Caledonian (St. Johnsbury, Vermont)
Camden Confederate (Camden, South Carolina)
Charleston Daily News (Charleston, South Carolina)
Charleston Mercury (Charleston, South Carolina)
Chattanooga Daily Rebel (Chattanooga, Tennessee)
Chicago Tribune (Chicago, Illinois)
Christian Recorder (Philadelphia, Pennsylvania)
Cincinnati Gazette (Cincinnati, Ohio)
Cincinnati Daily Press (Cincinnati, Ohio)
Civilian and Telegraph (Cumberland, Maryland)
Clarksville Chronicle (Clarksville, Tennessee)
Clayton Herald (Clayton, Delaware)
Cleveland Leader (Cleveland, Ohio)
Cleveland Plain Dealer (Cleveland, Ohio)
Colored Citizen (Cincinnati, Ohio)
Columbia Democrat and Bloomsburg General Advertiser (Bloomsburg, Pennsylvania)
Columbia Herald (Columbia, Tennessee)
Constitution (Atlanta, Georgia)
Cretan (Boston, Massachusetts)
Crisis (Columbus, Ohio)
Cultivator and Country Gentleman (Albany, New York)
Daily Alta California (San Francisco, California)
Daily Columbus Enquirer (Columbus, Georgia)
Daily Chronicle and Sentinel (Augusta, Georgia)
Daily Dispatch (Richmond, Virginia)
Daily Exchange (Baltimore, Maryland)
Daily Nashville Patriot (Nashville, Tennessee)
Daily Press (St. Paul, Minnesota)
Daily State Register (Des Moines, Iowa)
De Bow's Review (New Orleans, Louisiana)
Democratic Enquirer (M'arthur, Ohio)
Elevator (San Francisco, California)
Enquirer (Columbus, Georgia)

Essex County Republican (Keeseville, New York)
Evening Star (Washington, D.C.)
Fairfield Herald (Winnsboro, South Carolina)
Fayetteville Observer (Fayetteville, Tennessee)
Fortnightly Review (London, United Kingdom)
Frank Leslie's Illustrated Newspaper (New York, New York)
Gallipolis Journal (Gallipolis, Ohio)
Gazette and Sentinel (Plaquemine, Louisiana)
Green-Mountain Freeman (Montpelier, Vermont)
Harper's New Monthly Magazine (New York, New York)
Harper's Weekly (New York, New York)
Highland Weekly News (Hillsborough, Ohio)
Holmes County Republican (Millersburg, Ohio)
Hours at Home (New York, New York)
Indiana State Sentinel (Indianapolis, Indiana)
Ithaca Journal (Ithaca, New York)
Lamoille New Dealer (Hyde Park, Vermont)
Liberator (Boston, Massachusetts)
Lincoln County Herald (Troy, Missouri)
Living Age (Boston, Massachusetts)
Local News (Alexandria, Virginia)
Marysville Daily Appeal (Marysville, California)
McClure's Magazine (New York, New York)
Memphis Daily Appeal (Memphis, Tennessee)
Memphis Daily Avalanche (Memphis, Tennessee)
Mobile Nationalist (Mobile, Alabama)
Morning Republican (Little Rock, Arkansas)
Nashville Daily Union (Nashville, Tennessee)
Nashville Union and Dispatch (Nashville, Tennessee)
National Anti-Slavery Standard (New York, New York)
New Englander (New Haven, Connecticut)
New Era/New National Era/New National Era and Citizen (Washington, D.C.)
New Orleans Daily Crescent (New Orleans, Louisiana)
New Orleans Republican (New Orleans, Louisiana)
New Orleans Tribune (New Orleans, Louisiana)
New-York Daily Reformer (Watertown, New York)
New York Herald (New York, New York)
New York Sun (New York, New York)
New York Times (New York, New York)
New York Tribune (New York, New York)
New York World (New York, New York)

Old and New (Boston, Massachusetts)
Old Guard (New York, New York)
Ohio Statesman (Columbus, Ohio)
Orleans Independent Standard (Irasburg, Vermont)
Ottawa Free Trader (Ottawa, Illinois)
Overland Monthly and Out West Magazine (San Francisco, California)
Pacific Commercial Advertiser (Honolulu, Hawaiian Islands)
Philadelphia Enquirer (Philadelphia, Pennsylvania)
Pomeroy Weekly Telegraph (Pomeroy, Ohio)
Public Ledger (Memphis, Tennessee)
Public Ledger (Philadelphia, Pennsylvania)
Putnam's Magazine (New York, New York)
Revolution (New York, New York)
Richmond Enquirer and Sentinel/Enquirer and Examiner (Richmond, Virginia)
Round Table (New York, New York)
Sacramento Daily Union (Sacramento, California)
Salt Lake Weekly Tribune (Salt Lake City, Utah)
San Antonio Express (San Antonio, Texas)
San Francisco Bulletin (San Francisco, California)
Star of the North (Bloomsburg, Pennsylvania)
Stark County Democrat (Canton, Ohio)
Tarboro' Southerner (Tarboro', North Carolina)
Troy Weekly Times (Troy, New York)
Weekly Lancaster Gazette (Lancaster, Ohio)
Weekly Louisianian (New Orleans, Louisiana)
White Cloud Kansas Chief (White Cloud, Kansas)
Woman's Advocate (New York, New York)
Zion's Herald (Boston, Massachusetts)

Government Documents

39th Congress, 2nd session. House of Representatives Executive Document, no. 38, *Revolution in Candia.*

39th Congress, 2nd session. House of Representatives Miscellaneous Documents, no. 58, *Sympathy for the Greeks: Concurrent Resolution of the Legislature of New York, expressive of Sympathy for the Greeks, who are now struggling for freedom.*

39th Congress, 2nd session. Miscellaneous House Document, no. 75, *Utah Territory.*

40th Congress, 2nd session, House of Representatives Miscellaneous Documents, no. 9, *Resolutions of the legislature of Maine expressing sympathy for the Cretans in their struggle for independence.*

40th Congress, 2nd session, House Miscellaneous Documents, no. 153, *Affairs in Utah and the Territories.*

Congressional Globe.

Despatches from Crete. General Records of the Department of State, RG 59, National Archives, Washington, D.C.

Despatches from Zante. General Records of the State Department, RG 59, National Archives, Washington, D.C.

Report of the Joint Committee on Reconstruction at the First Session Thirty-Ninth Congress. Washington, D.C.: Government Printing Office, 1866.

Report of the Secretary of the Navy. December 1867. Washington, D.C.: Government Printing Office, 1867.

Contemporary Publications and Published Documents

Adams, George. "Society of Natural History." *Massachusetts Register* 91 (1857): 203–4.

Anderson, Benjamin J. K. *Narrative of a Journey to Musardu, the Capital of the Western Mandingoes.* New York: S. W. Green, 1870.

Arrington, Leonard J. "Crusade against Theocracy: The Reminiscences of Judge Jacob Smith Boreman of Utah, 1872–1877." *Huntington Library Quarterly* 24, no. 1 (November 1960): 1–46.

Arnakis, George Georgiades. *American Consul in a Cretan War.* Austin, Tex.: Center for Neo-Hellenic Studies, 1966.

———. *Articles and Despatches from Crete.* Austin, Tex.: Center for Neo-Hellenic Studies, 1976.

Baskin, Robert. *Reminiscences of Early Utah.* Salt Lake City: Tribune-Reporter, 1914.

Beadle, John H. *Life in Utah; or the Mysteries and Crimes of Mormonism: Being an Exposé of the Secret Rites and Ceremonies of the Latter-Day Saints, with a Full and Authentic History of Polygamy and the Mormon Sect from Its Origins to the Present Time.* Philadelphia: National Publishing Company, 1870.

———. *Brigham's Destroying Angel: Being the Life, Confession, and Startling Disclosures of the Notorious Bill Hickman, the Danite Chief of Utah.* New York: G. A. Crofutt, 1872.

Bellows, Henry W. *The Old World in Its New Face: Impressions of Europe in 1867–1868,* vol. 2. New York: Harper and Brothers, 1869.

Bennett, Norman. *Stanley's Despatches to the New York Herald, 1871–1872, 1874–1877.* Boston: Boston Univ. Press, 1970.

Boston Natural History Society, *Anniversary Memoirs of the Boston Society of Natural History, 1830–1880.* Boston: Boston Natural History Society, 1880.

Bowles, Samuel. *Across the Continent: A Summer's Journey to the Rocky*

Mountains, the Mormons, and the Pacific States, with Speaker Colfax. Springfield: Bowles, 1865.

Buckley, Charles Burton. *An Anecdotal History of Old Times in Singapore,* 2 vols. Singapore: Fraser and Neave, 1902.

Clemenceau, Georges. *American Reconstruction, 1865–1870.* Edited by Fernand Baldensperger. Translated by Margaret MacVeagh. New York: L. MacVeagh, Dial Press, 1928.

Cleveland Leader. *Then and Now: The Story of the Cleveland Leader and the Cleveland News.* Cleveland: Art Engraving and Electrotyping, 1913.

Clodd, Edward. *Memories.* New York: G. P. Putnam's Sons, 1916.

Codman, John. *The Mormon Country: A Summer with the "Latter-Day Saints."* New York: United States Publishing Company, 1874.

———. *Ten Months in Brazil.* Boston: Lee and Shepard, 1867.

Coffin, Charles Carleton. *Our New Way Round the World.* Boston: Fields, Osgood, 1869.

Convention of Colored Newspaper Men. Cincinnati: N.p., August 4, 1875.

Cuban Anti-Slavery Committee. *Slavery in Cuba: A Report of the Proceedings of the Meeting Held at Cooper Institute.* New York: Powers, MacGowan and Slipper, 1872.

Dixon, William Hepworth. *New America.* Philadelphia: J. B. Lippincott, 1867.

Du Chaillu, Paul. *Explorations and Adventures in Equatorial Africa.* New York: Harper and Brothers, 1861.

———. *A Journey to Ashango-Land: And Further Penetration into Equatorial Africa.* New York: Appleton, 1867.

Fisher, Humphrey, ed. *Journeys to Musadu.* London: Frank Cass, 1971.

Fogg, William. *"Round the World": Letters from Japan, China, India, and Egypt.* Cleveland: *Cleveland Leader,* 1872.

Fredeman, William E., ed. *The Correspondence of Dante Gabriel Rossetti.* Vol. 7, *The Formative Years, 1835–1862,* Part 2, *1855–1862.* Cambridge, UK: D. S. Brewer, 2002.

Gosse, Edmund, and Thomas James Wise, eds. *The Letters of Algernon Charles Swinburne.* 2 vols. New York: John Lane, 1919.

Henry, Joseph. *The Papers of Joseph Henry.* Vols. 10–11. Edited by Marc Rothenberg. Washington, D.C.: Smithsonian Institution Press, 1972–2008.

Herzberg, Emanuel. *Gorilla Catechism.* New York: American News Company, 1869.

Howe, Julia Ward. *From the Oak to the Olive: A Plan of a Pleasant Journey.* Boston: Lee and Shepard, 1868.

———. *Reminiscences, 1819–1899.* Boston: Houghton Mifflin, 1899.

Howe, Samuel Gridley. "An Appeal to the People of the United States to Relieve from Starvation the Women and Children of the Greeks of the Island of Crete." Boston: N.p., 1867.

———. *The Cretan Refugees and Their American Helpers.* Boston: Lee and Shepard, 1868.

Hunt, James. *On the Negro's Place in Nature.* London: Trübner, 1863.

Johnson, Andrew. *The Papers of Andrew Johnson.* Vol. 8. Edited by Paul Bergeron. Knoxville: Univ. of Tennessee Press, 1989.

Kneeland, Samuel. "Introduction." In Charles Hamilton Smith and Samuel Kneeland, *The Natural History of the Human Species,* 15–98. 1851. Reprint, Boston: Gould and Lincoln, 1859.

Lincoln, Abraham. *The Collected Works of Abraham Lincoln.* Compiled and edited by Roy P. Blaser. Vol. 7. New Brunswick, N.J.: Rutgers Univ. Press, 1953.

"Marching through Zion." In "Political Parties," *Heart Throbs of the West.* Vol. 10. Salt Lake City: Daughters of the Utah Pioneers, 1949. Page 18.

Maurice, Paul, ed., *The Letters of Victor Hugo from Exile, and After the Fall of the Empire.* Boston: Houghton, Mifflin, 1898.

Montgomery, James E. *Our Admiral's Flag Abroad: The Cruise of Admiral D. G. Farragut, Commanding the European Squadron in 1867–68, in the Flag-Ship Franklin.* New York: G. P. Putnam and Son, 1869.

Nordhoff, Charles. *California: For Health, Pleasure, and Residence: A Book for Travellers and Settlers.* New York: Harper and Brothers, 1874.

Owen, Richard. *The Life of Richard Owen.* 2 vols. London: John Murray, 1894.

Pond, J. B. *Eccentricities of Genius: Memories of Famous Men and Women of the Platform and Stage.* New York: G. W. Dillingham, 1900.

Porter, Kirk H., and Donald Bruce Johnson, comp. *National Party Platforms, 1840–1956.* Urbana: Univ. of Illinois Press, 1956.

Pratt, Orson, and John P. Newman. *Great Discussion! Does the Bible Sanction Polygamy!* Milwaukee: N.p., 1875.

Proceedings of the National Conference of Colored Men of the United States. Washington, D.C.: Rufus H. Darby, 1879.

Reade, W. Winwood. *Savage Africa.* Harper and Brothers, 1864.

Rhodes, William H. "John R. McConnell." In Oscar T. Shuck, *Representative and Leading Men of the Pacific.* 529–33. San Francisco: Bacon, 1870.

Richards, Laura E., and Maud Howe Elliot. *Julia Ward Howe, 1819–1910.* Boston: Houghton Mifflin, 1916.

Richardson, Albert D. *Beyond the Mississippi: From the Great River to the Great Ocean.* Hartford, Conn.: American Publishing, 1867.

Rothenberg, Marc, ed. *The Papers of Joseph Henry.* 12 vols. Washington, D.C.: Smithsonian Institution Press, 1972–2008.

Rossetti, William Michael, ed. *The Family Letters of Christina Georgina Rossetti.* New York: Charles Scribner's Sons, 1908.

———. *Rossetti Papers, 1862–1870.* New York: Charles Scribner's Sons, 1903.

———. *Some Reminiscences of William Michael Rossetti,* 2 vols. New York: Charles Scribner's Sons, 1906.

[Ryan, John George]. *Life and Adventures of Gen. Ryan, the Cuban Martyr.* Chicago: Scully, 1876.

Rusling, James F. *The Great West and the Pacific Coast.* New York: Sheldon, 1877.

Sala, George Augustus. *Notes and Sketches of the Paris Exhibition.* London: Tinsley Brothers, 1868.

Seward, Olive Risley. *Around the World Stories.* Boston: D. Lothrop, 1889.

Seward, William H. *The Papers of William Henry Seward* (microfilm). Woodbridge, Conn.: Research Publications, 1981.

———. *William H. Seward's Travels around the World.* Edited by Olive Risley Seward. New York: Appleton, 1873.

Sheppard, Samuel T. *The Byculla Club, 1833–1916, A History.* Bombay: Bennett, Coleman, 1916

Skinner, J.E.H. *Roughing It in Crete in 1867.* London: R. Bentley, 1868.

Stenhouse, T.B.H. *"Tell It All": The Story of a Life's Experience in Mormonism.* Hartford, Conn.: A. D. Worthington, 1874.

Stephens, Henry Louis, and James Fuller Queen. *The Adventures of a Conscript as Told by Himself.* Library of Congress, Washington, D.C., circa 1863.

Stillman, William J. *Autobiography of a Journalist.* 2 vols. London: G. Richards, 1901.

———. *The Cretan Insurrection of 1866–7–8.* New York: Holt, 1874.

Sumner, Charles. *The Papers of Charles Sumner* (microfilm). Compiled by Beverly Wilson Palmer. Alexandria, Va.: Chadwyck-Healey, 1988.

Swinburne, Algernon. "Ode on the Insurrection in Candia." *Fortnightly Review,* March 1867, 284–89.

Train, George Francis. *My Life in Many States and in Foreign Lands.* New York: Appleton, 1902.

Tuckerman, Charles Keating. *Personal Recollections of Notable People at Home and Abroad.* 2 vols. London: Richard Bentley and Sons, 1895.

Twain, Mark. *The Innocents Abroad, or the New Pilgrim's Progress.* San Francisco: Bancroft, 1869.

———. *Roughing It.* New York, 1872. Reprint, New York: Oxford Univ. Press, 1996.

Waite, Catherine V. *The Mormon Prophet and His Harem; or an Authentic History of Brigham Young, His Numerous Wives and Children.* Cambridge, Mass.: Riverside Press, 1866.

Ward, Jean M., and Elaine A. Maveety, eds. *"Yours for Liberty": Selections from Abigail Scott Duniway's Suffrage Newspaper.* Corvallis: Oregon State Univ. Press, 2000.

Ward, John Dean. *Biographical Sketch of George Mountfort, Esq.* Boston: N.p., 1886.

Waters, William Elkanah. *Life among the Mormons, and a March to Their Zion:*

To Which Is Added a Chapter on the Indians of the Plains and Mountains of the West. New York: Moorehead, Simpson and Bond, 1868.

Welles, Gideon, and Edgar Thaddeus Welles. *Diary of Gideon Welles: Secretary of the Navy under Lincoln and Johnson.* 3 vols. Boston: Houghton Mifflin, 1911.

Woodford, Stewart L. *Crete: An Address.* Albany, N.Y.: Weed, Parsons, 1868.

Online Resources and Repositories

The Seward Family Digital Archive. https://sewardproject.org/.

The Colored Conventions. http://coloredconventions.org/.

Secondary Sources

Abbott, Richard. *For Free Press and Equal Rights: Republican Newspapers in the Reconstruction South.* Athens: Univ. of Georgia Press, 2004.

Adas, Michael. *Dominance by Design: Technological Imperatives and America's Civilizing Mission.* Cambridge, Mass.: Belknap Press of Harvard Univ. Press, 2006.

Akpan, M. B. "Black Imperialism: Americo-Liberian Rule over the African Peoples of Liberia, 1841–1964." *Canadian Journal of African Studies* 7, no. 2 (1973): 217–36.

Alexander, Thomas G. "Federal Authority versus Polygamic Theocracy: James B. McKean and the Mormons, 1870–1875." *Dialogue: A Journal of Mormon Thought* 1, no. 3 (1966): 85–100.

Anderson, M. S. *The Eastern Question, 1774–1923: A Study in International Relations.* New York: St. Martin's Press, 1966.

Andrews, J. Cutler. *The North Reports the Civil War.* 1955. Reprint, Pittsburgh, Pa.: Univ. of Pittsburgh Press, 1983.

Appel, Toby A. "Jeffries Wyman, Philosophical Anatomy, and the Scientific Reception of Darwin in America." *Journal of the History of Biology* 21 (1988): 69–94.

———. "A Scientific Career in the Age of Character: Jeffries Wyman and Natural History at Harvard." In *Science at Harvard: Historical Perspectives,* edited by Clark A. Elliott and Margaret W. Rossiter, 96–120. Bethlehem, Pa.: Lehigh Univ. Press, 1992.

Appleby, Joyce. "Republicanism and Ideology." *American Quarterly* 37, no. 4 (1985): 461–73.

Armitage, David, et al. "Interchange: Nationalism and Internationalism in the Era of the Civil War." *Journal of American History* 98, no. 2 (September 2011): 455–89.

Armstrong, William M. *E. L. Godkin: A Biography.* Albany: State Univ. of New York Press, 1978.

Arrington, Leonard J. "Kate Field and J. H. Beadle: Manipulators of the Mormon Past." American West Lecture, Salt Lake City, March 31, 1971.

Arrington, Leonard J., and Davis Bitton. *The Mormon Experience: A History of the Latter-day Saints,* 2nd ed. Urbana: Univ. of Illinois Press, 1992.

Arrington, Leonard J., and John Haupt. "Intolerable Zion: The Image of Mormonism in Nineteenth Century American Literature." *Western Humanities Review* 22 (1968): 243–60.

Ash, Stephen V. *A Massacre in Memphis: The Race Riot That Shook the Nation One Year After the Civil War* (New York: Hill and Wang, 2013).

Axeen, David. "'Heroes of the Engine Room': American 'Civilization' and the War with Spain." *American Quarterly* 36 (1984): 481–502.

Bailey, Thomas A. *A Diplomatic History of the American People,* 8th ed. New York: Appleton-Century-Crofts, 1969.

Baker, Jean H. "From Belief into Culture: Republicanism in the Antebellum North." *American Quarterly* 37 (1985): 532–50.

Baker, Jim. *The Eagle in the Lion City: America, Americans and Singapore.* Singapore: Landmark Books, 2005.

Banning, Lance. "Jeffersonian Ideology Revisited: Liberal and Classical Ideas in the New American Republic." *William and Mary Quarterly* 43 (1986): 3–19.

Barnes, L. Diane. *Frederick Douglass: Reformer and Statesman.* New York: Routledge, 2013.

Bay, Mia. *The White Image in the Black Mind: African-American Ideas about White People, 1830–1925.* New York: Oxford Univ. Press, 2000.

Beasley, Delilah. *The Negro Trail Blazers of California.* Los Angeles: Times Mirror Print and Binding House, 1919.

Bederman, Gail. *Manliness and Civilization: A Cultural History of Gender and Race in the United States, 1880–1917.* Chicago: Univ. of Chicago Press, 1995.

Belasco, Susan. "The Cultural Work of National Magazines." In *A History of the Book in America,* vol. 3, ed. Scott E. Casper et al. Chapel Hill: Univ. of North Carolina Press, 2007.

Bender, Daniel E. *American Abyss: Savagery and Civilization in the Age of Industry.* Ithaca, N.Y.: Cornell Univ. Press, 2009.

Bender, Thomas, *A Nation among Nations: America's Place in World History.* New York: Hill and Wang, 2006.

———, ed. *Rethinking American History in a Global Age.* Berkeley: Univ. of California Press, 2002.

Bendixen, Alfred. "American Travel Books about Europe before the Civil War." In *The Cambridge Companion to American Travel Writing,* ed. Alfred Bendixen and Judith Hamera, 103–26. New York: Cambridge Univ. Press, 2009.

Bennett, James A. "'Until this Curse of Polygamy Is Wiped Out': Black Methodism,

White Mormons, and Constructions of Racial Identity in the Late Nineteenth Century." *Religion and American Culture* 21, no. 2 (summer 2011): 167–94.

Bennett, Norman Robert. "David Livingstone: Exploration for Christianity." In *Africa and Its Explorers: Motives, Methods, and Impact,* edited by Robert I. Rotberg, 39–62. Cambridge, Mass.: Harvard Univ. Press, 1970.

Bentley, Nancy. "Marriage as Treason: Polygamy, Nation, and the Novel." In *The Futures of American Studies,* edited by Donald E. Pease and Robyn Wiegman, 341–70. Durham, N.C.: Duke Univ. Press, 2002.

Bergeron, Paul. *Andrew Johnson's Civil War and Reconstruction.* Knoxville: Univ. of Tennessee Press, 2014.

Binning, F. Wayne. "Carpetbaggers' Triumph: The Louisiana State Election of 1868." *Louisiana History* 14, no. 1 (winter 1973): 21–39.

Blight, David W. *Frederick Douglass: Prophet of Freedom.* New York: Simon and Schuster, 2018.

———. *Frederick Douglass' Civil War: Keeping Faith in Jubilee.* Baton Rouge: Louisiana State Univ. Press, 1989.

Blum, Edward J. *Reforging the White Republic: Race, Religion, and American Nationalism, 1865–1898.* Baton Rouge: Louisiana State Univ. Press, 2005.

Bowden, Bruce. *The Empire of Civilization: The Evolution of an Imperial Idea.* Chicago: Univ. of Chicago Press, 2009.

Brantlinger, Patrick. "Victorians and Africans: The Genealogy of the Myth of the Dark Continent." *Critical Inquiry* 12, no. 1 (autumn 1985): 166–203.

Breaux, Peter J. "William G. Brown and the Development of Education: A Retrospective on the Career of a State Superintendent of Public Education of African Descent in Louisiana." Ph.D. diss., Florida State University, 2006.

Broadhead, Richard H. *Cultures of Letters: Scenes of Reading and Writing in Nineteenth-Century America.* Chicago: Univ. of Chicago Press, 1993.

Brock, Lisa. "Back to the Future: African-Americans and Cuba in Time(s) of Race." *Contributions in Black Studies* 12 (1994): 9–32.

Brock, William R. *An American Crisis: Congress and Reconstruction, 1865–1867.* New York: St. Martin's, 1963.

———. "The Image of England and American Nationalism." *Journal of American Studies* 5 (1971): 225–45.

Brown, Joshua. *Beyond the Lines: Pictorial Reporting, Everyday Life, and the Crisis of Gilded-Age America.* Berkeley: Univ. of California Press, 2003.

Brown, Thomas J., ed. *Reconstructions: New Perspectives on the Postbellum United States.* New York: Oxford Univ. Press, 2006.

Brubaker, Rogers. "Ethnicity without Groups." *European Journal of Sociology* 43, no. 2 (2002): 163–89.

———. *Nationalism Reframed: Nationhood and the National Question in the New Europe.* New York: Cambridge Univ. Press, 1996.

Bryan, Carter R. "Negro Journalism in America before Emancipation." *Journalism Monographs* 12 (September 1969): 1–29.

Bucher, Henry, Jr. "Canonization by Repetition: Paul Du Chaillu in Historiography." *Revue Française d'Historie d'Outre-Mer* 66 (1979): 15–32.

Bullock, Penelope L. *The Afro-American Periodical Press, 1839–1909*. Baton Rouge: Louisiana State Univ. Press, 1981.

Burgett, Bruce. "On the Mormon Question: Race, Sex, and Polygamy in the 1850s and the 1990s." *American Quarterly* 57, no. 1 (March 2005): 75–102.

Burlingame, Michael. "Introduction." In *With Lincoln in the White House: Letters, Memoranda, and Other Writings of John G. Nicolay, 1860–1865,* edited by Michael Burlingame, xi–xxi. Carbondale: Southern Illinois Univ. Press, 2000.

Burton, O. Vernon, David Herr, and Matthew Cheney. "Defining Reconstruction." In *A Companion to the Civil War and Reconstruction,* edited by Lacy Ford, 299–322. Malden, Mass.: Blackwell, 2005.

Butchart, Ronald E. *Schooling the Freedpeople: Teaching, Learning, and the Struggle for Black Freedom, 1861–1876*. Chapel Hill: Univ. of North Carolina Press, 2010.

Butler, Leslie. *Critical Americans: Victorian Intellectuals and Transatlantic Liberal Reform*. Chapel Hill: Univ. of North Carolina Press, 2007.

———. "Reconstructions in Intellectual and Cultural Life." In *Reconstructions: New Perspectives on the Postbellum United States,* edited by Thomas J. Brown, 172–205. New York: Oxford Univ. Press, 2006.

Byrd, Brandon. "Black Republicans, Black Republic: African-Americans, Haiti, and the Promise of Reconstruction." *Slavery and Abolition* 36 (December 2015): 545–67.

Calhoun, Charles W. *Conceiving a New Republic: The Republican Party and the Southern Question, 1869–1900*. Lawrence: Univ. Press of Kansas, 2006.

Cannon, Charles A. "The Awesome Power of Sex: The Polemical Campaign against Mormon Polygamy." *Pacific Historical Review* 43, no. 1 (February 1974): 61–82.

Cannon, Mark W. "The Mormon Issue in Congress 1872–1882: Drawing on the Experience of Territorial Delegate George Q. Cannon." Ph.D. diss., Harvard University, 1960.

Cardyn, Lisa. "Sexual Terror in the Reconstruction South." In *Gender and Sexuality in the American Civil War,* ed. Catherine Clinton and Nina Silber, 140–67. New York: Oxford Univ. Press, 2006.

Carpenter, Kenneth E. "Libraries." In *A History of the Book in America,* vol. 3, ed. Scott E. Casper et al. Chapel Hill: Univ. of North Carolina Press, 2007.

Carriere, Marius. "An Irresponsible Press: Memphis Newspapers and the 1866 Riot." *Tennessee Historical Quarterly* 60 (2001): 2–15.

Casper, Scott E. "The Census, the Post Office, and Governmental Publishing." In

A History of the Book in America, vol. 3, ed. Scott E. Casper et al. Chapel Hill: Univ. of North Carolina Press, 2007.

Casper, Scott, Jeffrey Groves, Stephen Nissenbaum, and Michael Winship, eds. *A History of the Book in America.* Vol. 3, *The Industrial Book, 1840–1880.* Chapel Hill: Univ. of North Carolina Press, and Worcester, Mass.: American Antiquarian Society, 2007.

Catsiyannis, Timotheos. *The Greek Community in London.* London: Zeno, 1993.

Chang, Gordon H. "Whose 'Barbarism'? Whose 'Treachery'? Race and Civilization in the Unknown United States-Korean War of 1871." *Journal of American History* 89, no. 4 (March 2003): 1331–65.

Chapin, James Burke. "Hamilton Fish and American Expansion." Ph.D. diss., Cornell University, 1971.

Chaplin, Joyce E. *Round About the Earth: Circumnavigation from Magellan to Orbit.* New York: Simon and Schuster, 2012.

Chatziioannou, Maria Christina. "Greek Merchants in Victorian England." In *Greek Diaspora and Migration since 1700: Society, Politics and Culture,* edited by Dimitris Tziovas, 45–60. Abingdon, UK: Ashgate, 2009.

Ciment, James. *Another America: The Story of Liberia and the Former Slaves Who Ruled It.* New York: Hill and Wang, 2013.

Clark, Elizabeth B. "'The Sacred Rights of the Weak': Pain, Sympathy, and the Culture of Individual Rights in Antebellum America." *Journal of American History* 82 (1995): 463–93.

Connor, William P. "Reconstruction Rebels: The *New Orleans Tribune* in Post-War Louisiana." *Louisiana History* 21, no. 2 (spring 1980): 159–81.

Conroy-Kurtz, Emily, et al. "Interchange: Globalization and Its Limits between the American Revolution and the Civil War." *Journal of American History* 103, no. 2 (September 2016): 400–433.

Contopolous, Michael. *The Greek Community of New York City: Early Years to 1910,* with a forward by Constantine G. Hatzidimitiriou. New Rochelle, N.Y.: Aristide D. Caratzas, 1992.

Cooley, Everett L. "Carpet-bag Rule—Territorial Government in Utah." *Utah Historical Quarterly* 26, no. 2 (April 1958): 107–29.

Cordell, Ryan. "Reprinting, Circulation, and the Network Author in Antebellum Newspapers." *American Literary History* 27, no. 3 (2015): 417–45.

Cordell, Ryan, and David A. Smith. "Viral Texts: Mapping Networks of Reprinting in 19th-Century Newspapers and Magazines." http://viraltexts.org/. Accessed January 3, 2016.

Cornelius, Janet. "'We Slipped and Learned to Read': Slave Accounts of the Literacy Process, 1830–1865." In *Literacy and Historical Development: A Reader,* edited by Harvey J. Graff, 315–33. Carbondale: Southern Illinois Univ. Press, 2007.

Cresswell, Stephen. *Mormons and Cowboys, Moonshiners and Klansmen: Federal Law Enforcement in the South and West, 1870–1893*. Tuscaloosa: Univ. of Alabama Press, 1991.

Csergo, Zsuzsa. "Review Essay: Do We Need a Language Shift in the Study of Nationalism and Ethnicity? Reflections on Rogers Brubaker's Critical Scholarly Agenda." *Nations and Nationalism* 14, no. 2 (2008): 393–98.

Curtin, Philip. *The Image of Africa: British Ideas and Action, 1780–1850*. Madison: Univ. of Wisconsin Press, 1964.

Curtis, L. Perry, Jr. *Apes and Angels: The Irishman in Victorian Culture*, rev. ed. Washington, D.C.: Smithsonian Institution Press, 1997.

Dakin, Douglas. *The Unification of Greece, 1770–1923*. London: Ernest Benn, 1972.

Danky, James P. "Reading, Writing, and Resisting: African American Print Culture." In *A History of the Book in America*, vol. 4, *Print in Motion: The Expansion of Publishing and Reading in the United States, 1880–1940*, ed. Carl F. Kaestle and Janice A. Radway, 339–58. Chapel Hill: Univ. of North Carolina Press, 2009.

Dann, Martin E., ed. *The Black Press, 1827–1890*. New York: G. P. Putnam's Sons, 1971.

Davis, David Brion. "Some Themes of Counter-Subversion: An Analysis of Anti-Mason, Anti-Catholic, and Anti-Mormon Literature." *Mississippi Valley Historical Review* 47, no. 2 (September 1960): 205–24.

Davison, Roderic H. *Nineteenth Century Ottoman Diplomacy and Reforms*. Istanbul: Isis Press, 1999.

———. "Ottoman Public Relations in the Nineteenth Century: How the Sublime Porte Tried to Influence European Public Opinion." In *Historie Économique et Sociale de l'Empire Ottoman et de la Turquie (1326–1960)*, ed. Daniel Panzac, 593–603. Paris: Peeters, 1995.

Delaye, Karine. "Singapore: A Model for Indochina? (1860s–1920s)." In *Singapore from Temasek to the 21st Century: Reinventing the Global City*, edited by Karl Hack and Jean-Louis Margolin, with Karine Delaye, 185–209. Singapore: National Univ. of Singapore Press, 2010.

DeLombard, Jeannine Marie. "African American Cultures of Print." In *A History of the Book in America*, vol. 3, ed. Scott Casper et al. Chapel Hill: Univ. of North Carolina Press, 2007.

Denning, Michael. *Mechanic Accents: Dime Novels and Working-Class Culture in America*. New York: Verso, 1987.

Detorakis, Theocharis E. *History of Crete*, trans. John C. Davis. Iraklion, Crete, Greece: Detorakis, 1994.

Detweiler, Frederick G. *The Negro Press in the United States*. Chicago: Univ. of Chicago Press, 1922.

Dew, Charles B. *Apostles of Disunion: Southern Secession Commissioners and the Causes of the Civil War*. Charlottesville: Univ. Press of Virginia, 2001.

Dickason, David Howard. *The Daring Young Men: The Story of the American Pre-Raphaelites.* Bloomington: Indiana Univ. Press, 1953.

Dickenson, John. "The Naturalist on the River Amazons and a Wider World: Reflections on the Centenary of Henry Walter Bates." *Geographical Journal* 158, no. 2 (July 1992): 207–14.

Dickerson, Donna L. "George T. Ruby: Reconstruction Politician/Journalist." *American Journalism* 15, no. 1 (winter 1998): 51–68.

Dobbs, Stephen. "The Singapore River/Port in Global Context." In *Singapore in Global History,* edited by Derek Heng and Syed Muhd Khairudin Aljunied, 51–65. Amsterdam: Amsterdam Univ. Press, 2011.

Donald, David Herbert, Jean Harvey Baker, and Michael F. Holt. *The Civil War and Reconstruction,* 3rd ed. New York: Norton, 2001.

Dontas, Domna N. *Greece and the Great Powers, 1863–1875.* Thessalonike: Institute for Balkan Studies, 1966.

Downs, Gregory P. "The Mexicanization of American Politics: The United States' Transnational Path from Civil War to Stabilization." *American Historical Review* 117, no. 2 (2012): 387–409.

Downs, Gregory P., and Kate Masur. "Introduction: Echoes of War: Rethinking Post–Civil War Governance and Politics." In *The World the Civil War Made,* edited by Gregory P. Downs and Kate Masur, 1–21. Chapel Hill: Univ. of North Carolina Press, 2015.

Doyle, Don H. *The Cause of All Nations: An International History of the American Civil War.* New York: Basic Books, 2015.

———. "The Global Civil War." In *A Companion to the U.S. Civil War,* edited by Aaron Sheehan-Dean, 2 vols., 2:1103–20. Malden, Mass.: Wiley-Blackwell, 2014.

Drescher, Seymour. *Abolition: A History of Slavery and Antislavery.* New York: Cambridge Univ. Press, 2009.

Dudden, Faye E. *Fighting Chance: The Struggle over Woman Suffrage and Black Suffrage in Reconstruction America.* New York: Oxford Univ. Press, 2011.

Dwyer, Robert. "The Gentile Comes to Utah: A Study in Religious and Social Conflict." Ph.D. diss., Catholic University of America, 1941.

Dyson, Stephen L. *The Last Amateur: The Life of William J. Stillman.* Albany: State Univ. of New York Press, 2014.

Efford, Alison. *German Immigrants, Race, and Citizenship in the Civil War Era.* New York: Cambridge Univ. Press, 2013.

Egerton, Douglas. "Rethinking Atlantic Historiography in a Postcolonial Era: The Civil War in Global Perspective." *Journal of the Civil War Era* 1 (2011): 79–95.

———. *The Wars of Reconstruction: The Brief, Violent History of America's Most Progressive Era.* New York: Bloomsbury Press, 2014.

Ellingson, Ter. *The Myth of the Noble Savage.* Berkeley: Univ. of California Press, 2001.

Ekirch, Arthur Alphonse. *The Idea of Progress in America, 1815–1860.* New York: Peter Smith, 1951.

Fabi, M. Giulia. "Reconstructing Race: The Novel after Slavery." In *The Cambridge Companion to the African American Novel,* ed. Maryemma Graham. New York: Cambridge Univ. Press, 2004.

Fairhead, James, Tim Geysbeek, Svend E. Holsoe, and Melissa Leach, eds. *African-American Exploration in West Africa: Four Nineteenth-Century Diaries.* Bloomington: Indiana Univ. Press, 2003.

Fanuzzi, Robert. "Frederick Doulgass's 'Colored Newspaper': Identity Politics in Black and White." In *The Black Press: New Literary and Historical Essays,* edited by Todd Vogel, 55–70. New Brunswick, N.J.: Rutgers Univ. Press, 2001.

Farnie, D. A. *East and West of Suez: The Suez Canal in History, 1854–1956.* Oxford: Clarendon Press, 1969.

Faulkner, Carol. *Women's Radical Reconstruction: The Freedmen's Aid Movement.* Philadelphia: Univ. of Pennsylvania Press, 2004.

Faust, Drew Gilpin. *This Republic of Suffering: Death and the American Civil War.* New York: Vintage Books, 2008.

Ferrer, Ada. *Insurgent Cuba: Race, Nation, and Revolution, 1868–1898.* Chapel Hill: Univ. of North Carolina Press, 1999.

Field, James A., Jr. *America and the Mediterranean World, 1776–1882.* Princeton, N.J.: Princeton Univ. Press, 1969.

Firebaugh, Dorothy Gile. "The Sacramento Union: Voice of California, 1851–1875." *Journalism and Mass Communication Quarterly* 30, no. 3 (1953): 321–30.

Fitzgerald, Michael W. "Reconstruction Politics and the Politics of Reconstruction." In *Reconstructions: New Perspectives on the Postbellum United States,* edited by Thomas J. Brown, 91–116. New York: Oxford Univ. Press, 2006.

———. *The Union League Club Movement in the Deep South: Politics and Agricultural Change during Reconstruction.* Baton Rouge: Louisiana State Univ. Press, 1989.

———. *Urban Emancipation: Popular Politics in Reconstruction Mobile, 1860–1890.* Baton Rouge: Louisiana State Univ. Press, 2002.

Fleche, Andre M. *The Revolutions of 1861: The American Civil War in the Age of Nationalist Conflict.* Chapel Hill: Univ. of North Carolina Press, 2012.

Fletcher, Max E. "The Suez Canal and World Shipping, 1869–1914." *Journal of Economic History* 18, no. 4 (December 1958): 556–73.

Fluhman, J. Spencer. *"A Peculiar People": Anti-Mormonism and the Making of Religion in Nineteenth-Century America.* Chapel Hill: Univ. of North Carolina Press, 2012.

Foner, Eric. *Free Soil, Free Labor, Free Men: The Ideology of the Republican Party before the Civil War.* New York: Oxford Univ. Press, 1970.

———. *Nothing but Freedom: Emancipation and Its Legacy.* Baton Rouge: Louisiana State Univ. Press, 1983.

———. *Reconstruction: America's Unfinished Revolution, 1863–1877.* New York: Harper and Row, 1988.

———. "Reconstruction Revisited." *Reviews in American History* 10 (1982): 82–100.

———. "'The Tocsin of Freedom': The Black Leadership of Radical Reconstruction." In *Slavery, Resistance, Freedom,* edited by Gabor Boritt and Scott Hancock, 118–40. New York: Oxford Univ. Press, 2007.

Foner, Eric, et al. "Eric Foner's 'Reconstruction' at Twenty-Five." *Journal of the Gilded Age and Progressive Era* 14, no. 1 (January 2015): 13–27.

Foner, Philip S. "Black Participation in the Centennial of 1876." *Phylon* 39, no. 4 (1978): 283–96.

Ford, Lacy K., ed. *A Companion to the Civil War and Reconstruction.* Malden, Mass.: Blackwell Publishing, Ltd., 2005.

Fox-Genovese, Elizabeth, and Eugene Genovese. *The Mind of the Master Class: History and Faith in the Southern Slaveholders' Worldview.* New York: Cambridge Univ. Press, 2005.

Fredrickson, George. *The Black Image in the White Mind: The Debate on Afro-American Character and Destiny, 1817–1914.* New York: Harper Row, 1971. Reprint, Hanover, N.H.: Wesleyan Univ. Press, 1987.

Frost, Mark Ravinder, and Yu-Mei Balasingamchow. *Singapore: A Biography.* Hong Kong: Hong Kong Univ. Press, 2009.

Fuhlhage, Michael. "'To Limit the Spread of Slavery': A *Boston Journal* Correspondent's Multiple Roles in the Kansas Free State Movement." *Journalism History* 43, no. 3 (2017): 143–53

Gallman, J. Matthew. *America's Joan of Arc: The Life of Anna Elizabeth Dickinson.* New York: Oxford Univ. Press, 2006.

Gardner, Eric. *Unexpected Places: Relocating Nineteenth-Century African American Literature.* Jackson: Univ. Press of Mississippi, 2009.

Gates, Paul H., Jr. "Toward a Common Goal: Jean-Charles Houzeau, P.B.S. Pinchback and New Orleans' Black Press, 1862–1882." In *Proceedings of the American Journalism Historians' Association Conference (Salt Lake City, Utah, October 5–7, 1993),* Part 2, *Issues of Race,* 175–99. Salt Lake City: N.p., 1993.

Gemme, Paola. *Domesticating Foreign Struggles: The Italian Risorgimento and Antebellum American Identity.* Athens: Univ. of Georgia Press, 2005.

Genovese, Eugene. *The Slaveholders' Dilemma: Freedom and Progress in Southern Conservative Thought, 1820–1860.* Columbia: Univ. of South Carolina Press, 1992.

Gillette, William. *Retreat from Reconstruction, 1869–1879.* Baton Rouge: Louisiana State Univ. Press, 1979.

Goggans, Jan. "What Workers Were Reading, 1830–1890." In *A History of American Working-Class Literature,* ed. Nicholas Coles and Paul Lauter, 163–76. New York: Cambridge Univ. Press, 2017.

Gong, Gerrit W. *The Standard of "Civilization" in International Society.* New York: Oxford Univ. Press, 1984.

Goodyear, Frank H. "'Beneath the Shadow of Her Flag': Philip A. Bell's *The Elevator* and the Struggle for Enfranchisement, 1865–1870." *California History* 78, no. 1 (spring 1999): 26–39.

Gordon, Sarah Barringer. "'The Liberty of Self-Degradation': Polygamy, Woman Suffrage, and Consent in Nineteenth-Century America." *Journal of American History* 83, no. 3 (December 1996): 815–47.

———. *The Mormon Question: Polygamy and Constitutional Conflict in Nineteenth Century America.* Chapel Hill: Univ. of North Carolina Press, 2002.

Gott, Ted, and Kathryn Weir. *Gorilla.* London; Reaktion, 2013.

Gould, Philip. *Barbaric Traffic: Commerce and Antislavery in the 18th Century Atlantic World.* Cambridge, Mass.: Harvard Univ. Press, 2003.

Gourey, Hannah. "Poetics of Memory and Marginality: Images of the Native American in African-American Newspapers, 1870–1900 and 1970–1990." In *The Black Press: New Literary and Historical Essays,* ed. Todd Vogel, 104–22. New Brunswick, N.J.: Rutgers Univ. Press, 2001.

Grant, Susan-Mary. *North over South: Northern Nationalism and American Identity in the Antebellum Era.* Lawrence: Univ. Press of Kansas, 2000.

Gray, Elizabeth Kelly. "'Whisper to Him the Word 'India': Trans-Atlantic Critics and American Slavery, 1830–1860." *Journal of the Early Republic* 28, no. 3 (fall 2018): 379–406.

Green, Michael S. *Freedom, Union, and Power: Lincoln and His Party during the Civil War.* New York: Fordham Univ. Press, 2004.

Greenberg, Amy S. *Manifest Manhood and Antebellum American Expansion.* New York: Cambridge Univ. Press, 2005.

Griffis, William Elliott. *Charles Carleton Coffin: War Correspondent, Traveller, Author, and Statesman.* Boston: Estes and Lauriat, 1898.

Gross, Robert. "The Transnational Turn: Rediscovering American Studies in a Wider World." *Journal of American Studies* 34, no. 3 (December 2000): 373–93.

Groves, Jeffrey D. "Introduction" to chapter 7 of *A History of the Book in America,* vol. 3, ed. Scott E. Casper et al. Chapel Hill: Univ. of North Carolina Press, 2007.

Guyatt, Nicholas. "America's Conservatory: Race, Reconstruction, and the Santo Domingo Debate." *Journal of American History* 97, no. 4 (March 2011): 974–1000.

Hager, Christopher. *Word by Word: Emancipation and the Act of Writing.* Cambridge, Mass.: Harvard Univ. Press, 2013.

Hahn, Steven H. *A Nation under Our Feet: Black Political Struggles in the Rural South, from Slavery to the Great Migration.* Cambridge, Mass.: Belknap Press of Harvard Univ. Press, 2003.

Hale, William. *Turkish Foreign Policy, 1774–2000.* London: Frank Cass, 2000.

Hall, Richard. *Stanley: An Adventurer Explored.* Boston: Houghton Mifflin, 1975.

Han, Eunsun Celeste. "Making a Black Pacific: African Americans and the Formation of Transpacific Community Networks." *Journal of African American History* 101, no. 2 (winter–spring 2016): 23–48.

Handlin, Lilian. *George Bancroft: The Intellectual as Democrat.* New York: Harper and Row, 1984.

Hardy, B. Carmon. *Solemn Covenant: The Mormon Polygamous Passage.* Urbana: Univ. of Illinois Press, 1992.

Harrington-Lueker, Donna. "Finding a Market for Suffrage: Advertising and *The Revolution,* 1868–1870." *Journalism History* 33, no. 3 (fall 2007): 130–39.

Harris, Brayton. *Blue and Gray in Black and White: Newspapers in the Civil War.* Washington, D.C.: Brassey's, 1999.

Haskins, James. *Pinckney Benton Stewart Pinchback.* New York: Macmillan, 1973.

Hawkshawe, Dorothy Drinkard. "David Augustus Straker, Black Lawyer and Reconstruction Politician, 1842–1908." Ph.D. diss., Catholic University of America, 1974.

Haynes, Alan. "The Federal Government and Its Policies Regarding the Frontier Era of Utah Territory, 1850–1877." Ph.D. diss., Catholic University of America, 1968.

Heidler, David S., and Jeanne T. Heidler, eds. *Encyclopedia of the American Civil War: A Political, Social, and Military History.* New York: Norton, 2000.

Henkin, David M. "City Streets and the Urban World of Print." In *A History of the Book in America,* vol. 3, ed. Scott E. Casper et al. Chapel Hill: Univ. of North Carolina Press, 2007.

Henning, Joseph. *Outposts of Civilization: Race, Religion, and the Formative Years of American-Japanese Relations.* New York: New York Univ. Press, 2000.

Hickey, Dennis, and Kenneth C. Wylie. *An Enchanting Darkness: The American Vision of Africa in the Twentieth Century.* East Lansing: Michigan State Univ. Press, 1993.

Higham, John. *Strangers in the Land: Patterns of American Nativism, 1860–1925.* New Brunswick, N.J.: Rutgers Univ. Press, 1955.

Hildebrand, Reginald F. *The Times Were Strange and Stirring: Methodist Preachers and the Crisis of Emancipation.* Durham, N.C.: Duke Univ. Press, 1995.

Hobsbawm, Eric. *The Age of Capital: 1848–1875.* London: Weidenfeld and Nicolson, 1995.

Honeck, Mischa. *We Are the Revolutionists: German-Speaking Immigrants and American Abolitionists after 1848.* Athens: Univ. of Georgia Press, 2011.

Hoare, James. *Japan's Treaty Ports and Foreign Settlements: The Uninvited Guests, 1858–1899.* Folkestone, Kent, UK: Japan Press, 1994

Horner, Charles F. *The Life of James Redpath and the Development of the Modern Lyceum.* New York: Barse and Hopkins, 1926.

Horsman, Reginald. *Race and Manifest Destiny: The Origins of American Racial Anglo-Saxonism.* Cambridge, Mass.: Harvard Univ. Press, 1981.

Howard, Victor B. *Religion and the Radical Republican Movement, 1860–1870.* Lexington: Univ. Press of Kentucky, 1990.

Howe, Daniel Walker. "The European Sources of Political Ideas in Jeffersonian America." *Reviews in American History* 10 (1982): 28–44.

Hubbell, Jay B. "Charles Chauncey Burr: Friend of Poe." *PMLA* 69, no. 4 (September 1954): 833–40.

Hudson, Nicholas. "From 'Nation' to 'Race': The Origin of Racial Classification in Eighteenth-Century Thought." *Eighteenth-Century Studies* 29 (spring 1996): 247–64.

Hunt, Alfred N. *Haiti's Influence on Antebellum America.* Baton Rouge: Louisiana State Univ. Press, 1988.

Hunter, F. Robert. "Egypt under the Successors of Muhammad 'Ali." In *The Cambridge History of Egypt*, vol. 2, *Modern Egypt from 1517 to the End of the 20th Century*, edited by M. W. Daly, 180–97. New York: Cambridge Univ. Press, 1998.

Hurd, John, and Ian J. Kerr. *India's Railway History: A Research Handbook.* Leiden, The Netherlands: Brill, 2012.

Huston, James L. "The American Revolutionaries, the Political Economy of Aristocracy, and the American Concept of the Distribution of Wealth, 1765–1900." *American Historical Review* 98 (1993): 1079–1105.

Jackson, Debra. "'A Cultural Stronghold': The 'Anglo-African' Newspaper and the Black Community of New York." *New York History* 85, no. 4 (fall 2004): 331–57.

Jacobson, Matthew Frye. *Barbarian Virtues: The United States Encounters Foreign Peoples at Home and Abroad, 1876–1917.* New York: Hill and Wang, 2000.

Jeffrey, Julie Roy. *The Great Silent Army of Abolitionism: Ordinary Women in the Antislavery Movement.* Chapel Hill: Univ. of North Carolina Press, 1998.

Johanningsmeier, Charles. "Newspaper Syndicates of the Late Nineteenth Century: Overlooked Forces in the American Literary Market-Place." *Publishing History* 37 (1995): 61–82.

John, Richard. *Spreading the News: The American Postal System from Franklin to Morse.* Cambridge, Mass.: Harvard Univ. Press, 1995.

Johnson, Maizie Harrison. "European Reaction to the Cretan Insurrection, 1866–1869." Master's thesis, George Washington University, 1961.

Johnson, Walter, *River of Dark Dreams: Slavery and Empire in the Cotton Kingdom.* Cambridge, Mass.: Belknap Press of Harvard Univ. Press, 2013.

Jordan, Winthrop. *White over Black: American Attitudes towards the Negro, 1550–1812.* Chapel Hill: Univ. of North Carolina Press, 1968. Reprint, Baltimore: Pelican, 1969.

Jung, Moon-Ho. *Coolies and Cane: Race, Labor, and Sugar in the Age of Emancipation.* Baltimore: Johns Hopkins Univ. Press, 2006.

Kachun, Mitch. "Interrogating the Silences: Julia C. Collins, 19th-Century Black Readers and Writers, and the *Christian Recorder.*" *African American Review* 40, no. 4 (winter 2006): 649–59.

Kaestle, Carl F., and Janice A. Radway, eds. *A History of the Book in America.* Vol. 4, *Print in Motion: The Expansion of Publishing and Reading in the United States, 1880–1940.* Chapel Hill: Univ. of North Carolina Press, 2009.

Kallivretakis, Leonidas. "A Century of Revolutions: The Cretan Question between European and Near Eastern Politics." In *Eleftherios Venizelos: The Trials of Statesmanship,* ed. Paschalis M. Kitromilides. Edinburgh, UK: Edinburgh Univ. Press, 2006.

———. "Jules Verne's Captain Nemo and French Revolutionary Gustave Flourens: A Hidden Character Model?" *Historical Review/La Revue Historique* 1 (2004): 207–43.

Kaplan, Amy. *The Anarchy of Empire in the Making of U.S. Culture.* Cambridge, Mass.: Harvard Univ. Press, 2002.

Kaplan, Richard L. "The Economics and Politics of Nineteenth-Century Newspapers." *American Journalism* 10 (1993): 84–101.

———. "From Partisanship to Professionalism: The Transformation of the Daily Press." In *A History of the Book in America,* vol. 4, *Print in Motion: The Expansion of Publishing and Reading in the United States, 1880–1940,* ed. Carl F. Kaestle and Janice A. Radway, 116–39. Chapel Hill: Univ. of North Carolina Press, 2009.

Katz, Philip M. *From Appomattox to Montmartre: Americans and the Paris Commune.* Cambridge, Mass.: Harvard Univ. Press, 1998.

Kelley, Robert L. *The Transatlantic Persuasion: The Liberal-Democratic Mind in the Age of Gladstone.* New York: Knopf, 1969. Reprint, New Brunswick, N.J.: Transaction Publishers, 1989.

Kennedy, Dane. *The Highly Civilized Man: Richard Burton and the Victorian World.* Cambridge, Mass.: Harvard Univ. Press, 2005.

Kerber, Linda K. "The Abolitionist Perception of the Indian." *Journal of American History* 62, no. 2 (September 1975): 271–95.

Kester, Matthew. "Race, Religion, and Citizenship in Mormon Country: Native Hawaiians in Salt Lake City, 1869–1889." *Western Historical Quarterly* 40, no. 1 (spring 2009): 51–76.

Klein, Maury. *The Power Makers: Steam, Electricity, and the Men Who Invented Modern America.* New York: Bloomsbury Press, 2008.

Kloppenberg, James T. "The Virtues of Liberalism: Christianity, Republicanism, and Ethics in Early American Political Discourse." *Journal of American History* 74 (1987): 9–33.

Kolchin, Peter. "The South and the World." *Journal of Southern History* 75, no. 3 (August 2009): 565–80.

Kramer, Paul. "Power and Connection: Imperial Histories of the United States in the World." *American Historical Review* 116 (December 2011): 1348–91.

Kring, Walter Donald. *Henry Whitney Bellows*. Boston: Skinner House, 1979.

Lamson, Peggy. *The Glorious Failure: Black Congressman Robert Brown Elliott and the Reconstruction in South Carolina*. New York: Norton, 1973.

Larson, Gustive O. *The "Americanization" of Utah for Statehood*. San Marino, Calif.: Huntington Library, 1971.

———. "The Mormon Gathering." In *Utah's History*, ed. Richard D. Poll, 175–91. Provo, Utah: Brigham Young Univ. Press, 1978.

Lawson, Melinda. *Patriot Fires: Forging a New American Nationalism in the Civil War North*. Lawrence: Univ. Press of Kansas, 2002.

Livingstone, David N. *Adam's Ancestors: Race, Religion, and the Politics of Human Origins*. Baltimore: Johns Hopkins Univ. Press, 2008.

Love, Eric T. *Race over Empire: Racism and U.S. Imperialism, 1865–1900*. Chapel Hill: Univ. of North Carolina Press, 2004.

Lupfer, Eric. "The Business of American Magazines." In *A History of the Book in America*, vol. 3, ed. Scott E. Casper et al. Chapel Hill: Univ. of North Carolina Press, 2007.

MacCann, Donnarae. *White Supremacy in Children's Literature: Characterizations of African Americans, 1830–1900*. New York: Garland, 1998.

Mahmud, Khalil. "Introduction." In *The People of Africa: A Series of Papers on Their Character, Condition, and Future Prospects*, compiled by Henry Schieffelin, edited by Khalil Mahmud, v–xxiii. Ibadan, Nigeria: Ibadan Univ. Press, 1974.

Malmquist, O. N. *The First Hundred Years: A History of the* Salt Lake Tribune, *1871–1971*. Salt Lake City: Utah State Historical Society, 1971.

Manning, Chandra. *What This Cruel War Was Over: Soldiers, Slavery, and the Civil War*. New York: Knopf, 2007.

Marcoglou, Emmanuel E. *The American Interest in the Cretan Revolution, 1866–69*. Athens: National Center of Social Research, 1971.

Marszalek, John F. *Sherman's Other War: The General and the Civil War Press*. Kent, Ohio: Kent State Univ. Press, 1999.

Mason, Patrick Q. *The Mormon Menace: Violence and Anti-Mormonism in the Postbellum South*. New York: Oxford Univ. Press, 2011.

Masur, Kate. "'A Rare Phenomenon of Philological Vegetation': The Word

'Contraband' and the Meanings of Emancipation in the United States." *Journal of American History* 93, no. 4 (March 2007): 1050–84.

———. *An Example for All the Land: Emancipation and the Struggle over Equality in Washington, D.C.* Chapel Hill: Univ. of North Carolina Press, 2010.

May, A. J. "Crete and the United States, 1866–1869." *Journal of Modern History* 16, no. 4 (December 1944): 286–93.

Mazlish, Bruce. *Civilization and Its Contents.* Stanford, Calif.: Stanford Univ. Press, 2004.

McAfee, Ward M. *Religion, Race, and Reconstruction: The Public School in the Politics of the 1870s.* Albany: State Univ. of New York Press, 1988.

McCarthy, Michael. *Dark Continent: Africa as Seen by Americans.* Westport, Conn.: Greenwood, 1983.

McDaniel, W. Caleb. *The Problem of Democracy in the Age of Slavery: Garrisonian Abolitionists and Transatlantic Reform.* Baton Rouge: Louisiana State Univ. Press, 2013.

McGerr, Michael. *The Decline of Popular Politics: The American North, 1865–1928.* New York: Oxford Univ. Press, 1986.

McKivigan, John. *Forgotten Firebrand: James Redpath and the Making of Nineteenth-Century America.* Ithaca, N.Y.: Cornell Univ. Press, 2008.

McLeod, Mark W. *The Vietnamese Response to the French Intervention, 1862–1874.* New York: Praeger, 1990.

Meyer, Lysle E. *The Farther Frontier: Six Case Studies of Americans and Africa, 1848–1936.* Selinsgrove, Pa.: Susquehanna Univ. Press, 1992.

Merriam, George. *The Life and Times of Samuel Bowles.* 2 vols. New York: Century, 1885.

Miller, William. "George Finlay as a Journalist." *English Historical Review* 39, no. 156 (October 1924): 552–67.

Montgomery, David. *Beyond Equality: Labor and the Radical Republicans, 1862–1872.* Urbana: Univ. of Illinois Press, 1981.

Mott, Frank Luther. *A History of American Magazines, 1865–1885.* Cambridge, Mass.: Harvard Univ. Press, 1957.

Mulder, William. "Immigration and the 'Mormon Question': An International Episode." *Western Political Quarterly* 9 (1956): 416–33.

Munn, Christopher. *Anglo-China: Chinese People and British Rule in Hong Kong, 1841–1880.* Richmond, Surrey, UK: Curzon, 2001.

Murphy, Kevin C. *The American Merchant Experience in Nineteenth-Century Japan.* London: RoutledgeCurzon, 2003.

Murray, Cara. "Imperial Ways: The Victorians, the Suez Canal, and Narrative." Ph.D. diss., City University of New York, 2005.

Nerone, John. "Newspapers in the Public Sphere." In *A History of the Book in*

America, vol. 3, ed. Scott E. Casper et al. Chapel Hill: Univ. of North Carolina Press, 2007.

Nichols, Jeannette P. "The United States Congress and Imperialism, 1861–1897." *Journal of Economic History* 21 (1961): 526–38.

Ninkovich, Frank. *Global Dawn: The Cultural Foundation of American Internationalism, 1865–1890.* Cambridge, Mass.: Harvard Univ. Press, 2009.

———. "Theodore Roosevelt: Civilization as Ideology." *Diplomatic History* 10 (summer 1986): 221–45.

Nye, David E. *The American Technological Sublime.* Cambridge, Mass.: MIT Press, 1994.

Okker, Patricia. *Our Sister Editors: Sarah Hale and the Tradition of Nineteenth-Century American Women Editors.* Athens: Univ. of Georgia Press, 1995.

O'Leary, Cecilia. *To Die For: The Paradox of American Patriotism.* Princeton, N.J.: Princeton Univ. Press, 1999.

Opal, J. M. "The Labors of Liberality: Christian Benevolence and National Prejudice in the American Founding." *Journal of American History* 94 (2008): 1082–1107.

Paddison, Joshua. *American Heathens: Religion, Race, and Reconstruction in California.* Berkeley: Univ. of California Press, 2012.

Paix, Catherine. "Singapore as a Central Place between the West, Asia and China: From the 19th to the 21st Centuries." In *Singapore from Temasek to the 21st Century: Reinventing the Global City,* edited by Karl Hack and Jean-Louis Margolin, with Karine Delaye, 210–42. Singapore: National Univ. of Singapore Press, 2010.

Patrick, Rembert W. *The Reconstruction of the Nation.* New York: Oxford Univ. Press, 1967.

Patterson, K. David. "Paul B. Du Chaillu and the Exploration of Gabon, 1855–1865." *International Journal of African Historical Studies* 7 (1974): 647–67.

Pearce, Roy Harvey. *The Savages of North America: A Study of the Indian and the Idea of Civilization.* Baltimore: Johns Hopkins Univ. Press, 1965.

Pécout, Gilles. "The International Armed Volunteers: Pilgrims of a Transnational Risorgimento." *Journal of Modern Italian Studies,* Special Issue: International Volunteers and the Risorgimento 14 (2009): 413–26.

———. "Philhellenism in Italy: Political Friendship and the Italian Volunteers in the Mediterranean in the Nineteenth Century." *Journal of Modern Italian Studies* 9, no. 4 (2004): 405–27.

Penn, I. Garland. *The Afro-American Press and Its Editors.* Springfield, Mass.: Willey, 1891. Reprint, New York: Arno Press and the New York Times, 1969.

Perakis, Manos. "Muslim Exodus and Land Redistribution in Autonomous Crete." *Mediterranean Historical Review* 26, no. 2 (December 2011): 135–50.

Perman, Michael. "The Politics of Reconstruction," in *A Companion to the Civil War and Reconstruction,* edited by Lacy K. Ford, 322–41. Malden, Mass.: Blackwell, 2005.

Peterson, Carla. *"Doers of the Word": African-American Women Speakers and Writers in the North (1830–1880).* New Brunswick, N.J.: Rutgers Univ. Press, 1998.

Pitre, Merline. "Frederick Douglass and American Diplomacy in the Caribbean." *Journal of Black Studies* 13, no. 4 (June 1983): 457–75.

Poll, Richard D. "The Political Reconstruction of Utah Territory, 1866–1890." *Pacific Historical Review* 27, no. 2 (May 1958): 111–26.

———, ed. *Utah's History.* Provo, Utah: Brigham Young Univ. Press, 1978.

Pride, Armistead Scott. "A Register and History of Negro Newspapers in the United States: 1827–1950." Ph.D. diss., Northwestern University, 1950.

Priest, Andrew. "Thinking about Empire: The Administration of Ulysses S. Grant, Spanish Colonialism and the Ten Years' War in Cuba." *Journal of American Studies* 48, no. 2 (May 2014): 541–58.

Prior, David. "After the Revolution: An Alternative Future for Atlantic History." *History Compass* 12, no. 3 (March 2014): 300–309.

———, ed. *Reconstruction in a Globalizing World.* New York: Fordham Univ. Press, 2018.

Prior, David M., et al. "Reconstruction in Public History and Memory." *Journal of the Civil War Era* 7, no. 1 (March 2017): 96–121.

Prior, David M., et al. "Teaching the Civil War in Global Context." *Journal of the Civil War Era* 5, no. 1 (March 2015): 97–125.

Provatakēs, Theocharēs M. *Monastery of Arkadi: History, Art, Traditions.* Athens: Graphic Arts of Michalis Toubis, 1980.

Quarles, Benjamin. *Frederick Douglass.* New York: Da Capo Press, 1997.

Quigley, David. "Emancipations, Empires, and Democracies." In *Globalizing American History: The AHA Guide to Re-Imagining the U.S. Survey Course,* edited by Peter Stearns and Noralee Frankel, 73–92. Washington, D.C.: American Historical Association, 2008.

Quigley, Paul D. "Secessionists in an Age of Secession: The Slave South in Transatlantic Perspective." In *Secession as an International Phenomenon: From America's Civil War to Contemporary Separatist Movements,* edited by Don H. Doyle, 151–73. Athens: Univ. of Georgia Press, 2012.

———. *Shifting Grounds: Nationalism and the American South, 1848–1865.* New York: Oxford Univ. Press, 2012.

Rankin, David E. "Introduction." In Jean-Charles Houzeau, *My Passage at the New Orleans* Tribune*: A Memoir of the Civil War Era,* edited by David E. Rankin, translated by Gerard F. Denault, 1–67. Baton Rouge: Louisiana State Univ. Press, 1984.

Ray, Angela G. *The Lyceum and Public Culture in the Nineteenth-Century United States*. East Lansing: Michigan State Univ. Press, 2005.

Reel, Monte. *Between Man and Beast: An Unlikely Explorer, the Evolution Debate, and the African Adventure that Took the Victorian World by Storm*. New York: Doubleday, 2013.

Reeve, W. Paul. *Religion of a Different Color: Race and the Mormon Struggle for Whiteness*. New York: Oxford Univ. Press, 2015.

Reid, James J. *Crisis of the Ottoman Empire: Prelude to Collapse, 1839–1878*. Stuttgart: Franz Steiner Verlag, 2000.

Repousis, Angelo. *Greek-American Relations from Monroe to Truman*. Kent, Ohio: Kent State Univ. Press, 2013.

Richardson, Heather Cox. *The Death of Reconstruction: Race, Labor, and Politics in the Post–Civil War North, 1865–1901*. Cambridge, Mass.: Harvard Univ. Press, 2001.

———. *The Greatest Nation of the Earth: Republican Economic Policies during the Civil War*. Cambridge, Mass.: Harvard Univ. Press, 1997.

———. "North and West of Reconstruction: Studies in Political Economy." In *Reconstructions: New Perspectives on the Postbellum United States*, edited by Thomas J. Brown, 66–90. New York: Oxford Univ. Press, 2006.

———. "Reconstruction and the Nation." In *A Companion to the Civil War and Reconstruction*, edited by Lacy Ford, 447–67. Malden, Mass.: Blackwell, 2005.

———. *West from Appomattox: The Reconstruction of America after the Civil War*. New Haven, Conn.: Yale Univ. Press, 2007.

Richardson, Joe M. *Christian Reconstruction: The American Missionary Association and Southern Blacks, 1861–1890*. Tuscaloosa: Univ. of Alabama Press, 1986.

Ricklefs, M. C. *A History of Modern Indonesia Since c. 1200*, 4th ed. New York: Palgrave, 2008.

Roberts, B. H. *A Comprehensive History of the Church of Jesus Christ of Latter-day Saints: Century I*, vol. 5. Provo, Utah: Brigham Young Univ. Press, 1965.

Roberts, Timothy Mason. *Distant Revolutions: 1848 and the Challenge to American Exceptionalism*. Charlottesville: Univ. of Virginia Press, 2009.

Robson, Maureen M. "Lord Clarendon and the Cretan Question, 1868–9." *Historical Journal* 3, no. 1 (1960): 38–55.

Rodgers, Daniel T. *Contested Truths: Keywords in American Politics since Independence*. New York: Basic Books, 1987.

———. "Republicanism: The Career of a Concept." *Journal of American History* 79 (1992): 11–38.

Rodogno, Davide. *Against Massacre: Humanitarian Interventions in the Ottoman Empire, 1815–1914*. Princeton, N.J.: Princeton Univ. Press, 2015.

Ross, Dorothy. "'Are We a Nation?': The Conjuncture of Nationhood and Race in the United States, 1850–1876." *Modern Intellectual History* 2, no. 3 (November 2005): 327–60.

———. "Historical Consciousness in Nineteenth-Century America." *American Historical Review* 89, no. 4 (1984): 909–28.

Ross, Felecia G. Jones. "Democracy's Textbook: A History of the Black Press in Ohio, 1865–1985." In *The Black Press in the Middle West, 1865–1985,* edited by Henry Lewis Suggs, 243–66. Westport, Conn.: Greenwood, 1996.

Rotter, Andrew J. "Saidism without Said: Orientalism and U.S. Diplomatic History." *American Historical Review* 105, no. 4 (October 2000): 1205–17.

Rubin, Anne Sarah. *A Shattered Nation: The Rise and Fall of the Confederacy, 1861–1868.* Chapel Hill: Univ. of North Carolina Press, 2005.

Rugemer, Edward Bartlett. *The Problem of Emancipation: The Caribbean Roots of the American Civil War.* Baton Rouge: Louisiana State Univ. Press, 2008.

Rupke, Nicholaas. *Richard Owen: Biology without Darwin.* Chicago: Univ. of Chicago Press, 2009.

S., T. D. "Lewis R. Packard." *American Journal of Philology* 5, no. 3 (1884): 403–6.

Saab, Ann Pottinger. "The Doctors' Dilemma: Britain and the Cretan Crisis, 1866–1869." *Journal of Modern History* 49, no. 4, supplement (December 1977): D1383–D1407.

Said, Edward. *Orientalism.* 1979. Reprint, New York: Vintage, 1994.

Samito, Christian G. *Becoming American under Fire: Irish Americans, African Americans, and the Politics of Citizenship during the Civil War Era.* Ithaca, N.Y.: Cornell Univ. Press, 2009.

Sarafianos, Aris. "The Diaspora of Greek Painting in the Nineteenth Century: Christou's Model and the Case of Marie Spartali-Stillman." *Historien* 6 (2006): 150–69.

Schwartz, Harold. *Samuel Gridley Howe: Social Reformer, 1801–1876.* Cambridge, Mass.: Harvard Univ. Press, 1956.

Sebrell, Thomas, II. *Persuading John Bull: Union and Confederate Propaganda in Britain, 1860–1865.* Lanham, Md.: Lexington, 2014.

Sehat, David. "The Civilizing Mission of Booker T. Washington." *Journal of Southern History* 73 (2007): 289–323.

Sexton, Jay. "Toward a Synthesis of Foreign Relations in the Civil War Era, 1848–1877." *American Nineteenth Century History* 5, no. 3 (2004): 50–77.

———. "The United States, the Cuban Rebellion, and the Multilateral Initiative of 1875." *Diplomatic History* 30, no. 3 (June 2006): 335–65.

———. "William Seward in the World." *Journal of the Civil War Era* 4, no. 3 (September 2014): 398–430.

Sicherman, Barbara. "Ideologies and Practices of Reading." In *A History of the Book in America,* vol. 3, ed. Scott E. Casper et al. Chapel Hill: Univ. of North Carolina Press, 2007.

Silbey, Joel H. *The Partisan Imperative: The Dynamics of American Politics before the Civil War.* New York: Oxford Univ. Press, 1985.

———. *A Respectable Minority: The Democratic Party in the Civil War Era, 1860–1868.* New York: Norton, 1977.

Sinha, Manisha. *The Slave's Cause: A History of Abolition.* New Haven, Conn.: Yale Univ. Press, 2016.

Sizeranne, Robert de la. *The Pre-Raphaelites.* New York: Parkstone International, 2012.

Slap, Andrew. *The Doom of Reconstruction: The Liberal Republicans in the Civil War Era.* New York: Fordham Univ. Press, 2006.

Smith, Mark M. "The Past as a Foreign Country: Reconstruction, Inside and Out." In *Reconstructions: New Perspectives on the Postbellum United States,* edited by Thomas J. Brown, 117–40. New York: Oxford Univ. Press, 2006.

Smithers, Gregory D. "The 'Pursuit of the Civilized Man': Race and the Meaning of Civilization in the United States and Australia, 1790s–1850s." *Journal of World History* 20 (2009): 245–72.

Snay, Mitchell. *Fenians, Freedmen, and Southern Whites: Race and Nationality in the Era of Reconstruction.* Baton Rouge: Louisiana State Univ. Press, 2007.

———. "Freedom and Progress: The Dilemma of Southern Republican Thought during Radical Reconstruction." *American Nineteenth Century History* 5 (2004): 100–114.

———. "The Imagined Republic: The Fenians, Irish American Nationalism, and the Political Culture of Reconstruction." *Proceedings of the American Antiquarian Society* 112 (2002): 291–313.

———. "Transatlantic Liberalism: Radical Republicans and the British Reform Act of 1867." In *Reconstruction in a Globalizing World,* ed. David Prior, 74–93. New York: Fordham Univ. Press, 2018.

Sneider, Allison L. *Suffragists in an Imperial Age: U.S. Expansion and the Woman Question, 1870–1929.* New York: Oxford Univ. Press, 2008.

Stahr, Walter. *Seward: Lincoln's Indispensable Man.* New York: Simon and Schuster, 2012.

Stampp, Kenneth M. *The Era of Reconstruction, 1865–1877.* New York: Knopf, 1965.

Stanton, William. *The Leopard's Spots: Scientific Attitudes toward Race in America, 1815–1859.* Chicago: Univ. of Chicago Press, 1960.

Stevenson, Louise. "Homes, Books, and Reading." In *A History of the Book in America,* vol. 3, ed. Scott E. Casper et al. Chapel Hill: Univ. of North Carolina Press, 2007.

Summers, Mark Wahlgren. *The Ordeal of the Reunion: A New History of Reconstruction.* Chapel Hill: Univ. of North Carolina Press, 2014.

———. *The Press Gang: Newspapers and Politics, 1865–1878.* Chapel Hill: Univ. of North Carolina Press, 1994.

Sutcliffe, Marcella Pellegrino. "British Red Shirts: A History of the Garibaldi Volunteers (1860)." In *Transnational Soldiers: Foreign Military Enlistment in the Modern Era*, edited by Nir Arielli and Bruce Collins, 202–18. Basingstoke, UK: Palgrave Macmillan, 2012.

Takaki, Ronald. "The Tempest in the Wilderness: The Racialization of Savagery." *Journal of American History* 79, no. 3 (December 1992): 892–912.

Teal, Christopher. *Hero of Hispaniola: America's First Black Diplomat, Ebenezer D. Bassett*. Santa Barbara, Calif.: Praeger, 2008.

Terzuolo, Eric. "The Garibaldini in the Balkans, 1875–1876." *International History Review* 4, no. 1 (February 1982): 111–26.

Thomas, Amy M. "Literacies, Readers, and Cultures of Print in the South." In *A History of the Book in America*, vol. 3, ed. Scott E. Casper et al. Chapel Hill: Univ. of North Carolina Press, 2007.

Thompson, Julius E. *The Black Press in Mississippi, 1865–1985*. Gainesville: Univ. Press of Florida, 1993.

Thornton, Willis. *The Nine Lives of Citizen Train*. New York: Greenberg, 1948.

Trelease, Allen. *White Terror: The Ku Klux Klan Conspiracy and Southern Reconstruction*. Westport, Conn.: Greenwood, 1971.

"Tuckerman, Charles Keating." *The National Cyclopedia of American Biography*. New York: J. T. White, 1910.

Turner, John G. *Brigham Young: Pioneer Prophet*. Cambridge, Mass.: Belknap Press of Harvard Univ. Press, 2012.

Tyrrell, Ian. "American Exceptionalism in an Age of International History." *American Historical Review* 96 (1991): 1031–55.

———. "Reflections on the Transnational Turn in United States History: Theory and Practice." *Journal of Global History* 4, no. 3 (November 2009), 453–74.

Ulrich, Laurel Thatcher. *A House Full of Females: Plural Marriage and Women's Rights in Early Mormonism, 1835–1870*. New York: Knopf, 2017.

Van Deusen, Glyndon. *William Henry Seward*. New York: Oxford Univ. Press, 1967.

Van Doren, Charles. *The Idea of Progress*. New York: Praeger, 1967.

Vaucaire, Michel. *Paul Du Chaillu: Gorilla Hunter*. New York: Harper and Brothers, 1930.

Verhoeven, Timothy. "Transatlantic Connections: American Anti-Catholicism and the First Vatican Council (1869–1870)." *Catholic Historical Review* 100, no. 4 (autumn 2014): 695–720.

Vincent, Charles. *Black Legislators in Louisiana during Reconstruction*. Carbondale: Southern Illinois Univ. Press, 2011.

Walker, Ronald W., et al. *Mormon History*. Urbana: Univ. of Illinois Press, 2001.

Walters, Ronald G. *The Antislavery Appeal: American Abolitionism after 1830*. Baltimore: Johns Hopkins Univ. Press, 1978.

Walther, Karine V. *Sacred Interests: The United States and the Islamic World, 1821–1921*. Chapel Hill: Univ. of North Carolina Press, 2015.

Wang, Xi. *The Trial of Democracy: Black Suffrage and Northern Republicans, 1860–1910*. Athens: Univ. of Georgia Press, 1997.

Wasti, Syed Tanvir. "Ahmed Rüstem Bey and the End of an Era." *Middle Eastern Studies* 48, no. 5 (September 2012): 781–96.

Watson, Elmo Scott. *A History of Newspaper Syndicates in the United States, 1865–1935*. Chicago: [Watson], 1936.

Weisberger, Bernard A. "The Dark and Bloody Ground of Reconstruction Historiography." *Journal of Southern History* 25 (1959): 427–47.

West, Elliot. *The Last Indian War: The Nez Perce Story*. New York: Oxford Univ. Press, 2009.

———. "Reconstructing Race." *Western Historical Quarterly* 34, no. 1 (February 2003): 6–26.

White, O. Kendall, Jr., and Darryl White. "Polygamy and Mormon Identity." *Journal of American Culture* 28, no. 2 (2005): 165–77.

Wiebe, Robert H. *Who We Are: A History of Popular Nationalism*. Princeton, N.J.: Princeton Univ. Press, 2002.

Wilkerson, Isabel. *The Warmth of Other Suns: The Epic Story of America's Great Migration*. New York: Vintage, 2010.

Wilkins, Christopher. "'They had heard of emancipation and the enfranchisement of their race': The African American Colonists of Samaná, Reconstruction, and the State of Santo Domingo." In *The Civil War as Global Conflict: Transnational Meanings of the American Civil War*, edited by David T. Gleeson and Simon Lewis, 211–34. Columbia: Univ. of South Carolina Press, 2014.

Wilkins, Joe B. "Window on Freedom: The South's Response to the Emancipation of the Slaves in the British West Indies, 1833–1861." Ph.D. diss., University of South Carolina, 1977.

Williams, Gilbert Anthony. "The 'A.M.E. Christian Recorder': Forum for the Social Ideas of Black Americans, 1854–1902." Ph.D. diss., University of Illinois at Urbana-Champaign, 1979.

Williams, Heather Andrea. *Help Me Find My People: The African American Search for Family Lost in Slavery*. Chapel Hill: Univ. of North Carolina Press, 2012.

Williams, Raymond. *Keywords: A Vocabulary of Culture and Society*, rev. ed. New York: Oxford Univ. Press, 1985.

Williams, Walter L. "The United States Indian Policy and the Debate over Philippine Annexation: Implications for the Origins of American Imperialism." *Journal of American History* 66 (1980): 810–31.

Williamson, Joel. *After Slavery: The Negro in South Carolina during Reconstruction, 1861–1877*. New York: Norton, 1965.

Wilson, Ivy G. "The Brief and Wondrous Life of the *Anglo-African Magazine*; Or,

Antebellum African American Editorial Practice and Its Afterlives." In *Publishing Blackness: Textual Constructions of Race since 1850*, edited by George Hutchinson and John K. Young, 18–38. Ann Arbor: Univ. of Michigan Press, 2013.

Wilson, James Grant, and John Fiske, eds. *Appleton's Cyclopædia of American Biography* 6 vols. New York: Appleton, 1899.

Wiltse, Charles M. "A Critical Southerner: John C. Calhoun on the Revolutions of 1848." *Journal of Southern History* 15 (1949): 299–310.

Winship, Michael. "Distribution and the Trade." In *A History of the Book in America*, vol. 3, ed. Scott E. Casper et al. Chapel Hill: Univ. of North Carolina Press, 2007.

Withey, Lynne. *Grand Tours and Cook's Tours: A History of Leisure Travel, 1750 to 1915.* New York: William Morrow, 1997.

Wolseley, Roland E. *The Black Press, U.S.A.*, 2nd ed. Ames: Iowa State Univ. Press, 1990.

Wong, Edlie L. *Racial Reconstruction: Black Inclusion, Chinese Exclusion, and the Fictions of Citizenship.* New York: New York Univ. Press, 2015.

Wood, Forrest G. *Black Scare: The Racist Response to Emancipation and Reconstruction.* Berkeley: Univ. of California Press, 1968.

Wood, Gordon S. "Ideology and the Origins of Liberal America." *William and Mary Quarterly* 44 (1987): 628–40.

———. *The Radicalism of the American Revolution.* New York: Random House, 1991.

Wrobel, David M. *Global West, American Frontier: Travel, Empire, and Exceptionalism from Manifest Destiny to the Great Depression.* Albuquerque: Univ. of New Mexico Press, 2013.

Young, Elizabeth. *Disarming the Nation: Women's Writing and the American Civil War.* Chicago: Univ. of Chicago Press, 1999.

Zagarri, Rosemarie. "The Significance of the 'Global Turn' for the Early American Republic: Globalization in the Age of Nation-Building." *Journal of the Early Republic* 31 (spring 2011): 1–37.

Zboray, Ronald J. *A Fictive People: Antebellum Economic Development and the American Reading Public.* New York: Oxford Univ. Press, 1993.

Index